UNSETTLING ACTS

FORMATIONS: ADOPTION, KINSHIP, AND CULTURE
Emily Hipchen and John McLeod, Series Editors

UNSETTLING ACTS

PERFORMING TRANSNATIONAL ADOPTION

Jieun Lee

THE OHIO STATE UNIVERSITY PRESS
COLUMBUS

Copyright © 2025 by Jieun Lee.
All rights reserved.
Published by The Ohio State University Press.

This work is licensed under a Creative Commons Attribution-NonCommercial-NoDerivatives 4.0 International License. To view a copy of this license, visit https://creativecommons.org/licenses/by-nc-nd/4.0/legalcode. Note to users: A Creative Commons license is only valid when applied by the person or entity that holds rights to the licensed work. This work may contain components to which the rightsholder in the work cannot apply the license. It is ultimately your responsibility to independently evaluate the copyright status of any work or component part of a work you use in light of your intended use.

This book is freely available in an open access edition thanks to the generous support of Emory University and the Andrew W. Mellon Foundation. https://kb.osu.edu/home

Library of Congress Cataloging-in-Publication Data
Names: Lee, Jieun, 1986– author.
Title: Unsettling acts : performing transnational adoption / Jieun Lee.
Description: Columbus : The Ohio State University Press, 2025. | Series: Formations: adoption, kinship, and culture | Includes bibliographical references and index. | Summary: "Analyzes how contemporary theater and performance works about Korean transnational adoption intervene in long-standing transnational adoption narratives, which have essentialized adoptees through ethnonationalist, gendered, and postwar humanitarian themes. Shows how multiple adoptee-centered works performed in South Korea, the United States, the United Kingdom, Belgium, and Denmark reimagine and remake the adoptee experience"—Provided by publisher.
Identifiers: LCCN 2024048281 | ISBN 9780814215838 (hardback) | ISBN 9780814284056 (ebook)
Subjects: LCSH: Drama—21st century—History and criticism. | Intercountry adoption in literature. | Koreans in literature. | Theater—History—21st century.
Classification: LCC PN1650.A36 L44 2025 | DDC 809.2/05—dc23/eng/20241108
LC record available at https://lccn.loc.gov/2024048281

Other identifiers: ISBN 9780814259382 (paperback)

Cover design by Laurence J. Nozik
Text composition by Stuart Rodriguez
Type set in Minion Pro

To adoptee artists, activists, and academics whose works about transnational adoption create change onstage and offstage

CONTENTS

List of Illustrations   viii

Acknowledgments   ix

Notes on Terminology and Transliteration   xv

INTRODUCTION	Unsettling Transnational Adoption in Contemporary Theater and Performance	1
CHAPTER 1	Maternal Resurrection: Birth Search and Reunion on Korean Stages	39
CHAPTER 2	Bodily Testimony: Korean American Women Adoptees' Autobiographical Solo Performances	81
CHAPTER 3	Contingent Belonging: Korean Adoptees and Adoption Communities Imagined in US Theater	114
CHAPTER 4	Decolonial Discomfort: Extraordinary Adoption Stories beyond the Korea–US Cartography	159
POSTSCRIPT	Onstage and Offstage: Imagining Transnational Adoption within and beyond Birth Search and Reunion	207

Bibliography   221

Index   241

ILLUSTRATIONS

FIGURE 1	Josh and two men with the emcee on the search-and-reunion TV show in *Airport Baby*	61
FIGURE 2	Sun Mee Chomet wearing feminine accoutrements in *How to Be a Korean Woman*	98
FIGURE 3	Gabe and Billy with their Korean names overwritten by new American names in *Middle Brother*	126
FIGURE 4	*Re-enacting the Transnational Adoptee,* performance by Yong Sun Gullach	194
FIGURE 5	*Shadow Child,* by Wonsook Kim	209
FIGURE 6	*Mother's Arms,* by Kwanghyun Wang	210
FIGURE 7	Memory wall padlock	211

ACKNOWLEDGMENTS

Writing this book has been a journey filled with inspiration, support, and collaboration, and I am deeply grateful to everyone who has contributed to its realization. On this note, first and foremost, I would like to express my gratitude to the theater and performance artists who shared their time, artistic visions, and personal stories with me during our meetings and interviews for this research: Marissa Lichwick, Sun Mee Chomet, Amy Mihyang Ginther, Eric Sharp, Leah Cooper, Debra Kim Sivigny, Cathy Min Jung, In-Sook Chappell, and Yong Sun Gullach (by order of chapters). Their works and our discussions about the performances of Korean transnational adoption in the US and Europe plunged me deep into what it means to be an artist as well as an adoptee. To you, all the theater and performance artists who have touched my life in countless ways, thank you for your talent and commitment to the arts. This book is a testament to your works.

Looking back with gratitude, I would like to share a moment. In 2020 COVID-19 blazed through the world, and the theater worldwide was not spared. The South Korean performing arts industry responded to this outbreak by still offering theatrical events but limiting both the size of audiences and the number of performances while enforcing strict social distancing, mask wearing, mandatory temperature taking, and QR code checks. Even with such restrictions, audience members continued attending theater performances. I would like here to express my personal thanks to the performers, ushers, stage and technical crew for still making theater happen, with safety and care during those extremely precarious times. During this perilous period, my gratitude goes out as well to the following Korean archives for staying open and facilitating my research with very careful measure and boundless kindness: The National Theater Company of Korea 박으뜸, Arko Art Archives 조만자 (in Hyehwa), 이한솔 (in Seocho). My research shined thanks to their labor behind the footlights.

This book is the sum of numerous layers of learning from professors and scholars in several fields and levels for many years. I am indebted for their support and encouragement and wish to thank them. Especially, during the period at my alma mater, the University of Georgia (UGA), words cannot express my thankfulness to Marla Carlson, my academic advisor and my role model. Her inestimable mentorship persistently guided me on my scholarly and professional path. I am also grateful to my dissertation committee members David Saltz, Farley Richmond, and external member Esther Kim Lee. At UGA, I wish to also thank Hyangsoon Yi in the Department of Comparative Literature for her unwavering support. Still at UGA, I cannot express enough appreciation and love for the Institute for Women's Studies, a constant source of feminist knowledge and practice. There, I was lucky to meet Cecilia Herles, Pat Del Rey, Juanita Johnson-Bailey, Chris Cuomo, and Patricia Richards. These women steered my growth as a feminist teacher-scholar in what became my initial interdisciplinary research field of theater and performance studies and women's, gender, and sexuality studies. I also made fantastic friends at UGA. During numerous accountability meetings and writing sessions, my beloved friends Kristyl Tift and Jamie Palmer showed me professional and passionate ways of doing research and teaching. More than a decade overdue, I extend my thanks to Jinhee Lee, Jisung Yoo, and Jae Kyoung Kim.

As an assistant professor during my time at Wake Forest University (WFU), it has been my privilege to be part of its erudite intellectual communities. I am most thankful to my colleagues and friends in and outside the Women's, Gender, and Sexuality Department: Julia Jordan-Zachery, Wanda Balzano, Kristina Gupta, Jeffrey Solomon, Jayati Lal, Rian Bowie, Erica Still, Dean Franco, Cindy Gendrich, Sharon Andrews, Brook Davis, Mari Ishida, Simone Caron, Mir Yarfitz, Robert Hellyer, and Miho. During the Humanities Institute Interdisciplinary Faculty Workshop Seminar (2021–22), I received priceless feedback from T. H. M. Gellar-Goad, Amy Mars (Lather), Guillaume Coly, Lucy Alford, Katherine Shaner, Brittany Battle, and Qiaona Yu. Many thanks to all. Still at WFU, I met my dear friend Kimberly Wortmann. I cannot imagine how I could have survived those years without her intellectual companionship in research, teaching, and our Artivism@Wake series.

At my current academic institution, Emory University, I am grateful for the invaluable support and enthusiasm of the wonderful faculty, students, and staff in the Theater Studies Department. A special thanks goes out to Michael Evenden and Lisa Paulsen, who have shown such trust in this book project, and to all my fabulous colleagues. Your passion and vision for theater arts are truly admirable.

Researchers and participants whom I met at the following associations' annual, biennial, or triennial conference panels, working sessions, workshops, (in)formal meetings, and in journal and book chapter publishing have helped me shape this book. I am so thankful to have networked with worldwide esteemed scholars in various areas of studies and received their intellectual engagement with my research, especially at conference and symposium sites for the American Society for Theatre Research (ASTR), Association for Theatre in Higher Education (ATHE), International Federation for Theatre Research (IFTR), National Women's Studies Association (NWSA), Association for Asian American Studies (AAAS), International Symposium on Korean Adoption Studies of the International Korean Adoptee Associations (IKAA), and the Alliance for the Study of Adoption and Culture (ASAC). I would be remiss not to acknowledge the following people who also helped me in so many ways as mentors, colleagues, and friends during these events and more than once: Dorothy Chansky, Tracy Davis, Elizabeth Son, Jessica Nakamura, Donatella Galella, Ji Hyun (Kayla) Yuh, Soo Ryon Yoon, Ilka Saal, Hosu Kim, Jiyeon Jo, Yonson Ahn, Katelyn Hemmeke, and Seon Myoung Yoo. To all of you who have stood by me during this research and writing period, I wholeheartedly thank you.

This book was nourished by a chain of important eye-opening conversations and discussions at various special in-person and virtual conferences and invited talks. My special thanks to the following: The World Congress of Korean Studies, University of Pennsylvania (2016), International Conference of Korean Studies, Goethe University of Frankfurt, Germany (2018), The Research Center for Korean Community Conference, Queens College of the City University of New York (2019), Realisms in East Asian Performing Arts Conference, University of California, Santa Barbara (2020), Carolina Asia Center Talk, University of North Carolina, Chapel Hill (2023). I am very grateful for the feedback from the Graduate Student Fellow Pre-conference (2016) and First Book Bootcamp (2020), both hosted by the American Theatre and Drama Society (ATDS), and the AAAS Asian American Feminism Section's Book Proposal Workshop (2021).

I would like to thank the following institutions for their grants, awards, and fellowships over these many years: UGA's Interdisciplinary and Innovative

Research Grant (2015), Summer Doctoral Research Fellowship (2016), Willson Center Graduate Research Award (2016), Janelle Padgett Knight Graduate Award (2016), Sylvia Hillyard Pannell Travel Award (2016), Dissertation Completion Award (2017), Korean Student Association Research Award (2018), and Robert C. Anderson Memorial Award (2019); WFU's Archie Fund for the Arts and Humanities (2019 & 2020), Junior Faculty Research Leave (2020–21), Humanities Institute Summer Research Grant (2022), and Publication Fund (2023). Also, I am very grateful to have received support for my research and publication for this book from the Korean American Scholarship Foundation's Seoul National University Alumni Association & Joong Sik Cho Scholarship (2016) and the ATDS Publication Subvention Award (2024).

Finally, this book would not have reached its ultimate objective without the feedback and encouragement of the following scholars in the field of critical adoption studies: Kim Park Nelson and Kimberly McKee. I am most thankful for your irreplaceable support and guidance. Your dedication to the area of research continues to impassion me. I am also indebted to my editor, Kristen Elias Rowley, who helped me launch this voyage with The Ohio State University Press (OSUP). My thanks as well to the Formations: Adoption, Kinship, and Culture series editors Emily Hipchen and John McLeod, OSUP editors Elizabeth Zaleski, Meghan Tarney, and Becca Bostock, and my manuscript readers, whose insightful comments and suggestions greatly contributed to the refinement of this book. I also wish to mention my appreciation to copyediting masters whose skills and knowledge honed this manuscript's syntax, grammar, and flow over the years: Kristen Ebert-Wagner, Liz Laurie, Kathy Haake, and Alexander Leonard.

On a familial level, I am profoundly grateful for the confidence and patience about this research and book publication process from my parents Soohyun Lee, Eunyoung Choi, sister Jiae Lee, and brother-in-law Taehun Park. On this personal note, I cannot forget to mention Claudine Laperdris and also my four-legged lucky charms. Their irresistible cuteness has given me immeasurable comfort during the process of writing this book. Finally, to Alain G. Cloarec, a.k.a. "Rufus T. Firefly," without whom I would not have been able to finish or even start this book, words fail to express how beholden I am to you.

The world of theater is a vibrant tapestry woven by the dedication and artistry of myriad individuals and groups. To all those who breathe life into stories and push the boundaries of expression, I offer my deepest gratitude. Thank you for creating worlds where I have walked with you and hope to continue to do so far into the future.

•

Sections of the introduction and chapter 2 were previously published as "Performing Transnational Adoption: Korean American Women Adoptees' Autobiographical Solo Performances," *Theatre Annual* 70 (2017): 60–80. Published by the College of William & Mary.

Parts of chapters 2 and 3 were previously published as "Transnational Journey into Belonging: Korean American Adoptee's Birth Search and Reunion in Eric Sharp's *Middle Brother*," in *Transnational Mobility and Identity in and out of Korea*, ed. Yonson Ahn (Rowman & Littlefield / Lexington Books, 2020), 23–35. Reproduced with permission of The Licensor through PLSclear.

NOTES ON TERMINOLOGY AND TRANSLITERATION

While there are different types of adoption (for example, domestic adoption, private and public adoption), this book focuses on private transnational adoption, particularly from South Korea. Theatrical works regarding Korean domestic adoption and adoptees are not the focus of this book. Unless otherwise specified, adoptees and adoption in this book refer to Korean transnational adoptees and adoption. Also, the words "search and reunion" imply adoptees' search and reunion with birth families, often termed as "birth search and reunion." I use both terms.

In this book I use the words "transnational" to highlight international adoption's migratory component by which adoptees come from another country, and "transracial" when referring to racial difference between adoptive parents and adopted children. Moreover, the word "adoption" refers to both transnational and transracial adoption unless otherwise specified. "International," "intercountry," and "overseas adoption" are used interchangeably to refer to transnational adoption.

When writing Korean names, I follow the order of given name followed by last name (for example, Jieun Lee) with the exception of the names of presidents. I also follow the Korean artists' way of using English when writing their names and works; otherwise, I romanize their names and translate the titles of their works in English following the original Korean titles. When artists romanize Korean words in their scripts, I keep these as such. Elsewhere, this book follows the "Revised Romanization of Korean" (Republic of Korea Standard, Ministry of Culture and Tourism Notice No. 2000-8, 2000. 7.7). For other languages, I use the original language followed by English translation.

INTRODUCTION

Unsettling Transnational Adoption in Contemporary Theater and Performance

In 2015 I traveled to Chicago to see the autobiographical solo performance *Yellow Dress* by Marissa Lichwick, a Korean American adoptee theater artist. This event was organized by the local adoptee affinity group Korean Adoptees of Chicago (KAtCH). Lichwick's work unpacked her search-and-reunion story using her own heartwarming and heartbreaking memories of being and becoming a Korean transnational adoptee in and out of the United States. With thirty to forty emotionally engaged audience members, Lichwick's performance filled the small, windowless space with a sense of community. The spectators seemed to experience moments of sadness, joy, and shock collectively, as I saw them at times shed tears, at times burst out in laughter, while always gazing intently in concert. This event and its impact on the audience and me strongly reaffirmed my belief in the value and power of performance, and the significance and effectiveness of telling the stories of Korean transnational adoption on stage. The experience—my first as a teacher-scholar writing about the theater and performance of the Korean diaspora—propelled me to seek out more works by Korean adoptee theater artists within and beyond the boundaries of the US. This book about Korean transnational adoption plays and performances is my way of showing solidarity with the talented theater and performance artists—most of them, but not all, Korean adoptees—whom I met during this project's long journey into a conflicting and conflicted part of the world of adoption.

In the aftermath of the Korean War (1950–53), South Korea (hereafter Korea) sent approximately two hundred thousand children to foreign countries for transnational adoption.[1] While adoption is a long-standing practice, large-scale transnational adoption—or the mobilization of children from mostly non-Western nations to adoptive families in the West—is a post–Korean War phenomenon. These adoptees became the largest group of Asian-born children adopted mostly by North Americans and Western/Northern Europeans and raised mainly by white adoptive parents.[2] During the early stages of the Cold War, US promotion of the adoption of Korean children allowed the American Empire to rewrite its history, leaving behind the role of destroyer and taking on the role of protective kin.[3] For decades, the representation of Korean children in US media as war orphans waiting to be saved helped facilitate transnational adoption to the United States while also spreading the message of American salvation.[4] Korean transnational adoption was also buttressed by advertising the easy assimilation of Korean children into American culture.[5] Yet, starting in the 1990s, when the early generation of Korean transnational adoptees came of age, adoptees who returned to Korea were framed by the Korean government as cultural representatives or economic ties.[6] Embracing this ethnonationalist outlook, Korean TV programs and commercial films frequently featured Korean transnational adult adoptees seeking biological family members and reuniting with them, resulting in happy and tearful reunions. In sum, ever since the end of the Korean War, the portrayal of Korean adoptees as pitiful orphans and grateful rescuees has been ubiquitous, and the idea that adult adoptees' search and reunion would result in an unquestionably satisfying ending has been prevalent. This book tackles these essentialized notions of what it means to be a transnational adoptee by focusing on theater and performance works that challenge them.

---

1. Depending on the source, the number of Korean children officially adopted overseas fluctuates from 150,000 to 200,000. E. J. Kim, *Adopted Territory*; Hübinette, "Adopted Koreans"; and R. M. Lee et al., "Comparing the Ethnic Identity."

2. According to a 2009 United Nations report from the Department of Economic and Social Affairs, China and Guatemala have replaced Korea in terms of numbers of children sent overseas for adoption. United Nations Department of Economic and Social Affairs, *Child Adoption: Trends and Policies*. Between 1953 and 2008, the United States ranked first among receiving countries, taking in 109,242 Korean children, more than half the total while other rankings of Korean adoptees by nationality include France, 11,165 from 1968 to 2008; Sweden, 9,051 from 1957 to 2005; Denmark, 9,297 from 1965 to 2008; and Norway, 6,295 from 1955 to 2008. E. J. Kim, *Adopted Territory*, 21. Kim draws from Hübinette and the Korean Ministry of Health, Welfare and Family Affairs (MIHWAF).

3. Woo, *Framed by War*.

4. Pate, *From Orphan to Adoptee*, 21–40.

5. Pate, 134.

6. E. J. Kim, *Adopted Territory*, 244.

Unsettling Acts: Performing Transnational Adoption highlights the staging of Korean transnational adoptees' birth search and reunion as a generative catalyst to open critical dialogues about the predicament and possibility associated with the process of the search and reunion. While examining the selected works, I argue that performing transnational adoption is an act of unsettling dominant discourses about Korean transnational adoption and adoptees. To be specific, birth search and reunion onstage unsettles postwar humanitarian, colorblind multicultural, and ethnonationalist adoption scripts that have pathologed adoptees in both adoptive and birth cultures. These predetermined scripts have not only restricted the scope of stories of transnational adoption from Korea but also reduced the subjectivity of worldwide Korean adoptees. Each of the theater and performance works analyzed in this book contests the historical and ongoing essentialist scripts imposed upon Korean adoptees, thus contributing to a greater understanding of the lives of transnational subjects—adoptees. In this creative realm where the possibilities of expression are boundless, the selected theater and performance works defy the compulsory demarcations of transnational adoptees and delineate a performative potential for the exploration of Korean transnational adoption in all its intricacy. Hence, this book presents the theater and performance of birth search and reunion as a transformative location where myths about Korean transnational adoption are disrupted and the ongoing process of making and unmaking adoptees' kinship, identity, and belonging in the twenty-first century can be reimagined.

As a close reading of Korean adoptee representations in theater and performance, this book poses this main question: by whom, how, and why is Korean transnational adoption performed onstage? To answer this question, I survey twelve contemporary theater and performance works mostly from the 2010s depicting Korean transnational adoptees' birth searches and reunions. In these works, the performance of birth search and reunion has brought to light the complexities of Korean transnational adoption's history and practices. In terms of geographical origin and genre, the works are fairly diverse: they come from Korea, the United States, the United Kingdom, Belgium, and Denmark, and include plays, a musical, autobiographical solo performances, community-based and immersive theater, and performance art. Of particular significance is the conversation this book enters into with artists of works produced in the 2010s, a decade when Korean adoptee artists continued their production and dissemination of consciousness-raising scholarship and activism on adoption issues from adoptees' viewpoints launched in the 1990s. These artists' explorations question previous and concurrent appropriations of adoptees in representation and assert their agency over how and by whom they are represented. Their adoptee-centered artworks illuminate the path for the next generation of adoptee artists and artists who are cathected to adoption-related topics beyond unquestioned essentialist adoption scripts. In this book, I also acknowledge the diversity of spectatorship, which includes adoptees, adoptive and birth family members, as well as the larger public, who react in various ways to these performances.

Tracing links between adoption and Western dramatic fiction from premodern to contemporary times in such works as Sophocles's *Oedipus Rex*, Shakespeare's *The Winter's Tale*, and Edward Albee's *The American Dream*,[7] Marianne Novy finds that theater can bring together people "with every relation to adoption, including total ignorance" and allow them to experience various perspectives on adoption.[8] Novy also writes that Western theater presents different representations of adoption and enables public discussions on the subject to take place while adding a new dimension to television and news media depictions of adoption.[9] Whereas adoption in general has appeared as a subject matter in theater, Karen Shimakawa notes that "the predicament of Korean American adoptees is a topic not frequently acknowledged or discussed within Asian American theatre/studies (let alone mainstream theatre/culture)."[10] Given this lack of acknowledgment, SooJin Pate's insistence on the importance of widening the scope of critical adoption studies, specifically through the lens of Korean adoptee artists' performances focusing on their own Korean transnational adoption experiences, is apt.[11] Peggy Phelan also asserts that "other art forms—song, dance, painting, video, spoken word, performance—should be more fully embraced by critical adoption studies because these forms allow more access points for more people involved in the adoption complex."[12]

While calls for more discussion about adoption in theater and performance or about theater and performance in critical adoption studies are welcome, the premise of this project emerged from a realization of the dearth of Korean transnational adoption scholarship in theater and performance

---

7. See chapters 2, 3, and 6 of Novy, *Reading Adoption*.
8. Novy, 187.
9. Novy, 187.
10. Shimakawa, *National Abjection*, 65.
11. Pate, *From Orphan to Adoptee*, 158–61. Note: a main concern of the field of critical adoption studies is to identify the race, class, age, and language doctrines that underpin master adoption narratives and to center adoptees' voices and viewpoints in adoption stories. Suh and Hemmeke, "What CDA/CDS Scholars Are Doing," 364. For more information about critical adoption studies, see Homans et al., "Critical Adoption Studies," in which the authors write about the intersection of their research with the field of study.
12. Phelan, "Letter to the Special Issue Editor," in Homans et al., "Critical Adoption Studies," 8.

studies on the one hand and scholarly consideration of theater and performance in adoption studies on the other.[13] Marking the intersection between the two fields of research—theater and performance studies and critical adoption studies—this book pinpoints theater and performance as a vital site for contextualizing Korean transnational adoption and adoptees' experiences in conversations about the formations of identity, kinship, and belonging across Korea, the United States, and beyond. *Unsettling Acts* thus contributes to both theater and performance studies and adoption scholarship by showing how the selected artists' works utilize the imagination, immediacy, and intimacy of theater and performance to unsettle normalized ideas and long-standing myths about Korean transnational adoption. Writing about performance, Richard Schechner highlights the importance of examining "every aspect of gathering/performing/dispersing . . . from the point of view of the performers and that of the spectators."[14] For Schechner, such thorough examination leads to a fuller understanding not only about the process of making art "but also about social life because theater is both intentionally and non-consciously a paradigm of culture and culture-making."[15] In this sense, the theater and performance works in this book from inception to production present adoption culture-making that values adoptees' experiences. Moreover, adoption is not just about practices but also about feelings, and theater, with its multitude of affects that are immediately shared with audiences, provides a powerful lens for the examination and exploration of feelings. Within this framework, this book aims to serve as an epistemological nodal point for adoption discourses, demonstrating how theater and performance can harness the power of knowledge, emotion, and empathy. *Unsettling Acts* thus seeks to amplify adoption culture–changing voices and visions that resonate strongly with those who care about transnational adoption and adoptees both on and offstage.

Novy identifies three representative narratives of adoption in literature and culture: the search for birth parents (with sometimes dire consequences), the joyful reunion, and the blissful adoption.[16] Novy states that most adoptees depicted in "canonical literature, fairy tales, and folklore . . . find their

---

13. As of this writing, previous scholarship regarding Korean transnational adoption and adoptee theater and performance includes chapter 2 in Shimakawa, *National Abjection*, 64–65; Bryant, "Performing Race and Place in Asian America"; Miseong Woo, "Performing the Diasporic Sensibility of Displacement"; Na, "Empathic Imagination" (ch. 4); Na, "Re-made in Korea"; Jieun Lee, "Performing Transnational Adoption"; Jieun Lee, "Transnational Journey into Belonging"; and Ginther, "Dramaturgy of Deprivation."

14. Schechner, *Performance Theory*, 202–3.

15. Schechner, 203.

16. Novy, *Reading Adoption*, 7.

identity in meeting their birth parents."[17] Using *Oedipus Rex* as an example of search and reunion in literature, Novy views Oedipus's birth search as a heroic quest, even though it leads to tragedy.[18] However, she finds the play problematic because it "emphatically defines genetic parenthood as the only real parenthood."[19] Furthermore, as the first story about adoption written in the Western world,[20] the play suggests that adoptees can come to terms with their identity when finding their birth families, since Oedipus, according to Novy, defines his parentage as his identity when he affirms to himself that he will know who he is.[21] In contrast to Oedipus's quest, the stories of Korean adoptees' birth search and reunion performed in the works discussed in this book present uneasy encounters that complicate identity and kinship rather than provide the adoptees a definite sense of who they are and where they belong. In this context, the Korean adoptee characters, performers, and playwrights analyzed here unpack complex issues, such as unequal motherhood, reproductive and racial injustice, gender and sexual violence toward adoptees. Often overlooked, these issues are nonetheless deeply entangled with transracial and transnational adoption stories that favor nonbiological family-making practices. Thus, I contend that the performances of Korean adoptees' birth search and reunion examined in this book involve more than a search for origins or a surpassing of biological family structure toward a postmodern adoptive kinship. Rather, they exercise unsettling acts that dismantle mythicized transnational adoption narratives while neither essentializing biological blood-relatedness as real kinship nor romanticizing birth search and reunion as a journey toward individual or familial wholeness.

Richard Weil conceptualizes international adoption as "quiet migration,"[22] referring to the predominance in transnational adoption narratives from the adoptive parents' point of view, and the silencing of adoptees' own voices. Starting in the 1990s, a number of academics, activists, and artists, many of them adoptees themselves, have contested this silencing and worked on

---

17. Novy, 1.
18. Novy, 45.
19. Novy, 33.
20. Novy quotes Jean Paton, who wrote that *Oedipus Rex* was "the first adoption life history." Paton, *Orphan Voyage*, 15, as quoted in Novy, 37.
21. Novy, 48. Oedipus sets out to find his birth parents and identity only indirectly, since his direct intention is to find the cause or person responsible for the plague ravaging Thebes. He eventually finds out that he himself is the culprit. According to Margaret Homans, Oedipus does not so much realize his need to know himself by reconnecting with his birth parents, but that "interpreting his wound[,] the feeling of injurious loss itself, rather than lost objects, makes Oedipus who he is." Homans, *Imprint of Another Life*, 222.
22. Weil uses the words "quiet migration" in the sense that works about international migrations of adults or groups of people have usually overshadowed writings about transnational migration of children relinquished for adoption. Weil, "International Adoptions."

personal and collective levels using diverse means of communication and in various artistic genres, to express the multiplicity of transnational adoption experiences. Among these international adoptee artists are filmmakers Deann Borshay Liem and Glenn Morey; writers Jane Jeong Trenka, Sun Yung Shin, Jennifer Kwon Dobbs, and Maja Lee Langvad; graphic novelist Lisa Wool-Rim Sjöblom; visual and multimedia artists kate-hers RHEE, kimura byol lemoine, and Jane Jin Kaisen; hip-hop musician Dan Matthews; and stand-up performer Joel Kim Booster. According to Kimberly McKee, by sharing their experiences through artistic means, adoptee artists disrupt master narratives and change perceptions about transnational adoptees, and in the process find kinship and affinity as part of a larger group with access to unlimited ways of defining themselves and their belonging.[23] Also discussing Korean transnational adoptee artists, Pate states that "by highlighting the contradictions of Korean adoption, these artists produce personal narratives that act as counterhegemonic narratives."[24] It is in light of these premises that *Unsettling Acts* examines the theater and performance works of adoptee artists who portray their own experiences, understandings, and imaginations of birth search and reunion to audiences who then formulate a bodily testimony and community of care (chapters 2 and 3). While the greatest number of Korean adoptees reside in the United States, transnational adoption to Western and Northern Europe from Korea is also significant, and this book acknowledges the voices of Korean adoptee theater and performance artists from outside North America as well (chapter 4). One of my aims in this book is to gain new insights into adoption and birth search and reunion from the point of view of those most concerned—adoptees themselves, whose counterhegemonic voices can break the silences of adoption. To this end, I view Korean adoptee-centered plays and performances engaged in explorations of search-and-reunion narratives which encompass and express the historical, sociocultural, and emotional complexities of Korean transnational adoption as what Eleana Kim terms "the transnational Korean adoptee counterpublic."[25]

Along with the US- and Europe-based Korean adoptee theater and performance counterpublic, contemporary non-adoptee Korean playwrights have also formed a theatrical counterpublic in Korea, notably from the 2010s. Korean theater works that represent nonnormative family formations existed

---

23. McKee, *Disrupting Kinship*, 81–82.
24. Pate, *From Orphan to Adoptee*, 9.
25. E. J. Kim, *Adopted Territory*, 9. Citing Michael Warner, Kim states that community, culture, and kinship should be viewed as effects of "contingent performances and world-making practices" rather than considered "natural or preexistent." E. J. Kim, 100; and Warner, *Publics and Counterpublics*, 56, 124.

before the 2010s,[26] but theatrical depictions of Korean transnational adoption and adoptees began appearing much more frequently and pronouncedly in the 2010s.[27] These works have foregrounded nuanced Korean transnational adoption experiences in an attempt to offset the essentialized exposés of adoptees' birth search and reunion that were common in Korean television shows and films from the 1990s to the 2010s (chapter 1). The exposés tended to repeat formulaic depictions of adoptees' birth search and reunion as a return that guaranteed reunion with their biological family and hence discovery of their authentic identity and place of belonging. By contrast, a handful of Korean theatrical pieces utilized different ways of telling Korean transnational adoption stories to reveal the enduring intricacies of adoptees' birth search and reunion as well as transnational adoption's entanglement with postwar Korean culture and history. The works chosen for this book situate transnational adoption within critiques of the systems of sexism, patriarchy, and US militarism that have propelled Korea's involvement in the transnational practice of sending away babies and children for adoption. The works' staged counterpublics allow Korean audiences to not only consider the complicated experiences of returning Korean adoptees but also wrestle with their societal responsibility for the systemic marginalization of disenfranchised women, children, and families.

Unsettling Acts illuminates the importance of contemporary theater and performance of Korean transnational adoption. The vigor of their acts contests the distorted imaginations and skewed ideologies imposed on Korean transnational adoption and adoptees, allowing audiences to better grasp adoptees'

---

26. Before the 2010s, Korean playwrights wrote about family from a critical perspective. For example, Sukkyung Kim argues that playwright Geun Hyung Park's plays from 1988 to 2009 contest hegemonic family ideologies and familism in Korea. S. Kim, "A Study on Critical Understanding of Family Ideologies in Geun Hyung Park's Plays."

27. Korean search engine news archive results using the keywords "입양" (adoption) and "연극" (theater) show few theatrical production records from the 1990s, reflecting the recentness of interest in adoption as a focal point for the theatrical expression of social critique. 나는 알고싶다 (*I Want to Know*, 1991), about orphan adoption from a ten-year-old boy's view of the world of adults, was written by Sangrye Lee and staged at a one-act-play festival. *Yonhap News*, "One-Act Play Festival." Specifically regarding transnational adoption from Korea, Jangun Kim's play 캠프 케이시 문 밖에서 (*Outside of Camp Casey*, 1996) is the first notable production that discusses adoption and prostitution linked to the US military presence in Korea. Other productions include 나는 빠리의 택시운전사 (*Taxi Driver in Paris*, 1997), in which a Korean expat encounters a Korean French adoptee in Paris, and 바리: 잊혀진 자장가 (*Bari: Forgotten Lullaby*, 1999), which employs the Korean myth of *Baridegi* (the Abandoned Princess Bari) to set up the narrative of a Korean transnational adoptee's experience. 헬로우 마미 (*Hello, Mommy*, 2010) by JinWol Yoo primarily follows a Korean transnational adoptee's reunion with her birth mother. While these dramatizations of adoption show an interest in depicting adoption and adoptees in theater, the works from the 2010s analyzed in chapter 1 engage with Korean transnational adoption as a major theme and Korean transnational adoptees as main characters in recurring productions rather than sporadic and one-time special performances.

lived experiences. This in turn makes audiences recognize identity, kinship, and belonging as historically and transnationally configured and connected to social constructions and injustices of race, class, gender, sexuality, ethnicity, and nationality. In this book, I present theater and performance as an impetus with which artists and audiences together can rethink human mobility and possibility in relation to transnational adoption from Korea and, by extension, Asia and the Global South to the Global North.[28] The unsettling acts in theater and performance I examine here flip the script of transnational adoption and lay a path to radical forms of adoption-related representation, imagination, and collaboration across media, genres, and nations.[29] My hope is that this book will encourage present and future adoptee and non-adoptee artists and activists to pursue works and actions aimed at bringing about adoption justice on a global scale.

A Historical Trajectory of Transnational Adoption from South Korea to the United States

To enhance understanding of the selected artists' iterations and interventions with Korean transnational adoption, a historical explanation will be helpful since Korean transnational adoption has been driven by several significant historic factors. Through this brief history, the trifecta of postwar humanitarian, colorblind multicultural, and ethnocentric nationalist ideologies can be better understood, particularly in how the United States, as the largest receiving country of Korean adoptees, has shaped the discourse surrounding Korean transnational adoption. On the Korean side, the prevalent belief in racial purity led to the relinquishment to the American adoption market of mixed-race children born of Korean women and American soldiers following the Korean War.[30] At the same time, on the US side, Christian American narratives of salvation boosted demand for foreign children, allowing the postwar supply from Korea to be readily absorbed.[31] At the forefront of this movement

---

28. Homans, *Imprint of Another Life.*
29. The phrase "flip the script" forms the broad title of the adoptee-centered anthology *Flip the Script: Adult Adoptee Anthology.* The phrase is a nod to an adoptee movement established in 2014 around the concept of "flip the script." See "It Took the #FliptheScript Village . . . ," *Lost Daughters.* This movement started with a Twitter hashtag (#FliptheScript and #NationalAdoptionMonth) by Rosita González at *Lost Daughters,* an "independent collaborative writing project founded in 2011," during National Adoption Month. The founder of *Lost Daughters,* Amanda Transue-Woolston, originated the phrase in a video clip for the independently published book. See "#FliptheScript 2014 (the Origins)," *Lost Daughters.*
30. Oh, *To Save the Children,* 48–75.
31. Oh defines Christian Americanism as a "fusion of vaguely Christian principles with values identified as exceptionally 'American': an expansive sense of responsibility and a strong belief in the importance of family." Oh, 79.

was the Holt Adoption Program, founded by Harry and Bertha Holt, an evangelical couple from rural Oregon whose adoption program understood its mission as saving Korean orphans by Christianizing them.³² With the involvement of several Catholic, Seventh-day Adventist, and other religious organizations, an international adoption movement emerged with religious and sociopolitical strings attached.³³ During the Cold War era, adopting Korean children came to be viewed as a patriotic as well as a Christian act—saving children from atheistic Communism.³⁴ In this sense, international adoption was ideologically linked to American values, according to which adoption gave "individual Americans a chance to participate in spreading democracy abroad."³⁵ During this period, transnational adoption became an industry, buoyed by the post–Korean War relationship between the United States and Korea, allied in their staunch anticommunist stance and Christian missionary ideology.

The US media participated in linking adoption with these ideologies, through print, newsreels, and even Hollywood films. Susie Woo documents a newsreel showing US servicemen at an orphanage giving out clothes to "South Korean War waifs," as the film's voice-over describes the children.³⁶ The 1957 Hollywood movie *Battle Hymn* depicts the story of Dean Hess (portrayed by Rock Hudson), a real-life minister from an Ohio church who as a US Air Force pilot during the Korean War participated in the 1950 airlift rescue of more than nine hundred Korean children. Woo describes the climactic scene of desperate, grimy-faced Korean children dressed in tatters running barefoot across an airfield and being lifted by US pilots into huge planes, which then soar away to safety.³⁷ While widely disseminated in mass media, such images of Korean children as war orphans were no more than images, as war orphans adopted by Americans during the post–Korean War period made up less than

---

32. Oh quotes Harry Holt, who declared that he wished to fulfill "a three-fold purpose: to save lives, to get these children into homes, and to get them into Christian homes." Oh, *To Save the Children*, 96. Also see the Holt International website, which describes itself as "a Christian organization committed to expressing God's compassion for children." "Gifts of Hope," Holt International. According to David Ray Papke, the Holt adoption agency "required that the adoptive parents be church-going Protestants, and they referred Catholics and Jews who wanted to adopt Korean children to other agencies." Papke, "Transracial Adoption in the United States."

33. McKee, *Disrupting Kinship*, 4.

34. Park Nelson, *Invisible Asians*, 43.

35. McKee, *Disrupting Kinship*, 8.

36. Woo records the full narration over these shots in the newsreel: "Spring is a bloody time in Korea, . . . but the spirit of spring is unbound in the hearts of these South Korean War waifs. They line up in one of the most heartwarming fashion shows this uncertain spring season." Woo, *Framed by War*, 40–41.

37. Woo, 77.

4 percent of all Korean adoptions before 1962.[38] The perpetuation of images of Korean children rescuees and American saviors in US media reflects the instrumentalization of transnational adoption to serve worldwide American postwar humanitarian dogma. Moreover, the persistence of the narrative of rescuing Korean War orphans concealed the reality of America's responsibility for the division of Korea, US military massacres of Korean civilians, American GI- and Korean government–controlled prostitution, and the ensuing proxy adoption industry.[39] As Eleana Kim states, in the postwar context of burgeoning Korean transnational adoption, "This Janus-faced nature of the American military occupation—exploitative and humanitarian—has characterized the neocolonial relationship between America and Korea since the 1950s."[40]

On the surface, Korea's participation in international adoption seems to have been driven by the simple need to find homes for its "unwanted" and "unfortunate" children. Rather than celebrating transnational adoption as an admirable mission to save children from poor "Third World" environments, however, it is important to consider *why* so many Korean children were unable to find a home in their own country and were raised overseas, and *why* Korean adoptees have come to form one of the largest groups in the Korean diaspora through this systemic form of transnational adoption that continues long after the end of the Korean War. A closer look at postwar Korean society finds that the foreign relief aid institutionalized in the immediate postwar period included financial support, technical assistance, and the establishment of foster care and adoption practices. This dependence on external sources of welfare from Western countries prevented Korea from establishing an internal social welfare system of its own.[41] Moreover, the regime of Park Chung-hee (1963–79) espoused a Cold War ideology that held that the country should commit to economic development based on capitalistic values.[42] This belief in "growth first" and the need to chase after profits facilitated exports by major Korean conglomerates but hampered the creation of a sustainable safety net

---

38. Park Nelson, *Invisible Asians*, 41. Park Nelson uses demographics from Hübinette's dissertation, "Comforting an Orphaned Nation," as well as from Weil, "International Adoption."

39. Established in the 1950s, proxy adoptions let US citizens adopt foreign children by assigning a proxy agent to make decisions on their behalf while they stayed in America. The proxy agent in Korea did all the legal paperwork following Korean law, and the child was subsequently sent to the United States as the legal child of the American family. The Korean government favored the fact that the child was legitimately adopted before emigration, and adoptive parents also liked the time and cost savings involved. Proxy adoptions took only three months or so to complete because there were fewer (or no) administrative and social welfare requirements. Due to a lack of accountability in regard to the children, Congress banned proxy adoptions in 1961. Oh, *To Save the Children*, 95, 99.

40. E. J. Kim, *Adopted Territory*, 51.

41. Hübinette, "Comforting an Orphaned Nation," 54.

42. J. K. Lee, *Service Economies*.

for socially disadvantaged Koreans. By the 1960s, the dire economic situations of birth families were one of the main reasons for the relinquishment of children for international adoption.[43] In this social climate, many birth families tended to believe that their "unwelcomed" children in Korea would certainly have more opportunities for a better life in a wealthier country, the United States.[44]

During this era of feverishly rapid industrialization in Korea, scores of young rural women moved to urban areas to become workers.[45] Despite women's growing participation in the economy, Korean culture and society continued to prioritize patrilineal kinship, reinforcing established family structures with the male as head of the household. In other words, while many young women joined the industrial forces during these times of great change, patriarchal values and misogynistic familism endured. In 1962 the Korean government introduced family planning and population control programs to lower the fertility rate, usurping women's reproductive rights by exerting medical power over their bodies.[46] As part of this control regime, the male-preferring culture enforced the practice of sex-biased abortion, with the support of the government.[47] Moreover, children from families outside the "norm" of the heteropatriarchal married blood-related family—especially in unwed or single mother households—were discriminated against.[48] As the normal family myth became the ideological seedbed of the transnational adoption industry, children born of ostracized women came to be readily viewed as a source for the propagation of transnational adoption.[49] Tobias Hübinette observes that during the twenty-five or so years starting from the early 1960s, young

---

43. Oh, *To Save the Children*, 126.

44. Oh, 126.

45. O. Cho, "Modernization Experiences," 210–11; and M. Kim, "Gender, Work and Resistance."

46. Eunjung Kim, *Curative Violence*.

47. In consequence of this project, "the average number of children per woman had decreased from 6.3 in 1960 to 1.6 in 1990." Hübinette, "Comforting an Orphaned Nation," 65.

48. E. J. Kim, *Adopted Territory*, 25. Drawing on data from MIHWAF, Kim identifies the circumstances that from 1958 to 2008 caused Korean adoptions overseas as single mothers (102,433), broken homes (28,956), and abandoned children (29,975). Also see C. H. Park, *Korean Family and Misogyny*.

49. Children of what Korean society views as nonnormative families are marginalized because they are considered "abnormal" at various levels of both private and public spheres. For example, mass media outlets use discriminatory language and attitudes about children who are orphaned or nurtured by one parent (mostly single women) or relatives, misleadingly reporting that such children tend to become criminals since their familial backgrounds are "improperly" built or broken and are unable to adjust to "normal" life. Pathologizing children from "abnormal" families serves to perpetuate the myth of the "normal" family in Korea. For more on criticism of normalized family structure and government policy in Korea, see H. K. Kim, *Strange Normal Family*.

women factory workers relinquished the most children for adoption of all the segments of Korean society.[50] In sum, largely poor working-class unwed and single women's children were steered for overseas adoption by profit-oriented adoption agencies.

McKee dubs this business the "transnational adoption industrial complex (TAIC)—a neocolonial, multi-million-dollar global industry that commodifies children's bodies [. . . reflecting] the intersections and connections of the Korean social welfare state, orphanages, adoption agencies, and American immigration legislation."[51] The Korean TAIC provided a significantly less expensive, faster, and less bureaucratic process than in other countries, placing Korea at the top of the list for the exportation of children, and rendered international adoption in the 1960s and '70s "almost synonymous with adoption from Korea."[52] This trend increased under the succeeding regime of Chun Doo-hwan (1980–88), whose deregulations in the 1980s eliminated the quota system for adoption agencies and enabled greater economic competition among them. As a result, the 1980s witnessed the peak in transnational adoption from Korea, with a total number of 66,511 adoption cases.[53] In summary, from the 1960s to the 1980s, under two consecutive Korean military dictatorships, the Korean transnational adoption industry was buttressed by a patriarchal culture and nationalistic developmentalist agenda. During these decades of prosperity for the adoption business, Korea not only dismissed the rights and needs of the poor and working class but also marginalized and stigmatized single and unwed motherhood. The nation thus perpetrated a multilayered oppression of disadvantaged Koreans for the benefit of a transnational adoption industry whose success depended on the mass relinquishment of children.

Across the Pacific, under the flag of US multiculturalism in the 1970s and '80s, transnational adoption from Asia to the United States further increased as Native American and African American communities took to protesting against domestic adoption of Native American and African American children by white parents.[54] In the 1970s, the National Association of Black Social Workers (NABSW) asserted that the removal of Black children for transracial adoption was an act of cultural and racial genocide.[55] Along with this

---

50. Hübinette, "Comforting an Orphaned Nation," 32.
51. McKee, *Disrupting Kinship*, 2.
52. Hübinette, "Comforting an Orphaned Nation," 69.
53. Hübinette, 71. Regarding the surge in international adoption from Korea in the 1970s and '80s, Eleana Kim uses sources from MIHWAF to document these figures. E. J. Kim, *Adopted Territory*, 35, table 4.
54. Park Nelson, *Invisible Asians*, 92–120.
55. R. M. Lee, "Transracial Adoption Paradox."

objection to adoptions of children of color by white adoptive parents, another reason transnational adoption was favored over domestic adoption was the idea of a so-called clean break. Barbara Yngvesson writes how American and European adoption laws and policies "privilege so-called strong or plenary adoptions in which there is a legal 'clean-break' between the adopted child and its preadoptive kin."[56] Kit Myers notes that the clean break allows a trope in which the adoptee resurfaces as a different individual with a fresh identity, completely detached from past connections.[57] These developments in the US cultural landscape resulted in an increase in overseas adoptions of Asian children, especially as Asian Americans came to be regarded as the model minority. In the 1960s and '70s, East Asian Americans, particularly Chinese Americans and Japanese Americans, became the quintessential signifiers of this model minority, whose desirable features for inclusion in American society included "hard work, family solidarity, discipline, delayed gratification, nonconfrontation, and disdain for welfare."[58] In the eyes of white America, Asian children gained appeal in adoptability due to this stereotype. As Arissa Oh further explains, as "Korean adoptees were part of this reformulation of Asianness [to 'model' citizens]—as malleable children who could be raised to be good Americans, they not only refuted arguments about unassimilable Asians but also were recast as the most desirable of immigrants."[59]

According to Kim Park Nelson, Korean adoptees raised in colorblind white families were rendered racially invisible yet nevertheless viewed themselves "in every possible permutation of Asianness, Whiteness, and racelessness."[60] Park Nelson analyzes a 1975 article published in the *Seattle Times* entitled "Adopted Koreans Fully 'Americanized,'" and explains how the article's title not only praised the Korean child for easily assimilating into American culture but also commended the adoptive family for its effective erasure of the child's Asian origins.[61] Park Nelson also points out that this assimilationist narrative portrays the American story of transnational adoption from Asia as "a win-win situation for Asian adoptees and their White American parents."[62] In this light, Korean adoptees can be seen to have been recruited to promote the notion of colorblindness, which reflected only the mostly white adoptive

56. Yngvesson, "Transnational Adoption and European Immigration Politics," 328.
57. Myers, "'Real' Families," 179.
58. Lee and Zhou, *Asian American Youth*, 18. Also see Laybourn, "Adopting the Model Minority Myth."
59. Oh, *To Save the Children*, 12.
60. Park Nelson, *Invisible Asians*, 10.
61. Skreen, "Adopted Koreans Fully 'Americanized.'" As quoted in Park Nelson, *Invisible Asians*, 4.
62. Park Nelson, *Invisible Asians*, 5.

parents' point of view of their parenting and adoption experience as a celebratory multicultural American practice.[63] In the field of psychology, research led by Oh Myo Kim, Reed Reichwald, and Richard Lee reveals that adoptive parents have a tendency to overvalue their adopted children's cultural socialization to birth culture. While leading them toward social activities related to their birth culture, adoptive parents often overlook their children's very real and consequential experience of racial discrimination in the United States.[64] On the other hand, some adoptive parents, whether through lack of access to information or lack of interest, neglected governmental regulations and failed to obtain properly documented immigrant status for their adopted children, who as a result faced the prospect of deportation as adults.[65] In all, the colorblind multicultural adoption script tended to overlook the real social conditions and needs of transnational and transracial adoptees, erasing their race and origins while failing to address the inevitable issues they would face on account of being considered "other" than white in a white-normative culture. When considering this history, it is important to note that the representation and understanding of Korean transnational adoptees in terms of a colorblind multicultural narrative in a white-normative culture occurred not only in the US context but in Western and Northern Europe as well.[66]

In the late 1980s, Korea was compelled to change its views and policies on transnational adoption. In 1988 the Seoul Olympic Games put Korea under a worldwide spotlight. Focusing not only on the Olympic Games but also on diverse facets of Korean life, international media outlets highlighted Korea's remarkably rapid recovery from the destruction and chaotic aftermath of the Korean War, showcasing the period of soaring economic growth known as the "Miracle on the Han River." However, some Western journalists reported on Korea's practice of international adoption and provoked uproar with criticism of the Korean government for its aggressive and deregulated international

---

63. Park Nelson writes that adoption studies in the 1970s and '80s were centered on adoptive parents' experiences, with positive narratives, but omitted problems associated with adoptees' adjusting to their adoptive environments. Park Nelson, 74–76.

64. Kim, Reichwald, and Lee, "Cultural Socialization in Families."

65. Although the Korean Special Adoption Law passed in 2013 made Korean adoptees eligible for a visa that gave them automatic US citizenship, the law is not retroactive for Koreans adopted before the year 2000 who were eighteen or over at that time. McKee, *Disrupting Kinship*, 47. In chapter 3, one of the adoptee characters in Debra Kim Sivigny's site-specific immersive theater *Hello, My Name Is . . .* is based on a Korean adoptee's deportation as an undocumented adult.

66. For more on the historical, social, and cultural implications of Korean transnational adoption in Western and Northern Europe, see chapter 4.

adoption policy that promoted the child-export business.⁶⁷ North Korean media also condemned South Korea's involvement in international adoption, declaring the "selling [of] Korean offspring to Westerners for profit as an appalling example of 'flunkeyism.'"⁶⁸ Concerned with the deterioration of the national image, over the following decade the South Korean government attempted to regulate the annual number of international adoptions by downsizing adoption agencies and encouraging domestic adoptions through tax reductions. Though in decline, the trend in international adoption continued even after 1996, when Korea became eligible to join the Organisation for Economic Co-operation and Development (OECD), whose stated mission is to "build better policies for better lives [. . . and] shape policies that foster prosperity, equality, opportunity and well-being for all"⁶⁹—a paradoxical statement within the framework of Korea's ongoing transnational adoption industry.

The 1990s marked Korea's entrance to the stage of globalization, termed *segyehwa*. During this period, President Kim Young-sam's (1993–98) administration launched Korea's globalization drive (the Promotion of Globalization Committee [*segyehwachujinwiwonhoe*] was officially formed in 1995), emphasizing a liberal economy and deregulation. This globalization drive encompassed the building of a worldwide Korean community by embracing ethnic Koreans living abroad, including Korean overseas adoptees. Consequently, it came to be generally assumed that returning adoptees innately embodied Korean identity. This assumption stemmed from the ethnonationalist belief in the crucial role of blood ties and consanguineous relationships in identifying Koreanness.⁷⁰ As part of this effort to build a worldwide Korean community, at the turn of the millennium, President Kim Dae-jung (1998–2003) publicly apologized to Korean overseas adoptees for what Korea had done to them. President Kim's speech at a reception for twenty-nine adult adoptees in 1998 reflected this sentiment: "So, we sent you away. Imagining all the *pain* and psychological conflicts that you must have gone through, we are *shamed*. We

---

67. Hübinette lists examples of newspapers that disparaged South Korea's intense participation in international adoption: *New York Times* (April 21, 1988), *International Herald Tribune* (April 22, 1988), and *Washington Post* (December 12, 1988). All discussed South Korea's adoption practice as a trade in human capital. Hübinette, "Comforting an Orphaned Nation," 86.

68. Hübinette, "Comforting an Orphaned Nation," 82; and Hübinette, "North Korea and Adoption."

69. "About," Organisation for Economic Co-operation and Development (OECD).

70. Hübinette, "Comforting an Orphaned Nation," 196–98. Yet the belief in blood-relatedness does not equally apply to other diasporic groups from Korea, such as Koreans from China, Russia, or former Soviet satellite states, revealing the arbitrariness of ethnonationalism. Park Nelson writes about the differences between Korean adoptees' ethnic return and other groups of returnees. Park Nelson, *Invisible Asians*, 188.

are *grateful* to your adopted parents, who have loved you and raised you, but we are also filled with *shame*."[71] Hosu Kim comments: "Kim acknowledged the pain and loss suffered by Korean adoptees. This unprecedented official apology is indicative of how the adoption discourse in South Korea is often deeply associated with negative affects, such as shame and guilt."[72] The Korean government subsequently invited Korean transnational adoptees to Korea, branding them cultural and economic "ambassadors and bridges connecting Korea to the West."[73] Hübinette problematizes these gestures, which, while shining a spotlight on adoptees, did not bring about action to change Korea's involvement in the transnational adoption industry. Rather, by using adoptees to "uphold friendly ties with Western host countries" as a means of expanding Korea's diaspora policy,[74] the overture primarily served the government. Hosu Kim further criticizes the government's offer, observing, "through the return and subsequent reclaiming of their [adoptees'] Koreanness, the adoptee narrative highlights the Korean adoptee as a harbinger of a competitive global Korea," a concept the government utilized to identify Korean adoptees as potential assets for its global neoliberal mission.[75] While the ethnonationalist extension of Koreanness utilizing adoptees may have expanded the Korean geographical imagination of belonging from the 1990s onward, it has not advanced practical discussions of how to support Korean adoptees to achieve betterment and a sense of belongingness within and beyond Korea. Indeed, upon returning to Korea, adoptees still confront a harsh reality—in the words of Park Nelson, a "cultural chasm that separates them from Korean nationals."[76] For instance, looked upon as Korean, adoptee returnees are expected to not only speak the language but also be culturally proficient and are often shamed for their inability to speak their mother tongue.[77]

Also around the turn of the millennium, Korean media increased their coverage of prominent Korean overseas adoptees. The phantasmagoric ethnonationalist exposés produced during this period reflected Korean media's

---

71. Speech cited in H. Kim, *Birth Mothers*, 128–29. Italics added by H. Kim. Translated from Korean into English from "President Kim Dae Jung's Speech."

72. H. Kim, *Birth Mothers*, 129.

73. E. J. Kim, "Our Adoptee, Our Alien," 507.

74. Hübinette, "Comforting an Orphaned Nation," 103. Under Kim Dae-jung's presidency, interest in adoption-related issues grew, leading to the organization of a human rights symposium on Korean adoptees (1998), the establishment of a government-sponsored Adoption Information Center in Seoul (1999) to serve as a resource for visiting adoptees, and the promotion of Korean culture to Korean adoptees in Northern Europe, for example by sending a famous *samulnori* music group to tour that region (2000). Hübinette, 99.

75. H. Kim, *Birth Mothers*, 137.

76. Park Nelson, *Invisible Asians*, 188.

77. Park Nelson, 173.

fascination with success stories and fetishization of returned adoptees. For example, Korean French politicians Fleur Pellerin and Jean-Vincent Placé, Korean Norwegian taekwondo practitioner Nina Solheim, and Korean American mogul skier Toby Dawson have all been made famous in both Korea and their adoptive countries. Toby Dawson, who won a bronze medal at the 2006 Olympic Games in Torino, Italy, appeared with his birth father on *The Oprah Winfrey Show* in 2007 and 2009. Dawson's search-and-reunion story was loosely made into the Korean commercial film and box-office hit *Take Off*.[78] In 2012 Fleur Pellerin was appointed Minister Delegate for Small and Medium Enterprises, Innovations and Digital Economy in the government of President François Hollande. The following year, when Pellerin visited Korea for the first time since her adoption at the age of six months, the Korean media went into a frenzy, touting her as a proud and successful returned Korean woman.[79] Thus, successful Korean transnational adoptees who return to Korea have been proudly hailed and publicized by the media as honorable overseas Koreans, reflecting "an almost exclusive interest in [Korea's] 'model citizen' adoptees."[80] Hübinette points out that this enduring selective interest in up-and-coming Korean diaspora stories can be viewed as a refusal to contend with transnational adoption's negative associations, a refusal that aims "to not be entangled in even more guilt, and [represents] a somewhat cynical way of taking credit for 'model citizen' adoptees in order to raise the country's national prestige and pride in the Western countries."[81]

Aside from these recurring (re)presentations framing the return of Korean overseas adoptees as a model Korean diaspora's homecoming, transnational adoption as a part of contemporary Korean history is hardly discussed, and adoptees still rarely appear in the history of the Korean people as a whole,[82] with a few notable exceptions. In 2011 Korea's legislature amended the adoption law, intending to center efforts on family preservation instead of overseas adoption and to strengthen the rights of birth mothers and adoptees. Specifically, the law required birth parents to wait for a period of seven days

---

78. Herskovitz, "Olympic Star in Tearful Reunion with Korean Dad." Kyung-Sook Boo points out that the Korean title of the film means 국가대표 (*National Team*) and holds a nationalistic connotation. The change to the English title *Take Off* serves a global market, replacing the sense of Korean nationalism with an innocuous ski-jump term. Boo, "Intersections of Historical Remembering."
79. Chun, "From Adopted Child to French 'Fleur'"; and Koo, "From Korean Adoptee to French Minister."
80. Hübinette, "Comforting an Orphaned Nation," 92–93.
81. Hübinette, 105.
82. Rasmussen, "Sublime Object of Adoption," 12.

before consenting to relinquishment, offered counsel on available resources if parents wished to keep the child, and made family court mandatory for birth parents relinquishing a child, thus leaving a governmental record of the adoption.[83] In 2013 the Korean government also signed the Hague Convention on the Protection of Children and Co-operation in Respect of Intercountry Adoption.[84] Originally created in 1993, this measure was meant to safeguard the "best interests of children" and stipulated that children should first be considered for adoption by families in their birth country.[85] Although Korea has signed the convention, it has yet to ratify it at the time of this writing. While Korea has dropped from its top position in the list of sending countries, it continues to practice transnational adoption.[86] In 2019 the top five countries sending children to the United States for adoption were, in descending order, China, Colombia, India, Korea, and Bulgaria.[87] Over the past three decades, during which Korea's position regarding ongoing transnational adoption practices has fluctuated, significant numbers of overseas adult adoptees have returned to Korea to conduct birth searches in the hope of possible reunion with their birth families. As I detail in the next section, the search-and-reunion experiences that these adoptees recount through academic, activist, and artistic works reveal how Korean public and private institutions have represented and misrepresented them through culture and media products.

On Birth Search and Reunion: A Master Script for Korean Adoptee Return

Since the 1990s, search-and-reunion stories shown in Korean reality programs, films, TV dramas, and in some literary works, have become the ubiquitous

---

83. S. K. Kim, "Abandoned Babies."

84. "The Republic of Korea Signs the 1993 Hague Intercountry Adoption Convention," Hague Conference on Private International Law (HCCH).

85. Oh, *To Save the Children*, 206. Also see "33: Convention of 29 May 1993 on Protection of Children and Co-operation in Respect of Intercountry Adoption," Article 33, HCCH.

86. "Expert Discussion on the Hague Convention on Intercountry Adoption Held," Ministry of Health and Welfare. In 2016 the nation spent only 10.4 percent of its GDP on social welfare, ranking thirty-fourth among the thirty-five OECD member countries. D. S. Kim, "Korea Ranks Bottom in OECD for Welfare Spending."

87. US Department of State Bureau of Consular Affairs, "FY 2019 Annual Report on Intercountry Adoption." For a discussion of adoption policy in China, see Johnson, *China's Hidden Children*; and Wang, *Outsourced Children*.

master narrative of Korean transnational adoption's "odyssey."[88] The trope of long-lost children reuniting with their biological parents already contains an element of spectacle, but the spectacular aspects of desperate searches and dramatic reunions are arbitrarily heightened when mediatization occurs. For instance, reality TV programs often cover search-and-reunion stories by presenting the actual first meeting after years of separation, attempting to move viewers to joyful, tear-filled catharsis. These experiences appear to be consumed as a sort of rite of passage for returned adoptees, promising complete affective belonging when they are confirmed as Korean daughters and sons through the search-and-reunion process. Audiences experience vicarious pleasure watching these representations that depict adoptees' searches and reunions as successful and happy, thus providing temporary emotional fulfillment instead of the senses of sadness, loss, or longing attached to the hidden side of Korean transnational adoption. As a result, audiences tend to view Korean transnational adoption in a simplistic light rather than as a critical issue that should evoke their concern about what birth search and reunion means to adoptees, birth families, and society at large. These spectacularized searches and reunions continue to appear in Korean TV dramas and films that have recently gained worldwide popularity as part of the *Hallyu* Korean wave of cultural products aimed at global audiences.[89] One early example, the 2004 Korean TV drama 미안하다, 사랑한다 (*I'm Sorry, I Love You*), presents the story of a Korean man relinquished as a child and adopted by an Australian couple. As an adult, having learned that his birth mother is still alive in Korea, is a successful actress, and has another son, he seeks revenge for his abandonment.[90] So Young Park discusses how the Korean transnational adoptee figure has "entered into the transnational imaginary" through *Hallyu*[91] and

---

88. See Hübinette's analysis of Korean popular cultural texts, including films, news media, and photography in the 1990s and 2000s. Hübinette particularly explores fiction films that include representations of Korean adoptees, such as *Susanne Brink's Arirang* (1991), directed by Gil-su Jang; *Berlin Report* (1991), written and directed by Kwang-su Park; *Wild Animals* (1997), written and directed by Ki-duk Kim; and *Love* (1999), directed by Jang-su Lee. Hübinette, "Comforting an Orphaned Nation." More contemporary commercial films include *Champion* (2018), directed by Yong-wan Kim. In literature, see Eundeok Hwang's novel 우리들, 킴 (*We, Kim*, 2017) and Haejin Cho's 단순한 진심 (*Simple Sincerity*, 2019), the winner of the Daesan Literary Award.

89. *Hallyu* denotes South Korea's rapid growth in cultural (and other) products, which have found worldwide popularity since the late 1990s. These products include music (K-pop), films, TV shows (K-drama), and video games, as well as food, fashion, and even medical services such as plastic surgery. D. Y. Jin, *New Korean Wave*.

90. More recent examples of Korean adoptees represented in Korean TV drama are discussed in the conclusion; see *Guardian: The Lonely and Great God* (2016) and *Vincenzo* (2021).

91. S. Y. Park, "Transnational Adoption, 'Hallyu,' and the Politics of Korean Popular Culture," 152.

notes that returning adoptees are depicted in a melodramatic way, which transforms the "personal and political trauma of transnational adoption into a new form of cultural commodity."[92] Analyzing contemporary US media's stereotypes of Asian American adoptee women and girls, McKee also delves into search and reunion, questioning its fantasized depiction as a happy object.[93] I would assert that such highly packaged (re)presentational commodities have become the archetype for search-and-reunion stories in and out of contemporary Korea, a master script for Korean transnational adoption which flattens Korean adoptees' experiences and deters them from other narrative paths.

In contrast to spectacularized media and cultural representations insinuating that every adoptee experiences this dramatic event, not all Korean transnational adoptees conduct a birth search. Andrea Kim Cavicchi writes that "since the early 2000s, approximately 3,000 to 5,000 adult adoptees return to their birth country each year for short-term or long-term visits or to reside."[94] Park Nelson points out that a great many of the adoptees who visit Korea do not travel with the intent of conducting a birth search and reunion.[95] While adoptees come to Korea for many reasons other than birth search and reunion,[96] for those who do search for their birth family, a happy reunion is far from certain. Citing statistics from the Adoption Institute and a 2010 International Korean Adoptee Association (IKAA) survey report, Sara Docan-Morgan writes that "only 22% of Korean adoptees have actively searched for their birth parents and less than eight percent of Korean adoptees who search for their families are able to reunite."[97] Many adoptees' actual experiences of birth searches do not result in a reunion because of lack of information, original documentation mistakes, or the unwillingness of birth family members to reunite. Illuminating the communicative strains that Korean transnational adoptees experience surrounding the entire gamut of their reunions, Docan-Morgan further calls attention to the availability of proper support and resources for adoptees involved in reunions.[98]

---

92. S. Y. Park, 159.

93. McKee, *Adoption Fantasies*. The use of the words "happy object" here is a nod to Sara Ahmed, who writes of "the family as a happy object," and that we are "directed by the promise of happiness." Ahmed, *Promise of Happiness*, 21, 14.

94. Cavicchi, "Power, Resistance, and Subjectivity."

95. Park Nelson, *Invisible Asians*, 157.

96. According to Park Nelson, aside from searching for their birth families, Korean transnational adoptees return to Korea "to connect to their Korean-ness," to meet other adoptees, and simply for vacation. Park Nelson, 162. Also see Choe, "An Adoptee Returns to South Korea, and Changes Follow"; and Jones, "Why a Generation of Adoptees Is Returning to South Korea."

97. Docan-Morgan, "Korean Adoptees' Birth Family Reunions," 596.

98. Docan-Morgan, *In Reunion*, 254–62.

Going back to the narrative of birth search and reunion, Hosu Kim criticizes its failure "to provide a discursive framework for meaningful reparation for sixty-five years of transnational adoption practice."[99] In my view, allied with Kim, the conspicuous repetition of the skewed search-and-reunion narrative leads spectators to expect happy endings for all Korean transnational adoption stories, resulting in an affective and cognitive stasis. The preordained dénouements celebrate adoptees' blood-relatedness while dismissing their actual experiences with adoptive and birth families and cultures. Moreover, the habitual catharsis of tearful but joyful search-and-reunion stories eliminates the need for or possibility of adoptee-generated conversations about what should change and come next for adoptees. By ignoring or glossing over adoptees' complex and diverse realities, these lopsided search-and-reunion stories, which the public is encouraged to believe are typical, prevent the development of multifaceted understandings of transnational adoption and adoptees' experiences.

From another perspective, discussing the meanings of adoptees' search and reunion, Betty Jean Lifton writes that "the very idea of search and reunion is empowering. . . . Healing begins when adoptees take control of their lives by making the decision to search [. . . to embark] on this forbidden journey toward self."[100] Kimberly Leighton develops this notion of search for identity in adoption by pointing out that "as a desire to know the self through *genealogical*—rather than *genetic*—narratives of identity, the adoptee's 'search' is a continuous and open-ended *process of identity-making*."[101] In a similar vein, from her analysis of both private/interpersonal and public/collective dimensions of Korean adoptees' return to Korea, Elise Prébin contends that, cultural differences notwithstanding, adoptees' family searches, reunions, and post-reunions with their biological families are valuable to themselves and their birth families. Prébin suggests that reunions in Korea are "a process of recognition of blood ties that, at the same time, reestablishes symbolic continuity and aims at the acceptance of difference and loss in order for individuals to 'live better'—that is, without overwhelming feelings of resentment or sadness."[102] By looking specifically at biological parents' environments, principles, and representations, Prébin reveals the different kinds of "relatedness" that can arise for adoptees from these reunions.[103] Her focus on birth parents' point of view and adoptees' alternative relatedness to their birth families

---

99. H. Kim, "Reparation Acts," 323.
100. Lifton, *Journey of the Adopted Self*, 128.
101. Leighton, "Adoption and Critical Models of Identity," 40. Italics in original.
102. Prébin, *Meeting Once More*, 15–16.
103. Prébin, 16.

produces unique insights into the adoptive parent–centric relationships of transnational adoption.[104] This is not to say that biological connection is the only authentic and viable form of adoptees' relatedness, but to recall the possibility of a constructive outcome of search and reunion that reconfigures the severed other side of their relatedness. Referencing Yngvesson, Prébin further observes that relatedness "combines and accepts a plurality of belongings and fluidity of identities—no matter the outcome of the meeting."[105]

Moreover, Park Nelson notes that for adoptees who want to seek out their birth family, the ongoing "stigmatization of adoptee birth search is a disabling factor."[106] But to assume that adoptees are unwilling or lack the interest to search because they are "well-adjusted" in their adoptive settings is to disregard many adoptees' need and interest to search.[107] Jenny Heijun Wills further illustrates ways in which Asian adoptees are deemed "embodiments of anti-essentialism and even social constructivism—and yet within their life narratives, not only does the specter of essentialism linger, but essentialism is also a major plot driver."[108] Wills calls this effect "paradoxical essentialism," wherein essentialism, anti-essentialism, and constructivism are simultaneously present and connected as "complementary qualities in individuals' understandings of their subjectivity."[109] Thus, living with this paradoxical effect per Wills' theorization, adoptees who are drawn to undertake birth search and reunion can accept the contradiction within the process, wherein anti-essentialism and essentialism not only coexist but can also be experienced as complementary.

Drawing on the viewpoints outlined above, I contend that the adoptees' birth searches and reunions depicted in the theater and performance works discussed in this book shed light on their potential to engender adoptees' multiple relatedness rather than seek an essentialized permanent wholeness. Furthermore, the artists who are themselves adoptees use the search-and-reunion narrative to revisit their pre- and post-adoption experiences as well as their adoptive and birth cultures. Against the nationally popularized and globally commercialized representations of adoptees, these artists show how stereotypical search-and-reunion stories limit audiences' knowledge and reduce adoptees' subjectivity to a simplistic spectacle. Rejecting the objectification

---

104. Sorensen explains that "parent-centric" refers to discourse from the perspective of adoptive parents, who occupy a dominant position relative to birth parents and adoptees, whose viewpoints are often silenced or not represented. Sorensen, "Korean Adoption Literature and the Politics of Representation," 161.
105. Prébin, *Meeting Once More*, 179–80.
106. Park Nelson, "Disability of Adoption," 301.
107. Park Nelson, 301.
108. Wills, "Paradoxical Essentialism," 204.
109. Wills, 204–5.

of adoptees as an inter/national postwar humanitarian, colorblind multicultural, and ethnonationalist apparatus, with their theatrical works these artists shatter the passive state of the discourse on adoptees' birth search and reunion, thereby reclaiming the initiative to tell their own stories. In this sense, the staging of birth search and reunion is not a sensationalist iteration that usurps adoptees' experiences but a performative intervention into Korean transnational adoption by and for adoptees. The playwrights, performers, participants, and spectators of these works are, in effect, rewriting the Korean transnational adoption master script and re-evaluating the manifolded aspects of what it means to be a Korean transnational adoptee undertaking a birth search and reunion.

Bodily and Emotional Scripts Unsettled

In this book, "unsettling acts" are doings that can disrupt the previous bodily and emotional inscriptions so that a different "script" can be written over them. Scripts are embedded in people's behavior, physical reactions, language, feelings, and attitudes toward other people, often specifically toward people's gender, race, and ethnicity. For instance, in a highly gendered society, women and men are expected to perform specific gender roles and to act in scripted ways. The concept of script here is influenced by Judith Butler's idea of bodily inscription (in relation to gender), in which the "'body' often appears to be a passive medium that is signified by an inscription from a cultural source figured as 'external' to that body."[110] In other words, if the body is a blank slate, gender can be imposed on it through actions, gestures, and desires that are inscribed on the body itself by external influences or forces.[111] As such, the body becomes a topography where power and discourses map their mark.[112] In the context of staging Korean transnational adoption, Butler's notion of bodily inscription can help to explain the ways in which gender, racial, and ethnic scripts have been inscribed upon Korean transnational adoptees' bodies to reveal the contours of Asianness, Koreanness, whiteness, womanness, foreignness and somewhere in between. Thus, the selected theater and performance works can be seen to foreground corporeal responses to the inscription of adoptive and birth cultures and ideologies on adoptees' bodies.

As a means of categorization, scripts produce and reinforce unbalanced power relations between dominant and disenfranchised groups. For example,

---

110. Butler, *Gender Trouble*, 164.
111. Butler, 173.
112. Butler, "Foucault and the Paradox of Bodily Inscriptions," 601.

whiteness itself can become a behavioral script that white privilege writes for other racial groups to follow.[113] Borrowing from Julia Kristeva's notion of abjection, Shimakawa investigates Asian/Americanness in theater and performance and finds the history of the Asian body in the United States to be a history of exclusion and distortion, a venue of national abjection.[114] For Shimakawa, Americanness defines itself through the exclusion of Asian Americans who are regarded as either "foreigners/outsiders/deviants/criminals or as domesticated/invisible/exemplary/honorary whites."[115] Shimakawa suggests that "Asian Americanness functions as *abject*" in contrast to Americanness and examines how Asian American theater groups and artists respond to this abjection in imaginative ways on stage.[116] Shimakawa describes how these groups and artists (among which is Minnesota Twin City–based Theater Mu) challenge "the abjection of Asian Americanness by representing Asian Americans as fully formed and fully materialized *subjects,* in stark contrast to the abjected . . . representations imposed by dominant culture."[117] While theatrical and performing arts indeed reflect the omission and misrepresentation of the Asian body in US history, I would emphasize the power of the theater and performance of Korean transnational adoption to jettison the ways in which Asian/Korean adoptee bodies and their embodied experiences have been constructed and conventionalized as an object of abjection.

Along with deciphering the selected works' unsettling of imposed scripts through embodied performance, this book pays great attention to emotive aspects. Offstage, transnational adoption encompasses in-depth emotional inscription and labor for those involved in its process—from adoptive, birth, and foster family members to social workers in both countries as well as adoptees themselves.[118] In regard to Korean adoptees specifically, Jessica Walton discusses the ways in which adoptees negotiate their transracial and cultural identities via embodiment processes that create emotional labor. Walton assesses Korean adoptees' emotional labor as stemming from dealing with the disconnect between their present adoptive life in a white family and what

---

113. According to Peggy McIntosh, white privilege is the lack of awareness of the racial privilege that white people have due to their unearned privilege even as they make their advantages visible and felt to nonwhite people. McIntosh, "White Privilege and Male Privilege."
114. Shimakawa, *National Abjection,* 1–22.
115. Shimakawa, 15.
116. Shimakawa, 3, 58. Italics in original.
117. Shimakawa, 20. Korean adoptee artists at Theater Mu are discussed in more detail in chapter 3.
118. The term "emotional labor" was coined by Arlie Russell Hochschild to describe how employees hide their emotions to align themselves with what employers, institutions, and social entities demand of them. Hochschild, *Managed Heart.* Elizabeth Raleigh writes about the emotional labor that adoption social workers take on as they manage prospective adoptive parents' expectations, vulnerability, and hope. Raleigh, *Selling Transracial Adoption,* 64–93.

they experienced in their past lives or imagine their past lives to have been.[119] Walton also writes that adoptees' substitution of negative emotions ("grief, sadness or anger") for positive ones ("gratitude, happiness and contentment") to minimize feelings of loss associated with adoption "contributes to the justification of adoption as being in the so-called 'best interests' of adoptees and birth parents."[120] As McKee points out, this emotional script is accountable for the one-dimensional outline of gratefulness and happiness that adoptees are supposedly required to feel, having been "saved" by adoptive families.[121] The compulsory script of gratitude and happiness that adoptees are meant to subjugate themselves to, even if doing so leaves them with a feeling of unbelonging, is an affective form of oppression.

The theater and performance works analyzed in this book portray adoptees' search and reunion not as an obligatory route to feelings of gratefulness and happiness but more as a labor, triggering various other emotions, such as guilt, loneliness, and sadness, related to "failed" assimilation, familial dissolution, separation, and loss. Cathy Park Hong defines "minor feelings" by associating them with "the racialized range of emotions that are negative [. . . and express] the trauma of a racist capitalist system that keeps the individual *in place*."[122] Exploring a cornucopia of muted minor emotions about Korean transnational adoption—including sympathy, sorrow, shame, guilt, fear, anger, pain, and discomfort—I probe the selected theater and performance works' deconstruction of repressively simplistic emotion-laden scripts. In this way, *Unsettling Acts* charts how the selected works disrupt the scripts of happiness and gratitude imposed upon Korean adoptees' bodies and minds by performing their (un)makings of family, identity, and belonging on stage. Through various dramaturgic modalities, these works elucidate the heterogeneous affective dimensions of transnational adoption by expressing the embodied experiences of adoptees, as well as adoptive and birth families and adoption communities, particularly those that stem from birth search and reunion. Considering theater as a dynamic process of feeling, Martin Welton finds that the particularities of method that affect people in theatrical events "invite or allow us to define world and self differently," even if only on a temporary basis.[123] In the context of this book, performers' bodies, characters, plots, movements, production processes, sets, lighting, and props can all become temporary elements that offer audiences different feelings and deeper understandings of Korean transnational adoption.

119. Walton, *Korean Adoptees and Transnational Adoption*, 12.
120. Walton, 28.
121. McKee, *Disrupting Kinship*, 8–13.
122. Hong, *Minor Feelings*, 55–56. Italics in original.
123. Welton, *Feeling Theatre*, 26.

Staging Accountability and Making Accountable Memory

Performing transnational adoption imagines ways of problematizing the postwar humanitarian and colorblind multicultural ideologies that inform transnational adoption practices, and of questioning ethnonationalist notions of what it means to be a Korean transnational adoptee returning for a birth search and reunion. In this regard, this book focuses on artists whose works represent the complexity and precarity of adoptees' experiences and identities. These works do so not to simply denounce adoption practice altogether but to challenge the white middle-class heteronormative way of making families that hides the realities of adoptees' lives and makes birth mothers and families invisible. By unsettling historical and cultural norms, these theater and performance works provoke audiences to question facile, celebratory narratives of adoption and family formation. The research in this book joins concurrent debates about transnational adoption issues such as adoptees without citizenship, adoptees' experiences of racism and sexism in receiving countries, and the patriarchal suppression of poor and unwed birth mothers' reproductive rights in sending nations. This book's contribution to these debates is the argument that Korean transnational adoption theater and performance is an artistic practice that raises awareness of and facilitates resistance to the gendered, racialized, and economic power underlying the unequal treatment of women, children, and adoptees in both birth and adoptive environments. Hence, *Unsettling Acts* underscores the efficacy of the theater and performance of Korean transnational adoption in creating accountability for, with, and by adoptees.

The significance of this accountability lies in its offer of potential redress for the unjust political, socioeconomic, and cultural structures and exercises embedded in Korean transnational adoption's history and industry. Accountability in this book is conceptually aligned with Jessica Nakamura's use of the term *response-ability*.[124] Nakamura uses this term to analyze performance as a method of answerability in relation to Imperial Japanese war crimes during the Asia-Pacific War. As a way for performance to engage younger generational audiences in responding to and remembering the war, Nakamura conceptualizes the notion of "transgenerational remembrance" to characterize how memories moved across generations during and after the war.[125] The idea of accountability also connects with Elizabeth Son's analysis of the capacity of performative acts for justice to bring about redress in relation to the euphemistically named "comfort women"—the estimated two hundred thousand predominantly Korean young women and girls pressed into sexual slavery

---

124. Nakamura borrows the term "response-ability" from Japanese philosopher Takahashi Tetsuya. Nakamura, *Transgenerational Remembrance*, xvi–xvii.
125. Nakamura, xi, xvi–xvii.

by the Imperial Japanese Army during the 1930s through the end of the Asia-Pacific War.[126] Son's notion of "embodied reckonings" captures the corporeal pain of "comfort women" and communicates that pain to spectators to constitute redressive acts: "embodied practices that involve multiple audiences in actively reengaging with traumatic pasts to work toward social, political, cultural, and epistemological change."[127] Drawing on these ideas about Asian and Asian American theater and performance as acts of redress and remembrance, I consider Korean transnational adoption theater and performance to be unsettling acts that engender a redressive accountability in the remembrance of the past and present practices of Korean transnational adoption.

As theater serves as a site for remembrance that does not simply re-enact the past but assembles numerous and different "histories of loss through the experiences and re-experiences of affect,"[128] the selected works featured in this book revisit Korean transnational adoption to make audiences experience and re-experience the memories of adoption that still live with us. Thus, the works offer countermemories that challenge commodified and depoliticized spectacles of adoption. In the process, they join Korean adoptee activists in rejecting both infantilized depictions of adoptees as lamentable orphans and essentialized portrayals of adoptees as successful transnational individuals—both of which, according to Eleana Kim, constitute "forms of symbolic violence that cancel the inherent complexity and ambivalence of adoptees' experiences."[129]

These theatrical and performative works are also situated in the continuum of Korean diasporic memory critiques that complicate the remembrance of transnational adoption practice and adoptee presence shadowed and haunted by postwar neocolonialism, US militarism, and heteropatriarchal nationalism.[130] In her examination of kate-hers RHEE's videotaped public performance and Jane Jin Kaisen's experimental film, Crystal Mun-hye Baik finds that the adoptee return in Korea "ruptures dominant rhetoric and established policies that have sought to erase adoptee subjectivities from public sight and dominant national history."[131] Baik further maintains that adoptees as Korean diasporic bodies "problematize the twin projects of South Korean national development and American exceptionalism, while also refusing to be solely defined by or

---

126. Son, *Embodied Reckonings*.
127. Son, 3.
128. Trezise, *Performing Feeling in Cultures of Memory*, 4.
129. E. J. Kim, *Adopted Territory*, 259.
130. G. Cho, *Haunting the Korean Diaspora*; and Baik, *Reencounters*.
131. Baik, *Reencounters*, 102.

delimited to these dominant discourses."[132] In alignment with this understanding of the disruptive yet generative nature of Korean adoptee diasporic return in Korea, this book focuses on how each of the selected theater and performance works presents creative and critical ways of re-encountering adoptees' birth search and reunion, thereby unsettling the politics and poetics of Korean transnational adoption. Therefore, this book shows how the theater and performance of Korean transnational adoption can inspire artists and their audiences to remember Korean transnational adoption beyond "good intentions" and to join calls for responsibility bolstering transpacific justice.

I conceptualize these works, in which adoptees' experiences are re-encountered through theater and performance, as live creations of memory and collective remembrance of Korean transnational adoption with audiences. Marianne Hirsch uses the term *postmemory* to describe the experiences of the private, shared, and cultural sufferings that the "generation after" inherited but did not live through, yet these indirect histories are so vivid that they "*seem* to constitute memories in their own right."[133] I consider the transnational Korean adoptee characters and performers in the selected works who comprise the memories of their own past, as well as transnational adoption's past and present trajectory, as becoming what I call *live memorists* on stage. In this process, theater artists producing pieces about transnational adoption are making memories with audiences who are not necessarily involved with transnational adoption but who, after experiencing the performances, acquire their own memories of transnational adoption. Borrowing from Hirsch, I call these engaged theater audience members imbued with new understandings and feelings about transnational adoption the *audience after*. Affected by the productions, audiences themselves consequently become *postmemorists*, holders of a multitude of memories about transnational adoption. Performing transnational adoption thus reconstructs a cultural memory with live memorist artists and audiences after, who both contribute to a postmemory-making practice. In this way, artists and audiences together engender a collective countermemory of Korean transnational adoptees' birth search and reunion within and beyond the theater and performance spaces. Staging accountability and making accountable memory on stage, the selected works perform transnational adoption through living Korean adoptees' voices, thus imparting meaningful insights about the historical and ongoing impacts of transnational adoption to audiences engaged in artistic creation with the performers.

---

132. Baik, 122.
133. Hirsch, *Generation of Postmemory*, 5. Italics in original.

Identity Locations of Performing Transnational Adoption: Adoptees, Artists, and Academics

Engaging with interdisciplinary discussions on policy, law, literature, television, film, and newspapers, in *Unsettling Acts* I use a variety of methods. First, I analyze playscripts and live performances to unpack how representations of adoptees' birth search and reunion are written and performed in the selected theater and performance works. The live performances I attended over several years, both in the United States and Korea, have allowed not only for analysis of the actual productions but also for examination of audience response to the performances. Second, these analyses are complemented by archival materials, such as posters, program books, reviews, production photos, and videotaped performances. Last, and most importantly, I conducted in-person interviews with Korean adoptee theater and performance artists for deeper understanding of their work. Following oral history research methods used by critical adoption studies and ethnic studies scholar Kim Park Nelson—who interviewed an extensive number of Korean adoptees regarding their experiences in and out of their adoptive countries and cultures for her book—I tried to put Korean adoptees' own voices at the center of this study. Park Nelson chose oral histories as her research method because it gave her access to Korean adoptees and their intersecting communities' personal and political lived experiences both in the United States and the rest of the world.[134] Similarly, and with the purposeful intention of centering adoptee artists' voices, I conducted interviews in such a way as to facilitate an exchange of thoughts regarding the artists' artistic endeavors, personal connections to adoption and activism, the purpose of their work, and their positionality as adoptees, artists, and adoptee artists. When I could not attend some of these productions in person or find them in public performing arts archives, the artists graciously provided me with videotaped performances, scripts, and theatrical production materials. I am particularly indebted to the artists whose works are analyzed herein.

Korean adoptee artists, like adoptees in general, are not a monolithic group but rather have dissimilar and shifting perspectives on adoption-related issues and their own identity formation, and they attach differing levels of importance to being transnationally and transracially adopted. It is important to note that some artists who are adoptees resist the label *adoptee artists* because while the exploration of adoption is part of their artistic expression, neither is it solely the main focus of their art, nor is their art always based on their experiences, especially traumatic ones. In doing art, adoptee artists are

---

134. Park Nelson, *Invisible Asians*, 19, 21.

continuously negotiating and redefining the label of adoptee-identified artist. For chapters 2, 3, and 4—the majority of this book—I feature carefully chosen Korean transnational adoptee artists whose works are inspired by their own adoption experience centering on birth search and reunion. By specifically placing socially and culturally conscious adoptee artists at the center of this book, I do not mean to identify adoptee-ness as the singular core of their artistic identity but rather to examine meanings of being adopted in their works which explore birth search and reunion as part of their adoption experience or imagination.

In my interview with the playwright, performer, and Korean adoptee Eric Sharp, whose imaginative time-traveling play *Middle Brother* is examined in chapter 3, Sharp expressed hope that as a result of his play, people would "think about the entire process and all the people involved in adoption."[135] Furthermore, Sharp clarified that his own vision is to avoid being overly preoccupied with the dualistic identifications between being an adoptee and an artist while creating artistic works which entertain audiences and make them think about adoption: "We [adoptee artists] need to be able to make comments about adoption that are not based entirely on fact. . . . That's what I want to have happen as an artist. . . . I want them [audiences] to be entertained."[136] During my interview with dramatist, actress, and educator Amy Mihyang Ginther, whose autobiographical solo performance *Homeful* is analyzed in chapter 2, Ginther told me "[it's] a coming-of-age story, but it's told through the lens of being a Korean adoptee. I can never separate that from my experience, but it's not about just me being an adoptee."[137] As these artists concern themselves with adoptees' position in theater-making practices about adoption, the adoptee-authored works in this book show how adoptees create artistic pieces which tease out the tensions and distances between the autobiographical and the imagined, the personal and the political, the private and the public, without reinforcing a rigid demarcation between being an adoptee and being an artist.

Throughout the research and writing of this book, as a US-based Korean scholar I was often asked a specific question at conferences, while conducting

---

135. Sharp, interview with the author, Minneapolis, May 19, 2015.

136. Sharp, interview. It is worth noting that some adoptee-identified spectators might have a different view regarding personally relatable experiences staged for entertainment for non-adoptee audience members. For instance, during a talk back for *Middle Brother*, a Korean adoptee audience member stated "I didn't want to come tonight because this is such a close issue to my heart. I didn't want to sit in an audience with non–Korean adoptees who might laugh at something that is so personal and painful to me." Garza, "Mu Performing Arts' Lost and Found."

137. Ginther, interview with the author, New York City, October 22, 2018.

interviews, and in everyday conversations: "Are you an adoptee?" This question regarding my position was critical not only for my interviewees (mostly Korean adoptee artists) but also for myself as a researcher. First, this question alerted me to be aware of my identity location not as an adoptee but as a nonadoptee Korean researcher—an outsider. I was careful to analyze adoptee artists' theatrical and performative expressions from a non-adoptee interlocutor's perspective, and especially careful not to flatten the depth and breadth of their works but to expose the nuances that come with them. Several adoptee artists wanted to know my position on discourses regarding Korean transnational adoption and whether my research might simplify the complications and sensitivities they presented in their work. Their questions reminded me of the gravity that their work intends to bring to the changes in adoption discourse and public awareness.

While working on her ethnographic research, non-adoptee Korean American anthropology scholar Eleana Kim felt restricted at adoption conferences by her "'nonadoptee' status" and excluded "from 'adoptee-only' spaces."[138] Yet Kim also felt a commonality with adoptees who, sharing "a feeling of always being an outsider or misfit, inverted normative terms of social belonging and personhood to construct themselves as insiders."[139] With Kim's account of her experiences in mind, the further I learned about adoptees' artistic pieces, the more I also found a commonality with the structures of feelings of being outside societies and cultures expressed in their works, which unsettle inscribed insider identity, emotion, and belonging in Korea, the United States, and beyond. Sun Mee Chomet's *How to Be a Korean Woman* (chapter 2) particularly struck a chord with me, as, like Chomet in the performance work, I identify with the sense of estranged womanhood that I feel as a US-based Korean woman when temporarily returning to Korea, realizing, as Chomet presents so insightfully, that one's own femininity and selfhood can only be actualized by oneself. I also strongly resonated with Amy Mihyang Ginther's *Homeful* (also chapter 2) in which the artist reveals her encounters with racism and the experience of being "othered" as an Asian through the loaded question "Where are you from?" As performed in her work, Ginther's question serves not just to inquire about one's origin but to reinforce the perception that one does not belong. While watching her performance, which depicted the perpetual foreignness imposed on Asians and her frustration with this racializing question, I could not help to empathize enough about this damning identifier. However, this is not to say that these artists' embodied experiences in their works are the same as mine, but rather to point out that they evoke a sense of

138. E. J. Kim, *Adopted Territory*, 15.
139. E. J. Kim, 15. On her last point, Kim references Erving Goffman's *Stigma*.

mutual recognition among different but intersecting identity locations. In this sense, these theater and performance works of Korean transnational adoption become a stimulus for a conversation not limited to just adoption but encompassing what it means to be scripted with sociocultural norms, thereby leading adoptee as well as non-adoptee audiences to envision resistance against these dominant racial and gender scripts.

Although my position started as an outsider in adoption-related discourse and practice, as my research into Korean productions and my accessibility to Korean archives and plays progressed, my identity as a researcher fluctuated from outsider to insider. Studying adoption in theater and performance for this book eventually brought me to the alternating position of outsider/insider rather than a fixed position of either one or the other. As a non-adoptee researcher, I found the whole process to be a transformative experience during which I gradually came to feel allied with socially and culturally engaged adoptees, adoptee artists, and academics whose shared artistic and scholarly comradeship I deeply appreciated.

Interestingly, while discussing my book project with a non-adoptee public over the years, I was occasionally cautioned that my analysis could be considered injurious to adoptive parents because my focus centered on critically thinking adoptees whose ideas of the history and practice of transnational and transracial adoption go beyond celebratory and honorary scripts about adoptive parents. These encounters, seemingly meant to warn or silence me, reminded me of incidents Richey Wyver described in which adoptees' critical voices regarding adoption, corruption, and postcolonial feminist analysis were "crushed" due to their perceived threats.[140] I felt that in my allied position, while still thinking critically about transnational adoption reflected in adoptees' artistic oeuvres, I was also seen as a potential threat to adoptive parent–centric discourses rather than as a facilitator of critical dialogue and empathetic understanding of adoptees' perspectives. During these uncomfortable encounters, I strangely felt a stronger sense of alliance with critically thinking adoptee artists, activists, and academics. Nevertheless, I would like to clarify that this book is not intended as a source of polemics leading to the reductive duality of a pro or con opinion of adoption. Instead, with this book, I want to offer a comprehensive way of viewing the topic of Korean transnational adoption, centering on what Docan-Morgan terms a *proadoptee* position, via a theatrical and performing art form that engages with contesting and creative visions.[141]

---

140. Wyver, "Civilizing Missions and Mimicry," 142–43.
141. Docan-Morgan, *In Reunion*, 20. Italics in original.

Chapter Overview

The four chapters herein do not follow simple geographical demarcations based on the playwrights' nationalities but rather draw together common threads in themes, genres, and outputs. These include representations of Korean birth mothers, adoptee autobiographical solo performances, theater formations of the adoption community, and audience responses to extraordinary adoptee representations. Except for chapter 1, in which non-adoptee Korean theater artists and their works produced in Korea are discussed, my selection of adoptee artists' works reflects their heightened consciousness and care regarding Korean transnational adoption issues and adoptee representations. The non-adoptee artists in chapter 1 also connect their own theatrical imagination of Korean transnational adoptees' birth searches and reunions to the Korean context rather than unquestioningly affirming postwar humanitarian, colorblind multicultural, and ethnonationalist adoption scripts. The two-tiered structure of this book attempts to convey the different perspectives of and impacts on the artists' target audiences as well as to manifest a simultaneous view of how adoptee and non-adoptee artists achieve their shared goal of unsettling scripts.

Chapter 1 begins with a genealogy of spectacularizing searches and reunions in the Korean reality TV programs *Finding Dispersed Families* (1983) and *I Miss That Person* (1996), and the fiction film *Ode to My Father* (2014), which materialized a national sorrow and sympathy toward dispersed families, including Korean overseas adoptees. This chapter compares these screen cultural products with three plays—Sumin Ha's duo-drama 찰칵 (*Chalkak*, 2020), Soo-yang Jun and Hee-sun Chang's musical 에어포트 베이비 (*Airport Baby*, 2018, 2020), and Yang Gu Yi's play 일곱집매 (*Ilgopzipmae*, 2013)[142]— and examines the representation of adoptees' birth searches and reunions on the Korean stage, particularly focusing on birth mothers. Building on Hosu Kim's analysis of Korean birth mothers experiencing social and legal stigmatization comparable to the condition of "social death," this chapter argues that adoptees' birth searches and reunions symbolically "resurrect" birth mothers from the social death imposed by transnational adoption practices that render birth mothers "dead-to-others."[143] In each of the three examined works, specific performative actions—such as photographing, bodily gesturing, and voice recording—embody the birth mothers' belated motherhood that disrupts their assumed deaths. Chapter 1 thus conceptualizes these performances

---

142. Hereafter, I refer to these three plays by their English titles.
143. H. Kim, *Birth Mothers*, 8–9.

of birth search and reunion as a contact zone where adoptees and birth mothers encounter each other's experiences of systemized ostracization in racist, patriarchal, and militarized societies and cultures within and beyond Korea.[144] This chapter further unsettles the ethnocentric nationalism which showcases the birth mother's symbolically resurrected body as a recovery from the national shame and guilt represented by Korea's involvement in transnational adoption as a sending country. I also problematize the birth mothers' corporeal deaths at the ends of the three plays by theorizing what I refer to as *necropoetics*, the dramaturgical negation of any other possibility but death. While a shared precariousness becomes the impetus for the three theatrical works to imagine healing and reconciliation, the ultimate death of the birth mothers signals the absence of imagining a meaningful reparation for adoptees and birth mothers drawn into the circle of Korean transnational adoption.

Chapter 2 spotlights bodily testimonial acts in three Korean American women adoptees' autobiographical solo performances: Marissa Lichwick's *Yellow Dress* (2015), Sun Mee Chomet's *How to Be a Korean Woman* (2012), and Amy Mihyang Ginther's *Homeful* (2018). These three works perform pre- and post-adoption experiences garnered from the artists' own birth searches and reunions with their biological families in Korea. The artists' works set out to demythify the transnational and transracial adoption tales of multicultural American families and melodramatic search-and-reunion narratives, which overwrite the realities that adoptees actually confront. By utilizing their solo bodies, the performers demonstrate the systemic forms of racializing and gendering oppressions which produce and reinforce the normative expectations and discriminations of being a transnational and transracial female adoptee in both adoptive and birth countries. As the adoptee artists claim authority over their very personal (but political as well) and affectively intense life events, this chapter argues that their performances bring forth a form of bodily testimony that embodies racial, ethnic, and gender relations imposed on Korean women adoptees. Borrowing from Amanda Stuart Fisher's idea that the interimplication of physical witness and testimonial action is a way of engendering new learning and awareness,[145] I further claim that the solo body in the performances becomes a terrain of new knowledge and understanding of Korean transnational adoption, where the dualistic demarcations between Korea and the United States, lived experiences and constructed myths, and past and present are unsettled. Through constant bodily transitions and multiple mobilizations from self to other, present to past, and one

---

144. Pratt, "Arts of the Contact Zone."
145. Stuart Fisher, *Performing the Testimonial.*

culture to another, these performers' bodily testimonies effectively underline the power of fluid transformation that enables audiences to grasp the border-crossing experiences and emotions that Korean transnational adoption entails. In this way, the performers' bodies also function as an archive for their affective memories via different performance modes, including speedy bodily collage, body movements in slow motion, and aural and visual embodiment. Furthermore, analyzing audience response at adoptee-centered public events, such as adoption conferences and gatherings, I highlight the capacity of solo performance to provide a live intimacy shared with adoptee audiences whose physical witnessing of their fellow adoptees' transnational experiences resonates with theirs, thereby facilitating adoptee affinity and critical adoption spectatorship through performance.

Chapter 3 expands on the analysis of representations of Korean American adoptees' birth searches and reunions by examining three highly imaginative theater works: Eric Sharp's play *Middle Brother* (2014), Leah Cooper and Alan Berks's community-based theater production *In My Heart: The Adoption Play Project* (2016), and Debra Kim Sivigny's immersive theater production *Hello, My Name Is . . .* (2017). The adoptee characters in these three plays experience fantasylike worlds through time-traveling, fairy-tale narratives, and spiritual immersions, as their search for belonging reinvigorates a discussion on birth search and reunion. Using a discussion on biopolitics by SooJin Pate, who argues that adoptees' belonging is delineated on their body, I scrutinize how a sense of belonging in each play is shaped on the body, language, and space of adoptees.[146] I also apply Kimberly McKee's investigation of the connection between affect and adoption, through which gratitude is viewed as an indicator for gauging "good" adoptees from "bad" adoptees and conceives the "adoptee killjoy" as a subverter of happiness, rejecting the reification of a humanitarian adoption fantasy.[147] Building on Pate's and McKee's research, this chapter argues that adoptees' birth searches and reunions become a discursive and disciplinary process of (un)settling belonging contingent on the "performance" of being a "good," "bad," or otherwise "strange" adoptee. As I foreground adoptees' ties with siblings and peers beyond the child–parent bond, this chapter reveals how adoptee characters form, shift, and diverge in their relationships with adoptive and birth families and the adoption community, resulting in a transformation of kinship and citizenship. Departing from monolithic identification of the Korean adoption community, this chapter also interrogates the three theatrical works' actual and virtual constructions

---

146. Pate, *From Orphan to Adoptee*.
147. McKee, *Disrupting Kinship*, 72–86.

of community, in which performer, playwright, and participant/audience find a commonality by building various matrices of empathy on and offstage. By positing this community-making as an act of *kinning*, I further envisage theater as a nodal point generating intersections between Korean adoptees and other "kins," such as Asian American theater groups, Native American adoption circles, and Korean adoptee networks. In this sense, the theater works analyzed in this chapter impart a sense of community and care among these kins whose links enrich the meaning of belonging through theatrical work.

Starting with a historical overview of Korean transnational adoption in Western and Northern Europe, chapter 4 explores women adoptee artists' extraordinary imagination regarding Korean transnational adoption stories beyond Korea-US boundaries. In Cathy Min Jung's solo performance *Les Bonnes Intentions* (2011) from Belgium, In-Sook Chappell's play *This Isn't Romance* (2009) from the UK, and Yong Sun Gullach's performance art piece *Re-enacting the Transnational Adoptee* (2015) from Denmark, the artists disclose the racial and sexual violations experienced by the main adoptee characters: rape, incest, and whitewashing (figuratively and literally). All three works unpack the othering of Korean women adoptees' bodies to demonstrate the colonizing power that molded them into imagined adoptee-ness, Asianness, and exotic femaleness. While *This Isn't Romance* explicitly shares this book's main theme of birth search and reunion, *Les Bonnes Intentions* and *Re-enacting the Transnational Adoptee* connect to the act of searching via, respectively, fantasizing about a birth mother's story to escape from domestic violence, and enacting a personal experience of adoption forgery to expose institutional violence against adoptees. Moreover, as the three pieces of staging birth search and reunion depict physical, cultural, and systemic violence with regard to Korean/Asian adoptee women, the women in turn "violate" ethical and moral rules of propriety by appropriating violence and altering themselves from victim to aggressor. The adoptee characters and performers decide where, when, and how to exercise their agency to put an end to the vicious cycle of violation. Here I argue that their astonishing boldness of action transforms their embodied vulnerability from victimhood into resistance.[148] Furthermore, borrowing from Bretton White's analysis of audiences' discomfort when confronted with queer bodies portrayed on stage,[149] this chapter further contends that feelings of discomfort work toward a radical unsettling of senses and sensibility regarding the static perceptions of Korean transnational adoption. This chapter, therefore, foregrounds audience response as a possible realm

---

148. Butler, "Rethinking Vulnerability and Resistance."
149. White, *Staging Discomfort*.

for decolonizing the "feel-good" affect typically associated with the ways in which Korean transnational adoption is viewed. The extraordinary search-and-reunion stories discussed in this chapter attempt to awaken audiences' numbed imagination of Korean transnational adoption by presenting adoption and adoptees in vastly different—uncomfortable—ways than those of the "feel-good" master narratives. As these works shock audience members into a discomfort-induced state of uneasiness by conveying the pain of inflicted and inflicting violence on and by adoptees, performing the three boldly creative pieces becomes a decolonial practice.

I close out this book with a site observation of Omma Poom Park, a city-owned park located in a former US military camp in Paju, a one-hour drive north of Seoul (adjacent to the North Korean border). This memorial park was established to welcome returning Korean transnational adoptees with a sense of reunion with their birth land and birth mothers. I analyze this space as a site where visitors can experience birth search and reunion beyond the stage, as it engenders an embodied sense of Korean transnational adoption embedded in the ongoing postwar and neocolonial location of separation and loss. Visiting this site as an offstage search-and-reunion performance, I also question its curatorial choices, geographic isolation, and lack of accessibility. In the ambivalence of its spatial performativity, the site simultaneously commemorates adoptees' searches and reunions with imagined birth mothers and birth land, and disremembers them, as well as Korean transnational adoption at large. Considering the potentials and predicaments of this spatial performance, I conclude this book by envisioning the futures of performing transnational adoption within and beyond the dramatic arc of birth search and reunion. Finally, I leave my readers with the hope that this book presents performing transnational adoption as a strategic praxis offering a gesture of belonging, healing, and justice for adoptees.

CHAPTER 1

Maternal Resurrection

Birth Search and Reunion on Korean Stages

When the subject of transnational adoption is brought up in discussion, whether public or private, the first images evoked tend to be those of children, usually infants, followed by happy adoptive parents. The image of the birth mother, however, rarely enters the picture.[1] If it does, the image will often be tainted by preconceptions of irresponsibility and callousness. Margaret Homans writes, "A birthmother's story can be at least doubly unspeakable: as that of the illegitimate, rejecting, 'bad' mother, and as that the mutely material body, mother in body only."[2] In her work examining birth, foster, and adoptive mothers in Asian transnational adoption, Jungyun Gill identifies the gendered ideologies and oppressions that reinforce unequal motherhoods at the intersections of race, class, and nationality, stating: "The social injustice and inequality embedded in the international adoption system became invisible."[3] In this system of invisibility, birth mothers have often been the forgotten ones;

---

1. Hübinette maintains, "if anyone must be considered as marginalized and silenced subalterns within the Korean society... it must be the biological parents of the adoptees and particularly the mothers." Hübinette, "Comforting an Orphaned Nation," 32.
2. Homans, *Imprint of Another Life*, 253.
3. Gill, *Unequal Motherhoods*, 140. Gill writes that "it is also interesting to note that adoptive parents usually receive adoption documents that include brief information about the child's birth parents such as their names, age, education, family backgrounds, and their social circumstances, but the birth mother does not generally receive any information about the adoptive family—whether the child was placed domestically or abroad." Gill, 3.

it is notable, then, that Korean theater incorporates birth mother characters on the stage in connection to their relinquished children's search-and-reunion stories. Although many Korean stage productions have presented scenes or episodes featuring Korean transnational adoptee characters, they have not necessarily used transnational adoption birth search and reunion as the main storyline.[4] This chapter examines three Korean theatrical works which center on adoptees' stories of birth search and reunion with their birth mothers: Sumin Ha's close-knit duo-drama *Chalkak* (2020), Soo-yang Jun and Hee-sun Chang's musical *Airport Baby* (2018, 2020), and Yang Gu Yi's full-cast play *Ilgopzipmae* (2013). While some Korean plays have presented adoptees as main characters in search-and-reunion narratives,[5] I selected the three plays in this chapter due to their focus on birth mothers who are an integral part of the stories. Most notably, these three productions revolve around the experiences of birth mothers who have long lived in silence and shame due to having relinquished their children.[6]

In her analysis of social death, Lisa Marie Cacho takes the condition to involve a devaluing of certain populations deemed to be undeserving of being part of society, for example, criminalized people of color.[7] Hosu Kim compares the situation of Korean birth mothers in the transnational adoption process to the condition of social death on the basis of both the social stigma and the legal process of adoption, which deprive birth mothers of all custody rights.[8] These rights are transferred to the adoption agency when a child is relinquished, effectively rendering the birth mother "dead-to-others."[9] Indeed, Korean birth mothers are in a figurative sense "criminalized," most often through public judgment for the trifecta of being unwed, pregnant, and poor. Rather than allowing this discrimination to stand, the three plays analyzed in this chapter reclaim the agentic voices of these birth mothers as they interact with their once relinquished and reunited children. Drawing on Kim's concept, I argue that the staging of Korean transnational adoptees' birth

---

4. Such plays include *Follow the Railroads to the Sea of Canna* (2017, 2020) by Jina Kim, *Termites in the Desert* (2018) by Jeongeun Hwang, *Adoptee & Stranger* (2017) by Wanghyeok Lee, *Round, Round, Round* (2014) by Eunseong Kim, and *Bye Cycle* (2014) by Hyeontak Kim, based on a 1978 work by Taesuk Oh entitled *Bicycle*.

5. For example, *Hello, Mommy* (2010) and *La Lune en Papier* (2016), the puppet theater *A Box: An Untold Story* (2015), and the musical *Bravo, My Love* (2018).

6. Although not in theater, Korean birth mothers' voices have been available to US readers through their own letters and stories translated into English. See Dorow, *I Wish for You a Beautiful Life*; and Han, *Dreaming a World*.

7. Cacho, *Social Death*.

8. H. Kim, *Birth Mothers*, 8.

9. H. Kim, 8–10. Also see Patterson, *Slavery and Social Death*; and J. Kim, "An 'Orphan' with Two Mothers."

searches and reunions "resurrects" birth mothers from social death by putting them in a public spotlight on the stage.[10]

Motherhood has been staged in theater and performance to examine structures of race, class, gender, and sexuality in and outside family relations. For example, analyzing the staging of motherhood by British women playwrights from the mid-1950s to the present, Jozefina Komporaly contends that changes in women's private and public lives influenced women's theater, for instance, the themes and politics of the 1960s and the 1970s.[11] In their representations of motherhood, British women playwrights during that period predicted future transformations of women's lives. Although the depiction of motherhood on the Korean stage has been visible,[12] representations of birth mothers as central figures have been few and far between. The three theatrical representations of adoptees' birth searches and reunions examined in this chapter are thus all the more significant for their interrogation of motherhood in connection with Korean transnational adoption and their revival of birth mother characters from deathlike invisibility. The three plays defy the hiddenness of birth mothers by performing their visibility and openly accounting for their loss and pain. Giving special consideration to their ongoing sorrow due to the relinquishment of children for transnational adoption, these works also map out the procedure by which birth mother characters are brought to life and enabled to shed the shame and stigma associated with being a birth mother.

While Korean theater is the major site for this chapter's inquiry, I also look at Korean screen culture to understand the impact on the Korean public of two specific TV programs, *Finding Dispersed Families* (1983) and *I Miss That Person* (1996), and one feature film, *Ode to My Father* (2014). Two of the theater productions discussed in this book (*Airport Baby* in this chapter and *How to Be a Korean Woman* in chapter 2) contain scenes centered on televised search-and-reunion programs, demonstrating the influence of mediatized search and reunion on Korean adoptees. Thus, this chapter begins with a genealogy of spectacularized searches and reunions in TV programs and commercial films that tend not only to simplify birth search and reunion but also to silence adoptees and birth families. In comparison, Korean theater works herein across genres and styles attempt to present more nuanced

---

10. This concept of resurrection is metaphoric, not a reification of the actual death of birth mothers. The word "resurrection" as I use it has no religious connotation. I use it in the sense of bringing birth mothers back from social death. My use of the term is more in accordance with Andreas Huyssen's conceptualization of museums as resurrecting history and engendering counterhegemonic memory. Huyssen, "Metamorphosis of the Museal."
11. Komporaly, *Staging Motherhood*, 1.
12. Shim, "Recasting the National Motherhood."

search-and-reunion stories with adoptee and birth mother characters whose affective strength and psychological depth can be somewhat differently experienced by audiences. Not wanting to appear to champion theater as a more elevated form of artistic exploration, I rather propound that theater becomes a representational battleground where a push-and-pull between simple and complex narrativizations is foregrounded.

Furthermore, I view birth search and reunion as presented in the three works as a "contact zone" wherein the birth mothers perform their belated motherhood and (hope to) communicate with their children.[13] Here, I borrow the term *contact zone* coined by Mary Louise Pratt, which she states "invokes the space and time where subjects previously separated by geography and history are co-present, the point at which their trajectories now intersect."[14] I introduce this idea in order to discuss how stage productions of search-and-reunion stories create an intersecting space where adoptees' encounters with their birth mothers are performed. As a means of expressing belated motherhood, the playwrights and directors of the plays analyzed in this chapter use technology to convey the meanings of birth search and reunion to audiences through the sensorial experiences of sights and sounds. Delving into the varied performative actions of photography, bodily gesture, and voice recording in each of the three plays, my investigation reveals how birth mothers' belated motherhood and contested subjecthood are shown, heard, and felt through the differently rebuilt relationships with their now-adult children. The appeal to these senses is necessary to make certain that birth mothers remain visible and audible even after death. The performances of adoptees' searches and reunions thus situate birth mothers as perceptible as well as profound figures, connecting with adoptees' past and present lives as well as their futures.

The dramaturgical focus on birth mothers is also significant for its presentation of their reasons to "choose" relinquishment, their years shaped by that one single event from the past, and their experiences of reunion, whether achieved or not. The birth mother characters disclose not only how they viewed transnational adoption relinquishment as the only viable choice but also how their choice was related to systemized gender and class discrimination inflicted on them as women and mothers under patriarchal power in Korea. In actual adoption practices, while some birth mothers' choice of relinquishment was made under pressure, many other women did not make

---

13. H. Kim writes about Korean birth mothers' virtual mothering as a way in which they can find a "belated reconnection" with their children, whether the reconnection is "imagined or real." H. Kim, *Birth Mothers*, 13. I use the term "belated motherhood" to refer to the way in which the birth mother characters in these three plays take up mothering again once reunited with their relinquished children, reclaiming being mothers via performative acts.

14. Pratt, *Imperial Eyes*, 8.

the choice themselves. Hosu Kim unpacks the Korean transnational adoption industry's treatment of birth mothers, starting at the beginning of the practice when the birth mother's consent for relinquishment was not always required, as the father, relatives, or legal guardian could make the decision instead of the mother.[15] In other international contexts, Laura Briggs reveals how Black and Native American birth mothers in the United States and Indigenous and poverty-stricken Latin American women have also been pressured to relinquish their children for adoption.[16] Although the rhetorical emphasis on the choice of relinquishment of birth mothers of color may offer prospective adoptive parents in wealthier Western countries an opportunity to make a multicultural family, this viewpoint not only deprives women of color worldwide of the possibility of forming their own families but also erases society's responsibility to ensure a social safety net for disenfranchised families' kinship preservation.[17] While it is possible to criticize the resurrected voices and visibility of birth mothers as a re-essentialization of biological motherhood being "real" or "natural,"[18] this chapter tackles the politics of birth mothers' choice of relinquishment beyond the reductive dualistic view of motherhood as either fake or real. In this sense, I assert that the birth mother characters' transnational adoption stories revive the long-dismissed discussion of women's vulnerable reproductive rights and family-making environments. As audience members encounter a birth mother testifying about her situation in which she could only imagine herself to choose relinquishment, they are led to ponder what it means to give up one's own child without active participation.

For each of the three works, this chapter further problematizes the staging of the birth mothers' symbolically resurrected body imagined as a recovery from the national shame of Korea's involvement in transnational adoption. Extending this understanding to birth mothers involved in the process of the mediatized search-and-reunion narrative, Hosu Kim investigates how this discourse sheds light on the figure of the "now-visible birth mother" who, although taken "out of the shadows . . . is manipulated to serve a nationalistic rendering of loss, within an intricate dynamic of fantasy and exclusion in

---

15. H. Kim, *Birth Mothers*, 6.
16. Briggs, *Somebody's Children*, 60, 118, 209.
17. See McKee on the politics of "choice" of relinquishment and the failure to preserve Korean families in transnational adoption. McKee, *Disrupting Kinship*, 23–37.
18. Sara Ruddick brings up the idea that highlighting biology over motherhood would overlook all the different forms of nontraditional families whose members perform maternal work. Recognizing Ruddick's point, I am not setting up a hierarchy of motherhoods based on the essentialist ideal of blood-relatedness but rather attempting to reveal the overlooked narratives of birth mothers' relinquishment embodied by the three theatrical works. Ruddick, *Maternal Thinking*, 48–51.

the adoption narrative."¹⁹ Building on Kim's analysis, I elucidate the ways in which the three plays foreground the birth mothers' resurrections from shame associated with Korean transnational adoption yet also limit their significance because of the eventual corporeal death of the mothers. This outcome, common to all three of the plays, reiterates the exclusion of birth mother figures on stage. Even as these birth mothers recover from shame, secrecy, and silence, they ultimately die, thus denying hope for an enduring relationship between adoptees and birth mothers. From this analysis, I conceptualize *necropoetics* to show how the three plays portray the deaths of birth mother characters as necessary in the search-and-reunion context. By what I call a necropoetics of theater, I refer to the use of dramatic plots to "kill" characters whose fictional death also reinstates the social death of their identities. Hence, I view the birth mothers' deaths at the end of all three plays as instances of necropoetics that negate any other possibility for the birth mother characters but death.

The Genealogy of Search and Reunion in Korean Screen Cultures

The Korean War not only caused Korean infants and children to be sent to the West but also triggered an unprecedented dispersion and separation of Korean families. During the war and postwar chaos, a great number of families were separated by the delineated border at the 38th parallel and many did not know if their loved ones were still alive in either of the Koreas. An exact count of separated family members has not been possible, but estimates range from five to ten million for the entire Korean Peninsula.²⁰ *Cheonman isangajok* ("ten million separated families"), a Korean colloquialism referring to the largest estimate, has taken on a special significance in the minds of the majority of Koreans.²¹ To this day, this post–Korean War phenomenon of separated family units is still widespread, prompting former South Korean President Moon Jae-in (2017–22) to openly express his wish at the United Nations in 2021 for an official end to the Korean War and the restart of an inter-Korean program to reunite separated South and North Korean families.²²

In this historical context, the landmark Korean TV program *Finding Dispersed Families* (1983) witnessed unparalleled televised spectacles of real-life

---

19. H. Kim, *Birth Mothers*, 138.
20. Song and Moon, *Korean American Women*, 256.
21. N. Kim, *Memory, Reconciliation, and Reunions*, 2.
22. The last meetings between North and South Korean families occurred in 2018. Haas, "Tears Flow as Separated South and North Korean Families Reunite"; and Hincks, "'Moment We Met.'"

search-and-reunion stories of separated Koreans. Like the "emotion-generating machine" of cinema, television has been viewed and analyzed in its capacity as a medium to emotionally affect viewers.[23] Before the advent of the internet and its mass instant information-disseminating power, television was one of the central media venues that Koreans interacted with for public information and entertainment.[24] In this mediascape, *Finding Dispersed Families* has not only been recognized as the longest continuous live broadcast in the world (at 453 hours and 45 minutes long) but also had its archives listed by the United Nations Educational, Scientific and Cultural Organization (UNESCO) in 2015 as constituting a "documentary heritage of monumental value in world broadcasting history."[25] The archives of this special broadcast from the national public broadcaster Korean Broadcasting System (KBS), described by UNESCO as "an epic television humanitarian campaign,"[26] include 20,522 video records of live broadcasts of reunions of war-dispersed families from June 30 through November 14, 1983. During the 138-day live program, more than 50,000 applicants were selected for studio time as the program received an overwhelming number of requests to find lost family members.[27] Thousands of other people gathered in front of the KBS building and in Yeouido Square in Seoul with countless posters displaying their information including their lost ones' names, hometowns, and physical and personal traits. These people hoped their posters would be broadcast even for just one single moment or that their lost ones would come to the site and see their signs posted on walls and sidewalks. In the studio, the program's daily schedule included the introduction of a number of dispersed family stories and family reunions by phone, televised image, or in-studio meeting, accompanied by a very melodramatic or nostalgic song performed by a guest celebrity singer. The show even gained international importance when overseas Koreans looking for their lost ones were connected via satellite from various countries, such as the United States, Russia, and Japan.[28]

---

23. García, *Emotions in Contemporary TV Series*, 1–3.

24. By 1980, 80 percent of Korean households had television sets. Larson, *Telecommunications Revolution in Korea*, 204.

25. United Nations Educational, Scientific, and Cultural Organization (UNESCO), Archives of the KBS Special Live Broadcast "Finding Dispersed Families"; and W. Y. Lee, "Two Korean Documentary Heritage Holdings Inscribed in UNESCO's Memory of the World."

26. Archives of the KBS Special Live Broadcast "Finding Dispersed Families."

27. During the period of the broadcast of *Finding Dispersed Families*, KBS staff processed 100,952 candidates, with 53,536 of these appearing on the air, resulting in 10,189 reunions. The show drew an unprecedented 78 percent share of ratings. N. Kim, *Memory, Reconciliation, and Reunions*, 6.

28. Note that searches and reunions implemented through this program were specifically geared toward finding dispersed people within South Korea and the Korean diaspora abroad, not between North and South Korea.

Finding Dispersed Families seamlessly packaged the Aristotelian affects of pity and fear leading to catharsis as feelings of sorrow and suffering transformed into extreme joy and tearful release when successful reunions did occur.[29] This media event revealed the power of television to move masses of people to gut-wrenching emotion, almost in the vein of a national mass frenzy. According to Nan Kim, "the KBS telethon quickly became the object of binge-watching among riveted South Korean audiences and its public memory would endure in later decades as a cultural touchstone of family separation as national tragedy [. . . establishing television] as a medium for the transmission of intense affect."[30] The affair was almost comparable to a massive ritual performance, as the public shared the intimate bond of communal longing and collective purgation through intense visual, audible, and human spectacles seen on and off the television screen. As Kim puts it, through the program's witnessing of countless people in pain, *Finding Dispersed Families* became an archive of emotional repertoire in its "marathon" of recalling memories of Korean national suffering.[31] The program was a mediated national mourning that haunted the streets of Korea and filled the hearts and minds of Koreans with a sense of oneness. In other words, via the spectacles of search and reunion, *Finding Dispersed Families* created a sense of unity through the lamentation of painful memories in search of Korea's national identity and ethnic belonging. Ironically, the airing of *Finding Dispersed Families* coincided with the time of the largest transnational separation and dispersion of Korean children yet, which continued throughout the 1980s, forming another wave of dispersed Korean families.

From this time on, search and reunion of dispersed families, now including overseas adoptees, became a popular subject for the Korean TV and commercial film industries to spectacularize. Search-and-reunion TV shows about people drawn into transnational adoption, such as biological families and adoptees, continue to be broadcast even today. As a sort of sequel to *Finding Dispersed Families,* the nationally syndicated KBS program *I Miss That Person* initially aired in 1996 as a weekly segment within a TV morning show called 아침 마당 *Achim Madang* (*Morning Forum*). This program, which has had several incarnations over the years, became well known to Korean adult adoptees trying to find their biological families from all over the world. In her analysis of this program, Hosu Kim observes, "A television search-and-reunion narrative is an utterly fabricated social memory that has been

---

29. My observations on *Finding Dispersed Families* in this section is based on KBS's archived videos available on YouTube.
30. N. Kim, *Memory, Reconciliation, and Reunions,* 6.
31. N. Kim, 5.

serialized into various elements and arranged in a certain order, so as to construct a social memory of transnational adoption."³² Furthermore, Kim argues, "Television search shows offer a crucial site in which the Korean adoption story is incorporated into the collective national trauma of separated families, and then resolved with a family reunion in the framework of a particular narrative commitment."³³ Within this televised realm of social memories about transnational adoption, the viewer was meant to feel like the family members who were made whole again through their reunions and, on a larger scale, as part of a healing nation.

Unlike the sense of fulfillment that the televised search-and-reunion show gives to viewers, *I Miss That Person*'s treatment of Korean overseas adoptees is problematic in its objectification and use of the language barrier to render them into a passive spectacle. Almost all the adoptees who appeared on these series could not speak Korean fluently and only communicated with their biological family members through an interpreter who often left adoptees speechless or silenced following instructions from the show's host. One blatant way the program used this communication obstacle was through coaching non-Korean-speaking adoptees to speak Korean. In one episode, a Korean American woman standing in the studio in front of an audience was told that her biological mother was backstage waiting to meet her. The host and interpreter then asked the woman if she could say *Eomeoni* ("Mother" in Korean). The polite and flustered woman said *Eomeoni* but was directed again by the host and interpreter to say it louder. The nervous woman said *Eomeoni* one last time. Melodramatic music started playing, and the mother entered the studio area for her long-awaited initial reunion with her biological daughter.³⁴

While search-and-reunion shows such as *I Miss That Person* make great efforts to fabricate "spectacular" scenes, the partial knowledge given to viewers and selective ignorance about transnational adoption do a great disservice to the public by overlooking the lived experiences of birth families and adoptees. In some episodes, biological families describe domestic violence, patriarchal and capitalist oppression, and crushing poverty. Yet the show fails to provide viewers an in-depth examination of these or any other kinds of systemic difficulties and cultural discrimination that influenced biological families toward relinquishment. This leaves viewers uninformed as to what needs to be done (and could have been done) for the advancement of women, children, and adoptees' rights in terms of pre- and post-transnational-adoption practices.

---

32. H. Kim, *Birth Mothers*, 118.
33. H. Kim, 118.
34. This analysis is based on the 2008 episode of *I Miss That Person* uploaded on YouTube. "그사보 정희정," Global Overseas Adoptees' Link.

Furthermore, while avoiding those topics, a "reinstatement" of adoptees as blood-related Koreans was also staged. For instance, at one critical point in these TV programs, a deus ex machina moment occurs with the results of DNA tests or legal proof, irrefutably ending any confusion and anxiety.[35] In this part of the search-and-reunion adoption spectacle, the deus ex machina reveals the adoptee's proof of Koreanness, actualizing a dramatic but brief resolution to the long-standing Korean national tragedy of human separation. The pseudo-utopian reconciliation and quick dénouement achieved in that specific moment insinuate that blood-related Koreanness "solves" the complexity of adoptees' national and ethnic identity and affective belonging. The disclosure of an adopted Korean's identity as a "true" Korean is a spectacular tool used to obliterate the "old" image of the pitiful Korean orphan and instead replace it with a "new," joyous, and grateful Korean child. Returning adoptees thus become fully verified (scientifically, legally, or emotionally) as a future human token for the acceleration of Korea's image transformation.

Incorporating *Finding Dispersed Families* and *I Miss That Person* within its narrative, the Korean mega-hit commercial film *Ode to My Father* (2014) spans contemporary Korean history from the 1950s to the early 2010s. The film tells the story of a boy separated from his younger sister during the frantic December 1950 evacuation of Heungnam Port during the Korean War. The boy's father stays behind to search for the girl but makes his son promise to become the head of the family and save his mother and two younger siblings. Both father and daughter disappear. Years later as an adult, the man, who settled in South Korea, seeks out his sister through a search-and-reunion TV program (referring to *Finding Dispersed Families*) and discovers that she was adopted by an American family. Their first meeting to attempt verification that the adoptee woman in Los Angeles is in fact related to him is done via satellite in a TV studio in Seoul. This scene, which cuts back and forth between the siblings and other family members watching the live show at home, is filled with tears and is one of the most emotionally charged parts of the film. The following scene shows the joyful family and relatives reunited in Korea. In this blissful reunion scene, the long-lost sister and her American family wear traditional Korean outfits and bow in the traditional Korean way. The happy ending gives the impression that the "Americanized" adopted sister is or will willingly reassimilate into Korean ethnic culture and tradition without

---

35. Latin for "god from the machine," *deus ex machina* is a translation of a phrase first used in ancient Greek theater, *theòs ek méchanês*. The term describes the use of "a *mechane*—a mechanised lifting arm or crane to suspend gods over the concluding action of its tragedy." The term has widely been used to designate a plot device that quickly brings about a resolution to the dramatic problem of a play or situation. Baugh, *Theatre, Performance and Technology*, 2. Italics in original.

any problems. With its ethnonationalist qualities, *Ode to My Father* must have offered Korean viewers a deep sense of satisfaction, since an estimated fourteen million Korean viewers, about one-fourth of the Korean population, watched the film in movie theaters.[36]

Box-office success notwithstanding, some film critics have criticized *Ode to My Father* for the centering of its narration of a family story on a patriarchal and ethnocentric voice.[37] In the film's depiction of search and reunion as part of a rite of passage in the Korean brother's life, the adult adoptee sister character only serves to represent the human outcome of her male sibling's endurance and hardship. When the protagonist succeeds in reuniting his family at the end of the film, he also fulfills the promise he made to his father to become the surrogate head of the family. The adoptee woman's happy reunion therefore seems to communicate the message that even though Korea as a "father" (symbolized by the main male character) experienced such struggles, now as a developed country it has the paternal capability to welcome back and embrace even its lost children from abroad. However, the film gives no information about the adoptee's life in her adoptive country. Viewers only see the male protagonist's narrative of Korean contemporary history, which focuses on the pride and nostalgia of a patriarchal power that has endured postwar upheaval and been able to create a foundation for the "new" world. Though only a fictionalized mashup of *Finding Dispersed Families* and *I Miss That Person*, the search-and-reunion TV program sequence in *Ode to My Father* presents an "ideal" way for viewers to experience Korea's tragic past and postwar history as a central part of the male protagonist's—Korea's—bildungsroman. Moreover, the film makes no reference to the two long-lasting Korean dictatorships, which were not only guilty of human rights violations, particularly in the bloody crackdowns on students and other Korean citizens protesting for democracy in the 1980s, but also helped to streamline the institutionalization of the Korean transnational adoption industry with little or no accountability for adoptees, birth parents, and birth family members. By conveniently avoiding challenging issues regarding adoption and opting instead for a happy lost-and-found narrative, *Ode to My Father* contributes to the erasure of adoptees' and birth families' voices and their embodied experiences of loss and separation.

If these three media (re)presentations display a heightened theatricality in the staging of searches and reunions, then how do theatrical works of search and reunion differ from them? Whereas the previously discussed

---

36. This film has been recorded as the fourth-largest box-office hit in South Korean film history. D. S. Kim, "[History through Films] 'Ode to My Father.'"

37. One film critic, Chi-ung Hŏ, criticizes the film because it showed the Korean War generation as having suffered the most hardships as opposed to their offspring. K. H. Kim, "Korean War through Cinema."

media products present flattened spectacles of transnational adoptees and birth families, the Korean theater works examined in this chapter endeavor to present more sensitive and intricate depictions of transnational adoptee and family member characters. In this respect, the three Korean theater productions *Chalkak, Airport Baby,* and *Ilgopzipmae* portray varied iterations of Korean transnational adoptees' searches for and reunions with their birth mothers, giving voice and visibility to birth mothers who are central to the storylines. These theatrical productions also demonstrate the significance of onstage spatial arrangements and technological methods in portraying relationships between adoptees and birth mothers as they perform their belated motherhood.

One-Day Reunion in *Chalkak* (2020)

Chalkak dramatizes the first reunion between a Korean birth mother, Malsim, and a Korean German adoptee, Bongu, in Korea after a thirty-year separation by foregrounding simplicity: a bare set, two wooden chairs, a projection screen on the rear wall (on which subtitles and scenery are shown), and only two actresses. *Chalkak* was the last part of the *Tteodom* ("Wandering" in Korean) Trilogy, after *Good Day Today* (2014) and *Mu* (無) *Ra* (2016). All three works were written and directed by Sumin Ha of the theater group 즉각반응 (Immediately Reaction), based in Seoul.[38] *Chalkak* not only demonstrates the efficacy of its genre but also brings an intensity to the relationship between the two characters, centered on each of the characters' thoughts, feelings, and actions. In an interview about *Chalkak* regarding the two-person performance genre, Ha said that "by facing each other, the two human entities experience each other's sincerity and feel their aliveness. . . . 'Facing each other' is the smallest and the biggest intuitive language through which theater and human beings can interact with others and in a society."[39] Focusing on only two performers, the duo-drama pursues an expressiveness drawn from the minimum elements of human interaction.[40] Having the two characters face each other, communication and concentration are effectively used to depict an adoption story that starts with two intimately related but completely estranged women and ends

---

38. Selected as part of the 2020 STAGE UP series, a performing arts support program sponsored by the CJ Cultural Foundation, *Chalkak* featured intense performances by Aesim Kang as the birth mother and Jingyeong Lee as the relinquished daughter in a production that premiered during the first summer of the COVID-19 pandemic and was staged again later that same year. The analysis of *Chalkak* is based on the 2020 premiere in Seoul, which I attended.

39. H. J. Park, "*Chalkak*, the Final Work for the Wandering Trilogy." Translation by author.

40. Duo-drama is a theatrical term for a play having only two characters. Harrison, *Language of Theatre*, 91.

with a re-established mother–daughter bond as a result of their reunion. The choice of this performative format makes clear to the audience that the long-overdue reunion between the two women is *Chalkak*'s focal point.

Chalkak completely skips the search process and concentrates solely on the limited time that adoptee daughter and birth mother spend reunited in the course of one day. As Bongu and Malsim travel from a hotel café to a restaurant to a shantytown house and then to the seashore, their relationship steadily grows closer. Each location stages a different level of emotional engagement, as the relationship blossoms over the course of the day, and the play ends in a personal moment after both women purge the most vulnerable parts of their pasts. At the beginning of the play, on her arrival in Korea, Bongu directly addresses the audience, telling them she has come from Germany to meet her birth mother and ask why she relinquished her. At first excited by the reunion, which takes place at a hotel café, Bongu quickly becomes disappointed with Malsim's seemingly cold attitude, not making direct eye contact with her. Their conversation is initially limited due to the language barrier. Bongu attempts to speak Korean with difficulty and Malsim tries to communicate in English. As Bongu's frustration grows due to her speaking incompetence, she sometimes uses German words to express her feelings, and the Korean translations show up on the screen (much to the surprise of the audience when she uses curse words translated into Korean). The production gradually overcomes the language difficulties, for instance, by having Bongu speak Korean throughout with a German accent and surprisingly understand Malsim's Korean (which she intentionally speaks slowly, with exaggerated gestures to convey her meaning). After the uncomfortable and constrained first meeting at the café, Malsim and Bongu go to a Korean restaurant, where Malsim offers Bongu a special fermented fish dish, which she says she always orders when she wishes to celebrate. Malsim teaches Bongu how to eat the dish, and this becomes their first maternal lesson, even though Bongu barely eats due to the dish's pungent smell and taste. While communication between the two gradually improves at the restaurant, helping their relationship to develop somewhat, their rapport remains shallow as they talk about differences in their cultures.

Malsim and Bongu's next destination, however, makes for a dramatic change and an affective breakthrough between them. They arrive at a decrepit house that stands in an empty alleyway between two other buildings, shown in a photograph projected on the screen. On the front door, the Korean for "soon-to-be-demolished" is written in red spray paint. As they enter, they hear and feel an ominous wind. Once inside, the spotlight on the two characters in the dimmed performance space accentuating the eeriness of the setting, Malsim starts to prepare a ritual meal for the dead without telling Bongu who it is for. Startled and scared by this strange behavior, Bongu erupts and unleashes her repressed feelings on Malsim, who seems to be hiding something from Bongu. Following this emotional outbreak, both Bongu and Malsim open up to each other and share stories of their separate but parallel misfortunate lives. Bongu confesses to Malsim about her dead-end life in Germany, where she experienced racism, unfulfilling relationships with her transracial adoptive family, and an episode of homelessness and sex work leading to multiple abortions. After her monologue, Bongu starts to dance to rock music as if in trance, seeking purgation and finding a sense of freedom through her dancing. Malsim then shares her life story, including her parents' early death, her rape, teen pregnancy, and ostracism from her community. Losing her will to live, Malsim developed a fatal heart condition, but her life changed when she received a heart transplant from an organ donor who, she reveals, was the owner of the house they are currently in. Malsim then tells Bongu that she initially felt unable to directly face her until she had thanked the donor who had given her the chance to live and reunite with her relinquished daughter.

Aptly, this "haunted" house setting becomes a site for mother and daughter to reunite and unearth deep-rooted secrets that have had destructive impacts on each of their lives. Performing personal narratives is an essential way for people to interpret their own lives and present their selves to their audiences.[41] Julie Salverson views theatrical storytelling as expressing an intimate give-and-take of life stories, particularly when histories of violence and injury are recounted.[42] In this intensely emotional scene set in an unfamiliar space, mother and daughter seem to be drawing on the potential of their reunion to heal each other's painful past. Their relationship further deepens when Malsim takes Bongu to the seashore, where she can see the island where she was born and share memories of her childhood. In this outdoor setting, Malsim becomes physically freer and dances barefoot on the beach like a child. Just as in the previous scene in the house when Bongu danced and released her suppressed feelings, Malsim finds freedom from her repressed memories through dancing and jumping on the beach. Both characters are shown finding an emotional outlet through dance. Writing about the artform of dance throughout the nineteenth and twentieth centuries from a feminist perspective,[43] Sally Banes notes that women have used dance to establish their agency over their space both literally on stage and figuratively. When and where words cannot wholly express their feelings, Bongu and Malsim break out in dance, taking

41. Borland, "'That's Not What I Said.'"
42. Salverson, "Transgressive Storytelling or an Aesthetic of Injury."
43. Banes, *Dancing Women*, 1, 11.

full control of their bodies to channel their emotions accumulated over years of being an alienated adoptee and an ostracized woman.

Their excursion is short-lived, as Malsim shows symptoms of deteriorating physical health, and Bongu accompanies her to the hospital. After a weary and exhausted Malsim falls asleep in her hospital bed, Bongu, wearing a patient gown as pajamas, unfolds the handkerchief that Malsim has been holding throughout the day and sees what is inside: a dried umbilical cord with embroidery on which is written in Korean "Bongu's umbilical cord." In silence, Bongu slowly lies down next to Malsim, fitting her body with her mother's until they become one in perfect union, as reflected in the matching visual pattern of the gowns.[44] The tableau reifies Bongu's desire for reconnection with her mother. In her analysis of Korean American adoptee Jane Jeong Trenka's memoir *The Language of Blood* (2003), Margaret Homans observes, "Trenka, who does find refuge with her mother and sisters in *The Language of Blood*, describes a nearly womblike contact that mutes the visual and accentuates intimate bodily contact and care."[45] Homans also notes how Trenka views her birth mother through a "semiotic 'language of blood'" that connects the returning daughter to "the preoedipal mother."[46] Homans explains the language of blood as "the wordless bond between mother and daughter that transcends their geographic and linguistic distance."[47] Although for Homans this relationship can only come about after the mother's death, when language and cultural roadblocks disappear,[48] in the play's hospital bed scene, Bongu seems to achieve ultimate reunion with her preoedipal birth mother, as represented by their physical oneness, symbolizing the natal state of a baby in the womb, and by their "wordless bond." Mother and daughter's temporary reconnection brings to mind the image of Bongu in her mother's womb, in a state of embodied relatedness. In the following scene, all alone on stage, Bongu tells the audience about Malsim's death after their one-day reunion. Although the moments she spent with her mother were so brief, Bongu is nevertheless thankful that her memories of them will last a long time and resonate so strongly. *Chalkak* thus signifies the nucleus between adoptee and birth mother formed by their one-day reunion. This short-lived but intensely felt reunion creates a cocoon

---

44. Tellingly, throughout the entire performance both characters wear similar outfits—white blouses and beige-colored pants—creating a visual parallel to the two women.
45. Homans, *Imprint of Another Life*, 169.
46. Homans, 171. According to Freud, during the pre-Oedipal stage, the daughter feels love and a strong attachment to her mother. Also see Lamm, *Addressing the Other Woman*, 205.
47. Homans, *Imprint of Another Life*, 171.
48. Homans, 171.

that excludes the outside world, and this very intimate event reserved for the two women actualizes a belated motherhood and memory-making.

Chalkak uses photography to capture memories of Malsim, as Bongu takes photos of each location she and Malsim visit together, and these are shared with audience members. The play's title, *Chalkak,* is a two-syllable Korean onomatopoeia corresponding to the English-language "click," made by the press and release of a still camera's shutter button. At the very beginning of the play, Bongu takes a photo with a disposable camera (which emits a "click" each time she presses the shutter button), and the photos that Bongu seems to be capturing in real time show on the screen on the rear wall, transmitted by projector. The camera functions to expose Bongu's perspective—what she sees: Seoul streets, the scenery from the subway window, her first meal with Malsim, the strange house she visits with Malsim, Malsim's face, and Bongu's own dried umbilical cord. By integrating photography into the play, the playwright creates a symbiotic relationship between performing arts and photography. This encounter between theater and photography allows for a "nuanced form of interdisciplinarity," a duologue between two disciplines.[49] In the play, the camera essentially serves to enhance the projection of reality to create a visual experience from Bongu's point of view, which parallels the audience's visceral experience of the live performance. Theater thus transforms the medial essence of the photograph into a performative element. The use of a camera, however, brings more than just Bongu's perspective to the audience; it also conveys her chosen identity as an outsider in Korea. At one point, Bongu explains why she purchased a disposable camera at the airport. In carrying and using the camera, she says, she can protect herself by looking like a tourist, escaping unnecessary interactions with local Koreans who presumably will first make insensitive remarks about her inability to speak Korean and then take pity on her when they find out that she is adopted. By using a camera, Bongu performs being a non-Korean-speaking Asian tourist whose foreignness is understood as "normal." The camera thus becomes a shield that allows her to conceal her "relinquished" Koreanness and provides some form of protection for her adopted identity and self.

Bongu's use of a disposable camera also connects to the idea of the irreversible process of memory-making. Before the advent of digital cameras and cell phones, using disposable cameras was a convenient and inexpensive way to take photos, as opposed to purchasing an analog camera and film rolls and learning how to load and use them. The fact that even though digital cameras and cell phones are now ubiquitous Bongu still purchases a disposable camera

---

49. Anderson and Leister, "Theatre of Photography."

implies that she has chosen the limitations that come with it: the inability to immediately see how her photos come out and either retake or delete them. The inability to instantly evaluate quality means that, for disposable-camera users, acceptance of irreversibility is inherent. Indeed, irreversibility is also the main component of Bongu's reunion with Malsim, as their memories will be binding. These images seized by the camera are the newly created moments Bongu has chosen to keep in her memory. Thus, Bongu's camera becomes the pen with which she visually composes her journal and documents her memories of each place she and her mother visit together before death physically separates them forever. For Roland Barthes, a photo is a signifier that does not show what no longer exists but rather proves what has existed.[50] That is, a photo reveals an actual past in present time. In essence, Bongu's photo travelogue comes to be the witness to their irreversible reunion, their relationship, and the fact that Malsim was her birth mother.

In this process, the photos become performative objects that direct Bongu's act of archiving moments with her birth mother in the land of her birth. Photography, like film and video, is a technological way of archiving feelings in contemporary society. Ann Cvetkovich views cultural texts (including photographs) as "repositories of feelings and emotions, which are encoded not only in the content of the texts themselves but in the practices that surround their production and reception."[51] Bongu's photography archives emotions shared between her and Malsim over the course of their visits to the meaningful places of Malsim's past. Having reunited with her daughter, Malsim now reunites with her own past in order to reveal to Bongu how it has shaped both of their lives. However, instead of showing Bongu a scrapbook filled with photos of the past, Malsim brings Bongu to the actual sites where her memories still live, continuing to archive newly generated emotions, memories, and experiences of mothering together. Moreover, the staging of *Chalkak* itself is a means to share the affective archive of Malsim's motherhood with spectators in the immediacy of each performance, as the photos are instantly shared with audience members in the theater space. Susan Sontag describes photos as traces of pasts that are dead ("vanished past")[52] and notes that "people robbed of their past seem to make the most fervent picture takers."[53] Following Bongu

---

50. In Barthes's words, "The Photograph does not necessarily say *what is no longer*, but only and for certain *what has been.*" Barthes, *Camera Lucida*, 85. Italics in original.

51. Cvetkovich, *Archive of Feelings*, 7.

52. Sontag writes that photographs are *"memento mori,"* a reminder that we will all die. For Sontag, taking a photograph is "to participate in another person's (or thing's) mortality, vulnerability, mutability." Sontag, *On Photography*, 14.

53. Sontag, 9.

on her reunion, audiences come to realize that having been relinquished, she has indeed missed out on her past; just as importantly, however, audiences also come to understand (as Bongu does) that Malsim's mothering and Bongu's affective experience of Malsim's motherhood were also lost. Yet, because photos "furnish evidence," these pasts continue to have a life beyond their deaths: "there is always a presumption that something exists."[54] In this sense, Bongu's action of taking pictures is a way of validating her experience and of certifying that her birth mother's motherhood—although belated—actually occurred and gave meaning to both of their lives, as witnessed by the audience.[55]

Written on the back of the performance flyer is a question for audience members: "When is the brightest moment in life?"[56] The text answers the question by stating, "The brief moment of clicking when taking a photo can be the brightest moment in a painful life."[57] The flyer's introduction to the play thus immediately establishes two of the most prominent elements in *Chalkak*: the camera and light (or lighting), and the mechanism of photography itself used to materialize a sense of hope. At one point, Malsim expresses her hope that Bongu will always be "in the light." After Malsim's death, Bongu looks at the only photo Malsim took of her, using a flashlight when Bongu was dancing in the abandoned dark house, a reflection of Malsim's hope. Bongu's realization of the meaning of her mother's words is staged in a still tableau with Bongu sitting on a chair upstage where she recounted Malsim's death to the audience, fully illuminated from the side in her brightest-lit moment in the performance, symbolizing Malsim's wish for her daughter to always stay on the bright side of life. Moreover, the importance of the camera in *Chalkak* encompasses the idea of temporality, as time is seized in photography with moments frozen for as long as the digital photo or physical paper lasts. This idea of time standing still, or unending time, is illustrated at the end of the performance when Bongu points the camera toward the audience members as if to take their picture. The sound of an elongated *chal* when Bongu pushes down the camera button is heard, but the performance ends in darkness without the concluding release of the shutter's *kak*, which would indicate that the photo had finally been taken. The unending *chal* without the concluding *kak* implies that the photo remains in the continuous process of being taken. If the shutter button is not released, Bongu's life with the memories of her mother and their reunion will go on even after her death, and,

---

54. Sontag, 5.
55. Sontag, 8.
56. Author's translation of production flyer for *Chalkak* (2020).
57. Production flyer for *Chalkak* (2020).

consequently, Malsim's motherhood will also still be ongoing. Writing about Virginia Woolf, Louise Hornby notes that Woolf viewed photography as a type of enclosure, associating "the photographic containment of the world with maternal enclosure, drawing together light and mother, photographic development and gestation."[58] In this sense, Malsim's action of taking Bongu to all the significant places of her past frames the entire reuniting journey in an enclosure that contains both women in their own world of motherhood and womanhood, and remains in the brightest present as long as the *chal* sound lasts.

Search and Triple Reunions in *Airport Baby* (2018, 2020)

In the 2010s, eager to present a wider variety of topics for *changjak* musicals (newly composed musicals by Korean artists as opposed to imported works translated for Korean audiences), the Korean musical industry increased its efforts to find new sources of stories. During this period, Korean transnational adoption appeared as a subject for a new musical called *Airport Baby*.[59] *Airport Baby* is a co-production by playwright Soo-yang Jun and composer Hee-sun Chang. In 2013 both were among the first recipients of the Musical House Black and Blue Award for young artists creating new *changjak* musicals. This was followed by further financial support in 2015 from the Korean government for its development.[60] The 2016 premiere production, produced by Seensee Company, garnered publicity even before its opening with the addition of the well-known musical performer, director, and producer Kolleen Park, who joined as director.[61] In 2017 and 2018, the ShowBT production version started its national tour of Korea. The 2020 version of *Airport Baby* opened in Seoul, produced by For Kyyks Production Company with the original creative team and director. All three versions of the production follow the story of Josh Cohen, a Korean American adoptee who has always felt "different" and now as a young adult decides to come to Korea to find his birth mother.[62]

Before the 2020 performance of *Airport Baby*, the stage's backdrop showed the sky as seen from an airplane cockpit, with English and Korean words flying across like passing clouds: *Korea, America, police station, home,* among

---

58. Hornby, *Still Modernism*, 148.
59. G. Y. Kim, "Is That Material Like This?" Translation by author.
60. Choi, "Attempts Revealing Potential and Possibility." Translation by author.
61. Jackson, "Kolleen Park Presents New Musical 'Airport Baby.'"
62. The analysis of *Airport Baby* is based on both the videotaped 2018 production and the 2020 performance that I attended.

many others. Imitating a flight attendant's voice, the director of the play, Kolleen Park, announced important regulations and the start of the performance via the sound system, placing the audience in the setting of the play by saying, "We will be landing shortly." The projected screen image then showed a plane landing, and the play opened with Josh's arrival at Incheon International Airport. The airport setting holds an important spatial meaning, as it frames the beginning and ending of Josh's search-and-reunion story. In transnational adoption narratives, airports frequently appear as sites of perennial embodiment of the act of sending and receiving children. Borrowing from Marc Augé's concept of "non-places," such as public transport and commercial hubs where people are brought together but social life does not take place due to the spaces' liminal quality, Tobias Hübinette interprets the airport as "the (non-)place, where adopted children are bought and sold, and are going through their ethnic *rite de passage*."[63] Furthermore, Hamid Naficy writes that border spaces like airports are "representations, symbols, and allegories of elsewhere and of home, [. . . and] actual physical locations in which exilic narratives are enacted. For many exiles and refugees, airports are not just rhizomatic points of linkage to other points in an abstract network of relation and commerce [. . . but] are nodal sites of high intensity in which their belonging and unbelonging are juxtaposed."[64] Though Josh is neither an exile nor a refugee, his juxtaposed belonging and unbelonging are reflected in his airport arrival and expressed through the first song in the play, which Josh sings, an upbeat but yearning song about being an "airport baby."[65] Josh's entrance is dramatized in a bustling and hectic airport where travelers quickly pass by, eventually joining in the chorus at the end of the song. The transitional space of the airport serves as a "nodal site of high intensity" where Josh is temporally and spatially dislocated while still going on his hopeful way to reconnect with his mother, longing for belonging.

As the play's title and opening song are centered on both the airport as a site and the word "baby" as an identifier, particular attention should be paid to their connection to the idea of infantilizing adoptees. Referring to an adult adoptee as a "baby" follows the careless Korean colloquial practice of calling

---

63. Augé (1995) as cited in Hübinette, "Comforting an Orphaned Nation," 130. Italics in original.

64. Naficy, *Accented Cinema*, 245–46.

65. Singing is more emphasized than dancing in this musical play with a few exceptions. For example, in the 2020 version, a drag act by queer characters added vibrancy to the overall production, showcasing the performers, in bright vinyl, short pink dresses with shining spangles, sporting blonde wigs and singing and dancing to upbeat music like a K-pop girl group.

adoptees *ibyanga*, meaning an adopted "child" instead of an adult adoptee, *ibyangin*. Both examples, the play's title and the act of equating an adult adoptee with *ibyanga*, undermine adoptees' adulthood by delineating them as infants or children. Furthermore, Josh's arrival in Korea and his designation of himself as an airport baby constitute an intriguing switch on American adoptive families' practice of labeling the day their adopted child arrives at the airport in the United States as "Airplane Day" or "Gotcha Day."[66] Kimberly McKee observes that an adoptee's US "arrival celebration emphasizes the quintessential Americanness of the child without consideration for any residual memories or relations from Korea."[67] This rebirth as an American tucks away any biographical data from before adoption and overlooks the "biological mother's pregnancy and birth process."[68] In the play, Josh's arrival at Incheon International Airport and his declaration of being an airport baby affirms in reverse his "Airplane Day" or "Gotcha Day" from the United States to Korea, as if, on his first day back in his land of origin in search of his biological mother, he is reborn. The play thus establishes Josh's celebratory new beginning with, moreover, a flashback scene about Josh facing racism while growing up in the US. Without much investment in the complexity of these difficulties, this segment reflects a simple severance from his past life in the US.

While *Airport Baby* brings up several engaging discourses about transnational adoption, the musical makes a notably critical theatrical intervention about the objectification of adoptees' search and reunion in Korean television and commercial films. Craving the Jewish American food that he grew up with, Josh goes to Itaewon, a vibrant Seoul neighborhood famous for its small shops, cafés, restaurants, bars, and nightclubs, where foreign cultures and cuisines are more common than in other places in Korea. There Josh befriends Delia, the transgender Korean owner of the bar "Dilly Dally," who misses her long-lost American lover. Wanting to help Josh find his birth mother, Delia suggests that he participate in a TV show that helps lost family members reunite and accompanies Josh to the studio. The play's depiction of the TV program clearly references the nationally syndicated, long-running Korean reality show *I Miss That Person* (mentioned earlier in this chapter). Josh agrees to be on the show, although he expresses discomfort because the show is designed to make its Korean audience feel sorrow and show adoptees as pitiful. At the TV studio, along with Josh, two elderly men are made to hold placards with their missing persons' handwritten names, current age,

66. McKee, *Disrupting Kinship*, 86.
67. McKee, 86.
68. McKee, 86.

and when and where they were lost, recalling the live 1983 TV reality program *Finding Dispersed Families* (which was also fictionalized in *Ode to My Father*). A further connection to the television shows and film can be seen in the staging of the scene with the use of a live TV camera for the 2020 performance. This camera transmits the images of Josh and the two elderly men on multiple television screens in the background of the stage, as if the images were being broadcast simultaneously on Korean airwaves. Although Josh is visibly uncomfortable being part of this spectacle, he still manages to (in)voluntarily share his story, prompted by the show's emcee while his face is shown on the screens behind him. Josh and the two men are prodded and pushed onstage, bullied by the emcee, and framed on the screens in tight close-ups, all at a rapid pace that reflects the program's insensitive spectacularization of its participants (see figure 1). By using the technological element of a live camera onstage, *Airport Baby* effectively reveals how adoptees' searches are exploited through mass mediatization, for apparent "humanitarian" purposes that hide abusive aspects. Despite having been treated callously in the TV program, Josh discovers that his birth mother lives in Mokpo, a port city in the southern part of Korea.

Unlike most search-and-reunion stories, upon the discovery of Josh's birth mother, three reunions take place with her rather than one. Structured around these three reunions, the play takes time to gradually reveal the truth regarding Josh's adoption. Even though Josh attempts multiple visits to see his birth mother for the initial reunion, his efforts to build a relationship are futile, as his mother refuses to meet with him. Just as Josh is about to give up, an anonymous young male figure appears and encourages him to try one more time. This character, who only interacts with Josh, at first seems like a mirror of Josh's inner persona or a projection of his imagination. Thanks to the new character's prodding, Josh makes another attempt, and his mother finally agrees to meet him. Although the helpful Delia acts as a go-between and interpreter, this first reunion between Josh and his mother ends in utter disappointment. Josh's mother is mostly silent and distant, revealing only that she relinquished him because she was too poor to raise him, without giving further details. After this first bitter reunion, an angry Josh, bereft of emotional closure, sings a sad song entitled "No Heaven for Me" and decides to leave Korea. However, at the airport he receives a phone call from Delia informing him that his mother is critically ill. Josh initially refuses to stay, but the mysterious young male figure reappears convincing Josh not to leave.

In comparison to the 2018 version, the 2020 production differs specifically in a few scenes that present a birth mother character with a more pronounced motherly presence and outward expressions. In the 2018 production, Josh

FIGURE 1. Josh (at left) and two men with the emcee on the search-and-reunion TV show in *Airport Baby* (2018). Image Courtesy of For Kyyks Entertainment.

reunites for the second time with his mother, now in a wheelchair in a hospital. Happy to see Josh, she caresses him lovingly, calling him Junsu, before an attendant takes her away. The incident prompts Josh's Korean uncle to explain why his mother was initially adamant about not wanting to meet him. Her other son, Junsu, Josh's biological twin brother, had died six months earlier, and she had been agonizing over his death ever since. In the 2020 production's hospital scene, Josh's mother still retains all her mental faculties, and it is she who explains why she was so distant with him during their first encounter. Instead of Josh's uncle telling him of Junsu's existence, the mother tells Josh the details of Junsu's accidental death. As she recounts the incident, she seems to witness the dramatic re-enactment of Junsu's accident, with car headlights shocking her into a fainting spell. In this way, the 2020 version attempts to increase the birth mother's visibility, as she gives more information about her own agony over Junsu's death and engages more with Josh. In addition, in both productions, after this second reunion Josh realizes who the mysterious young male figure is. The spirit of Junsu then appears and the brothers sing a duet. Yet, instead of finding a compassionate brotherhood, Josh and Junsu engage in conflict, as symbolized by their song, which is vocalized as a duel whose two participants express differing ideas about what it means be transnationally adopted. Junsu notes bitterly that, as an adoptee, Josh was raised in a wealthier nation and acquired a higher standard of culture and lifestyle unavailable to him in Korea. Josh counters that his life as a Korean adoptee in the United States is full of confusion and struggle, due to racial discrimination, and is not to be desired. Their contrasting perspectives are intensified throughout the song by their stage positions on opposite sides of the balcony, upstage on the highest level of the set as if interacting on a separate plane from reality. At the end of the scene, their conflict remains unresolved.

Subsequently, a frustrated and enraged Josh breaks the windows of a building and is arrested by the police. At the police station, authorities find out that he overstayed his visit and had no visa allowing him to legally remain in Korea. Placed in the detention facility, Josh is informed about his mother's death, which is confirmed by a letter from his uncle. As Josh reads silently, his uncle enters and narrates the letter. Josh's young single mother from the past then appears, and the audience sees the moment when, having suffered from stigmatization and discrimination, heartbroken, she relinquishes both sons for adoption. Subsequently, while Josh was sent to the United States, Junsu fell sick and was given back to his mother. At this moment, she and Junsu reappear as spirits. Josh's mother approaches and caresses him in the heartfelt reunion he would have wished for had his mother, and the brother he never knew existed, not died. Both the 2018 and 2020 versions show the mother reassuring Josh that she and Junsu are leaving the world without regrets as she caresses Josh from his face down to his feet. In the 2020 version, however, she kneels in front of him also holding his two feet but for a longer time as if begging for his forgiveness. Both the mother's active role in detailing the story of Junsu's death and her emotion embodied in the act of kneeling in front of Josh reflect her deep-rooted sense of guilt. Judging by general audience reactions to the 2020 production I attended, the mother's emotional performance made quite an impact, leaving several audience members in tears.

The mother's act of kneeling in front of Josh is a forceful image. David McNeill states that gestures "exhibit images."[69] Applying McNeill's concept to this scene, we can see that the staging of the mother's motion and posture holds an almost biblical aspect, suggestive as it is of one of the iconic images of motherly grief: the Virgin Mary kneeling at the foot of Jesus on the cross. Although Josh is not physically dying, a metaphorical death is occurring, as

---

69. McNeill, *Hand and Mind*, 11.

Josh and his mother will soon be separated once more, this time unequivocally. In this tableau, the idea of deep sacrifice and profound lamentation is also powerfully embodied in the mother–son image. McNeill notes that gestures are a "person's memories and thoughts rendered visible."[70] By her gestures, Josh's mother makes her feelings about the relinquishment of her "airport baby" son visible. E. Ann Kaplan identifies two central patterns of representation of motherhood in American nineteenth-century novels and late twentieth-century films, which Kaplan calls "the angel/witch mother dichotomy," whereby the mother is seen as either a sacrificial angel or, at the other end of the spectrum, a domineering witch.[71] In this sense, the representation of Josh's mother as a sacrificial angelic figure leans into a view of mothers as necessarily devoting themselves to their children. Within Korean culture, as Joanna Elfving-Hwang states, "motherhood has become enshrouded in an almost sacred positivity," wherein the self-sacrificing mother is valorized as a major influence contributing to her son's success and the "driving force behind national or historical heroes."[72] The 2020 production of *Airport Baby* thus invested in restoring an emotive dimension to the reunion scenes in the course of elaborating the encounters between Josh, Junsu, and their mother, while also reinforcing the message of sacrificial and sacred motherhood.

An elaboration is also seen in the staging of a wistful celestial background effect that accentuates the mother's expressive gesture in the last moment of the imaginary reunion. Suddenly, a multitude of bright stars appears from below and rises in a dazzling backdrop visualization that evaporates like steam. Streaming into the Milky Way, the stars resemble thousands of flying fireflies, creating a dreamy atmosphere. In the theater, such fluctuations in lighting impact the spatial sense of audiences, as the backdrop overtakes the characters, highlighting their vulnerability within the grand scope of the effect.[73] As this occurs, the strong and determined tone of the trio's last song together, "I Don't Regret," contrasts with the visually mesmerizing background image symbolizing the ephemeral quality of time and space. This scene thus foregrounds the paradoxical parallel between the de-romanticization via the soundscape and the romanticization via the visualscape, allowing us to ponder the difficulty and challenge of depicting a reunion scene without sentimentalizing it or losing its message and impact on audience members.

Nevertheless, in its abstract and beautified visualization, this special effect not only associates death with the notion of heavenly eternity but also reminds

---

70. McNeill, 12.
71. Kaplan, *Motherhood and Representation*, 182.
72. Elfving-Hwang, *Representations of Femininity*, 99.
73. Abulafia, *Art of Light on Stage*, 145.

the audience of the opening backdrop, the clouds in the sky seen from an airplane cockpit, in effect linking the idea of death with ideas of voyage and passage to another level of life. With this elaborate visual force, the seemingly unworldly reunion is glamorized. While the theatrical tableau is strikingly staged, its sentimentalization of a birth mother and her death prompt the need for deeper reflection. As Arissa Oh points out, representing a birth mother "as a mythic, tragic-romantic heroine—is itself a kind of erasure that collapses all birth mothers into one poor woman, [and] strips her of agency."[74] Although the 2020 production of *Airport Baby* made the mother more visible, staging Josh's "ideal" reunion posthumously with his birth mother in this embellished way can be read as a type of effacement because it suggests the mother's unavoidable death as a tragic-romantic and glorious one, dismissing her lived individuality and autonomy. Finally, this third and last reunion suggests that Josh's solace and growth can only be achieved by transgressing the ultimate separation of death.

As the end of *Airport Baby* marks the conclusion to Josh's search for his birth mother and family in Korea, the quest narrative continues by transferring the hope for search and reunion from Josh to Delia, who decides to seek out her lost lover. In addition to the powerful mother–child bond that originally launches Josh to search for his birth mother, a quintessential mothering is suggested by the character of Delia and her relationship with Josh. Although just a supporting character in *Airport Baby*, as a nurturing person, Delia immediately bonds with Josh when he shares the reason for his trip to Korea and supports him throughout his search for his birth mother, functioning as friend, guide, coach, and counselor. As such, Delia becomes a surrogate mother for Josh, who finds comfort with her when suffering setbacks and rejections in trying to find and meet his birth mother. Delia is not only a facilitator of Josh's search and reunion but also a caretaker for two younger queer characters, Shasta and Chris, at her Dilly Dally bar. Just as the airport holds a strong significance as a border site in the story of Korean transnational adoption, Itaewon, where the bar is located, also carries its own special meaning as another type of border location. Situated in the vicinity of a former US military base in Seoul, Itaewon has become a pseudo-extraterritorial area where US soldiers, foreigners, and American and other foreign cultural products and lifestyles intermingle with local Korean communities, attracting racial and sexual minorities. Here, "true" Koreanness becomes delegitimized amid the activities and interactions of marginalized Koreans and foreigners:

---

74. Oh, *To Save the Children*, 171–72.

the neighborhood is a queer space.⁷⁵ Jieheerah Yun writes that many gay people consider Itaewon "a 'safe haven' where their sexual identities are better protected than in other places."⁷⁶ The long-standing Dilly Dally bar in the play, like other queer nightlife in Itaewon, has flourished in this now trendy, more commercial, and youthful neighborhood and has become a communal haven for minorities such as Shasta, Chris, and Delia, who share the experiences of prejudice and discrimination in a heteronormative Korean culture.

As Josh and Delia's friendship develops, Josh accepts Delia's offer to take up residence in a spare room at the Dilly Dally. Joined by Josh, Delia's bar also becomes an interstitial site where both the minority-ness of being a returning Korean American adoptee and being queer in Korea can find a home. Josh and Delia share the sense of being outsiders due to their "extraordinary" Koreanness, which does not conform to normalized standards of what it means to be a Korean: speaking and understanding the Korean language and customs, and following gender-conforming culture. Thus, the Dilly Dally bar is envisioned as a space of belonging and acceptance. Josh and Delia form an alternative mother–son pair, performing motherhood through their bonding as outcasts as well as via Delia's nurturing attitude toward young people, and Josh in particular, while not in a sexual or romantic way. In this sense, Josh and Delia constitute a "queer kinship" not built on a physical or sexual relationship but upon a "movement away from oppressive families of origin toward alternative structures of belonging that may offer intimacy, care, . . . and dependency in other forms."⁷⁷ Queer kinship thus constructs a deep sense of familial connection based on choice, expanding the idea of family and reorganizing gender norms; as David Eng suggests, focusing on queer diasporas can lead to an examination of "poststructuralist accounts of family and kinship."⁷⁸ Josh and Delia's queer kinship thus teases out the gendered rules of mothering to show that representations of motherhood and constructions of family are not fixed but fluid, and can be socially produced and queerly performed. Yet Josh and Delia's queer kinship somewhat confines them to a mother–son relationship, thus negating any other possible rapport, which could create anxiety in Korea's heterosexist society. In other words, presenting Josh and Delia in a mother–son liaison, the musical distances itself from the potential for queer

---

75. As Michael Fuhr describes it, Itaewon exists as a "contact zone with foreign cultures, a reminder of America's physical presence in Korea, a gateway for American pop culture, a space of social conflict with high criminalization and prostitution rates, and a place that signifies the freedom and the decadence of Western culture that many Koreans consider with mixed feelings." Fuhr, *Globalization and Popular Music in South Korea*, 216.

76. Yun, "Foreign Country in Seoul," 131.

77. Bradway and Freeman, "Introduction," 13.

78. Eng, *Feeling of Kinship*, 18.

desire between them, thereby gesturing that queerness is safe, but only in a nonsexual, motherly way.[79] While raising questions about what it means to create a performance that radically imagines queerness in Korean musical landscapes, overall, *Airport Baby* provides an engaging and entertaining representation of transnational adoption, addressing Korean transnational adoptee birth search and reunion via the musical genre.

Search but No Reunion in *Ilgopzipmae* (2013)

Ilgopzipmae premiered in 2012 and was revived in 2013 as part of the Seoul Theater Festival, produced by Yeonwoo Stage and directed by Samhwa Moon.[80] The play, written by Yang Gu Yi, theatricalizes the experiences of Sunyeong, an old Korean birth mother who happens to be a former *gijichon* woman who relinquished her Black biracial son Michael for transnational adoption.[81] As a racially mixed adoptee and GI who returns to Korea in search of Sunyeong (but only appearing at the end of the play), Michael embodies the Cold War intersection between US militarism and transnational adoption in and out of Korea. During and after the Korean War, racially mixed Korean American GI babies were relinquished because Korean society considered such children to be an "unacceptable racial mixture."[82] Kori Graves notes not only that children from white soldiers were made stateless by Korean laws and customs in a patrilineal family system but that children from Black American GIs met further ostracization.[83] Michael's appearance in the play reminds audiences about the exclusion of racially mixed babies who were subject to being sent away for international adoption from anti-biracial

---

79. Other musicals find a commonality with Josh and Delia's nonsexual pair that reifies a "safe" queerly relationship between main characters, for example, Charlie and Lola in *Kinky Boots*.

80. Yeonwoo Stage is a historical theater venue where newly written works are presented in Korea. In the 1980s, this theater produced works that reflected the sociopolitical upheavals sweeping the nation at the time. J. Park, "Yeonwoo Mudae and the Korean Theatre Movement in the 1980s." *Ilgopzipmae* was selected as the runner-up in the 2013 Seoul Theater Festival. The analysis of this play is based on the videotaped performance of the 2013 revival and the Korean script published that same year.

81. A biracial child appears in another Korean play, 주인이 오셨다 (*Master Is Here*, 2011), by Yeon-ok Koh. Both plays, *Master Is Here* and *Ilgopzipmae*, show how biracial or multiracial children of women sex workers were socially stigmatized in Korean society. My thanks to Ji Hyun (Kayla) Yuh for the source.

82. Oh, *To Save the Children*, 127. Also see J. Y. Lee, "Black-Korean Romance"; "Black Korea"; and Doolan, *First Amerasians*.

83. Graves, *War Born Family*, 1.

and anti-multiracial postwar Korea.[84] Ironically, as an outcast marginalized by Korean monoracial cultures, Michael returns to Korea as an insider of the US militaristic hegemony that enmeshed Korean territories and *gijichon* women's lives including his birth mother's.

The Korean word *gijichon* (literally, "camptown") refers to a town near a US army base, while *gijichon* women refer to Korean women who sexually or romantically served US soldiers. Under the dictatorships from the 1960s to the 1980s, which prioritized economic development as the nation's foremost mission, sex work was propagandized as a heroic act of sacrifice. Because they were paid in US dollars, *gijichon* women's sex work was deemed to be of the utmost importance to Korea's collaboration effort with the United States as a faithful and fraternal ally against North Korean Communism.[85] Under the blanket of this allied militaristic rule, *gijichon* women's sexuality and sexual labor were, however, exploited by governments and communities.[86] These women's involvement with sex work came to be also understood as a path for poor women to provide for their households during this period. Katharine Moon cites a 1965 US Army study, which reported that "of 105 prostitutes surveyed in the Yongsan area, all 'were supporting from one to eight members of their family.' Stories about young females working in camptown prostitution to pay for their brothers' high school and university education or their parents' medical expenses still abound in Korea."[87] Paradoxically, these women, often the sole supporters of their families, were also condemned for their participation in prostitution and derogatorily labeled as *"yanggongju,"* meaning "'Yankee whore,' 'Western princess,' 'UN lady,' and 'GI bride,'" among other translations.[88] In her study of the transpacific history of *yanggongju*, Grace Cho observes that these women's memories generated a "transgenerational haunting" due to their unspeakably traumatic experiences of serving and being stigmatized as *yanggongju*, "the bearer of secrets about the traumas of the Korean War and of U.S.-Korea relations—and, in many cases, about her [their] own past."[89] These women were not only defamed on account of their work but also stripped of their reproductive rights when pregnant and

---

84. T. S. Kim et al., "Research Report on the Status of Mixed-Blood People in Camp Towns."
85. Höhn and Moon, *Over There*.
86. US–Korea allied forces implemented policies forcing *gijichon* women into invasive medical checkups to prove that their bodies were free of STDs for safe sex with American soldiers. N. Y. Lee, "Construction of Military Prostitution." Korean governments profited from the *gijichon* women establishments, as the profits were also split between local officials and businessmen. K. Moon, *Sex among Allies*, 155.
87. K. Moon, 26.
88. G. Cho, *Haunting the Korean Diaspora*, 103.
89. G. Cho, 39, 14.

giving birth. Citing Eun Hye Shin and Hyun Hee Kim's report, Hosu Kim notes that only 25 percent of *gijichon* women raised their own children.[90] Kim further comments, "Transnational adoption operated as a population removal policy that was essentially institutionalized violence against the sex workers' motherhood, and racism against their mixed-race children."[91] In this context, exposing the ongoing aftermath of institutionalized GI military prostitution, *Ilgopzipmae* seeks Sunyeong and other *gijichon* women's autonomy over their right to form and maintain a family, a right that was taken away by social stigmatization and systemized discrimination marking them as shameful beings.

During field research for the play, the playwright, Yi, conducted interviews, informal meetings, and weekly visits as a volunteer for the Sunlit Sisters' Center, a Methodist Church–sponsored community center, located near US Camp Humphreys approximately 40 miles south of Seoul in Anjeong-ri, Pyeongtaek (where the story of *Ilgopzipmae* takes place). This center offers a safe space for former *gijichon* women, and it was here that Yi interviewed the older *gijichon* women.[92] Interview materials and data organized by sociologist Na Young Lee and her research team also helped Yi to understand what *gijichon* women had endured and, in particular, the positionality of these older women who worked and remained in camptowns.[93] In creating *Ilgopzipmae*, Yi attempted to explicate the unuttered reality of *gijichon* women living in poverty who were driven to sex work by means of nationalist and capitalist rhetoric. Regarding audience reaction, the performances of *Ilgopzipmae* brought about an affective response not only for ordinary spectators but also for actual former *gijichon* women whom Yi had met during the pre-production research and invited to the performance. Afterward, the women told Yi that they had never imagined their stories would resonate so strongly with others.[94] Sparked by the flame of the footlights that moved them beyond silence, these elderly former *gijichon* women decided to take up performance themselves and created their own autobiographical documentary and participatory theatrical work, entitled 숙자이야기 (*A Suk-ja Story*). While not part of this chapter's focus, this work deserves a brief look as it relates to the stories of *gijichon* birth mothers.

---

90. H. Kim, *Birth Mothers*, 46. Shin and Kim, "Report on Former Kijichon Sex Workers in Gyeonggi Do," 61.

91. H. Kim, *Birth Mothers*, 50.

92. The Sunlit Sisters' Center was established in 2002 by Soon-duk Woo, a Korean Methodist Church woman leader. Jeffrey, "Place for the Forgotten."

93. Yi, "Playwright's Note," 17; and Paik, "Interview with Artists." Translation by author.

94. Paik, "Interview with Artists." Translation by author.

Directed by Ji-hyang Noh, *A Suk-ja Story* premiered in 2012 at a community center in Pyeongtaek. In 2013 a revised production was staged as the opening production of the Seoul Marginal Theatre Festival. Produced by the Sunlit Sisters' Center, Happitory, and Theater Hae, *A Suk-ja Story* was co-created, without a written script, by actual former *gijichon* women, who also appeared on stage.[95] The performance depicts the story of two *gijichon* women whose names are coincidently identical: Suk-ja. One of the two Suk-jas is forced to relinquish her son because of Korean society's racism toward Black biracial children and patriarchal oppression toward unwed *gijichon* mothers. Although the play does not explicitly bring up Korean transnational adoption as a central theme, the issue took center stage when audience members were invited to participate in revising any part of the play after the first half of a 2013 performance. During the second half, the director, Noh, asked the audience to volunteer to change the part(s) during which they felt they wanted a change. One of the spectators chose to restage the scene in which Suk-ja decides to relinquish her son for transnational adoption. A young male spectator who volunteered to improvise as her son insisted on staying with her rather than be relinquished, thereby keeping the family united.[96] Through this action, the audience–former *gijichon* women performer production "rewrote" the hegemonic script of Korean transnational adoption that reifies relinquishment as a birth mother's best way to ensure a child's well-being. To this day, the former *gijichon* women continue to be involved in theater, with variations on their lives presented in works such as 문밖에서 (*Outside the Door*, 2020), also directed by Yi.

Returning to the discussion of *Ilgopzipmae*, its title is phonetically broken down: *ilgop* signifies seven, *zip* a house, and *mae* a sister, meaning seven houses standing adjacent to each other like sisters. In Anjeong-ri, two former Korean *gijichon* women, Sunyeong and Hunnam, are now old and living together with a current *gijichon* woman bar owner named Hwaja, a working *gijichon* woman from the Philippines going by the name of Seonhui, and a pro-US Korean man called Chungwon whose mother was a former *gijichon* woman. In this housing edifice laid out in a row under one roof and functioning as a small house, each person has only a small private room, indicating the residents'

---

95. Along with the Sunlit Sisters' Center, Happitory and Theater Hae work for the disenfranchised through theatrical expression and community engagement. Theater Hae with its catchphrase "Oppressed People's Theater Space" specializes in producing forum theater. See Theater Hae blog. Happitory is a private group that "seeks the way to happiness through introspection and contribution" via theater, meditation, and other means. "Introduction of Happitory." Translation by author.

96. This analysis of *A Suk-ja Story* is based on a videotaped 2013 performance. For a more detailed discussion, see Ju, "Autobiographical Documentary Theatre."

poor financial situation. A US-based Korean woman researcher named Hana temporarily joins their living arrangement, occupying the sixth room while documenting the stories of Korean *gijichon* women for her research. Except for a few instances, the last room's door stays closed throughout the play. The audience eventually learns that any person who rents this room ultimately dies there, leaving it empty. The closed wooden door of each small house signifies the disconnectedness between the residents. Yet this separation does not completely bar them from bonding, as their doors align under the same roof. The set suggests that even though the former and current *gijichon* women are separated, they are still linked to one another, sharing the ostracization that comes with being *gijichon* women. Only three outsiders—Hana, Sunyeong's relinquished son Michael, and an anti-American male activist, Sangcheol—come and go from the house. This limited access underscores the isolation of these camptowns, which Christine Hong describes as a "site of internal exile [. . . and] zones of transaction between notoriously disposable Korean labor and U.S. military personnel shielded by extraterritorial rights."[97] Moreover, Susie Woo writes how Korean sex workers, mothers of mixed-race GI babies, and those babies themselves were concealed in "camptowns, segregated schools, and orphanages."[98] The only time all the characters leave the enclosed setting is at the end of the play, when they go to the Fourth of July fireworks display at the US Army base, revealing just how much their lives are intertwined with US militarism. *Ilgopzipmae* resonates with the (in)voluntary seclusion of this solitary site, surrounded by invisible fences and barriers put up by a condemnatory Korean society, reflecting the isolation of *gijichon* women who have been hidden due to national shame but who still seek hope and healing. By situating the play as a search-and-reunion story, I argue, *Ilgopzipmae* not only materializes an intersection between *gijichon* women and their encounter with transnational adoption but also contests the shame and secrecy associated with being both a GI prostitute and a birth mother.

Through Hana's role as a researcher, *Ilgopzipmae* follows Sunyeong's life story. As Hana befriends Sunyeong, she comes to trust Hana and eventually agrees to a recorded interview with her. Significantly, *Ilgopzipmae* uses the dramatic situation in which a birth mother records herself as a *gijichon* birth mother to break the silence surrounding what it means to be a *gijichon* woman and a birth mother who relinquished her child. Playwright Yi points out that the interview scene between Sunyeong and Hana is the crucial part of the play because it revisits the past and present life experience of *gijichon* women

---

97. Hong, *Violent Peace*, 217.
98. Woo, *Framed by War*, 19–20.

and the searching voice of a *gijichon* birth mother, culminating in Sunyeong's life in the camptown.[99] In the interview scene, Sunyeong and Hana are seated downstage in a strong visual position, closer to the audience than in any other scene throughout the play. Staging the scene and placing the characters so close to the audience not only creates a sense of intimacy in which Sunyeong can privately and safely expose her story but also connects the spectators to this space as if they are actually in the yard with Sunyeong and Hana.

This intimate downstage staging is intriguing in that the interview scene is also set in the public space of the front yard of the seven houses. The play's main setting is the small yard: here, people mingle with each other and express themselves, while death sporadically occurs behind doors. This communal space, where most of the play's action takes place, generates a feeling of liminality between the private interior spaces of the seven houses and the public space of the world beyond the yard. As part of the seven-room house complex, the yard is public but still retains its private connection to the houses, their inhabitants, and their histories, and serves as a passageway to the outside world. That Sunyeong's interview should take place in this private–public realm suggests that her personal history as a *gijichon* birth mother is connected on a larger scale to the public history of contemporary Korea, wherein *gijichon* women's gender and sexuality became entangled with patriarchal and militaristic forces.

In this twenty-minute interview scene, Sunyeong discloses how she ended up living and working as a *gijichon* woman, what being a *gijichon* woman has meant to other women, the community members, and herself, why she relinquished her son, and how she avoided meeting him when he searched for her a few years prior. Invited by Sunyeong to be an auxiliary interviewee, Hwaja often interjects, amending and supplementing Sunyeong's episodes, revealing their longtime friendship and her importance as a witness to Sunyeong's life and relinquishment. Throughout the interview, Sunyeong and Hwaja both reconstruct the memories of their past as *gijichon* women who suffered from poverty and discrimination and who directly and indirectly were connected to transnational adoption. This paired interview scene reveals to the audience that the two women's experiences of adoption and prostitution exist not only on the personal level but also on the shared, collective level, where they find a sense of commonality and comradeship.

At the end of the interview, Sunyeong decides to record a voice message for Michael in Korean, not knowing if he will ever hear it:

---

99. Yi, "Use of the Date," 20. Translation by author.

SUNYEONG: Michael . . . may I refer myself to you as your mother? I am your mother. I am still alive. I am so sorry for having lied. . . . Since the day you came and people told you that I had died, I hoped that you would visit me once more. I hoped you would have known that your mother was not dead. . . . Or, I wish you would visit here, hoping you would stand on the land where your mother died. I have waited for you. . . . Dear Michael. God will protect you. I believe that.[100]

Sunyeong's action of recording a long-overdue revelation carries an emotional intensity beyond that of devastation from guilt. In the short recording, Sunyeong comes as close as she can to revealing the truth of what kind of life she has led and how Michael is connected to it. The psychological and emotional safety of distance via the use of technology allows Sunyeong to share her last words with him and reveal how she was doubly stigmatized as a *gijichon* woman and a birth mother who relinquished her child. The use of technology to express feelings otherwise repressed is explored by Hosu Kim, who writes about real-life Korean birth mothers' online posts. According to Kim, in these virtual forums, birth mothers document their experiences of relinquishment, loss, and grief, the internet functioning as a site where they feel safe enough to expose their vulnerabilities.[101] In *Ilgopzipmae*, the tape-recording interview scene not only captures Sunyeong's—and by extension *gijichon* birth mothers'—memories but also, through Sunyeong's calm and courageous voice, carves for her a testimonial legacy of sorts, a willful archive. Sunyeong's recorded voice conveys a transmittable determination to be heard by future generations, including Michael. On a similar note, Kim also posits that birth mothers can find ways to connect with their relinquished children via the internet, thereby creating a "virtual kinship" that can also offer the mothers agency as "a critical population of virtual mothers."[102] I consequently view Sunyeong's recording as an act of belated mothering, an attempt to restore and ensure a possible future kinship with the help of technology. While she would not be alive and could not be sure that Michael would even hear the recording, the play affirms her voice as a virtual motherly presence. In this sense, staging an interview in which Sunyeong tells her own story as a *gijichon* birth mother serves not to reify a sense of shame due to her past experience but to bring forth a sense of agency for herself and other *gijichon* birth mothers whose life story, once shared, can then be reckoned with. Ultimately,

---

100. Yi, "Ilgopzipmae," 212–13. Translation by author.
101. H. Kim, *Birth Mothers*, 145–87.
102. H. Kim, 146.

this scene creates its own documentation of undeservedly forgotten women's voices, generating long-awaited accountability for *gijichon* birth mothers.

Even though a vital part of Sunyeong's story, Michael appears only once at the end of the play when, a few years after her interview with Sunyeong, and Sunyeong's death, Hana revisits the house. There she accidently encounters a Black Korean American soldier who has come from his camp to pass out flyers about the Fourth of July fireworks that evening. Although Hana realizes he is Sunyeong's son, she does not tell him. A much older Hwaja then appears and recognizes Michael but also says nothing. Michael leaves without either Hana or Hwaja telling him about his mother. This intentional omission of a reunion scene can be understood as a "blank," like a blank space on a written page. Winfried Fluck explains that

> a blank is thus not a mere gap, or an ideologically instructive omission. It is an intentional, often carefully crafted, suspension of relations in order to make us provide links for what is disconnected. The difference is significant: A mere gap allows readers to indulge in their own projections, a blank compels them to set up relations between their own imaginary constructs and the text.[103]

The purposeful "blank" of a reunion—or, more precisely, the absence of a recognition scene—in *Ilgopzipmae* is a deliberate choice that compels the audience to form their own thoughts on the long-lasting scars of separated families. It is also meant to reflect on how conventional happy closures of adoptees' search-and-reunion narratives fail to represent the incommensurability of loss that has never found a clear-cut ending. Discussing the fictional search narrative in the novel *Somebody's Daughter* (2005) by Marie Myung-Ok Lee, Marina Fedosik interprets the chance meeting without recognition of a birth mother and her relinquished daughter as "destabiliz[ing] the conventional logic of the search narrative," and yet the characters still find a meaningful resolution to their search.[104] Through the absence of a recognition scene, *Ilgopzipmae* keeps a distance from the narrative of blissful reunion and reconciliation between birth mother and returned adoptee, suggesting to its audiences the ambiguity and open-endedness of birth mother search. The notion of a "blank" here gives the audience the opportunity to fill in the gap of the play's ending with their thoughts, wonderings, and wishes of what

---

103. Fluck, "Role of the Reader," 258.
104. Fedosik, "Representations of Transnational Adoption," 185–86.

could have happened if a reunion had occurred. Within the context of the story, however, this lack of a final reunion underscores a past search-and-reunion attempt. The audience finds out that when Michael was younger, he had searched for his mother, but the shame that Sunyeong had internalized due to her being a *gijichon* woman made her decide to avoid him. Following Sunyeong's instructions, Hwaja lied, telling Michael his mother had passed away. At the end of the play, when Michael revisits the house, the audience members are left unaware of whether he knows his mother had actually lived there. In a sense, by visiting the location of the seven houses, Michael is hoping for a confirmation of his mother's existence and some form of symbolic reunion with her through the site of her life. Thus, the play presents two failed searches and no reunion, postponing any fulfilling closure between Michael as an adoptee and Sunyeong as a birth mother.

While an adoptee–birth mother reunion does not occur as a melodramatic dénouement in *Ilgopzipmae*, the play's conclusion foregrounds a salient visual message. After Michael exits and the residents of the seven houses leave to see the fireworks at the base, Hana stands alone in front of Sunyeong's door, which opens. A bright white light emanating from inside enwraps Hana, seen in silhouette from behind. The light fades away and the fireworks are then seen through the tiny windows at the top of each of the closed doors. Unlike the romantic star stream backdrop in *Airport Baby*, this subtle and fleeting fireworks effect evokes a mixture of sadness, loneliness, contentedness, and lingering desire. In this final moment of the play, the ray of light streaming from Sunyeong's door reads as an expressionistic emblem of the lives of the *gijichon* birth mothers who, although they suffered terribly during their time on earth, still emit rays of hope. The bright white light shining out from the darkness of the room presents a visual catharsis, replacing the "blanked" reunion between Sunyeong and Michael. Although the play does not follow the conventional representation of birth search and reunion, *Ilgopzipmae* nevertheless delineates the knotted relationships between Korean *gijichon* birth mothers and transnational adoptees, locating them in the tapestries of camptown lives and deaths.

The Death of Birth Mothers: Necropoetics

The birth searches and reunions in *Chalkak, Airport Baby,* and *Ilgopzipmae* engender the "resurrection" of birth mothers' voice and visibility, as each of the birth mother characters reveals how she encountered and was affected by Korean transnational adoption. The birth mother characters' telling of their side of the adoption story is significant in its revelation of the hidden intricacies of relinquishment. Their stories address the conditions of stigma and poverty that prevented them from keeping and raising their children as young single and unwed mothers in a heteropatriarchal Korean society. During the interview scene in *Ilgopzipmae*, Sunyeong relates how an adoption agency worker visited her multiple times to convince her to give up her rights as a mother for the good of the child. Her recorded voice exposes the conspiratorial practices of Korean adoption agencies, whose industry-imposed gender and class discrimination renders mothers powerless. In this context, Sunyeong's act of recording her story can be seen as a conscious act, a deliberate breaking of the wall of shame that deprived her of her son. In *Chalkak*, Malsim, a survivor of sexual violence, had to convince herself throughout her life that her choice of relinquishing her daughter Bongu for adoption was the way to set Bongu free. Whether persuaded by others or self-convinced, the birth mother characters in all three plays believed that their choice was an act of love and care, but only because they had no other options, not realizing how much pain would permeate their lives, even after death, as the character of Josh's mother shows in *Airport Baby*. The birth mothers' resurrected voices and visibility challenge the preconceived and perpetuated images of birth mothers as irresponsible and uncaring, and complicate transnational adoption stories of birth search and reunion by widening the discourse on reproductive politics and justice for birth mothers who have been deprived of their rights. Furthermore, the three theatrical works imagine the mothers' healing and reconciliation with their children whether they have actually reunited or not. In *Chalkak*, Malsim and Bongu come to terms with each other's life during their very brief reunion period by sharing their experiences as marginalized women. When Josh realizes the truth of his birth mother's past in *Airport Baby*, their final imaginary reunion creates a heartbreaking but relief-filled sense of closure for him. While a reunion between Sunyeong and Michael is not actualized in *Ilgopzipmae*, Sunyeong's voice serves as a virtual archive in which her past and truth resonate through its potential power of redress in the remembrances of *gijichon* birth mothers' lives. Unfortunately, although their voices are heard and their visibility regained, healing and reconciliation for these women come at a harsh price, as all three die at the end of the plays.

Why do all the birth mothers have to die? Of course, playwrights have the privilege of killing off their characters to advance a plot, conclude it, or create empathy, anger, and any other feeling in an audience. Analyzing the demise of the three birth mothers in each play, I interpret the deaths of these characters through a *necropoetics* framework—a term borrowed from Carol Margaret Davison, who uses this term to describe Charlotte Brontë's interrelated themes of death, mourning, and the spirit world.[105] In the context of theater, I consider necropoetics a method for interpreting dramatic texts in which specific characters die. Necropoetics, in this sense, is a dramatic lens for contextualizing the narrative and staging of a character's death to convey a social, political, or cultural point. Within the framework of birth mothers and transnational adoption, the necropoetics of the three plays imply that the deaths of the birth mother characters are *necessary* for the termination of their own state of living death, that is, their condition of living with guilt and shame. In his book about race and immigration in Spanish theatrical works, Jeffrey Coleman discusses misrepresented theatricalizations of Latin American women working in the sex and domestic work industries. Coleman engages with Achille Mbembe's concept of necropolitics, in which masses of individuals are subjected to death-exposed living environments, relegating them to the "status of the *living dead*."[106] Coleman views the misrepresentation of women as a type of symbolic violence in a "necropolitical" state where "the captive is never killed but rather socially and mentally dead to the rest of society through isolation and marginalization."[107] In the three plays discussed in this chapter, the birth mother characters are, at first, imagined as resurrected from their necropolitical state of being in the Korean society that has isolated and marginalized them. Necropoetics, however, imply the inevitability of the mothers' deaths by means of theatrical imagination.

The use of necropoetics in the stories is twofold. First, it brings about forgiveness for the mothers' lingering guilt of relinquishment, and second, it expunges Korea's national shame of having sent away its children. As women have often been imagined as a gendered embodiment of the nation, and thus reduced to a nationalist symbol, they have become, in the words of Cynthia Enloe, "patriarchally sculpted symbols—of the nation."[108] In the context of the three plays, if the birth mothers are viewed as representing the nation, through their eventual deaths their shameful pasts are finally forgiven, and the nation's honor and pride restored. In the televised narratives of Korean adoptees' search and reunion with their birth mothers, Hosu Kim sees a shift from Korea's shame, which is symbolized by "unsuccessful" birth motherhood and the losses of transnational adoption, to its readiness to start the

---

105. Davison, "'Last Home.'"
106. Mbembe, *Necropolitics*, 92. Italics in original.
107. Coleman, *Necropolitical Theater*, 21.
108. Enloe, *Bananas, Beaches and Bases*, 87.

reconciliation process. As Kim notes, the "discourse of motherhood in 'origins,' 'roots,' and 'home' ... tends to appropriate the body of the birth mother, once more, in the service of national reconciliation, as part of South Korea's nation-building project in the global era."[109] Birth mothers who had "failed" to function as "good" mothers and citizens yet agree to reunite with their transnationally relinquished children. Publicly doing so on TV shows such as *I Miss That Person*, birth mothers could then be proudly considered, in nationalistic terms, as elevating Korea's globalization status. By reconciling with their children who return as part of the Korean diaspora, the birth mothers contribute to this (inter)national narrative. In the three plays, however, the necropoetic endings—the fetishizations of the birth mothers' death as a dramatic resolution—reaffirm the trope of the birth mother as a sacrificial figure, and buttress patriarchal cultural forces trying to preserve the social order of reinstalling the invisibility of birth mothers. In this line of thought, Korea can only find redemption from its "dishonorable" past at the cost of the birth mothers' deaths.

Just as importantly, the birth mothers' necropoetics of indispensable "dying" in the narrative takes away the prospect of envisioning solidarity oriented toward social change between birth mothers and adoptees within and beyond Korea. If the birth mother characters had not died, would the performances of adoptees' birth search and reunion have theatrically foregrounded an ending with the possibility of a sustainable mother–child relationship? As the necropoetics limit the potential for birth mothers to gain further agency, the actual moments of their deaths are also denied staging, thus rendering their deaths part of the very invisibility that permeated their lives. In all three plays, the birth mother characters' deaths are not staged but simply mentioned. Hence, the necropoetics disallow the possibility of imagining changing the pattern of erasing birth mothers from Korean transnational adoption narratives. In contrast to this fictional depiction, some returned adoptee activists and unwed mothers themselves, as well as non-adoptee Korean activist groups, advocate for the rights of adoptees and unwed mothers in real life.[110] These people form an affinity in their advocacy and activism to examine certain roots of transnational adoption from Korea: the patriarchal oppression of women, the disenfranchisement of women's autonomy over their bodies, and especially the deprivation of a woman's right to form a family by herself

---

109. H. Kim, *Birth Mothers*, 126.
110. Bae, "Radical Imagination," 300–315.

without fear of judgment and discrimination.[111] Could Korean theater imagine these acts of defiance rather than deaths for birth mothers?

Finally, the necropoetics of each of the three plays leave a sense of wanting at the end, as the adoptee characters are so quick to accept their birth mothers' deaths and move on with their lives. In *Chalkak*, in the scene immediately following Malsim's death, Bongu is at the airport preparing to leave Korea and seems to have already processed her mother's death. In *Airport Baby*, after the highly emotional reunion with the vision of his deceased mother, Josh, also at the airport, sings a happy song of acceptance before flying back to the United States. In *Ilgopzipmae*, Michael, having been told several years prior that his mother had died and accepted this as fact, seeks some memory of her at the camptown, but even right up until the end of the play he finds no concrete confirmation that his mother is dead. In all three plays, the adoptee characters' ready acceptance of their birth mothers' deaths functions to remove their mothers' existence and therefore the need to mourn for them from the adoptees' lives. As the necropoetics bring about the rapid acceptance of the death of birth mothers, the prospective metamorphosis of their shared vulnerability into mutual agency is delayed and eventually dismissed.

According to Jung-Soon Shim, while Korean theater in the 1990s and early 2000s brought feminist ideas to the stage, in its portrayals of motherhood it continued to draw on the ideal image of a "National Motherhood" that conformed to the "traditional stereotype of Good Wife/Wise Mother."[112] Shim argues that the powerful Confucian philosophy of family designating women solely as virtuous mothers is reflected in Korean theater, where the representation of an "individualistic Mother" is yet to be seen.[113] The representations of birth mothers in the three plays analyzed in this chapter somewhat continue this Korean national mother-making practice, but they also contest patriarchal boundaries of what it means to be a birth mother in the search-and-reunion narrative of transnational adoption. This effort in challenging patriarchal

---

111. For instance, the Seoul-based Global Overseas Adoptees' Link (G.O.A.'L) and Adoptee Solidarity of Korea (ASK), who fight for adoptees' rights, and the Korean Unwed Mothers Families Association (KUMFA), composed of "a coalition of internationally adopted people, unwed mothers, first parents, and their allies [who] started to work to revise South Korea's Special Adoption Act in late 2008. It was wholly revised in 2011 and enforced in 2012 to prioritize family preservation over adoption." Oparah, Shin, and Jeong Trenka, "Preface," *Outsiders Within*, xii. Bae also points out that "relationships between adoptees and KUMFA mothers and their children represent a creative form of kinship that can be seen as a product of a shared radical imagination." Bae, 310.

112. Shim, "Recasting the National Motherhood," 143.

113. Shim, 153.

representations of motherhood has appeared on the Korean theater scene.[114] For instance, a community play 미모되니깐 (*Because I Am an Unwed Mother*, 2015) by and about the stories of unwed Korean mothers raising their children by themselves was staged, confronting the idealized motherhood trapped in a patriarchal order with its normalized father-led and nuclear familial structure. The play, devised and directed by Hyeonjeong Kim, featured actual Korean unwed mothers on stage sharing their experiences of raising their children as unwed mothers in Korea. While the production did not explicitly focus on transnational adoption, the subject did come up, as unwed mothers are often prodded to choose adoption rather than offered support for their mothering and motherhood. In anticipation of a possible wind of change, I am hopeful that performances of Korean birth mothers' own stories of search and reunion will be produced and that such performances will overturn necropoetic dramatizations in which birth mothers are romanticized as sacrificial maternal figures whose inevitable destiny is death.[115] Hopefully, such performances and stories will lead audiences to engage in scholarly and socially relevant discussions about birth mothers' pre- and post-reunion experiences with their children that allow for and give thought to their present and future together.

•

From duo-drama to musical to full-cast play, this chapter has examined three theatrical works that present variations of Korean transnational adoptees' search-and-reunion stories on contemporary Korean stages. Centering the narratives of search and reunion on the experiences of birth mothers and their belated motherhood shines a light on their existence within a Korean transnational adoption industry that would prefer to keep them out of the picture. While the representations of birth mothers resurrected from social death in these three works might fall short of full-fledged agency, performing transnational adoption nevertheless opens an imaginative way of demanding the possibility of a life of coexistence for birth mothers and adoptees and social change involving full affirmation of single and unwed mothers and their motherhood. Furthermore, as to my knowledge no Korean birth mothers have penned and performed their own accounts of search and reunion in theater, I hope that Korean and other birth mothers worldwide will soon relate their stories on the stage in all their complexity. As SooJin Pate states, the focus on

---

114. Borowiec, "South Korean Single Mothers."

115. Korean fiction films featuring a birth mother character trying to search for her relinquished child include 육혈포강도단 (*Robbery*, 2010), directed by Hyo-jin Kang, and 영도다리 (*I Came from Busan*, 2010), directed by Soo-il Jeon.

birth families in the story of Korean transnational adoption will offer "other emergences and other genealogies" to be examined.[116] These other emergences and genealogies, as Pate calls them, are exactly what Korean theater's unsettling acts could aim to achieve through a critical and creative engagement with the historical, political, and social ramifications of Korean transnational adoption inclusive of birth mothers as well as adoptees.

---

116. Pate, *From Orphan to Adoptee*, 160.

CHAPTER 2

Bodily Testimony

*Korean American Women Adoptees'
Autobiographical Solo Performances*

Via various artistic media from poetry to visual arts, a handful of Korean American adoptee artists have explored their own search-and-reunion experiences with the public. Kim Park Nelson states that for these adoptee artists, "birth search and reunion with Korean family becomes a central part of their adoptee identities."[1] This chapter centers on Marissa Lichwick, Sun Mee Chomet, and Amy Mihyang Ginther, who chose the autobiographical solo performance genre to unpack their search-and-reunion stories in, respectively, *Yellow Dress* (2015), *How to Be a Korean Woman* (2012), and *Homeful* (2018). In these three works, the artists present a shared goal of finding and reconnecting with their birth mothers; yet rediscovery of birth mothers, in the words of Margaret Homans, can turn "from a source of comfort into a source of frustration."[2] In light of this ambivalent awakening, the works undermine the expectations of the romanticized narrative on Korean transnational adoptees' searches and reunions, which tends to oversimplify diverse situations and realities. This chapter discusses this staged counternarrative with reference to the three adoptee artists' performances of identity construction, following the trajectories of their birth searches and reunions between adoptive and

---

1. Park Nelson, *Invisible Asians*, 158.
2. Homans uses these words to describe Korean American adoptee Deann Borshay Liem's feelings when she reunites with her Korean birth family in Liem's film *First Person Plural* (2000). Homans, *Imprint of Another Life*, 170.

birth cultures. The conclusions of the artists' birth searches and reunions are not necessarily definitive, and the artists' identities remain unfinalized. Significantly, however, the process of autobiographical solo performance gives the artists a better understanding of who they were as adopted children and who they have become as adult adoptees, at the same time enabling them to accept the sense of impermanence and uncertainty they have felt in both their adoptive and their birth countries. As Chomet states with regard to her piece, "There's no answers in this show, it's all about questions."[3]

As Arissa Oh observes, "the birth searches that adoptees undertake are not just efforts to find their roots or acquire genetic information, but quests for elemental knowledge of who they are."[4] While this quest did inform the birth searches and reunions of Lichwick, Chomet, and Ginther, I contend that their autobiographical solo performances encompass much more than the quest motif. Their works foreground the hidden systemic mechanisms and cultural ideologies that complicate the process of transnational subject formation involved in becoming a Korean adoptee in the United States and returning as an "Americanized Korean" to Korea. Within this complex process, Park Nelson explains, "the experiences of discrimination that these adoptees face are transnational—for being Asian in appearance in the United States and for not being culturally Korean enough in Korea."[5] The performance works discussed in this chapter reveal the performers' experiences and understandings of their own vacillating positions as transnational outsiders, as they become aware of shifts in their own gender, race, and ethnicity both in and outside of Korea and the United States.[6] To present this awareness, the artists stage their personal interactions with adoptive and birth family members, as well as contentious encounters that racialize them or essentialize their being Asian, women, and adoptees. In this way, they demythify the typical transnational adoption tale that shows adoptees' smooth integration into a happy multicultural adoptive family and a newly found blood-related birth family. I intentionally use the word *demythify* here instead of *demystify* to explicitly convey the process of dispelling myths or misconceptions. Also, by using the word demythify, my analysis in this chapter recenters the solo performances' ways to defy the mythic adoptee-ness as they question what it means to be an adopted person

3. Chomet, interview with the author, Minneapolis, May 18, 2015.
4. Oh, *To Save the Children*, 207.
5. Park Nelson, *Invisible Asians*, 185.
6. In this chapter, race is discussed as a social and cultural construction about what it means to be Asian and/or white. All three performers theatricalize the experiences of being part of a white family in the United States without specifying any ethnic and religious background, except for Sun Mee Chomet, who mentions her adoptive family's Jewish background in her play.

in conjunction with their racial, gender, and ethnic identities. As such, the word directly relates to unsettling acts as the performances challenge the systemic forms of racialization and gendering oppression that reinforce the normative expectations and limitations of being and becoming a transnational adoptee in Korean and US cultures and beyond. This work of demythification thus illustrates how the actual experience of reality in search and reunion can facilitate the performative disruption of essentialized transnational adoption master narratives.

As a more intimate and individualistic form of theater, the solo performance genre derives its power and effectiveness from the intense focus that the solo performer must apply in order to sustain the narrative alone and from a heightened authority. Moreover, this genre carries a specificity wherein a single person takes responsibility on stage, being both vulnerable and accountable for their performative actions. This venue consequently allows for fuller agency to be exercised. Esther Kim Lee observes that Asian American solo performers view their work as a way toward self-empowerment through the expression of their identities.[7] According to Stacy Schultz, the performative works of Asian American women solo artists both expose and express resistance against abjection of Asian American women.[8] Lynette Goddard cites Catherine Ugwu, who underscores how the centering of cathartic experiences in Black women's solo performances engages artists and audiences in a type of purification.[9] Goddard further views the autobiographical aspect of Black women's performances as different from the often seen tropes in Black women's theater.[10] Echoing these scholars' ideas about the solo performances of women of color, I view Lichwick's, Chomet's, and Ginther's solo body as a conduit through which their actions produce an empowerment that propels them and their audiences to defy the racialized, ethnicized, and gendered notions that have made Korean American women adoptees an othered passive object. By performing their resistance and agency, these artists thus forge a path toward rewriting the processes and meanings of their own search-and-reunion experiences.

More pointedly, I argue that by placing their affective moments and critical thoughts center stage, each via a specific expression of collage in speed, slow movement, and aural and visual embodiment, the three artists engender bodily testimony. These actions transform their memories and feelings into an embodied new knowledge that they share with live audiences. Amanda

---

7. E. K. Lee, *History of Asian American Theatre*, 156.
8. Schultz, "Asian American Women Artists."
9. Ugwu as quoted in Goddard, *Staging Black Feminisms*, 154.
10. Goddard, *Staging Black Feminisms*, 177.

Stuart Fisher describes Anna Deavere Smith's performance of bearing witness as "an embodied, performative action," through which the physicalness of the witness and the corroborative action are inter-implicated as a way of "generating new knowledge and understanding."[11] Similarly, the three performers' bodily testimonies produce an empathetic understanding of Korean American transnational adoptees' border-crossing experiences, a crucial step in creating a discerning perception of international adoption, including the actuality of adoptees' "homecomings" across temporal and spatial borders. In other words, the lived experiences embedded into the artists' performing bodies engage audiences in a new way of viewing and contextualizing the narratives of birth search and reunion. Thus, both the artists and the audiences of the performances gain a renewed perspective from which to think differently about birth search and reunion and Korean transnational adoption at large. While all three plays were staged in several venues for a general public, they were also performed at Korean American adoptee associations' gatherings and adoption conferences. With reference to this production history, I look further into the act of incubating a critical adoption spectatorship and adoptee affinity through the theater space.

Autobiographical Search-and-Reunion Story

In the context of Korean transnational adoption, before turning to theater, Korean American women adoptee artists used documentary film and nonfiction writing to explore their experiences of birth search and reunion. Among these artists' works, Deann Borshay Liem's documentary film *First Person Plural* (2000) recounts Liem's life as a Korean adoptee in a white Californian family in the mid-1960s and her later search and reunion with her birth mother in Korea.[12] Jane Jeong Trenka's memoir *The Language of Blood* (2003) recalls her life as a Korean adoptee in a small Minnesota town and her journey as an adult to seek her mother and siblings in Seoul. Writing about adult adoptees' return memoirs, including Trenka's, Margaret Homans notes that the works tend to start with high expectations of idealized fictive versions of the birth country and to proceed through demythification by experience to a point where the initial expectations are "replaced, in qualified ways, by the acts of

---

11. Stuart Fisher, *Performing the Testimonial*, 165.
12. Note that two documentary filmmakers predate by just a few years Deann Borshay Liem's film. In both Tammy Chu's *Searching for Go-Hyang* (1998) and Jennifer Ardnt-Johns's *Crossing Chasms* (1998), the adoptee filmmakers seek answers to questions about their adoption through their birth search and return to Korea.

writing or filmmaking."[13] Park Nelson observes that both Liem's and Trenka's autobiographical works draw on personal experiences to produce and disseminate messages of dissent, critiquing the white parent-centered discourse of transnational adoption as a careless dismissal of adoptees' own voices.[14] Shelley Park also examines Liem's films, and finds that they reveal the deleterious effects of colorblindness, its erasure of adoptee histories and identities.[15] Kimberly McKee writes that Liem's films and Trenka's memoirs repossess and restore Korean adoptees' agency by contesting narratives of rescue and reunion.[16] This stream of adoptee-centered creative works has continued in cinema with more recent documentary films on Korean American women adoptees, including Liem's *In the Matter of Cha Jung Hee* (2010) and *Geographies in Kinship: The Korean Adoption Story* (2012), and Samantha Futerman and Ryan Miyamoto's *Twinsters* (2015).[17] My examination of Korean American adoptee solo performers' autobiographical theater works about birth search and reunion furthers these scholarly engagements with Korean American women adoptees' literary and cinematic dissension and contestation of prevailing adoption narratives.

According to Barbara Yngvesson and Maureen Mahoney, transnational adoptees who return to their country of birth in search of biological relatives are "caught in the pursuit of 'realness.'"[18] Yet adoptees often find themselves confronted with gaps in available information, such as their exact birth place or birth date, or even the name of their father or mother.[19] Analyzing search narratives like those found in Korean adoptee memoirs, Eli Park Sorensen interprets Yngvesson and Mahoney's findings to denote that "ultimately, there is always a *fictional* or *imaginary* element involved in this search, [. . . and] the meaning invested in the idea of birthplace is often exaggerated, . . . perhaps even delusional."[20] However, as Sorensen continues, a fictional account of an adoptee's search narrative (such as a memoir) that does not claim authenticity still remains "*plausible*" because it involves a "textual dynamic of truth-seeking—the search for the true circumstances, true information."[21]

13. Homans, *Imprint of Another Life*, 156.
14. Park Nelson, "'Loss Is More Than Sadness.'"
15. S. M. Park, "Queer Orphans and Their Neoliberal Saviors," in *Mothering Queerly*.
16. McKee, "Locating Adoptees in Asian America."
17. For an examination of how birth search and reunion complicates what it means to be a Korean adoptee, see McKee's discussion of Tammy Chu's *Resilience* (2009) and Deann Borshay Liem's *In the Matter of Cha Jung Hee* (2010) in her article "Rewriting History."
18. Yngvesson and Mahoney, "'As One Should, Ought, and Wants to Be,'" 82.
19. Yngvesson and Mahoney, 80.
20. Sorensen, "Korean Adoption Literature," 168–69. Italics in original.
21. Sorensen, 169. Italics in original.

In regard to Korean transnational adoption and adoptee identity, discussing this idea of authenticity brings forth the notion of slippage, as Korean adoptees experience the slipping away of their Korean culture when their ties to their biological origins are cut and their social and cultural histories become inaccessible.[22] Artistic works offer the possibility of addressing this slippage in creative explorations of adoptees' lived experiences, rather than in polemic discussions about authenticity versus inauthenticity. Ebony Coletu notes that even data—nonfictional documents—present "contingencies of identification as a porous and mediated process."[23] In this sense, the autobiographical performances of birth search and reunion discussed here can be seen to tease out the porous yet creative slippage of Korean adoptees' social and cultural experiences in artistic expressions rather than pursuing an impeccable, fixed authenticity. In regard to adoptee-authored works, McKee remarks that these hold the potential for adoptees to "assert their authority as experts on the adopted person's experience."[24] Sharing their experiences, the artists mark their own personal stamp of authority over how their stories are laid out, embodied, and expressed through staging. *What* exactly happened may be important, but *why* it is important to them and *how* they affect audiences is more noteworthy. Beyond asking whether these artists' accounts of search narratives are authentic or inauthentic, the question I want to pose in this chapter is: How effective and engaging are these adoptee-authored representations in creating a nuanced understanding of Korean transnational adoption?

In her examination of women's autobiographies, Leigh Gilmore shows how "women use self-representation and its constitutive possibilities for agency and subjectivity to become . . . subjects who exchange the position of object for the subjectivity of self-representational agency."[25] In this light, the three artists discussed in this chapter can be seen to construct their own subjectivity, claiming agency through their bodies over their intense experiences of transnational adoption. McKee observes, "Autobiographical texts illustrate how adult adoptees move toward a process of self-definition, even as ambivalence in a fixed identity is apparent. In their individual and collective states, the anthologies are narrative acts of insubordination, shifting and even rejecting the master narrative of the mythical adoptee."[26] Taking into account this idea

22. McKee, *Disrupting Kinship*, 27.
23. Coletu, "Introduction Biographic Mediation," 466.
24. McKee, "Locating Adoptees in Asian America," 358.
25. Gilmore, *Autobiographics*, 12.
26. McKee, *Disrupting Kinship*, 99. McKee's footnote regarding the rejection of master narratives as "narratives acts of insubordination" cites Hilde Lindemann Nelson's *Damaged Identities, Narrative Repair,* as her source. Lindemann Nelson, 8.

about autobiographical texts, I assert that Lichwick's, Chomet's, and Ginther's autobiographical performances of birth search and reunion become "a process of self-definition," a process they undergo throughout their performances and share with their audiences via the intimacy and immediacy of live theater. By this process of self-definition, which complicates their performances with important deliberations—what they thought of their own experiences, why their stories should be shared with both adoptee and non-adoptee audience members—the three artists produce "acts of insubordination" against mythical search-and-reunion narratives and mythic adoptee-ness. Hence, this chapter further develops the argument that an imperative function of these adoptee-authored autobiographical solo performances is to unsettle the racial, gender, and ethnic myths levied on the artists' bodies.

Performing Race and Ethnicity in *Yellow Dress* (2015)

As Park Nelson points out, transnational adoption is "a complicated exchange, where children, the governments of the two nations, both sets of parents (birth and adoptive), (usually) two adoption agencies, adoption workers, social workers, childcare providers, attorneys, and a host of other intermediaries may be involved."[27] This complexity is clearly illustrated in Chicago-based actress and playwright Marissa Lichwick's *Yellow Dress*.[28] In *Yellow Dress*, written and performed by the playwright, Lichwick portrays over twenty different characters, as she recounts her own experience of transnational adoption. In the play, Riss (the character representing Lichwick) returns as an adult to Korea to find her biological family. Lichwick also depicts her childhood in flashback scenes, showing how she was adopted as a young child from a Korean orphanage by a family in the United States. Lichwick's portrayal of her adoptive childhood in the United States, sometimes funny and sometimes shocking, problematizes what it means to grow up as a child of color in a white American family. Her scenes in present-day Korea likewise address

---

27. Park Nelson, "Shopping for Children," 89.
28. *Yellow Dress* previewed at the University of Washington School of Drama and the Guthrie Experience at the Guthrie Theatre in Minneapolis. In 2011 it made its West Coast debut at the Hollywood Fringe Festival and its East Coast debut at the New York International Fringe Festival. It was also performed at the 2015 Korean American Adoptee Adoptive Family Network Conference in St. Louis and produced by Silk Road Rising in Chicago in October 2015, directed by Lavina Jadhwani. In 2020 Lichwick wrote and produced a short animated version of *Yellow Dress*, which screened and won awards at several film festivals. In 2023 Lichwick wrote and directed her first feature film, *Searching for Yoo*. The analysis of *Yellow Dress* is based on the 2015 performance I attended and the unpublished script provided by the artist.

her position as an outsider. While Riss succeeds in reuniting with her biological family, she does not experience the powerful emotional bond she had expected to have with her birth mother. A little yellow dress, which she loved as an orphanage child and which had been taken away from her, is one of the few comforting memories that has stayed with her throughout her life. Thanks to her Korean uncle, who retrieved the dress from the orphanage and kept it all those years, Riss is able to find some type of closure to her past as she returns to the United States, clutching her yellow dress.

Lichwick takes the audience on a journey to her past, making public a number of sensitive issues hidden behind the façade of the grateful orphan to adoptee trope, such as racialization, sexual abuse, and the disciplinary function of orphanages.[29] In one scene, transforming her body into her relinquished child-self at the San Rok Orphanage, Lichwick shows audiences the harsh reality of orphanage life, where abuses like child molestation seem to have occurred, such as when a male employee plays "touch time" with Riss. In another scene, Lichwick depicts Riss's eager attempts to improve her English and shows her admiring the image of a white woman with blonde hair and blue eyes in a torn-out page from an American magazine. In her performance, Lichwick looks in awe at the photo, puts her hand over her eyes and nose and in the most admiring tone says, "Such big noses. Their eyes, so big and round." Full of wonder, she then says "Mee-guk," meaning America in Korean, shows the audience the image of the white woman and repeats "Mee-guk," as if blissfully longing for the utopia she will persevere to one day reach.[30] Focusing on the 1950s and '60s, SooJin Pate points out that orphanages essentially functioned as "a processing station," where an unwanted orphan was transformed into a desirable adoptee for American clients by learning English, converting to Christianity, and assuming a doll-like girliness.[31] Under the guise of adoption, orphanages in Korea promoted US nationalism, refashioning Korean children into "proper" future Americans.[32] In these scenes of practicing "proper" Americanness, Lichwick shows how Riss yearns to speak English, be docile, and aspires to "become" white. Lichwick's depiction of Riss's life at the orphanage recalls JinWol Yoo's characterization of orphanages as sites "where children start their lives already at the margin."[33]

Once in the United States, however, even after attempting to learn the ways to assimilate, at various moments this eager-to-adapt adoptee encounters the

---

29. Pate, *From Orphan to Adoptee*, 102–3.
30. Lichwick, *Yellow Dress*, 17.
31. Pate, *From Orphan to Adoptee*, 101–25.
32. Pate, 125.
33. Yoo, *Korean Diaspora beyond Margin from Margin*, 119. Translation by author.

latent racial bias of her adoptive family. Pate comments, "Orientalist fantasies, global capitalism, and the rise of a consumer commodity culture coalesced with the racially integrative politics of Cold War Orientalism to create a discourse of yellow desire that motivated Americans to imagine and welcome Korean children as a part of their national and private family."[34] According to the concept of yellow desire, a notion particularly associated with Korean adoptees, "the bodies of Korean children become desirable because of their potential to integrate successfully in American society and in their new American family."[35] Lichwick shows the audience the unstable demarcation between contrasting ideologies, whereby "yellow desire"—covertly inscribed on an Asian adoptee—can easily shift into a form of "yellow peril." Yellow peril is a historically constructed Western xenophobia reflecting fear of an Asian invasion of the Western World and marking Asian bodies as inassimilable subjects.[36] This switch from yellow desire to yellow peril is represented in *Yellow Dress* in a scene where Riss plays doctor with her adoptive white American younger brother in her new American home. As Lichwick depicts the children innocently kissing and tussling on the floor, she suddenly transforms herself from her previously caring and loving adoptive mother to a frantic one bursting into the room screaming, "Oh no oh no. Oh no. I knew something would be wrong with you Oriental kids. . . . There will be no Incest in my house!"[37] The lines are delivered in a slowly articulated voice-over, satirizing the adoptive mother's horror and abhorrent policing of her adopted Asian daughter's sexuality, as if her worst fear about transracial adoption has materialized in her home. Riss's adoptive mother views Riss through the racist stereotype of the lascivious female body, and reacts as if the little girl has become a "dragon lady," ensnaring her young brother in her depravity. Lichwick uses mimicry to show how her supposedly liberal adoptive mother subconsciously racializes her adoptive child, apparently subscribing to entrenched fantasies of sexual otherness based on Orientalist ideologies. This scene theatricalizes the point made by Homi Bhabha about "'otherness' which is at once an object of desire and derision, an articulation of difference contained within the fantasy of origin and identity."[38] In the context of this scene, Riss is the "other" due to her Asianness, which is accepted on the surface but on a deeper level is still marked as the embodiment of the desirable but derisive fantasy of the "Orient."

---

34. Pate, *From Orphan to Adoptee*, 17.
35. Pate, 88.
36. Tchen and Yeats, *Yellow Peril!*
37. Lichwick, *Yellow Dress*, 38.
38. Bhabha, *Location of Culture*, 67.

Lichwick also depicts the ethnocentric demarcation that she encountered during her visit to Korea. When Riss arrives at the airport in Korea, her first exchange is with an older Korean man who, on hearing her speak broken Korean, switches to English:

KOREAN MAN: Are you Korean?
RISS: Oh yes, I'm Korean American.
KOREAN MAN: Ah I see, you're American Korean.
RISS: No I'm Korean American. I was Korean First [sic] and then I became an American.
KOREAN MAN: You look American.[39]

Lichwick's performance of this confusion shows that the boundaries between nationality and ethnicity are unstable, and that the instability becomes amplified when an adoptee returns to Korea and encounters people who look ethnically identical but use a different language and manner. The Korean man generalizes Riss's identity due to her behavior and appearance, saying "You look American." The man misconstrues "American-looking" Koreans as Americans and not "authentically" Korean. This scene, disclosing how the Korean man immediately essentializes Riss as an American or as anyone other than an "authentic" Korean, shows the precarious identification process wherein "real" Koreanness is arbitrarily drawn. The scene continues with the man asking whether Riss is adopted or American born. When Riss answers that she is adopted, the man responds, "Oh. I'm very sorry for you."[40] According to Park Nelson, adoptees are often pitied by Koreans who feel sorry that adoptees were not brought up as Koreans in Korea or are seemingly ashamed that they themselves were not able to raise those adoptees.[41] Park Nelson notes that Korean adoptees live with the "cultural mismatch" of being perceived to be lucky to have been adopted into "loving American homes" in the United States but being pitied in Korea.[42] Riss's encounter with the Korean man exposes how adoptees are treated as culturally mismatched subjects whose ethnic assimilability is questioned in Korea.

If Riss's life as a Korean adopted child in America is shown as being marked by racialization, her adult adoptee experience of returning to Korea reflects her difficulties with the forced silence that Korean societal norms dictate on the issue of adoption. When Riss visits the orphanage, the owner asks

---

39. Lichwick, *Yellow Dress*, 8.
40. Lichwick, 9.
41. Park Nelson, *Invisible Asians*, 185.
42. Park Nelson, 185.

her why she wants to find her biological family; she answers: "I have to discover what's been missing my whole life."[43] When she finally meets her family, however, Riss is confronted with their persistent silence about her adoption. Although her uncle tries to help her as much as possible, Riss's meeting with her birth father brings no answers to her questions, as he claims to not remember the reasons for her and her biological brother's relinquishment. A separate reunion with her divorced birth mother is even more perplexing:

> RISS: I don't know where to start, just please tell me everything? Everything from your point of view.
> MOTHER: Too much.
> RISS: What do you mean too much. Ummm, why did you leave us?
> MOTHER: God. I chose God.
> RISS: Are you still a missionary?
> MOTHER: Oh yes. I have my own church. He is the only man in my life.
> RISS: Didn't you miss your kids?
> MOTHER: But he is my God. He is the man who saved me.
> RISS: But we were your kids.
> MOTHER: It was a long time ago.[44]

After this scene, because Riss's birth mother does not drive at night, Riss invites her to stay overnight. Sharing the same bed yet unable to sleep, Riss finds it inconceivable that the woman she had longed for her entire life was now "so close yet so far away."[45] By depicting such a dispassionate reunion, Lichwick's story deromanticizes the sentimental reunion scene often sensationalized by the media as highly emotional, with a perennially happy ending.

By the end of the play, Riss realizes that she has become a stranger in her own birth country and even to her birth mother: "I found almost all of them yet they didn't want to open up the past to me. Everything was an illusion. Just like my American-ness in Korea and my Korean-ness in America. So I decide to head back to the United States."[46] As Riss is packing to go back to the United States, a flood of memories comes back to her, expressed in a bodily collage of utterances from various persons she has encountered in her life's journey as an adoptee. Performing as Riss, Lichwick uses her body to archive her memories from childhood to adulthood, emitting short, rapid sentences to

---

43. Lichwick, *Yellow Dress*, 15.
44. Lichwick, 39–40.
45. Lichwick, 40.
46. Lichwick, 47.

create a fast collage of spoken words, movements, and characters from Riss's life, a collage in speed that flashes by in the manner of a fast-cut film montage:

"My memory escape me." [sic]
"I chose God."
"Rachel, I found your shoe." [Rachel is Marissa's orphanage given name]
"Welcome to McDonald's, how can I helps you?" [sic]
"A, B, She, D . . . !!"
"Such big eyes!"
"'Beat It' by Michael Jackson."
"Your name is Marissa."
"You are enough."
"Oma [mother]! I gotta go!!"
"It's not about your nose . . . you are enough."[47]

As she repeats these quotes from herself and other people, including her biological and adoptive mothers and adoptive sister, Lichwick evoke these characters by quickly changing her demeanor and posture from one line to the next. For example, on the line "Such big eyes," she transforms herself into the five-year-old Riss, widening her eyes while looking at the magazine image of a blonde American woman; she then suddenly becomes her teenage self, dancing to "Beat it" in her American home; next, she changes into her adoptive mother, telling Riss in a soothing voice that she has a new name, "Marissa." This sequence of utterances and body movements not only recaps what has happened in the performance but also compresses Riss's lifetime of being racially and ethnically shaped as a transnational adoptee in and out of the United States and Korea. In the visual arts, collages are works of a single composition created through "the gathering of materials from *different* worlds."[48] I view Lichwick's sequence as a visual and aural collage in which the materials are not physical but derive from the memories of her characters' worlds. Lichwick acts out this collage with speed and precision, presenting an urgency that evokes a sense of chaos and confusion as Riss attempts to find meaning in her life yet is unable to settle on a definite resolution.[49] While the collage style suggests a fragmented sense of self, this condensed moment of memories

---

47. Lichwick, 48. Ellipses in original.
48. Brockelman, *The Frame and the Mirror*, 10. Italics in original.
49. Brockelman states that "the experience of collage both insists that we learn to live without guarantees of meaning (the reality of 'knowing our place') and opens the possibility for a kind of meaningfulness that we ourselves produce through a process of judgment." Brockelman, 37.

nevertheless represents a significant breakthrough for Riss. On leaving Seoul, she tells the audience, "as I was riding away, I looked at the Yellow Dress and realized that Korea was not going to define me and America didn't define me; it wasn't about definition, it was about forgiveness."[50] Riss finds solace in the act of absolution and by accepting the incompleteness within herself.

Performing Gender in *How to Be a Korean Woman* (2012)

While Lichwick's *Yellow Dress* encompasses the stories of her pre-adoption and adoptive childhood prior to her birth search and reunion, Sun Mee Chomet's *How to Be a Korean Woman* focuses on the process of search and reunion with her birth family members.[51] Chomet is a St. Paul–based actress, dancer, director, and playwright whose two plays, *Asiamnesia* (2008) and *The Sex Show* (2016), deal with the intersecting experiences of race, gender, and sexuality as an Asian woman in the United States as well as in Asia. Chomet includes only women characters in *How to Be a Korean Woman* in order to reveal the powerful female element in her quest: "it's very much about this longing for mother.... For the most part all of the people who helped me to find her were women ... there was this theme of female connection."[52] Through her connection with other women, Chomet comes to realize that her position as a woman in Korea's intricate structure of gender dynamics and patriarchal power is different from her experience in America, where it is rooted in a liberal and feminist upbringing. Chomet's story boldly highlights the reality of returning Korean American women adoptees, who, in the words of Homans, "encounter Korean forms of androcentrism and sexism that they experience as even more toxic than those they suffered in the U.S."[53]

Chomet formulates a cautionary tale for Korean American women adoptees who meet their biological families and, in the process, encounter the

---

50. Lichwick, *Yellow Dress*, 51.
51. *How to Be a Korean Woman* premiered in 2012 at Dreamland Arts, directed by Zaraawar Mistry, as part of a collaborative work named "The Origin(s) Project: Memoirs in Motion" with Korean adoptee artist Katie Hae Leo's *N/A* in St. Paul, and was staged in 2013 at the Guthrie Theatre in Minneapolis. It was also performed at the Asian Art Initiative in Philadelphia as a part of an artist exchange program in 2012 and at the Rochester Civic Theatre in Minnesota in 2013. Chomet performed the piece at the Seventh Annual Philadelphia Theatre Research Symposium at Villanova University in 2013. More recently, the play was produced at Theater J in Washington, DC, in 2023 and 2024. The analysis of *How to Be a Korean Woman* is based on the 2012 unpublished script and a videotaped performance provided by the artist.
52. Chomet, interview.
53. Homans, "Adoption and Return," 189.

Korean construct of femininity and patriarchy that women adoptees are subjected to on returning to Korea.[54] Chomet (who in the play uses both her Korean name, Sun Mee, and her American name, Rachel) tells us that she was relinquished for adoption at the age of six months and that her American adoptive mother was "a tomboy, an ultra feminist."[55]

> MOM: Rachel, *(heavy sigh)* how many times do we have to go through this?!! I never bought you Barbies or dolls because they're oppressive representations of women! *(crossing around stage, picking up all remaining costume pieces as if cleaning)* I didn't let you try out for cheer-leading because whooping it up for boys is degrading! *(picking up lipstick and compact)* And you don't need make-up, because you are beautiful inside and that's all that matters. The same goes for SHOPPING! *(puts all props behind USR curtain and quickly crosses DSC, as if handing SUN MEE a football helmet)* Now put on this football helmet and go play with your brothers![56]

While growing up from a young age with a feminist mother may have empowered Chomet as a woman in the United States, it certainly did not prepare her for the "re-feminization" to which she would be subjected when she reunited with her biological family in Korea.

In contrast to Lichwick's high-speed bodily collage, Chomet's performance of the corporeality of her transnational adoption experiences occurs in slow motion. When Sun Mee participates in a Korean TV program looking for her biological family, sixteen people claim that they may be related to her.[57] To find out if any of them could be part of her biological family, Sun Mee prepares for a DNA test, as described in her stage directions: "As music plays, SUN MEE takes one strand of hair, places in an imaginary baggie, puts on hand and blows it to the sky."[58] The gesture suggests the importance of bodily materials like a single hair in proving her kinship. In the performance, Chomet does not

---

54. This chapter focuses on the performances of Korean American women adoptees and their engagement with femininity from girlhood to womanhood. For a discussion about the performance of masculinity, see Kimberly McKee's analysis of Korean adoptee internet persona and hip-hop artist Dan Matthew's birth search and reunion in the YouTube's docu-series *akaDAN* (2014) in her article "Gendered Adoptee Identities."

55. Chomet, *How to Be a Korean Woman*, 23.

56. Chomet, 23.

57. The TV program aired her search video, but their reunion did not occur on television. For a more detailed description of the search-and-reunion TV programs like *I Miss That Person*, see chapter 1.

58. Chomet, *How to Be a Korean Woman*, 12.

actually pull out a strand of her hair; however, the silent, stylized act of plucking out the single hair is the existential moment she counts on as an adoptee to prove both her "blood-relatedness" and her "adoptee-ness." Without any explanation to the audience of how to do the test, what it means to her, and what she envisages its result will be, she silently performs the preparation for the test in slow motion. By slowing down the act, Chomet gives it the aura of a ritualistic action, reflecting her profound wish and longing to find her biological mother.

In another scene, Sun Mee reacts to a letter from her real-life biological mother, projected on the backdrop wall. As the audience hears her recorded reading of the letter, Sun Mee performs slow movements in silhouette. The perfectly controlled slowness of her body demonstrates her feelings of excitement, happiness, shock, sorrow, and yearning to physically see her mother. Her embodiment of an array of emotions in reacting to the memorabilia of her biological mother's letter written in Korean is visually striking. The juxtaposition between the temporal slowness of Chomet's bodily movement and the fixed state of the object on the screen destabilizes time and space, as if the letter were a lifetime away and that lifetime was one Chomet spent waiting. Hans-Thies Lehmann writes, "When physical movement is slowed down to such an extent that the time of its development itself seems to be enlarged as through a magnifying glass, the body itself is . . . 'cut out' of the time–space continuum."[59] Precisely by being removed from the time–space continuum, Chomet's movements capture and amplify the moments that Chomet and her birth mother could have spent together and the long periods they have spent waiting for each other.

The body speaks more than words in Chomet's reunion in *How to Be a Korean Woman*. In a scene in which she describes her Korean grandmother hugging and holding her tightly, Chomet says, "My grandmother pours her body into mine, holding onto my arm, refusing to let go. . . . Somehow my muscle memory remembers this feeling and has been crawling back towards it all of my life."[60] She then re-enacts the hug in silence with a controlled and slow movement of her body, emphasizing the intensity of her embrace of her imaginary grandmother, producing an embodied visualization of her experience of this sensory moment recalled. As Diana Taylor writes, "Memory is embodied and sensual, that is, conjured through the senses."[61] In these moments in her performance, Chomet's body becomes the source and the

---

59. Lehmann, *Postdramatic Theatre*, 164.
60. Chomet, *How to Be a Korean Woman*, 20. Ellipsis in original.
61. Taylor, *The Archive and the Repertoire*, 82.

intermediary of her memory, conjuring her past feelings for audiences in the present of her performance.

When Sun Mee finally finds her biological mother, the adoption agency caseworker tells her that they can only meet in secret. This is because her biological mother is married, and her husband does not know of Sun Mee's existence; if found out, her mother would "lose everything including contact with her two sons."[62] Later, on her last night together with her mother, grandmother, and two aunts (one of whom speaks English), Sun Mee asks her mother when she might be able to sleep over at her house and meet her two sons. Her mother replies that maybe in twenty years Sun Mee will be able to sleep over, after her husband dies. As in Lichwick's realization of the silence that permeated her adoption, this scene illustrates the fear and secrecy that all these women are forced to live in. The two scenes with Chomet's female birth family members echo Homans's observation on Liem's film *First Person Plural* that "daughters returning to Korea often struggle to hear their mothers' broken, discredited voices behind the loudspeaker of public and private male authority."[63] Chomet thus exposes how patriarchal oppression is in full force in Korea, affecting women, including herself.

While both Lichwick and Chomet undercut the sentimentality typically associated with mediatized adoptee reunions, Chomet does so with humor. As her grandmother (*halmoni* in Korean) hugs Sun Mee when they reunite for the first time, kissing her and crying, she speaks in Korean. Sun Mee believes her to be saying, "Look at your beautiful skin and healthy body. Your family in America raised you well. I'm glad you're okay. . . . You look just like your mother. I want to never let you go!"[64] Even though Sun Mee does not understand Korean, she is happy and moved by this gush of emotions, and later asks her English-speaking aunt what her grandmother has said:

> HALMONI: You look TERRIBLE! She said you look like you were adopted by FARMERS because of your clothes. She said you need to wear more MAKE-UP and she asked why you're so TAN and why your hair looks SO BAD. She said she remembered when you were a baby, you had fair skin and you were PRETTY with BIG EYES and she wants to know WHAT HAPPENED? She said you look HORRIBLE! She wants us to take you SHOPPING![65]

---

62. Chomet, *How to Be a Korean Woman*, 18.
63. Homans, *Imprint of Another Life*, 169.
64. Chomet, *How to Be a Korean Woman*, 19.
65. Chomet, 21. All caps in original.

The grandmother's outcry goads the other family members into action. They whisk Sun Mee away in a whirlwind of shopping, hairdressing, exfoliating, and Korean baths, partly to make up for lost bonding time but also due to her mother's and aunts' conviction that it is because Sun Mee has failed to make herself attractive to her dates that she is still unmarried. Thanks to her biological family, Sun Mee soon discovers the requirements of being a Korean woman, which she shares by directly addressing the audience:

You must get married
You must have children
You must go to church
You must cook
You must take care of others more than yourself
You must not be too skinny
You must not be too fat
You must dress well
You must have an expensive purse and wallet *(gestures to purse)*
You must wear scarves when it is 80 degrees *(pulls scarf from purse and puts on with a flourish)*
You must strive for perfect skin
You must wear a visor *(pulls visor from purse and puts on, completely shielding face from view)*
You must color your hair, even if afterwards, it looks exactly the same *(shows hair)*
You must have straight thick eyebrows, not thin like Americans *(peeks from underneath visor to show eyebrows)*
You must use a lipstick brush to make the color stay *(points to lips)*
You must have amazing nail colors that are super cute *(dramatically shows fingers)*
You must wear fashionable shoes, even if they hurt a lot *(points to shoes, stumbling)*[66]

This hectic sequence of body movements—arranging a scarf and hat, dangling a purse, putting on high-heeled shoes—are all actions that supposedly engender a "Korean woman" (see figure 2).

Sun Mee's experience corresponds with an established beauty myth, a sociohistorical patriarchal construct that weds a notion of femininity to heteronormative claims about women, emphasizing the value of their physical

---

66. Chomet, 27.

FIGURE 2. Sun Mee Chomet wearing feminine accoutrements in *How to Be a Korean Woman* (2012). Photo by Charissa Uemura, June 2012. Courtesy of Sun Mee Chomet.

and emotional fragility, their social and economic reliance on men, their compliance with male authority, and a pleasing outer appearance.[67] These requirements reflect contemporary Korea's look-centered culture, in which highly commercialized visual cultural products, such as television dramas and K-pop music videos, have indoctrinated women to endorse the ideals of fabricated beauty. A culture of "lookism" has become a prodding for Korean women, who feel compelled to transform their bodies.[68] This lookism is also connected to Korean mothering as Sharon Heijin Lee notes, some Korean mothers also feel duty-bound to show their motherly care by having their children undergo plastic surgery.[69] Under the influence of this lookism, Chomet's female family members have unwittingly agreed not only to follow its materialistic and

67. Wolf, *Beauty Myth*.
68. S. H. Lee, "(Geo)Politics of Beauty."
69. Sharon Heijin Lee writes of how children receive plastic surgery, "typically given as high school or college graduation presents." S. H. Lee, "Beauty between Empires," 17.

mythic rules of beauty but also to transmit them to Sun Mee and, by extension, to the younger generation of women, who presumably will also need to "fabricate" their looks for survival and success in contemporary Korea's highly gendered and competitive society.

After her frenetic transformation, Sun Mee suddenly stops and declares, "But it's not me."[70] She then slowly takes off her hat, scarf, and high heels and looks straight into the audience in silence. Sun Mee's rejection of the accoutrements of Korean femininity symbolizes the removal of the culturally gendered signifier of her temporary, superficial Korean womanness. As a woman brought up in the United States, Sun Mee is not considered "Korean female enough" by the lookism-derived standards of Korean society that govern her biological mother and aunts. Sun Mee's feminine makeover—which her family members do to show their affection and to make Sun Mee more acceptable according to the norms of Korean society—contradicts her own ideas of what it means to be a woman and her self. To Sun Mee, these "how-to-*look*-like-a-Korean-woman" requirements are a recipe for oppression, which, at the end of her journey, she is unwilling to accept. Sun Mee realizes the hollowness of any attempt to be a different person: "I try hard to put on this idea of what it means to be Korean. For my umma, for my aunts and grandmother. . . . But it's not me."[71] By taking off her shoes and accessories, Chomet performs a deconstruction of what it means to be a Korean woman, rejecting the ideologically manufactured beauty standards that would have homogenized her.[72] Her act highlights the contradiction between being an ideal Korean woman and being herself and, in the process, enables her to reset her identity.

At the end of the piece, before leaving for the United States, Sun Mee finds comfort, freedom, and belonging with other adoptees in Seoul who have created their own community: "It was good to feel like myself again: like an outsider. Being in the margins felt familiar. It was my birth family's efforts to put me in the center, to *normalize* me, that was exhausting . . . They were trying to make me *pass*."[73] Sun Mee feels at home in this third space, liberated from Korean gender normativity and cultural fabrication of women. Among these other outsiders in Korea, Sun Mee sends the message to her audiences that adoptees are not relegated to wandering in either a culturally normative society or a stateless space, but rather can generate their own communal belonging.

---

70. Chomet, *How to Be a Korean Woman*, 28.
71. Chomet, 28.
72. Rodrigues, "Undressing Homogeneity," 43.
73. Chomet, *How to Be a Korean Woman*, 28. Ellipsis and italics in original.

Performing Race and Ethnicity in *Homeful* (2018)

While Lichwick's and Chomet's stories evolve around the initial process of birth search and reunion, in *Homeful,* Bay Area performer and educator Amy Mihyang Ginther presents a travelogue narrative depicting episodes of her life as an adult adoptee, connecting with her adoptive mother in the United States and meeting her birth mother in Korea for the second time.[74] Going beyond the geographical binary of Korea and the United States, *Homeful* takes audiences around the world, following the character of Amy (representing Ginther) to England, Ireland, Senegal, the Czech Republic, Argentina, and Korea where she trains, performs, and teaches. Amy serves as Ginther's alter ego and a means of sharing her personal experience of being a lifetime world traveler.[75] Ginther's performance contends that Korean and Asian adoptees explore the world beyond the route bound by their adoptive and birth countries. Capturing cultural differences while globetrotting far from her adoptive mother and before her second reunion with her birth mother and family in Korea, Ginther comes to a renewed understanding of her identity as a Korean, Asian, American, and adoptee.

Prior to *Homeful,* Ginther's first autobiographical solo performance, *between,* also dealt with her transnational adoption story through the character of Amy.[76] Although this chapter focuses on *Homeful,* because *between* presents the introduction of Amy and her life story, it needs to be discussed as a prequel to *Homeful.* In *between,* Ginther portrays several characters as the audience follows Amy on her plane trip to Korea to meet with her birth mother for the first time. While set mostly in the airplane's cabin, disjointed scenes intercut to show Amy at other ages in her life as well as other characters connected to adoption, including fellow adoptees and birth mothers in

---

74. Directed by Lisa Marie Rollins, the solo performance *Homeful* won a Best of Fringe Award at the San Francisco Fringe Festival in 2017. The analysis of *Homeful* is based on the 2018 New York City Solo Performance Festival performance I attended as well as the unpublished script provided by the artist.

75. Bloom, "5 Ways Travel Can."

76. Originating from Ginther's undergraduate thesis performance at Hofstra University, *between* was initially performed at the 2006 Edinburgh Fringe Festival. In the 2011 Korean production, Ginther performed in English and the production offered simultaneous Korean subtitles in association with the Seoul Players, a Seoul-based English-language theater. Ginther also donated the entire box-office receipts to KUMFA, a nonprofit organization based in Seoul established by and for unwed mothers, advocating for the rights and needs of unwed mothers and their children. Ginther interviewed by Tammy Ko Robinson, "Amy Mihyang's Play 'between.'" Also see Ginther's own reflection on her performative works including *between* in "Dramaturgy of Deprivation." Segments from a videotaped performance of *between* as well as its script were provided by the artist.

nonspecific time periods. In an interview, Ginther mentioned that the play's title, *between,* reflects the symbolic setting of a flight between the United States and Korea: "the symbolism about liminal space is reflective of my experiences as an adoptee. And it's very much in limbo, you're not in one country, you're not in the other, you're in the air. And so we had beautiful symbolism in that . . . kind of a dream space, so all these other voices get folded in."[77] In this liminal space, Ginther offers dissimilar viewpoints on transnational adoption from each of the different characters' perspectives. Near the end of *between,* Amy tells the audience her thoughts specifically about search and reunion: "Meeting my family in Korea did not complete me. Reunions are not ends. They are middles."[78] Still in the interview, Ginther said that she purposefully wrote the play without an actual reunion scene because she wanted to "subvert the narrative of the reunion for an adoptee being the climax and the resolution because so often in adoption narratives a reunion is the goal."[79]

Instead of a clear-cut climax and resolution, Ginther presents a scene toward the end of *between* which takes place at the airport in Detroit on Amy's way back from Korea. During a layover, Amy meets three women escorting Korean babies to meet with their new American families. One of the women, with a baby boy called Yeon-Ooh, says his new name is now Andrew Charles Jones. The woman goes on to say that Andrew is lucky to have left Korea to grow up in a Christian home in Michigan with a family "brave enough to strengthen our country by rescuing and raising children."[80] With this scene, the audience realizes that Ginther as a playwright points at the relentlessness of the American white savior narrative surrounding transnational adoption, driven by religious, patriotic, and nationalist sentiment that idealizes the rebranding of Asian infants to be raised in American homes. As Sorensen writes, "In a very literal sense, the Korean adoptees are 'reborn'—in airports and other transit spaces—while their previous identity is overwritten and, in some cases, entirely erased, whether by the adoptive parents or adoption agencies."[81] Sitting near Yeon-Ooh, Amy projects her fears of "rebirth" on the baby, whose identity and past have already been effaced, as Ginther closes out *between* with a monologue directed to the little boy. Amy takes a red blanket from her shoulders, crumples it, and puts it on a chair in front of her to make believe that the baby is wrapped in the blanket as she addresses him. In this final scene, it is as if Amy is reuniting with herself as a baby, seeing her own

---

77. Ginther, interview.
78. Ginther, *between,* 15.
79. Ginther, interview.
80. Ginther, *between,* 16.
81. Sorensen, "Korean Adoption Literature," 164n16.

past in the eyes of Yeon-Ooh, who now also finds himself in between. Amy dreads to think that he might go through the same experience she did and find himself constantly searching for acceptance of an identity that is perpetually elusive. Amy then tells the baby boy that she will protect him and that she hopes he will find belonging despite being in between. Foregrounding adoptee solidarity across generations, this self-reflexive moment ends the play with hope.

As Ginther points out, the main difference between *between* and *Homeful* is that "*between* was about the flying and the journey in that way, but *Homeful* is more often about arrival."[82] In this sense, *between* is a voyage between birth land and adoptive land, whereas *Homeful* is composed of multiple arrivals as Ginther travels around the world, always seeking a home and belonging. Ginther also states that *between* is very much a reflection on birth search and reunion, while *Homeful* is a coming-of-age story told through the conflicting and contesting lenses of a Korean adult adoptee, an adoptee artist, and an Asian American.[83] As shown in her plays, performing adoption is an ever-changing practice, with her perspectives and dramaturgical approaches evolving over time and throughout different stages of her life. Her serialization of performance serves as a remarkable exemplar for artists whose inquiries intersect with adoption.

In terms of *Homeful*'s performance style, unlike Lichwick and Chomet who physically re-enact their memories by embodying other characters, Ginther mostly recounts her interactions with other characters and expresses her thoughts and feelings directly to the audience throughout the performance. Ginther also gives the audience a handful of visual and audio clues, including emails, texts, photos, music, and sound effects, indicating the ways in which her views evolve during her search for belonging. For instance, she uses aural cues, such as music and sound effects, to re-create the feel of the nation and city she finds herself in and to represent her culturally diverse experiences as she travels around the world. However, Amy's stays in Europe, South America, Africa, and Korea are interrupted by racialized encounters, frequently involving her being questioned as to where she is from, accentuating her feeling of being other. More than a mere signifier of locality, the aural is used to conduct a racialized interrogation of being an adoptee, as character after character asks Amy the question: "Where are you from?" At every location, Amy asks this question out loud as it appears on a screen in the background. Often asked in the United States of people of Asian descent, the question represents

---

82. Ginther, interview.
83. Ginther, interview.

one of the mechanisms of othering by which racial minorities are designated as forever foreigners, and thereby excluded from full participation in mainstream US society and culture. Whereas the question acts to dispute people of color's membership in a white hegemonic society, for transnational adoptees it communicates an even more complex message, imposing displacement and uprootedness on their identities and sense of belonging, which the supposedly colorblind practice of adoption had once promised to guarantee. Ginther makes this expression of exclusion the central question of her play, as Amy is repeatedly asked where she "actually" comes from. Through Amy's understanding of this experience of othering, which deepens with each encounter, Ginther reproduces the intersection between racial politics and adoptee-ness in the United States. For Amy, this perpetual remarking of her foreignness debunks the myth of racial exceptionalism in which transracial adoptees are viewed as exceptional subjects "in terms of cultural assimilation, psychological adjustment, and social success."[84] Amy being marked as other further challenges this exceptionalism that reinforces the imagined immigration hierarchy, where transracial adoptees are placed at the top on account of their "proximity" to whiteness, which distances them from the experiences and situations of immigrants. As long as the question "Where are you from?" is asked to ethnic and racial others, including transracial adoptees, in the context of white hegemony, the answer will obligate an explanation of one's position "as deviant *vis-à-vis* the normal."[85] Furthermore, the question affects Amy not only as an Asian adoptee on US soil but also as she travels around the globe and must incessantly explain her origins to people who do not believe she is American and instead insist on knowing where she is "really" from. Throughout the performance, as the question appears on the screen in the background, Amy politely replies to all of the different characters who ask the question, from Argentinian cab drivers to elderly English ladies. Eventually, however, the relentless repetition of the question causes Amy to cry out in anger:

> No matter where I go in the world, I will feel displaced. People will ask me "Where are you from?"—doesn't matter if I'm in Amsterdam or the neighborhood I grew up in in New York, I will get people stopping in their car in front of this very fucking flat, rolling down their windows, and shouting at me on street, going CHING CHONG CHAE. I get it. That's how the world works.[86]

---

84. Park Nelson, *Invisible Asians*, 13, 42, 65–71.
85. Ang, *On Not Speaking Chinese*, 30. Italics in original.
86. Ginther, *Homeful*, 13.

Fu-Jen Chen argues that adoptees are affected "not so much by the absence of origin (the lack of knowledge of one's familial, ethnic roots) as by its over-presence (the excessive association with the origin)."[87] As multiple characters attempt to define Amy by racial and ethnic demarcation, the question becomes an excessive reminder of otherness: "I've heard this question my entire life as a Korean American adoptee. No one is asking me where I'm from, they are telling me I'm not from here."[88] Specifically writing about the question "Where are you from?" when asked of adoptees, Jessica Walton states that adoptees' "embodied sense of self goes from something subjectively experienced to a body/self that is racially objectified," profoundly challenging them on an "existential level, which involves contested belonging along racial, cultural and familial lines."[89] For Amy, the compulsory questioning of her origins becomes acts to inscribe unbelonging onto her wherever she goes. While the question itself represents a problematic discourse, the constant *repetition* of the question stands out more starkly than a simple reiteration: it becomes a loop generating a new meaning that dislocates Amy's past and present, and by extension her identity and belonging.[90]

Throughout her travels, what keeps Amy grounded in her sense of self is her adoptive mother back home in the United States. Through this long-distance mother–daughter relationship, Ginther's *Homeful* depicts mothering in a contemporary virtual world, dramatizing the practice of virtual mothering by email exchange. Emails sent by Amy's adoptive mother are projected onto the background screen during the performance for the audience to read. This allows the audience to feel Amy's mother's emotional state and care for Amy, mediated through internet communication. The email exchange scenes between Amy and her adoptive mother show how virtual mothering through invisible gestures can establish an affective bridge despite physical separation. Shelley Park argues that mothering in our contemporary world has become "inextricably intertwined with technology."[91] Park calls these modes of communication "*technologies of co-presence*" because they allow for virtual mothering, unattached to physical presence, permitting mothers and their children to coinhabit different spaces and times while still engaging in a form of intimacy.[92] Hosu Kim conceptualizes the idea of virtual mothering via video conference and online forum by Korean birth mothers whose biological children

---

87. Chen, "Maternal Voices in Personal Narratives of Adoption," 174.
88. Ginther, *Homeful*, 2.
89. Walton, *Korean Adoptees and Transnational Adoption*, 78.
90. Herrera, "Sonic Treatise of Futurity."
91. S. M. Park, *Mothering Queerly*, 27.
92. S. M. Park, 176. Italics in original.

have been adopted and live in other countries. Kim views such technology as effective in enhancing mothering's performative aspect and affective power.[93] In the performance, Amy's adoptive mother coinhabits Amy's life mostly within the digital world, becoming the one constant anchoring Amy to her adoptive family. Amy's life on stage is constantly interrupted by email notification sounds, a humorous annoyance that ends when her adoptive mother falls ill and passes away. As the audience has become accustomed to hearing the email notification sounds and seeing texts from Amy's mother, the abrupt silence and blank screen that follow her death, and thus the end of her virtual mothering, make the impact of Amy's loss all the more powerful.

Amy's grief turns to hope when she moves to Korea to reconnect with her biological mother and family she has met only once before. In contrast to the virtual connection Amy had with her adoptive mother, who communicated her care and affection for Amy by email, her reunion with her birth mother in Korea is tangible, with her birth mother expressing maternal care especially through food. The description of the physical mothering by Amy's birth mother contrasts sharply with the virtual mothering of Amy's adoptive mother. The use of technology by Amy's adoptive mother incorporates a digital literacy emphasizing the acts of hearing and reading only, whereas Amy's birth mother's corporeal presence conjures all five senses and creates a sensorial rendering of the birth mother's expression of love. In two scenes set during Korean Thanksgiving and on Amy's birthday, Amy's birth mother prepares large amounts of food for her and the other guests. Lovingly prepared, the meals represent more than just sustenance and the conventions of special occasions, but rather are affective emblems of the mother's affection, tears, regret, hope, and determination to nourish the long-lost daughter she was unable to take care of for so many years.[94]

During the Korean Thanksgiving celebration with her biological family members, Amy is asked to sing a song and chooses "Amazing Grace." During her performance, her aunt spontaneously chimes in with the well-known Korean folksong "Arirang."[95] While to some extent the two songs express essentialized religious and ethnonationalist sentiments, their blending together engenders a uniquely and powerfully emotional moment, particularly

---

93. H. Kim, *Birth Mothers*, 145–87.

94. Shannon Bae describes a bonding experience among transnational adoptees, unwed mothers, and their children over food for the Korean Thanksgiving, Chuseok. See Bae, "Radical Imagination," 300–301.

95. "Arirang" is one of the best-known folksongs in the entire Korean peninsula and among Korean diasporic communities outside of the country. For more information regarding the song in Korean popular music history, see Lie, *K-Pop*, 7–65. Also, for the cinematic use of the song in colonial Korea, see D. H. Kim, *Eclipsed Cinema*, 55–102.

as Amy sings the overlapping songs without accompaniment, her solo voice resonating throughout the performance space. The merging of the two songs symbolizes the interwovenness of Amy's transnational experiences and identity as a Korean adoptee who grew up in the United States and has reunited with her biological family in her birth country. The musical hybrid constitutes an aural expression of belonging, conveying a message neither song can fully deliver separately. As Amy tells the audience when the singing ends: "it's as if these two songs, transcending time and space, have somehow always meant to be sung together."[96] By performing this experience of sonic memory, Ginther makes audience members realize that adoptees' belonging is not just established through policy and legal implementation but also strengthened by deep sensory affirmations of who adoptees feel they are, where they choose to belong, and how they express their own feelings.

A striking visual embodiment serves to recontextualize Amy's pre- and post-search-and-reunion experiences. Near the end of *Homeful,* Amy has a conversation with her birth mother regarding *New York Times* coverage of their reunification story as part of an article on Korean adoptees' returning to their birth country.[97] Projected on the background screen is the actual *New York Times* photo of Ginther and her birth mother. In the photo, Amy's birth mother has her eyes closed and her head slightly tilted toward Amy's. Looking at this image, one can imagine the myriad of emotions that are entangled with the mother's loss of and longing for her daughter. The performance revisits the media-narrated reunion, transferring the story live from print to performance. In this way, audience members relive Amy's search story and re-experience her birth mother's voice, beyond the limitations of the previous printed material. When Amy tells her mother about the other adoptees in the article and their painful experiences, her mother repeatedly says *sangchaw* to Amy, who then learns its meaning: wound.[98] The *New York Times* article combined with Amy's explanation of the photo has the effect of revealing to the audience the unfathomable depth of the wounds of relinquishment. Sung Hee Yook and Hosu Kim write that a birth mother often views relinquishment as an action that "hollows her out and leaves her bruised."[99] Amy's birth mother thus perceives the wound as deriving from her relinquishment of Amy, which left her void and scarred. The idea of wounds, felt and shared by both Amy and her mother, binds them in what Amy defines to her mother in Korean as "pain

---

96. Ginther, *Homeful,* 31.
97. Jones, "Why a Generation of Adoptees Is Returning to South Korea."
98. Ginther, *Homeful,* 32.
99. Yook and Kim, "Decolonizing Adoption Narratives," 5.

in the family."¹⁰⁰ Similarly, James Kyung-Jin Lee discusses the "woundedness" as a symptom of the "systemic cruelty of transnational adoption that adult adoptees have been expressing very forcefully and compellingly."¹⁰¹ Wounds, however, contain the potential for regeneration: new "flesh" grows to form scars, and, while marks remain, wounds heal. In this light, Amy's performance piece can be seen as a way for her to heal the wounds of all affected by transnational adoption. In the photo from the *New York Times* article, Amy and her mother hold each other tightly, their bodies overlapping; the image seems to capture a moment when their wounds meld with each other's, transmuting into shared scars. In this tableau of their united body, Amy's and her mother's wounds seemingly transform into a regenerated mother–daughter relationship, the afterlife of the image breathing life into Ginther's ongoing story and performance.

Border-Crossing Bodily Testimony

In their solo performances, the three artists portray international adoptees' racial, ethnic, and gender experiences. Their bodies become the territory where dualistic demarcations between Korea and the United States, lived experience and constructed myth, and reality and fiction are unsettled. Foregrounding the body in their performances, Lichwick, Chomet, and Ginther offer their audiences opportunities to sensorially experience these border-crossings, which are not merely physical passages from one geographical location to another but also movements between multiple times, memories, and cultures. Lisa Marie Rollins, the director of *Homeful*, writes in the show's program:

> The ever-encompassing skin map that is the diasporic/adoptee search for home, and its sister emotion—longing—carve lines on this map of the adoptee body. I invite you to jump across the globe with us, breathe deep the power of this movement/moving, and the power of the body to remember and (re)member how to locate home.¹⁰²

---

100. Ginther, *Homeful*, 32.
101. J. K. J. Lee, "An Adopter and the Ends of Adoption," 283–84.
102. Rollins, program note for *Homeful*. Director Lisa Marie Rollins is a transracial adoptee herself. Rollins is a Black and Filipina playwright, performance artist, poet, dramaturg, and director who was adopted into a white family in the 1970s. Her solo performance *Ungrateful Daughter: One Black Girl's Story of Being Adopted into a White Family . . . That Aren't Celebrities* premiered in 2012 at the New York International Fringe Festival and was produced at several venues in the Bay Area.

The contours of what Rollins calls the "map of the adoptee body" shift with changing feelings and (re)membering. Through their constant transitions from self to other, present to past, and culture to culture, the three performers disrupt binary borders and reaffirm the power of fluid transformation, enabling their audiences to engage with the multifacetedly entangled experiences of Korean transnational adoptees. Lichwick's, Chomet's, and Ginther's border-crossing bodies function as contested terrain of birth search and reunion via different modes: Riss's bodily collage in speed; Sun Mee's body movements in slow motion; and Amy's sonic enactment and visual embodiment. Using motions, images, and sounds to map out their memories on their physiques, the performers create a bodily language with which to share their border-crossing stories with their audiences. Chomet remarks, "I wanted to tell the story to get it out of my body. And I think the audience can feel that."[103]

Stuart Fisher writes of testimonial theater that it is driven by "dramaturgical practices that foreground the act of witnessing itself, placing the experience of the witness at the heart of the dramaturgical process."[104] For Stuart Fisher, testimonial theater performances make witnesses "an ethical presence": the playwrights and performers of testimonial theater create ethical experiences for their audiences.[105] Furthermore, the combination of testimony with performance by the actual person (or people) who lived the events lends more credence to the representations of those events in the eyes of audiences. The testimonial works of Lichwick, Chomet, and Ginther carry the hope of empathy and the potential of producing witnesses out of spectators. The personal and powerful nature of these three artists' bodily statements allows audiences to experience a form of theatrical testimony, transforming spectators into witnesses to the complex transnational experiences of birth search and reunion from the adoptees' points of view.

The testimonial voices of transnational adoptee performers are particularly appealing to audience members who have also experienced transnational adoption. At the 2013 International Korean Adoptee Associations (IKAA) gathering in Seoul, Chomet's solo performance in *How to Be a Korean Woman* was so powerfully felt that after the performance she was besieged by adoptee audience members, who, in Chomet's words, were

> crying and so emotional and I just didn't understand why people would want to feel all that; but especially adoptees said that: it's articulated in the play,

---

103. Chomet, interview.
104. Stuart Fisher, *Performing the Testimonial*, 103.
105. Stuart Fisher, 104.

the inner life of the adoptees that they don't often talk about to their families and that they often can't articulate to themselves.[106]

In 2015 *Yellow Dress* was performed as a special event in Chicago, organized by the Korean Adoptees of Chicago (KAtCH) organization, in a small theater space packed with highly receptive adoptee audience members.[107] After the 2018 United Solo Theatre Festival performance of *Homeful* in New York City, a group of adoptee audience members from a local Korean adoptee affinity group called Also-Known-As (AKA) huddled with Ginther in a show of support, as if replying to Ginther's "love letter" to adoptees, as she describes her own play.[108] McKee notes that adult adoptee organizations offer in-person and online connections across the globe to an adoptee community whose interactions "reflect their assertion of autonomy and agency as they seek to 'flip the script' on adoption—centering adoptees' voices—and articulate their knowledges of what it is like to *be* adopted."[109] Witnessing performers' lived experiences in theaters, adoptee spectators see their own experiences—real, imagined, or prospective—reflected in performances that validate and value their unexpressed thoughts, emotions, and memories. In this critical adoption spectatorship, they also can come to understand that the status quo of silence as acquiescence is not a script they are obligated to follow; they, too, can express themselves and deal directly with conflict and confusion as Lichwick, Chomet, and Ginther do.

Theater, as a live artistic medium, stands as perhaps one of the most effective vehicles for this affective attestation that once felt cannot be unfelt. Writing about *How to Be a Korean Woman*, Eunha Na proposes that the "spectatorship in this kind of performance allows us to imagine the viewing public in terms of a kind of kinship even while the content of the play is about the disillusionment about kinship, biological and adoptive. In this case, kinship is a more expansive frame with ambiguous boundaries and hails the empathetic

---

106. Chomet, interview. Founded in Europe and the United States in 2004, the International Korean Adoptee Associations (IKAA) was created to unite the Korean adoptee adult community and to offer space to share information, resources, and services. See "Who We Are," International Korean Adoptee Association Network.

107. The Korean Adoptees of Chicago (KAtCH) organization offers "education and awareness about issues surrounding transracial, international adoption and multicultural issues" to the adult Korean adoptee community in the Chicago area. See "Mission," Korean Adoptees of Chicago.

108. Ginther, interview. Also-Known-As (AKA) serves to "empower the voice of adult international adoptees, build cultural bridges, transform perceptions of race, and acknowledge the loss of the birth country, culture, language and biological family experienced by international adoptees." See "About," Also-Known-As.

109. McKee, "Public Intimacy and Kinship," 41. Italics in original.

listeners in the audience."[110] When the artists act out their adoption stories on stage, spectators are compelled to respond by the performances' aspect of sharing, which gives them the sense of being part of an extended family—especially among adoptee audience members. The artists' live performances are thus meant to stir spectators to participate in temporary communion with one another even though they might have different degrees of engagement. Once acted out on stage, the stories no longer belong only to the artists; they become part of a larger community of adoptees newly bound by the affinity of caring in theater.

In this sense, the three plays discussed here engage audiences to become witnesses to the experiences of transnational adoptees and by doing so hope to inspire change. To borrow the words of Stuart Fisher, their performances become an act of "staging a mode of resistance to hegemonic narratives that suppress certain perspectives from being heard or being recognised."[111] Moreover, cultivating oneself as a member of critical adoption spectatorship could be, in Eleana Kim's words, a "politically engaged choice that is tied to contemporary politics of recognition and the production and circulation of counter-images and counternarratives [of transnational adoption]."[112] Talking about her counterperformance at the 2013 IKAA gathering, Chomet mentioned that her goal was to have her audience "experience this complexity of adoption, not just the adoptees' emotional life, inner life but also the complexity between the Korean government, between how adoption agencies hide information, and the repercussions."[113] For instance, in the play, Sun Mee finds out that the Holt Adoption Program actually hid her from her biological family while she stayed with a Korean foster family for six months before departing for the United States. This vital piece of information was kept from Sun Mee her entire life. The audience learns that her mother went back to get her from Holt but was told that Sun Mee was no longer there. The fact that Chomet shares this eye-opening story with adoptee and non-adoptee audiences alike gives this episode the power of testimony, making it one of the most commanding moments in the piece.

In reference to the visual works of Korean adoptee artists kimura byol lemoine and kate-hers RHEE, Kim Stoker argues that artistic expression by adoptee artists can be considered a form of "artivism," in that it reveals an element of activism within the artistic expressions of international adoption that

---

110. Na, "Empathic Imagination," 138. For another analysis of *How to Be a Korean Woman*, see M. Woo, "Performing the Diasporic Sensibility of Displacement."
111. Stuart Fisher, *Performing the Testimonial*, 145.
112. E. J. Kim, *Adopted Territory*, 137.
113. Chomet, interview.

envisions a mutuality between art and politicity.[114] Stoker stresses the activist aspect of art as a way of deconstructing obsolete knowledge and constructing new knowledge about international adoption to encourage social transformation. Chomet's portraying her experience of discovering that she was hidden from her mother at the foster family home is an act of artivism as it raises the question: how many other grieving birth mothers were lied to? In *Yellow Dress,* Lichwick performs Riss's experience of child molestation at the Korean orphanage not just to theatricalize child abuse but to have the audience seriously consider violations of the rights of children in orphanages—the processing stations for international adoption. In this sense, Lichwick's performative testimony can be seen to express an artistic and activist voice, in other words an artivistic call to attention to unjust doings in the process and practice of transnational adoption. In *Homeful,* the question that Ginther is repeatedly asked—"Where are you from?"—manifests a racial othering that adult Asian adoptees confront. The artists' sharing of their experiences of injustices consequently represents that which Chen maintains is needed in regard to transnational adoption: "not a politics of pity, but rather a politics of justice: to disrupt the underlying fantasy and traverse the elementary coordinates of unjust power structures rather than offering assistance out of pity at the spectacle of individual suffering."[115] By disclosing on stage their personal lives as they relate to search-and-reunion experiences, the three artists deliver theatrical testimony that upholds adoptees' rights to know, feel, and express themselves freely. Rather than a "spectacle of individual suffering," they call on their audiences to witness "a politics of justice."

When asked what kind of public impact she wanted her performance of *How to Be a Korean Woman* to have, Chomet emphasized, "It's like having a person come into the theater and thinking one thing and having them leave and be like, I can never think about this topic the same way again."[116] The testimonies staged by the three artists affect not only Korean adoptees but also other adoption community members, who can (re)contextualize them with their own adoption stories. Regarding solo performance, Taylor observes, "The humor, the intensity, the beauty of these performances often stems from taking the small, the personal, the confessional and making it speak to a community organized around (but not limited to) an 'identity.'"[117] Tellingly, audiences in the first run of Chomet's show were mainly composed of adoptees, while later runs largely comprised adoptive families spurred to attend by

---

114. Stoker, "Beyond Identity."
115. Chen, "Maternal Voices," 164.
116. Chomet, interview.
117. Taylor, *The Archive and the Repertoire,* 230.

their children.[118] Chomet recalls how after one of her shows, a couple whose adoptive daughter had committed suicide told her that had they seen her play while their daughter was alive, they might have better understood what she had wrestled with. Another interaction occurred several days after a show, when a couple who attended the performance with their preteen daughter, adopted from Guatemala, said that at home after seeing the show their daughter opened up to them for hours and asked them questions they had never thought about. Thus, the performative testimonies of Lichwick, Chomet, and Ginther engender earnest and profound conversations that increase awareness of the hidden challenges faced by Korean American (and other) transnational and transracial adoptees as well as their adoptive parents and audience members in and out of the adoption community, who might not previously have discussed such matters. As Chomet says, "it's about breaking silences."[119]

Archbishop Desmond Tutu writes: "Theatre is the ambitious sister of Testimony. It strives to heal through truth."[120] Tutu expands by remarking on the importance of witnesses (audiences), who come to hear the personal stories being shared and acknowledge the past in an act of resistance against "the silence of indifference or fear," healing those who talk as well as those who listen.[121] Ultimately, the three artists' autobiographical solo performances of their search-and-reunion stories call for a metamorphosis in spectators. This transformation in critical adoption spectatorship involves not only their reception of the issue of Korean adoption, but also their communication and engagement with other transnational and transracial adoptees waiting to be heard, to witness, and testify to their own adoption experiences on and off the stage.

•

Yellow Dress, How to Be a Korean Woman, and *Homeful* offer nuanced portrayals of birth search and reunion from adoptee artists' own perspectives and experiences. In their autobiographical solo performances, Lichwick, Chomet, and Ginther refuse to allow themselves to be objectified by ethnonationalist ideologies or the savior narratives of colorblind family-making practices; instead, they assert their positions as autonomous actors, authors, and agents of their own transnational adoption stories. Opening a realm of critical discussion about what it means to be international adoptee women of color within and beyond the United States, the three artists' border-crossing bodily

---

118. Chomet, interview.
119. Chomet, interview.
120. Tutu, "Foreword," in Farber, *Theatre as Witness,* 7.
121. Tutu, "Foreword," 7.

testimonies actively unsettle the dominant racializing and gendering discourses dictating Korean adoptee bodies and minds. Chomet emphasizes that dramatic fiction and performance about transnational adoption not only have "the greatest story that's interesting for people to hear but [. . . also] the story that will actually liberate you."[122] In this sense, the three Korean adoptee artists, whose autobiographical performances impart to audiences their uniquely insightful points of view, create a space of liberation from mythified adoption narratives and cultural reifications of what it means to be an adoptee. In these Korean American women adoptees' stories of transnational adoption, performance itself becomes an epistemological, ethical, and political act. Through this undertaking, the experiences of these transnational adoptees usher audiences into an emancipatory world of theater, offering the glimpse of a transformative moment.

---

122. Chomet, interview.

CHAPTER 3

Contingent Belonging

*Korean Adoptees and
Adoption Communities Imagined in US Theater*

In this era of globalization, where the global and local seamlessly intermingle through increasingly flexible mobilities, our sense of permanence and security often fluctuates. In this light, this chapter examines the concept of (in)flexible belonging, as illustrated in Eric Sharp's play *Middle Brother* (2014), Leah Cooper and Alan Berks's community-based theater project *In My Heart: The Adoption Play Project* (2016), and Debra Kim Sivigny's immersive piece *Hello, My Name Is* . . . (2017). All three plays are highly imaginative works, presenting fantasylike worlds through time travel, a fairy-tale narrative, and otherworldly immersion, respectively. A common thread running through the three works is the convergence of reality and imagination in the main characters' worlds, foregrounding the staging of birth search and reunion as a compression of time and space. As Eleana Kim points out, "The project of return . . . has been enabled by globalizing flows and postmodern 'time-space compression.'"[1] Kim further theorizes that "the 'time-space compression' of adoptee returns . . . sets in motion possible transformations in the understanding and practice of transnational adoption, paradigms of citizenship, and the re-membering of the national body."[2] The three works unsettle the meanings of adoption and

---

1. E. J. Kim, *Adopted Territory*, 13. Kim cites here David Harvey's notion of "time-space compression." Harvey, *Condition of Postmodernity*.

2. E. J. Kim, *Adopted Territory*, 246.

belonging in the narratives of Korean transnational adoptees who crisscross through imagined time-space compressions, especially during their search-and-reunion processes. The heightened imagination thus deterritorializes the demarcated spatiality and temporality in which Korean American adoptee characters transgress the multiple dichotomies of domestic/private versus public, visible versus invisible, material versus spiritual, inner versus outer, and real versus imagined.

While theatricalizing the fluid mobility of their characters, the three plays depict belonging as something ambiguous, in-between, and unsettled. Applying SooJin Pate's analysis of body politics, wherein Korean adoptees' belonging is delineated upon their bodies, I scrutinize the transtemporal and transspatial forging of a sense of belonging in the bodies, language, and space of the plays' adoptee characters.[3] I also employ Kimberly McKee's notion of affect politics, which uses gratitude as a barometer to distinguish "good" adoptees from "bad" adoptees and conceptualizes the "adoptee killjoy" as a disruptor of happiness who refuses to reify a humanitarian adoption fantasy.[4] Building on these concepts, I contend that the staging of Korean transnational adoptees' birth search and reunion reveals a discursive and disciplinary process of (un)settling belonging that is contingent on the adoptees' "performance" of being "good," "bad," or otherwise "strange" adoptees.

Each in its own way, the three plays discussed in this chapter explore the idea that adoptees' sense of belonging is contingent on how they behave and feel, and what they search for in and beyond their given circumstances. This contingency of belonging demands that the adoptee characters in the plays conform to, or contest, their social environments, where they are categorized as "good," "bad," or "strange" adoptees, depending on whether they are considered grateful/assimilated or ungrateful/estranged. Regarding the options for behavior, self-presentation, and assessment available to children and adolescent adoptees within their adoptive homes, Betty Jean Lifton argues that the "good" adoptee must be docile, dutiful, mostly unquestioning, and "sensitive to his parent's needs," whereas the "bad" adoptee is "rebellious and continually acting out at home and in school."[5] Furthermore, according to Lifton, "good" adoptees tend to view their parents' home as a safe harbor—as opposed to "bad" adoptees, who are inclined to feel imprisoned in their adoptive environment.[6] Given the demanding and conflicting conditions of their situations, it

---

3. Pate, *From Orphan to Adoptee*, 101–25.
4. McKee, *Disrupting Kinship*, 11–12.
5. Lifton, "Good Adoptee—Bad Adoptee," 54.
6. Lifton, 59.

should be no wonder that some adoptees might come to feel—as the Korean American character Jennifer says in *In My Heart*—"stuck between worlds."[7]

Another point I wish to make about these works, closely related to the contingency of belonging, has to do with the double state of hope and fear their characters inhabit—a twofold state incorporating both the hope of belonging and the fear of unbelonging. According to Barbara Yngvesson and Maureen Mahoney, for many adoptees the feeling of displacement brought about by this double state is relentless, and the sense of not belonging can even translate into a sense of "not 'existing.'"[8] Therefore, I intend for my analysis in this chapter to unpack the three plays' treatment of adoptees' (un)attainable sense of belonging to family, community, and society, and their expression of adoptees' claims to their very existence.

In her review of search memoirs written by adoptees seeking their birth families in Korea, Taiwan, and Nigeria, Margaret Homans notes that while most adoptees in these works generally search for birth parents, many are surprised to find siblings instead.[9] Similarly, the three works discussed in this chapter focus on adoptees' relationships with siblings—whether adoptive, birth, or imagined—rather than parents. Kinship propels the reunion with a biological brother in *Middle Brother*, unearths conflict with a transracial adoptive sister in *In My Heart*, and generates siblinghood among non-blood-related adoptees in *Hello, My Name Is. . . .* Explicating the concept of "adoptee kinship," Eleana Kim describes that the powerful bonds among adoptees are not based on biological origin, ethnic background, or national belonging but rather on their shared displacement.[10] In other words, Korean transnational adoptees, Kim observes, find kinship beyond familial structures by developing connections based on their collective experiences of racial marginalization and alienation.[11] In this chapter, I draw on these ideas about adoptee kinship to understand how the three plays imagine and perform Korean adoptees' sense of relatedness. I thus argue that their performances transform the theater into a site of adoptee kinship-making through the act of *kinning*. Signe Howell writes that kinning is "the process by which a foetus [sic] or newborn child (or a previously unconnected person) is brought into a significant and permanent relationship with a group of people that is expressed in a kin idiom."[12] I contend that kinning in the selected plays enacts adoptee kinship

---

7. Cooper and Berks, *In My Heart*, 39.
8. Yngvesson and Mahoney, "'As One Should, Ought, and Wants to Be,'" 82.
9. Homans, "Reunions with Siblings in Search Memoirs across Cultures."
10. E. J. Kim, *Adopted Territory*, 86.
11. E. J. Kim, 95, 100.
12. Howell, *Kinning of Foreigners*, 63.

through interaction with Asian American theater, Native American communities, and Korean adoptee peers.[13] Hence, the plays configure multiple adoptee relatedness that departs from the singular identification of Korean adoptees and adoption communities.

The idea of community takes on further significance in the three works in individual participants' willingness to emphasize responsibility to the group in exchange for a sense of belonging and feelings of communal connection that last beyond the duration of the performance.[14] As Jill Dolan puts it, "Theater and performance offer a place to scrutinize public meanings, but also to embody and, even if through fantasy, enact the affective possibilities of 'doings' that gesture toward a much better world."[15] Sharing a world of adoption narratives and imagination throughout the production, preparation, and performance of these works, adoptee and non-adoptee performers, community members, and audiences become temporal kin.[16] In this sense, the momentary kinship, developed between all who experience these theaters and performances, creates the possibility of imagining a better world, "a gesture of commitment toward community."[17] Ultimately, then, this chapter highlights the three works' processes and impacts of making search-and-reunion stories as they bring forth a community of care.

Search-and-Reunion Fantasy

Orphanhood and adoption have often been represented in Western literature, theater, and film in fairy-tale and fantasy stories with characters such as Rapunzel, Snow White, Annie in *Little Orphan Annie*, Dorothy Gale in *The Wonderful Wizard of Oz*, and Harry Potter.[18] Through such stories of orphaned or adopted children, Western authors have explored themes of loss, relinquishment, self-reliance, class divisions, and societal norms. Focusing on nineteenth-century American and English literature, Hana Wirth-Nesher states that in American literature, orphanhood is often depicted as belonging

---

13. For consistency, I follow *In My Heart*'s use of the term "Native American" to designate the Indigenous people of North America.
14. Snyder-Young, *Theatre of Good Intentions*, 100.
15. Dolan, *Utopia in Performance*, 6.
16. For spectators forming kinship through the viewing of adoption stories, see Na, "Empathic Imagination."
17. Dolan, *Utopia in Performance*, 44.
18. Other well-known orphan or adoptee characters, though not all set within a fantasy setting, include Oliver Twist, Heidi, Cosette (in Victor Hugo's 1862 novel *Les Misérables*), Peter Pan, Rudyard Kipling's Mowgli, and Jane Eyre.

to a romanticized America where courageous self-determination and charming solitude sustain "the myth of eternal fresh starts."[19] Also according to Wirth-Nesher, in English literature, orphans are "usually on a quest to find a place for themselves in society rather than arranging for a romantic exit," signifying a process of maturation and enlightenment with regard to social class.[20] In both cases, orphan or adoptee characters, such as Pip in Charles Dickens's *Great Expectations* (1861) and Huckleberry Finn in Mark Twain's *The Adventures of Huckleberry Finn* (1885), face a choice between fabricating a past suited to their ambitions and maintaining their blood ties in a society where social classes are constantly changing.[21]

Diana Loercher Pazicky observes that in American melodrama of the mid-1800s, orphan characters were highly "unrepresentative of society's real orphans," with typical rags-to-riches fantasies of the time depicting orphans originally thought to be poor eventually being revealed to actually be the children of wealthy parents.[22] According to Loercher Pazicky, the American sentimental novel of the time told the same formulaic orphan story while also expressing an ideology that "establishe[d] the orphan tale as an allegory of middle-class survival," in which the central characters fell from their social class but regained their middle-class status by the story's end.[23] In twentieth-century North American literature, Kristina Fagan discusses the novels *The Diviners* (1974) by Margaret Laurence and *Pigs in Heaven* (1993) by Barbara Kingsolver, which Fagan views as "nationalistic fantasies [. . . that] revolve around orphaned characters who achieve, through literal or metaphorical adoptions, cross-cultural identities that include both Native and white cultures."[24] For Fagan, the fantasy aspect of these two novels functions as a metaphor reflecting the wish for reconciliation of racial and cultural differences in the United States and Canada to be attained through adoption.[25]

Examining adoption plots in nineteenth-century British novels, Marianne Novy finds that adoption is often ascribed a "mythic dimension," becoming "the fantasy that people develop to deal with uncongenial parents by imagining better parents elsewhere."[26] Novy further notes the fantastical character of plots wherein adoptees discover their unknown selves and homes when they

---

19. Wirth-Nesher, "Literary Orphan as National Hero," 260–61.
20. Wirth-Nesher, 261.
21. Wirth-Nesher, 260.
22. Pazicky, *Cultural Orphans in America*, 149–50.
23. Pazicky, 150.
24. Fagan, "Adoption as National Fantasy," 251.
25. Fagan, 251.
26. Novy, *Reading Adoption*, 123.

find their birth parents.[27] Discussing theatrical works, Novy writes that while some plays like Jane Anderson's *The Baby Dance* (1991) and Kristine Thatcher's *Emma's Child* (1995) remain within "the mode of realism," other playwrights, such as Lanford Wilson with *Redwood Curtain* (1992) and Rick Shiomi with *Mask Dance* (1995), use magical realism to theatricalize cross-cultural adoption.[28] For instance, in *Redwood Curtain*, the adoptee character possesses a magical ability and awareness of her ancestors. In *Mask Dance*, two imaginary characters, Spirit and Mask Dancer, occasionally speak for the adoptee characters and often interact with them. For Novy, Wilson's and Shiomi's works examine American society, history, and adoptee experiences through theatrical fantasy presentations of the birth search narrative.[29] Thus, fantasy has been ideologically utilized in a diverse range of stories about orphanhood and adoption, from rags-to-riches and restored social status and racial harmony stories to fantasies as dramatic devices for the revelation of origins and ancestral connections.

What makes the Korean adoptee characters in the three plays examined in this chapter alike is their decision to conduct a birth search. This vital action, involving neither a romantic view of a fresh start nor aspiration or a quest for social advancement, brings to light conflicts within both the characters themselves and their adoptive and birth cultures, which do not readily accept them as their own. In comparison with previous literature of orphanhood and adoption, these characters reveal more complicated aspects of adoptees' lives, thus unsettling persisting notions of what it means to be adopted in English and American literature. Furthermore, the three plays' use of fantasy does not reify their adoptee characters as allegorical receptors of adoption fantasies. Rather, fantasy serves the dramaturgical purpose of destabilizing the mythic dimension of adoptees' search-and-reunion stories. Achieved through the portrayal of temporal and spatial transgressions in fantastical situations, events, and relationships, this destabilization compels audiences to reflect, somewhat paradoxically, on the adoptee characters' realities and their unique ways of seeking belonging.

Works of fantasy incorporate disturbing and even alienating qualities that can cause readers or audiences to view things from new and different perspectives, thus subverting their reality. As Diana Taylor observes, "phantoms, fantasy, and performance have traditionally been placed on the opposite side of the 'real.'"[30] Although inspired by their own experiences of birth search and

---

27. Novy, 28.
28. Novy, 186.
29. Novy, 34.
30. Taylor, *The Archive and the Repertoire*, 141.

reunion and the real-life voices of other adoptees, the adoptee playwrights whose works are discussed in this chapter choose to present their pieces through the prism of heightened imagination. In this sense, fantasy presents a more intricate and intimate "real" world—or, as Rebecca Schneider puts it, "fantasy gestures toward reality, tells us something *about* reality."[31] Thus, the three plays use fantasy to represent adoptees' real experiences, and to communicate their ideas about transnational and transracial adoption and adoptees' birth search and reunion, as well as to encourage audiences to rethink the meanings of kinship and citizenship. By placing adoptee protagonists in fantastical and alienating settings, the plays transcend realistic representations and offer alternative views beyond the "fantasization" of adoption as a postwar humanitarian, colorblind multicultural, and ethnonationalist script.[32]

In My Heart borrows elements of a well-known fantasy narrative (Lewis Carroll's classic *Alice in Wonderland*) to help audiences understand the complexities and unknown aspects of adoption. For instance, in act 2, the play uses a fantasy sequence to represent pertinent historical and sociocultural information about adoption within and beyond the United States. The information is delivered in a quixotic and humorous way by familiar and phantasmal characters from *Alice in Wonderland*. A recital of the same information by characters in the realistic sections of the play might have come across as didactic exposition. In *Hello My Name Is . . .* , fantasy is used to reveal the untold and unseen in commenting on the social deaths of Korean birth mothers. The deceased birth mother of a Korean adoptee child is depicted as a spirit who follows her daughter to the United States and hovers around her, hoping her child can feel her presence and undying love. Thus, *Hello, My Name Is . . .* utilizes fantastical representations of the spirit world to depict the banishment of motherhood and the separation of children. Disorienting time and displacing space, the fantasy components of *Middle Brother* illustrate the fragility of the sense of belonging as it grows unsettled during the search-and-reunion process. While the main character, Billy, searches for his sibling in the present, he also navigates the imagined past of Korea's Joseon Dynasty (1392–1910). The transhistorical aspects of these fantasy scenes in *Middle Brother* represent the fleetingness of Billy's sense of belonging in his present life. Every time Billy confronts questions he cannot answer, he falls into a fantasy world of the Joseon Dynasty, hoping to be able to fill the gaps in his own narrative. In these scenes, Billy does not explicitly travel back to the exact time but rather imagines what the Joseon Dynasty could have been like with him in it. This

---

31. Schneider, *Explicit Body in Performance*, 95. Italics in original.
32. McKee, *Adoption Fantasies*.

oscillation between the real and the imaginary reflects Billy's way of finding answers about his birth, relinquishment, and separation from his birth family, while also illustrating the burdens adoptees face in negotiating their sense of belonging in the process of birth search and reunion. Ultimately, the three plays exemplify the idea that "fantasy is the vehicle for our construction of the real"[33] and affirm that fantasy can serve as a valid interpreter of reality, offering, in this context, vital insights and imaginative interventions into transnational adoptees' experiences of birth search and reunion.

The "Good" Adoptee in *Middle Brother* (2014)

Eric Sharp's *Middle Brother* was produced by Theater Mu and premiered at the Southern Theater in Minneapolis in 2014.[34] The play follows the story of Billy (performed by Sharp), a Korean American adoptee in Waterloo, Iowa, who was adopted at the age of seven and decides to move to Seoul in his late twenties. Once in Korea, Billy discovers he has a biological brother, Young-Nam (also called Hyung in the play, meaning "older brother" in Korean). Inspired by Sharp's own birth search and reunion, Billy's story includes his two brothers: his biological brother in Korea, Young-Nam, and his Korean adoptive younger brother in the United States, Gabe (not biologically related). The play's title refers to Billy, who becomes a middle brother as a result of his search and reunion, indicating his position within his newly composed brotherhood.

Lifton's notion of the "good" adoptee as one who does not rebel against their adoptive parents or environment finds a subtle rendering in *Middle Brother*, as Billy's adoptive parents are never seen or mentioned. With no background information regarding how Billy grew up, nor about his relationship with his adoptive parents, his decision to go to Korea cannot be understood to stem from a rejection of his adoptive parents or life; rather, it is, as Billy says, more like "going on a long vacation."[35] Even though he plans to visit the adoption agency that placed him to find out more about his birth family, Billy does not have a burning desire to discover his roots—until he finds out about the existence of his older brother. At this point, Billy's longing for belonging drives him to become a "good" returning adoptee in the land of his birth. As Billy undergoes this process, the audience also witnesses through flashbacks

---

33. Schneider, *Explicit Body in Performance*, 104.
34. The analysis of *Middle Brother* is based on the 2014 videotaped performance as well as the unpublished script provided by the playwright.
35. Sharp, *Middle Brother*, 6.

how he struggled to become a "good" adopted child in his adoptive country. In its representation of the demarcating forces Billy is subjected to in becoming a "good" adoptee, *Middle Brother* explores his complicated kinship and citizenship, as the social and cultural position he occupies changes into the liminal position of middle brother. Billy's sense of belonging becomes contingent on his ability to deal with this new position while adjusting to his Korean birth family and culture in the course of his birth search and reunion.

Robert Rosen, the director of the 2014 premiere of *Middle Brother*, has said that what struck him the most about the play was "the idea of an adoptee on a very intense personal journey whose story is hijacked by just about everyone he meets. Their stories seem to supersede his own and he is relegated to the position of caretaking or placating everyone else."[36] To theatricalize the "hijackings" in *Middle Brother*, Sharp interweaves flashbacks to the 1980s, when Billy was first a young boy in Korea and then a young adult adoptee in the United States, with the present time of the play set in the 2010s. Sharp incorporates an element of temporal mobility by interspersing Billy's current search and reunion with an imagined story about a royal family of the Joseon Dynasty, with Billy as the Queen's second son.[37] In this setting, Billy imagines that his mother has sent him away to study so that he will not pose a potential threat to his older brother's right to the crown. Rapid scene changes between present-day urban sites and premodern Korean royal court settings accentuate Billy's sense of displacement and disorientation. For example, the private singing room (*noraebang*) Billy goes to when he first lands in Korea transforms in the next scene into a Joseon Dynasty royal court setting, complete with the musical sounds of traditional instruments and royal family members wearing *hanbok*.[38] The contrast between the bowing and florid language and honorifics of royal courtiers in the Joseon-period scenes and the everyday mannerisms and language of characters in the present-day scenes is extreme, jarring Billy's sense of reality. Writing about the return of adoptees (and deportees) to their homelands, Barbara Yngvesson and Susan Coutin consider how their travels encompass "multidirectional movements," not only from "present to past or future, but sometimes from one present to another."[39] Similarly, the multidirectional time changes in *Middle Brother* cause the temporal line between

---

36. Rosen, "Director's Notes," program for *Middle Brother*, 5.

37. The early 1980s and the Joseon Dynasty period are mixed, accentuating the fantasy element of the flashbacks, as the Joseon period is purposely fictionalized rather than following historical accuracy.

38. The modified *hanbok* costumes in this play suggest a historical sense of temporality, not an accurate representation of Joseon-period attire, thus functioning as an imagined signifier of Korean royal lineage in history.

39. Yngvesson and Coutin, "Backed by Papers," 184.

Billy's imagined transhistorical past and his present-day reality to oscillate, evoking the fragility of his sense of belonging.

The physical spaces in *Middle Brother* also expose the challenged flexibility of Billy's transnational connection. In the 2014 production, Billy's transpacific mobility was actualized through an open spatial configuration of the set. At the beginning of the play, the words "한국 (Korea), 태평양 (Pacific Ocean), 아이오와 (Iowa)" are drawn on the floor with white chalk by members of a chorus. Using a cartlike chariot, Billy and the chorus move back and forth between the two countries marked on the stage floor, dramatizing Billy's mobility on this newly created topography. When Billy travels to Korea, the chorus brings the cart over to Iowa (stage left), picks him up, and wheels him across the Pacific to the Korean side (stage right). In one scene, Billy in the United States summons the chorus from Korea. The chorus members then wheel over a small bridge and crawl on top of it, crossing the Pacific Ocean from Korea to Iowa. This staging of transpacific movements makes Billy's birth search and reunion across borders legible for audience members. As Eunha Na points out, the theatricalization of transnational mobility in *Middle Brother* is more complex than a mere theatrical depiction of flexibility.[40] In effect, the chorus-guided circuit of unfolding spatiality magnifies Billy's liminal state between Korea and the United States, making his sense of belonging even more uncertain. Consequently, the movements imagine the disruption of the spatial stability and temporal linearity of Billy's search for belonging, as Billy gets lost between two times, two locations, and two brothers.

Aiwha Ong theorizes that enhanced transnational connection due to advances in technology and transportation has caused mobility and nationhood to become increasingly flexible.[41] Although contemporary transnational mobility offers Korean adoptees the opportunity of connecting and reconnecting with kin, it does not necessarily entail their acquisition of a transcultural sense of belonging. Unable to settle down, Billy embarks on a birth search and reunion, during which he encounters forces intent on shaping his identity as either American or Korean. *Middle Brother* thus reveals the oppressive bifurcated cultural configuration that Korean American adoptees confront, being placed in an in-between position where they are expected to easily assimilate into either culture or both. In the opening scene of the play, Billy practices speaking basic Korean in his apartment. He tells the chorus of his simple plan for his return to Korea: "Find an apartment. . . . Get a job. . . . Eat Korean barbecue. . . . Apply for a visa, learn Korean, then walk around and blend into

---

40. Na, "Re-made in Korea." In Korean.
41. Ong, *Flexible Citizenship*.

society."[42] As a reminder of Billy's position as a returned adoptee in Korea, the chorus responds by commenting on his belonging. One of the chorus members mimics him sarcastically, "Oh look at me, I am Billy and I'm blending in to Korean society."[43] By ridiculing Billy's naïve belief that his forthcoming assimilation into Korean society will be trouble-free, the chorus warns him that his unbelonging to Korean culture will make his integration nearly impossible. Billy sees himself as Korean but is mocked by the chorus members, who perform "real" Koreanness by identically donning the culturally specific outfits ubiquitous in Korean saunas (*jjimjilbang*) and speaking English with a Korean accent. The chorus members are an ethnicized reminder of the reality of Korean American adoptees returning to Korea and being viewed as "Korean foreigners," distanced from "authentic" Koreans.[44] Thus, *Middle Brother* expresses the dual actuality confronted by those adoptees who desire Korea to be "a site of plenitude and true familial or ethnic belonging" but become despondent on realizing the difficulty of being accepted as fellow Koreans in the face of "dominant ethnic nationalism that equates Koreanness with cultural, linguistic, and ethnic homogeneity."[45]

Emphasizing the idea of "foreignness" in the matter of adoptees' belonging, the chorus members tell Billy that to apply for a long-term visa, he must bring his US citizenship naturalization documents to prove that he is, in fact, *not* Korean and that his name is no longer on the *hojuk*:

BILLY: Hojuk, hojuk . . . Okay, what's a hojuk?
CHORUS 3: Korean family registry. You no longer part of family. You no longer Korean person. You now American person. Please prove that you are not Korean person.[46]

The information given by the chorus is significant, because for Korean children to become legally adoptable according to US Immigration Law, they must first gain "orphan status." As Eleana Kim writes, "For adoptees, an 'orphan *hojuk*,' or orphan registry, served to render the child as a legible, free-standing subject of the state in preparation for adoption and erasure as a Korean Citizen."[47] Kim adds that later in life, when adoptees apply for the overseas Koreans visa as adults, they can be informed that they have never been removed from their

---

42. Sharp, *Middle Brother*, 7.
43. Sharp, 7.
44. Park Nelson, *Invisible Asians*, 177.
45. E. J. Kim, *Adopted Territory*, 186.
46. Sharp, *Middle Brother*, 7.
47. E. J. Kim, "Our Adoptee, Our Alien," 521.

birth family registry and that in order to be eligible for the visa they must carry out the process of erasing themselves from the registry and annul their Korean citizenship.[48] In other words, in some cases, returning adoptees' legal recognition by the Korean government involves negating their "Koreanness," represented by the family registry. For those adoptees, the bureaucratic kinship and citizenship markers of both Korean and US authorities serve as identifiers that strictly and arbitrarily demarcate their belonging. *Middle Brother*'s dramatization of the hard facts faced by a Korean transnational adoptee who decides to return and stay in Korea debunks the romanticized idea of flexible mobility and belonging with which adoptees are often associated. As Billy's "Koreanness" is subject to cultural evaluation and legal verification processes, his liminal position gradually increases his sense of insecurity, statelessness, and unbelonging.

Examining the historical process by which unwanted Korean orphans were made into desirable adoptees, Pate argues that "the orphan's body was subjected to different methods of biopower—techniques and procedures that governed life and subjugated bodies and that worked to protect the health and appearance of incoming orphans so that they may be made useful (that is, adoptable)."[49] Taking a cue from Pate's Foucauldian analysis, I conceive of *Middle Brother* as an exposure and critique of biopower as the means through which Korean transnational adoptees are indoctrinated into being de-Koreanized and re-Koreanized. In this way, the play interrogates how the adoptees' bodies are marked with and for compulsory membership in and outside Korea. Each of the cultures Korean adoptees enter scrutinizes, disciplines, and demarcates their bodies and "tongues," forcing them to conform to the role of "good" adoptees. In *Middle Brother,* the demarcation of adoptees' bodies and language becomes a dramatic apparatus for the illumination of the ways in which belonging is constructed and contested as well as the evocation of fear and anxiety surrounding this process of de-Koreanization and re-Koreanization.

In an imaginative scene set in the Joseon-period past, the chorus rushes in and violently strips off Billy's *hanbok*, a symbol of his royal family lineage, revealing a faded orphanage uniform. Billy is then quickly transported to 1980s Waterloo, Iowa, where he meets a young Gabe for the first time. The chorus hangs a large white placard around his neck with his Korean name crossed out in red marker and his newly given American name written

---

48. E. J. Kim, 521.
49. Pate, *From Orphan to Adoptee,* 103. Also see Michel Foucault, *History of Sexuality.*

FIGURE 3. Gabe and Billy with their Korean names overwritten by new American names in *Middle Brother* (2014). Courtesy Theater Mu. Photo Credit: Michal Daniel.

underneath. Gabe also wears similar orphanage garb and has a name placard around his neck (see figure 3).

Naming is a way of sculpting identity, and people identify each other through this linguistic practice. As a visualized written form representing Billy and Gabe's identity and family lineage, the names in this scene become a performative interpellation for them to inscribe on themselves and recognize themselves as belonging to their new adoptive culture and customs—even as the involuntary loss of their birth names and heritage only makes their sense of belonging more unattainable. This interpellation becomes a defining moment in the formation of Billy's identity, a reinforcement in the Althusserian sense of the invisible power of the new culture to which Billy and Gabe have been forcefully taken, which by interpellation transforms them into its subjects.[50]

In the same scene, Billy's fear of re-relinquishment and unbelonging makes him desperately desire acceptance, and he instructs Gabe to give up speaking Korean, to only speak English, and to eat any food they are given, even if it tastes bland. Here, to assimilate in the United States as a "good"

---

50. Althusser, Jameson, and Brewster, "Ideology and Ideological State Apparatuses."

adoptee, Billy and Gabe must negate the names and tastes that evoke Korea, self-disciplining themselves to conform to their new environment. Their integration into North American culture and a new home is also demonstrated by Billy's desire to learn English. When Gabe calls Billy by his Korean name, Billy hastily hushes him as if Gabe has said a taboo word. Along with naming and being named, learning a language is a crucial part of acquiring the cultural and communicative tool to produce and reinforce one's selfhood and identity. However, in the play, the obligation for adoptees to acquire a new language for assimilation can be interpreted as a way of coercing them to give up their native tongue and submit instead to a new linguistic and cultural hegemony—in this case, English-speaking Americanness. Billy internalizes this requirement to become American and demands that his Korean adoptive brother abandon his Korean language and desire for Korean food as well. This scene reveals the anxiety and oppression that "good" Korean adoptees might feel for a "successful" belonging in their adoptive environment. The banishment of Billy and Gabe's mother tongue reflects the invisible authority working to reshape them from Korean orphans into "model" American adopted children. In other words, this scene presenting Billy and Gabe's compulsion to belong underscores how the assimilationist ideology of adoption requires the erasure of the child's name, language, and memories, and transformation into a trouble-free, docile American adoptee.[51]

According to Sharp, his goal for *Middle Brother* was to have the audience gain an understanding of "what it's like to be separated from your flesh and blood when that's not your choice" and to give voice to "this feeling of confusion that adoptees have when they go back to Korea," where they are constantly reminded every day that they do not belong there.[52] Foregrounding this sense of confusion for adoptees on their way back to Korea, in a dream sequence set on a Korean Air flight, Billy and Gabe's bodies become an exhibition of discipline as they comply with the Korean flight attendants' specific instructions on being accepted as returnees. Sporting Korean Air flight attendant outfits and impeccable manners, the two flight attendants "extend a special greeting to Billy and Gabe" on behalf of the captain.[53] While Billy and Gabe talk to each other, the attendants perform a "ritual dance in lieu of going through the various safety features verbally."[54] The two women then interrupt Billy and Gabe to give them special instructions for when they meet their biological family members in Korea:

51. Pate, *From Orphan to Adoptee*, 145.
52. Sharp, interview with the author, Minneapolis, May 19, 2015.
53. Sharp, *Middle Brother*, 51.
54. Sharp, 52.

Your seat cushion can be used as a weapon to suffocate your family members. . . . Korean Airlines would like to remind you that Hanguk mal [Korean] is the official language of your home country. By speaking English, you are causing your ancestors pain. . . . In the unlikely event you know two shits about your culture, you would realize that your older brother should be referred to as hyung-nim as a sign of respect.[55]

The attendants then take hold of Billy and, in a dancelike ritual, give him more special instructions for when he reunites with his biological father: "When the abbeoji [father] light is illuminated, please bow in that very specific way that you were never taught to bow. Helpful hint: If you think you're low enough to the ground—go even lower."[56] One of the attendants physically forces Billy to bow almost to the ground. "It is against Korean federal regulations to drink soju in front of your abbeoji. Please turn you [sic] red face away while getting drunk with family members."[57] The two attendants use their hands to force Billy's face away. This choreographed movement, coercing and controlling Billy's body to abide by Korean cultural standards he is unfamiliar with, embodies his apprehension about reuniting with his biological family, acclimatizing to Korean hierarchical structures, and learning to follow the regulatory social codes of his birth land. Eleana Kim points out that many adoptees who think about returning to Korea experience anguish due to the "fear of experiencing a second rejection."[58] In this sense, the ritual dance with the flight attendants is a somatic expression of Billy's fear of possible rejection and failure to become a "good"—properly Koreanized—returnee in time for his reunion with his biological family.

Whereas Billy did successfully adapt to his adoptive culture, *Middle Brother* makes it clear that this accomplishment is disadvantageous in Korea, where re-Koreanization in the form of acculturation through the Korean language becomes an insurmountable obstacle. In a Korean market scene, chorus members playing street vendors tell Billy that he is not blending in because, having lived in Korea for more than one year, he still does not know how to "even make one sentence in Korean."[59] Beyond this mockery, Billy's inability to communicate and assimilate comes to a distressing consequence toward the end of the play. The Queen of the Joseon Dynasty tells him that he can only take the throne if he is able to recount the entire tale of his journey, but

---

55. Sharp, 51–53.
56. Sharp, 54.
57. Sharp, 54.
58. E. J. Kim, *Adopted Territory*, 186.
59. Sharp, *Middle Brother*, 28.

Billy is unable to because he cannot speak Korean. Billy, whose self-discipline helped him learn English as a "good" adopted child, has failed to retain his birth country's language and loses his proper lineage in the Korean royal family. As Billy is deprived of his rights to the throne in the imagined royal court setting, another punishment is inflicted on him in the present when his biological brother, Young-Nam, refuses to talk to him about the past. Billy says to his brother, "I don't get it, Hyung. We spent all this time catching up with abbeoji [father], but the past is still off limits. When can I ask the big questions?"[60] Young-Nam answers, "There are things I can only tell you when we speak the same language."[61] As long as language is considered a marker of authenticity,[62] Billy's deficiency in the Korean language causes him to lose his "authentic" Koreanness, leading him to feel excluded from his birth family and, most importantly, be deprived of access to memories and the truth. Both scenes show how the actions of disciplining and punishing through language demarcate adoptees' sense of belonging. Thus, Billy's censored body and lost language actualize the contentious biopolitics of (un)making belonging, in the acts of inscribing him as a "good" de-Koreanized and re-Koreanized adoptee.

The postponed answers to Billy's questions about his past also connect to sociopolitical inquiry into the prevailing silence about transnational adoption in Korea. As he tries to understand why he was separated from his brother as a child, hoping to find a sense of justice, Billy's frustration and anguish grow. When he reunites with his biological brother in Korea for the first time, he asks, "Why didn't you look for me?"[63] At the end of a flashback scene, in which Young-Nam is found in a hospital following an accident and transported to a home for boys, Billy asks the chorus, "Why didn't our parents look for him?"[64] And in a scene set during the fictional Joseon period, when the royal court characters realize the older brother is missing, Billy, physically present but imperceptible to others, an invisible witness, yells, "Why didn't you look for him? . . . He's in Saint Andrew Kim's Boys Home. It's just one town over. Why didn't you look for him? Why didn't you look for me?"[65] This recurring questioning that punctuates the main time periods depicted in the play invites the audience members to contemplate Korea's lack of a social safety net for children. Why did Korean society so readily accept the relinquishment of lost children, like Billy and Young-Nam, to orphanages for

---

60. Sharp, 55.
61. Sharp, 55.
62. Lo and Kim, "Manufacturing Citizenship."
63. Sharp, *Middle Brother*, 31.
64. Sharp, 37.
65. Sharp, 40.

possible transnational adoption? This practice went largely unchallenged in the 1980s, the period during which Billy and Young-Nam went missing. The repeated questions serve as poignant prompts for audience members about the children who were lost during the peak of transnational adoption from Korea to the United States in that decade, as well as the tacit approval of the nations involved. Billy's repetition of the questions, which come to sound like demands for belated justice, creates a sense of urgency in the audience. Every piece of information he uncovers moves him one step closer to reconstructing the puzzle of his childhood. Each new discovery, however, also adds to his sense of loss and injustice. Sara Ahmed emphasizes that "justice involves feelings, which move us across the surfaces of the world, creating ripples in the intimate contours of our lives. Where we go, with these feelings, remains an open question."[66] At the end of the play, Young-Nam tells Billy that none of their family members ever told him that Billy had been relinquished and that they destroyed all traces of him: "All your pictures. All your clothes. Vanished."[67] The play's ending offers no satisfying answers to Billy's questions about his past, and no sense of justice is achieved. The lingering feelings of injustice and uncertainty leave audiences with open questions and the need to challenge the silence forced upon Billy and by extension other adoptees when they search and reunite with their birth families.

The "Bad" Adoptee in *In My Heart: The Adoption Play Project* (2016)

Conceived, compiled, and directed by Leah Cooper and Alan Berks, *In My Heart* was produced by the Minneapolis-based Wonderlust Productions, a theater company specializing in telling community stories through performance.[68] This full-length play, accompanied by songs and choreography, was created in collaboration with over 450 members of the Minnesota adoption community and premiered in 2016.[69] The project brought together adoptees,

---

66. Ahmed, *Cultural Politics of Emotion*, 202.
67. Sharp, *Middle Brother*, 68.
68. See "Mission," Wonderlust Productions. Other community projects created by Wonderlust include *The Veterans Play Project* (2013), culled from stories of more than one hundred military veterans in Minnesota, and *The Labyrinth and the Minotaur: The Incarceration Play Project* (2020), inspired by stories from Minnesota's incarceration community on both sides of the prison system. The analysis of *In My Heart* is based on the 2016 videotaped performance as well as the unpublished script provided by Leah Cooper. The graphic novel version of *In My Heart: The Adoption Story Project* was published in 2021.
69. Cover page of Cooper and Berks, *In My Heart*.

adoptive parents, birth parents, foster families, and social workers using their own words, recorded and transcribed, to formulate a playscript.[70] Cooper and Berks developed the play over two years, ensuring an inclusive process by asking participants open-ended questions and having them take part in workshops, story circles, improvisations, and staged readings. The play's involvement with the community created what Charlotte McIvor calls an "active citizenship," accentuating "community engagement as a necessary feature of dealing with increased ethnic and cultural diversity."[71] Diversity seemed to be first and foremost on the minds of Cooper and Berks as they incorporated characters based on interviews and research concerning the experiences of teenagers, adults, and senior citizens from the Korean American, Native American, and African American adoption communities, among others.[72] With *In My Heart*'s multiracial and multigenerational cast of performers, musicians, technical crew, and administrative team, all exercising their active citizenship in the adoption community, Cooper and Berks aimed to create a broader picture of adoption.[73]

In My Heart is set and performed in an actual banquet room where audience members assume the roles of guests at an engagement party for Alice and her fiancé Lewis. In the 2016 production, spectators sitting at dining tables shared the space with actors performing around and among them. Nonprofessional actors (members of the adoption community) performed most of the roles alongside five professional actors. Musicians on a platform both performed as the story's engagement party band and provided the play's musical accompaniment.[74] The story follows the narrative of *Alice in Wonderland* but changes the premise to tell the story of Alice as a white adoptee in a family where tensions arise when Alice's Korean adoptive sister Jennifer (abbreviated to Jen in the script) shows up after a long stay in Korea. After Alice and Jennifer drink a beverage given to them by a waitress who represents the White Rabbit with the power to "help people find their origins,"[75] they journey together through a magical world. During their dreamlike voyage, Alice and Jennifer encounter various figures from Lewis Carroll's story, including the Duchess, the Gryphon, the Mock Turtle, the Queen of Hearts, the Dor-

---

70. Cooper, interview with the author, Minneapolis, November 21, 2018.
71. McIvor, "Community Theatre as Active Citizenship," 185–86.
72. Although Cooper and Berks are not Korean adoptees (Cooper is adopted), *In My Heart* features a Korean adoptee character based on their research, interviews, and workshops with Korean adoptees in Minnesota.
73. Espeland, "Poignant 'Adoption Play Project' Is a Labor of Love."
74. Note: although *In My Heart* is a play with music, it is not a musical per se.
75. Cooper and Berks, *In My Heart*, 26.

mouse, the Cheshire Cat, and the Caterpillar. Additionally, they meet adoptees, adoptive and birth parents, social workers, policymakers, politicians, philanthropists, bureaucrats, priests, and various other characters. Thus, the play introduces diverse perspectives on adoption practices from characters with differing and often conflicting positions on racial, gender, and sexual issues and policies as well as birth search. Traveling through this not-such-a-Wonderland with its cacophony of voices and adoption stories, Alice and Jennifer come to realize the complexities of domestic and international adoption in and out of the United States and the differences between them as adopted persons and adoptive sisters.

At the beginning of the play, disparities over adoption narratives emerge among "real" characters in the engagement party setting. During the reception, Eddie (Alice and Jennifer's uncle) and Sue (Lewis's sister), a state legislator, discuss the subject of open and closed adoption records. Eddie tells Sue that he would like to find Alice's birth mother to tell her how much they all love her for having relinquished Alice because she has brought so much joy to their lives. Sue responds that perhaps Alice's birth mother does not want to be found and that adoption records are purposely closed to protect a woman's privacy. Eddie believes adoption records should be open and that Alice's birth mother should know what a wonderful person Alice has become. The issue of access to adoption records, on which the scene centers, has long been and still is a source of debate and division in adoption communities in the United States. The subject has become all the more complex as different values and criteria have been put into law by states across the country.[76] The issue is addressed again from Alice's and Jennifer's perspectives in the second act of the play in a debate over what are the best interests of a child. As a subject matter, the issue of access to adoption records becomes more crucial to the play, as it sets up the conflict between the two sisters, foregrounds the trope of the "good" versus the "bad" adoptee, and propels the story forward.

Act 2 opens in the same banquet room setting, now transformed into a fantasy world with wild and disorderly vegetation resembling a jungle. The band members are semidressed as Gryphons and Mock Turtles. Alice and

---

76. For more information, see Wegar, *Adoption, Identity, and Kinship*, 30–32; Carp, *Jean Paton*; Herman, *Kinship by Design*; Creagh, "Science, Social Work, and Bureaucracy"; and Leighton, "Being Adopted and Being a Philosopher." Novy makes an interesting connection between the open/closed adoption record question and theater by writing about Edward Albee, an adoptee actively involved in the adoptee rights movement, who featured adoption in his early play, *The American Dream* (1960). According to Novy, Albee gave a keynote address in 1995 at the Congress for Equal Rights in Adoption annual gathering, speaking in favor of open adoption records. Novy, *Reading Adoption*, 159, 180.

Jennifer, who have both drunk the magic potion from the White Rabbit, enter holding hands. They see three Bureaucrat characters dressed in playing card-patterned suits doing some form of paperwork, which involves switching and painting flowers. The Bureaucrats tell Jennifer and Alice that these are the rules of the game set by the Queen of Hearts, who desires harmony, happy families, and flowers. The White Rabbit then enters and introduces the game: "Find the child a home. We call it 'Best Interests.'"[77] "In the best interests of the child" is a phrase often mentioned in the field of adoption. The United Nations repeatedly used that phrase during its 1989 Convention on the Rights of the Child to set rules for the protection of children through social and legal principles.[78] From the convention's discussion of the topic of adoption, however, leading activist Jean Paton responded that this phrase was "a manual to deprive poor families of their children."[79] As part of this "Best Interests" game in the play, a lengthy overview of US adoption history from the 1850s to the present is given by the White Rabbit, the Philanthropist, the Social Workers, the Bureaucrats, a Priest, the Cheshire Cat portraying an Academic and a Scientist, and a couple from the 1950s. The characters' discussion topics include the inception of orphanages as part of a social control apparatus in the 1850s and the involvement of adoption practices in slavery and the genocide of Native American people. The story moves chronologically from the 1950s to the 1980s, addressing issues concerning culture keeping, reproductive rights, and the institutionalization of transnational adoption from Asia, Latin America, and Eastern Europe, all presented with informative dialogue. This educational section is reminiscent of Bertolt Brecht's *Lehrstücke* (learning-plays), the series of plays he wrote from the late 1920s to the mid-1930s. In its intent to "instruct" audiences about adoption history, *In My Heart* shares Brecht's idea that the task of the learning-play "is to show the world as it changes (and also how it may be changed)."[80]

The question of a child's "best interests," however, is left unresolved in the play. When the history lesson reaches the present day, Jennifer interrupts and demands to see her birth records, but the Social Worker refuses to give a straight answer:

> JEN: I'm just asking whether you are looking at my records?
> SOCIAL WORKER (obviously holding file): I might be.

---

77. Cooper and Berks, *In My Heart*, 61.
78. UN Convention on the Rights of the Child.
79. Paton, cited by Carp, *Jean Paton*, 297.
80. Brecht, *Brecht on Theatre*, 79.

> JEN: So you know who my birth parents are?
>
> SOCIAL WORKER: I might.
>
> JEN: Well don't you think it's just wrong for you to know more about me than I do?
>
> SOCIAL WORKER: We didn't know who you'd turn out to be when we made the rules. But believe me, when I tell you, sincerely, we've always tried to figure out your best interests.[81]

The dispute over the accessibility of birth records in this dramatization serves not only to reveal the history of adoption in the United States but also to show how this history endures and continues to silence adoptees and deny their right to access their birth and adoption records. As the scene continues, Jennifer's insistence on seeing her birth records triggers havoc in Wonderland. The other characters refuse Jennifer's demands and become frantic in their determination to prove that closed adoption records are in a child's best interests. The theatrical foregrounding of the historical and ongoing debate about open versus closed adoption records in *In My Heart* exposes the tensions and anxieties surrounding this discourse, in which there are no simple, straightforward answers that perfectly work for both sides. The disparate views and factional conflicts among participants in the debate serve to deromanticize the idea of a unified adoption community.

In My Heart mainly depicts a division between the two adoptive siblings: Jennifer, who wants access to her birth records, and Alice, who repeatedly asserts that she does not wish to know about her birth parents. In a prelude, the play introduces Jennifer's quest for her birth mother. On the darkened stage, Jennifer's voice is heard saying, "Do you know me?"[82] A character described in the script as "Old Woman" answers Jennifer in Korean, asking if she speaks Korean. When Jennifer answers, "I'm Jen. I think my mother named me Yu-jin," the woman replies, "Choe-song-ham-ni-da. Mot A-ra-deut-get-sseum-nee-da. [I'm sorry. I don't understand]."[83] When Jennifer asks in English whether the Old Woman is her mother, there is only silence. Jennifer's adoptive mother, Rebecca, then says, "I'm your mother, Jen. I raised you," but Jennifer does not answer her.[84] This short exchange introduces Jennifer's side of her adoption story and longing for her birth mother, a source of conflict with her adoptive mother, as well as the trope of the "bad" adoptee

---

81. Cooper and Berks, *In My Heart*, 75.
82. Cooper and Berks, 3.
83. Cooper and Berks, 3–4.
84. Cooper and Berks, 4.

explored through the characterization of Jennifer. The play portrays the adoptive sisters in antithetical terms, depicting Jennifer as an angry and upsetting "bad" adoptee whose sense of unbelonging in her adoptive environment compels her to seek and demand knowledge of her origins. Jennifer's actions stand in sharp contrast to those of her adoptive sister Alice, the "good" adoptee, whose secure trust in her adoptive parents makes her uninterested in learning about her past and origins—until the climax when an unexpected reunion is thrust upon her.

Early in the play, with the engagement party beginning, Jennifer arrives from Korea after a two-year absence and proceeds to openly express her bitterness about her life as an adoptee. Overhearing her, Lewis's parents, Beth and Frank, who were not aware that Jennifer was adopted, interrupt with insensitive remarks: "She doesn't look like any of you." "So you're not her real mother." "You're Korean."[85] Jennifer corrects them, "I'm sorry you're confused. Imagine how I feel. In Korea, I'm American. But here—Thank you so much, Mom and Dad for raising me to be the example of the Other everywhere I go."[86] Frank, thinking he is being polite but actually unknowingly condescending, bows to Jennifer and speaks to her slowly, as though to a non-English-speaking Asian person (while also incorrectly saying her name), "Nice to meet you, Kim. We're glad you could make it to your adopted sister's engagement. How do they say 'Congratulations' in Korean?"[87] Beth also exhibits her (un)conscious biases as she matter-of-factly remarks that Jennifer has "different vocal cords because she's Korean."[88] Jennifer's encounters with this type of racism while growing up in North America have intensified her sense of being othered and forged her into the rebellious person she is, angry at people's ignorance and the privilege of white Americans who blatantly categorize other races. Jennifer's anger also derives from having been lied to about her birth mother—it is said she was a prostitute, although Jennifer finds no one who can corroborate this during her time in Korea. As Frank continues to speak ignorantly and insensitively, Jennifer lets out her feelings of resentment toward her adoptive parents until Frank intervenes:

> FRANK: OK now OK. I'm sure you're a wonderful family to adopt two beautiful girls.

---

85. Cooper and Berks, 13.
86. Cooper and Berks, 13.
87. Cooper and Berks, 14.
88. Cooper and Berks, 14.

JEN: They bought us at the baby store. Don't act like they're Mother Theresa. They couldn't have a kid, so they got us instead.

ALICE: Why do you always have to be so mean, Jen?

JEN: Why do you always have to be so nice? Alice got nice people genes, but my third world birth family, well—

REBECCA: You looked for them?

JEN: What do you think I was doing in Korea for two years?

REBECCA: You already have a Mom and Dad.

JEN: Who lied to me about where I come from. . . .

REBECCA: What do you mean? We told you what we were told. We would never lie—

DAVID: Please, Jen, this is not the best time for this conversation. You see how much pain you're causing your mother.

JEN: Sorry! I forgot. Only happy stories in our house.[89]

Jennifer's position unravels the perception of adoption normalized as an act of salvation from an unbearable Korean motherhood leading to a dependably happy North American family-making ideal. Moreover, Jennifer's angry dialogue points to McKee's observation that "adoptees routinely discuss how their families failed to protect them from racism and racial microaggressions in their extended families and local communities. . . . Their testimonies expose the limits to color-blind thinking and the speciousness of multiculturalist idealism."[90] As the angry "bad" adoptee, Jennifer unwittingly fulfills her role as a disruptor of happiness. McKee takes her analysis of the "good" versus "bad" adoptee trope further by applying Ahmed's concept of the feminist killjoy to adoptees' affective experiences, wherein feminists "disturb the very fantasy that happiness can be found in certain places."[91] According to McKee, the notion of the feminist killjoy

> offers a lens to locate adoptees that fail to adhere to normative requirements of what it means to be a grateful adoptee. . . . In the eyes of mainstream society, ungrateful adoptees are failures—unfaithful betrayers of the nation for *failing and refusing to* embrace humanitarian narratives of adoption. Adoptees *kill* joy when they fail to adhere to the adoption fantasy—where adoptive parents save the orphan from poverty and degradation.[92]

---

89. Cooper and Berks, 15–16.
90. McKee, "From Adoptee to Trespasser," 151.
91. Ahmed, *The Promise of Happiness*, 66.
92. McKee, *Disrupting Kinship*, 11. Italics in original.

In *In My Heart,* Jennifer is depicted not only as an agitator who disrupts Alice and Lewis's wedding but also as a Korean adoptee killjoy who denounces the adoption fantasy of white America as the world's savior of children and maker of happy multicultural families.

The figure of the Korean adoptee killjoy stands in contrast to that which McKee conceptualizes as the "every adoptee," a kindly figure who does not challenge the adoption system, tends to be amenable to birth search and reunion, and maintains a strong bond with their adoptive family—in sum, a grateful and happy adoptee.[93] While the "every adoptee" is open to birth search and reunion in McKee's conceptualization, in my analysis of *In My Heart,* Alice, as the "every adoptee," must reject the idea and intent of birth search and reunion in order to remain loyal to her adoptive "forever family." The term "forever family" is used in the adoption industry to denote a relinquished child's final adoptive home. The term seems not only to guarantee an end to a child's recurring abandonment but also, as McKee points out, to express the happiness and gratefulness an adoptee should feel.[94] In *In My Heart,* Alice is portrayed as being eternally grateful to her forever family and rejects the idea of looking for her birth mother. Alice argues with Jennifer about birth search:

> ALICE: I don't want to think about all of this. I never thought about this before.
> JEN: I talk to you about it all the time.
> ALICE: Yes but I always thought of it as your problem, Jen, not mine.
> JEN: Awesome.
> ALICE: I didn't mean that the way it sounded. You have problems, Jen. I don't have problems. That doesn't sound right either. I'm the good adoptee, you're the ba—I don't know what's wrong with me.[95]

Alice's assertion that the desire to find one's birth mother is somehow not right, possibly even unethical, further distances Jennifer, whose need for her birth search is her "problem." Through her stance regarding birth search, Alice solidifies her image as the "good" adoptee. Noting the significance of the "good" and "bad" adoptee trope, Eli Park Sorensen observes that adoptees who wonder about their home nation or birth family or express interest in them, let alone lament the loss of their biological parents, potentially raise "subversive questions of loyalty and authentic belonging."[96] Earlier in the

---

93. McKee, 11–12.
94. McKee, 13.
95. Cooper and Berks, *In My Heart,* 78.
96. Sorensen, "Korean Adoption Literature and the Politics of Representation," 163.

play, when the White Rabbit tells Alice that it helps people find their origins, Alice replies that searching for her birth family "would kill my mother. The mother who raised me."[97] Although she considers the White Rabbit's offer, Alice remains indecisive and even apprehensive about trying to find her origins and birth mother. Her dread of being seen to be disloyal and her feelings of guilt far outweigh her unexplored birth search curiosity. Alice's reunion with her birth mother only happens in the Wonderland fantasy sequence at the end of the play, and not by her own doing—suggesting that she does not "betray" her forever family and remains faithful to her adoptive parents by prioritizing their happiness.

In contrast to Alice, Jennifer actively attempts to find her birth family, spending two years in Korea engaged in the search. In the Wonderland sequence, when the Queen of Hearts orders Alice and Jennifer to resolve their dispute, Jennifer insists on putting adoption on trial. At the trial, the White Rabbit describes the two adoptees as the victims and their adoptive parents as the accused. Appearing before the court, David gives an emotional testimony, asking, "Why were we being punished when all we wanted to do was build a loving family, to make a loving home?"[98] When other adoptive parents also voice similar feelings, Jennifer counters by telling Alice, "They shouldn't have adopted these children, Alice. They stole us from poor people."[99] Jennifer's accusation of theft, which evokes the disturbing fact of transnational adoption's dependence on the commodification of children enabled by unbalanced power dynamics, confirms her characterization as the adoptee killjoy.[100] However, Alice and Jennifer's adoptive parents' altruistic intentions and acts of love complicate matters through what Kit Myers calls "the violence of love."[101] Analyzing adoptive parents' statements about adoption and love, Myers observes an "'unmarked' symbolic violence that occurs in the process of making the transnational/racial adoptive family legible and how this violence *can be* produced by statements and acts of love."[102] Myers considers symbolic violence any declaration that tries to firmly and narrowly define the composition of an adoptive family as "real."[103] Despite hearing her adoptive parents' declarations of their good intentions, Jennifer remains belligerently adamant about

---

97. Cooper and Berks, *In My Heart*, 27.
98. Cooper and Berks, 82.
99. Cooper and Berks, 83.
100. McKee has called this commodification of children a "neoliberal pro-adoption regime that facilitates the actual buying and selling of children." McKee, *Disrupting Kinship*, 10.
101. Myers, "'Real Families,'" 176.
102. Myers, 176. Italics in original.
103. Myers, 176.

the hidden symbolic violence behind the façade of adoption as an act of love. Making her position clear, she points out that adoptive parents have the privilege of choice regarding their "real" family while adoptees do not. Jennifer's contentious attitude and harsh criticisms of adoption are not simply expressions of an adoptee's short-lived anger but an adoptee killjoy's fundamental unsettling of the adoption fantasy. As an adoptee killjoy, Jennifer takes on the leading role of disruptor of the "good" adoptee narrative that promises concrete and complete belonging. Moreover, through the events and revelations of the trial, Jennifer becomes the impetus for Alice's change of mind, as she comes to agree that adoptees deserve to know all sides of their adoption stories, even if the knowledge is potentially painful.

While the play's presentation of Jennifer as an embodiment of the Korean adoptee killjoy makes a significant point, its antithetical portrayal of the two adoptees can be seen to gloss over the nuances of what it means to be an adopted person. In particular, the depiction of Jennifer as an angry adoptee situated firmly in the dichotomous trope of "good" versus "bad" adoptee implies a moral judgment of her as "bad," an unbelonging troublemaker, dismissing her character's potential complexities. Toward the end of the play, the "good" and "bad" adoptee trope reappears when the Queen of Hearts announces her guilty verdict against the adoptive parents, followed by the sentence, "Off with their heads!"[104] Alice then intervenes as their protector, saying, "You can't judge these people. . . . I don't believe it. You are not thieves. You are not selfish. Or cowards. And we're not ungrateful or victims."[105] Conversely, Jennifer agrees with the judgment, confirming her role as the "bad" adoptee, ready to punish her adoptive parents. Although the dichotomy of "good" versus "bad" may be perceived as an axis on which a broad spectrum of adoptees can be represented, within a narrative structure—such as that employed here, where Jen is portrayed as a villain consumed by bitterness—it might encourage a reductionist assessment. At this point, as the Queen of Hearts decides to hear a final witness testimony, Alice's birth mother is forced to appear in court. The dire consequence of Alice's birth mother's appearance in court is the disclosure of sealed adoption records without her consent. Distraught at having been summoned against her will, she harshly reports the truth—that she was raped, and that the trauma of the experience made her decide to relinquish Alice. Alice's birth mother also declares her firm rejection of any possibility of a relationship with Alice. This startling revelation underscores Sue's earlier statement about closed adoption records' function of safeguarding a birth

---

104. Cooper and Berks, *In My Heart*, 83.
105. Cooper and Berks, 89.

mother's right to privacy. The posttraumatic stress resulting from such a brutal experience places an enormous psychological burden on a mother, particularly when compounded by the distress of relinquishing a child at birth. Alice is confronted by this painful truth because of "bad" adoptee Jennifer's belief in the necessity of birth search and her demand for open adoption records. In this sense, Jennifer is "sentenced" to play the role of the "bad" adoptee at the trial, rather than consciously and conscientiously choosing to embody the "badness" of an adoptee killjoy in order to represent a resistance to the narrow vision in which adoption has been viewed and delineated. While the inclusion of Korean adoptee characters in adoption community stories might increase Korean adoptee representation, it should not lessen the perceptively profound characterizations that are crucial to move audience members to ponder more nuanced ideas of what it means to be a Korean adoptee. In this analysis, I do not intend to discount the effort and energy community-based theaters put into the consideration of what it means to be part of an adoption community. It is challenging to produce work that both involves the entire community and innovatively represents it. Yet I would point out that it is important to recognize the thoughtful and thought-provoking ways in which Korean adoptees can be characterized in proximity with other racial and ethnic subjects. In this way, a more comprehensive depiction of Korean adoptees' humanity can be presented as part of a holistic picture of an adoption community.

In contrast to the feelings of uncertainty with which the ending of *Middle Brother* leaves its audience, *In My Heart* concludes differently. The ending of *In My Heart* occurs in the "real" world of Alice and Lewis's engagement party, where Jennifer and Rebecca come to a new shared understanding of their relationship. Jennifer, expressing her determination to continue searching for her birth mother in Korea, moves Rebecca to tears with her invitation for her to join the journey. The play closes on a joyful and hopeful mood, with Eddie making a toast expressing his gratitude for the fact that everyone, including Jennifer, is now present and happy. Jennifer, feeling accepted by Alice and Lewis, no longer holds any resentment against them or her parents, and Alice and Lewis each tell her, "You are in my heart. Welcome home."[106] The stage directions imply a happy-ever-after ending to this fairy-tale-like adoption story: "The WHITE RABBIT rushes on stage, and everyone freezes in a bug [sic] happy hugging tableau."[107] The play concludes with the White Rabbit speaking to the audience, repeating what Alice and Lewis told Jennifer: "You are in my heart. Welcome home."[108] Even though *In My Heart* attempts

---

106. Cooper and Berks, 103.
107. Cooper and Berks, 103.
108. Cooper and Berks, 104.

to achieve a balance of perspectives, the play's happy adoption dénouement falls into the trouble-free forever family trope, and the resolution it brings to Jennifer's sense of unbelonging and "bad" adoptee-ness feels hurried. The conclusion of *In My Heart* offers a momentary emotional suture to a divided adoption community, as the play seems to dream of seamless happiness and gratitude. Yet, after informing audiences about conflicts in the adoption community and adoption discourses within and beyond the United States, the play still seems to be needing a bold confrontation with its spectators about those contentions and divisions in the lives and relationships of adoptees and their families.

The "Good," "Bad," and "Strange" Adoptees in *Hello, My Name Is . . .* (2017)

Directed by Randy Baker and produced by Washington, DC–based playwrights' collective The Welders, Debra Kim Sivigny's immersive play *Hello, My Name Is . . .* had its world premiere in 2017, featuring Sivigny's own scenography.[109] *Hello, My Name Is . . .* was partly inspired by Sivigny's personal experience of using a post-adoption service agency in 2015 to search for her birth mother and biological family (to no avail).[110] The play follows, from childhood to adulthood, the dissimilar narratives of three Korean adoptees—Dana, June, and Bryan—whose life experiences in and outside the United States are shaped by their adoptions. Dana finds herself content with the affluent family that has taken her in; June, adopted by a Christian family, feels the need to learn about her birth mother; and Bryan, shuffled around foster homes, then finds out that his first adoptive family never legalized his status with US immigration authorities, which leads to his eventual deportation to Korea. Although Dana and Bryan feature prominently in the narrative, the story focuses more on June, from her arrival in her adoptive home at the age of six until as a young adult searching for her birth mother in Korea at the end of the play. While the play does not depict a typical search-and-reunion arc, all three characters are nevertheless shown to be emotionally and spiritually searching for their birth mothers. The outcome of their later search is illustrated toward the end of

---

109. The Welders' mission is to "establish an evolving, alternative platform for play development and production." See "Mission," the Welders, a Playwrights' Collective. In 2018 Sivigny received the Helen Hayes Award for Outstanding Set Design for the 2017 production of *Forgotten Kingdoms*. The analysis of *Hello, My Name Is . . .* is based on the 2017 videotaped performance as well as the unpublished script provided by the playwright.

110. Sivigny, interview with the author, Washington, DC, April 26, 2018.

the play in a scene set in Seoul, where all three adoptees find each other and discuss their failure to locate their birth families.

To tell the story of these three adoptees, Sivigny uses scenic design and visual language within an immersive performance space highlighting not only how these elements *perform* but also how they establish connections with human bodies and their actions.[111] In 2019 Sivigny's performance design for *Hello, My Name Is* . . . was selected as a US representative for the 14th Prague Quadrennial of Performance Design and Space (PQ), sponsored and organized by the Czech Republic Ministry of Culture and the Arts and Theatre Institute.[112] That Sivigny's work was selected for this event, the world's largest in the field of scenography, is significant, as it illustrates how adoption has become part of the transformational American landscape. Ten photos of Sivigny's design for *Hello, My Name Is* . . . were displayed, along with her statement regarding her personal upbringing, educational background, and research and design interests. In her statement, Sivigny wrote:

> My worldview grew from international travel and exploring the interplay between East and West. I wanted to reconcile my identities, and the Koreanness that I didn't acknowledge as a child. Growing up in a relatively racial vacuum, despite having Chinese influence, delayed my desire to seek out my origin story. I have never felt fully Korean, but I have also had trouble embracing an "American" identity in a nation that doesn't always embrace its immigrants. *Hello, My Name Is* . . . is a piece that explores the meaning of home and placemaking for those who feel caught in between worlds.[113]

Sivigny fittingly used her knowledge of stage design to imaginatively represent the "in-between worlds" the three main adoptee characters of her play inhabit. Sivigny says that she chose the immersive theater genre for her play in order to tell the story in "an altered space . . . creating an experience that immerses you with using all five senses."[114] Josephine Machon sees immersive theater as a diverse range of performance practices prioritizing human contact,[115] while Rose Biggin views the "immersive experience in relation to environment and space [. . . in which] the state of *immersion* exists in negotiation between the

---

111. Sivigny, interview. Emphasis added.
112. The 2019 Prague Quadrennial of Performance Design and Space Program (PQ) describes itself as "the largest international exhibition and festival event dedicated to scenography, performance design, and theatre architectures." *Prague Quadrennial of Performance Design and Space Program*, 5, 13.
113. Onsite exhibition description.
114. Sivigny, interview. Also see Sivigny, *Hello, My Name Is* . . . , 1.
115. Machon, *Immersive Theatres*, xvi.

found setting (the original building or site) and the designed set (the design, mise-en-scene, etc., created and installed by the artists)."[116] Acknowledging immersive theater's capacity to mediate between human interactions, space, and environment, for Sivigny's *Hello, My Name Is . . .* , I interpret immersive theater be a theatrical form in which audiences encounter a multilayered sensorial assemblage of private and public spaces wherein adoptee characters' life experiences, including adopted childhood and birth search, unfold. To create an all-encompassing immersive sensory experience, Sivigny's company rented an empty house in the Takoma neighborhood of Washington, DC, where audience members were led in and out of rooms by an actress playing the character of June's aunt. In the context of the play, the three adoptee characters' embodied experiences of transnational adoption and their settings merged in this one house. The settings included the characters' rooms in their US adoptive homes and other spaces, such as an airplane heading to Korea and a restaurant in Korea. Transported to different times and spaces in the characters' lives, audience members engaged in varying sensory experiences, such as partaking in food and drink, listening to music at a wedding party, and smelling burning incense in a Korean shaman's chamber, thus gaining individual and collective experiences through well-calculated mobile and sensorial interactions in this immersive setting. Hence, the house functioned as a rhizomatic space, in which the relationships, emotions, and memories of the three adoptee characters intertwined, allowing audience members to experience the spatial and sensorial embeddedness of being Korean transnational adoptees.

In terms of the play's story, the unique space of *Hello, My Name Is . . .* is filled with an extrasensory spirituality through the presence of June's two mothers: her birth mother in Korea and her adoptive mother in the United States. Interestingly, June's adoptive mother is never seen, only mentioned a few times by the aunt. Her presence, however, is felt through the house's set decor. At the beginning of the play, June's adoptive aunt greets the audience members as though they have arrived to welcome the six-year-old June to the United States. The audience enters the adoptive mother's house, which according to the script is decorated à la Laura Ashley but with a little more sophistication and also with "subtle hints of Christianity," while "Christian friendly" music can be heard playing.[117] These specific references to Christianity point to the connection between Korean transnational adoption and post–Korean War Christian Americanism, an evangelical movement with

---

116. Biggin, "Environment and Site-Specificity," 178. Italics in original.
117. Sivigny, *Hello, My Name Is . . .* , 3–4.

humanitarian savior beliefs.[118] Within this Christian domestic sphere, the otherworldly figure of June's Korean birth mother appears. Visible to audience members but not to June or the other characters, her birth mother, dressed in a traditional Korean outfit, silently moves around the space. Through her behavior, audiences understand that June's birth mother, in the form of her spirit, travels through time and space in the hope of connecting with her relinquished daughter in the world of the living. Toward the end of the play, the adult June in Korea, unable to find information about her mother from the adoption agency director, decides to consult a shaman.[119] The woman shaman channels June's mother, who tells June that she had to relinquish her because she was a single mother and was dying. Through casting, the otherworldly aspect of the play is further highlighted by the fact that the same actress plays the role of both the shaman and June's mother. Thanks to the shaman, June finally reunites with her deceased mother, though only spiritually channeled through the shaman.

June's birth mother's hovering is prominent throughout the play as she wanders around the young June, watching her but unable to speak to her. The distance and silence of June's birth mother, relegated to the state of a ghost, suggests the forfeited motherhood that haunts the world of adoptees, in which a mother figure exists but cannot interact with her relinquished child. Having entered her bedroom in her adoptive home for the first time, suitcase in hand, June takes a doll and curls up with it on the floor, then falls asleep crying. At this point, with dancelike movements, June's birth mother silently glides into the room, crouches next to June, and makes graceful soothing movements with her hand as if caressing her, until she stops crying. In the context of Korean transnational adoption, the invisibility of birth mothers reflects how their presence and rights have been discarded to the point where mothers become dead-to-others, a representation manifested in this play through the ghostly figure of June's birth mother.[120]

Jungyun Gill writes of an "unequal motherhood" forcefully imposed on birth mothers in Korea, where unwed single mothers have been stigmatized as "failed women," not abiding by a patriarchal society in which "a woman's reproductive activity should take place under the authority of her husband."[121] In the specterlike figure of June's birth mother, *Hello, My Name Is* . . . presents a character that is stigmatized by Korea's patriarchal society as a "failed" woman

---

118. Oh, *To Save the Children*, 79.
119. C. Kim, *Korean Shamanism*; and Kendall, *Life and Hard Times of a Korean Shaman*.
120. For more on Korean birth mothers and their representations in Korean theater, see chapter 1.
121. Gill, *Unequal Motherhoods*, 138.

and therefore is represented as no longer human. Janice Radway reflects on the continuing haunting of the present by past social forces, the ghosts that "tie present subjects to past histories."[122] In the play, the birth mother's yearning ties the domestic and the public, the tangible and the intangible, and the physical and the metaphysical. These distinctions merge in the birth mother's continuous, flowing movement, evincing her phantom motherhood while also moving forward her untold and still voiceless story. Furthermore, reclaiming the voices of mothers and reframing domesticity, Marilyn Francus introduces the concept of "spectral motherhood," which she defines in terms of mother characters who have been separated from their children by choice or through circumstances, haunting their children whether they (the mothers) are deceased or alive.[123] In this narrative of mothers' effacement, Francus sees a justification of domestic order that satisfies requirements for the preservation of a patriarchal social order.[124] Within the context of the play, June's birth mother as a spectral figure keeps appearing to remain in June's life, rather than disappearing into oblivion. While the social order of adoption removes birth mothers, her embodiment of spectral motherhood in her relinquished daughter's life is an act of resistance to the erasure.

The play's scenic design also accentuates audience members' experience of the extrasensory elements in its immersive spatial arrangement. For instance, in a scene set in the Seoul adoption director's office, spectators see the dramatic action taking place in the room through a sheer curtain. At one point in the scene, June's birth mother enters the room in Seoul and then passes through the curtain to the adoptive mother's living room in the United States, where everyone waits for June's arrival. The curtain creates a distancing effect between the audience and the birth mother character, rendering her presence all the more elusive, while also positioning audience members as ghostly figures to her life as a spirit, a condition they then share as they, too, pass through time and space into the next room. Moreover, the immersive element of the production brings audience members into close proximity with the performers, allowing an intimate as well as voyeuristic experience. For example, audience members are ushered into each adoptee character's small bedroom. They then watch the adoptees act out some private moment, invading their privacy without being acknowledged. The audience's proximity to the dramatic action in this unusual theatrical space permits audience members to become part of the story as observers and bystanders.

---

122. Radway, in the foreword to Gordon, *Ghostly Matters*, viii.
123. Francus, *Monstrous Motherhood*, 172.
124. Francus, 171, 200.

A significant portion of *Hello, My Name Is . . .* occurs with the audience situated in the three adoptee characters' rooms. As well as representing the adoptees' physical living spaces, these visually engaging spaces also illustrate the mindscapes and feelings of the three characters, their differing room designs identifying them respectively as "good," "bad," and "strange" adoptees. At first, Dana's room seems to have an atmosphere of happiness and affluence. Her bedroom, full of clothing and shoes, is described as "an overglorified walk-in closet" with mirrors and hangers and walls covered with "collages of the history of white Supermodel-pretty faces and bodies."[125] A wardrobe rack full of clothes stands in a corner while multicolored lights hang from the wall, on which the words "be grateful" can be read. Dana is the "good" adoptee, whose room illustrates her trouble-free assimilation into her adoptive family and seems to straightforwardly categorize her as firmly belonging to a happy adoptive environment. However, indications of an underlying uncertainty soon appear. At one point, Dana looks at herself in the mirror, and her mood darkens. Then she draws a traditional *hanbok* in a sketchbook and writes next to it: "Me?" This action suggests that she has started to wonder about her Korean origin, unsettling her seemingly assimilated self.

Bryan's foster home room appears twice in the play. The first of these scenes is set in 1995, indicated by a wall calendar. The script mentions that Bryan is a newly arrived twelve-year-old and that his bedroom has faded walls with spots, a faded rug, and an old painting. In the production, an old teddy bear and a small wooden hobbyhorse are the only objects pinned on the wall beside a coat rack. In the first scene, Bryan tries to write letters to his Korean mother, whom he cannot remember. The script describes "an overflowing trashcan across the room of crumpled attempts to write a letter."[126] The second time Bryan is shown in his room, he is twenty-four years old and still writing at his desk. The room is almost the same as before, except that now it is filled almost knee-deep with crumpled letters, rising to the lower level of Bryan's bunk bed and chair. The decrepit room, bare of personal objects, reveals not only Bryan's financial insecurity but also his lack of any meaningful attachments. Sitting at his desk, his back to the audience, Bryan writes yet another letter to his birth mother. Then he crumples up the letter and drops it on the pile, bangs his chair against his desk out of frustration, and collapses on his bed. The audience then hears a tape-recorded voice-over of Bryan reading a final letter to his birth mother before his deportation:

---

125. Sivigny, *Hello, My Name Is . . .* , 11.
126. Sivigny, 9.

Dear Omma,

For a long time growing up I hated you for sending me away, because nothing could be worse than where I grew up. I was thankful when my foster mother kicked me out when I was seventeen. I wanted nothing more than to be out of that hellhole of a home but I didn't know where else to go . . . So I tried punching my way out. I wanted to hurt people like they hurt me. I often wondered if you sent me away because I was a bad kid. That I deserved to be beaten and yelled at. Maybe that's what you thought I'd have in Korea too so anything could be better, right? I'm trying hard to understand that. I'm trying to write because this may be the last time I see U.S. soil. You may never even see this letter, but I feel like I have to write it now. Now or never. I am coming home. I'm being deported tomorrow. Will you be there to greet me?[127]

When the voice-over ends, Bryan digs deep into the piles of papers and lifts out a suitcase, into which he puts the letter and nothing else. He then sits on his chair facing the audience, his suitcase at his side, stares down, and turns off the light. Bryan represents the "bad" adoptee, who has failed to assimilate and remains attached (emotionally and imaginatively) to his birth mother. He is a troubled figure whose state of mind is illustrated by the piles of crumpled, unsent letters that surround him, filled with his disappointments, life struggles, and unresolved feelings about his past. According to Sivigny, the character of Bryan was inspired by the true story of a Korean American deportee she met in Seoul.[128] By basing the character of Bryan on the lived experience of an adoptee's unbelonging, Sivigny brings forth a sociopolitical message about deportation of transnational adoptees, which is seldom discussed.[129] As such, Bryan's "bad" adoptee-ness becomes associated with affective and institutional failure to ensure adoptees' belonging, leading finally to his physical removal from his adoptive country.

In contrast to Dana's and Bryan's rooms, which contain life-sized props, June's bedroom is decorated with oversized objects, including a bed with

---

127. Sivigny, 19. Ellipsis in original.
128. Sivigny, interview.
129. A 2015 *New York Times Magazine* article reported that "at least three dozen international adoptees had faced deportation charges or had been deported." Jones, "Adam Crapser's Bizarre Deportation Odyssey"; and Choe, "Deportation a 'Death Sentence.'" Moreover, a 2017 *Korea Times* article cites a Korean politician who stated that, out of "111,148 ethnic Koreans legally adopted into American families, 14,189, or 12.8 percent, have failed to obtain American citizenship and are left vulnerable to deportation." H. J. Kim, "14,189 Korean-Born Adoptees in US Undocumented." For more on Korean transnational adoptees' experience of deportation, see Laybourn, *Out of Place*, 77–110.

plush toys, a set of drawers, and dolls on shelves, which are all "white, blond, blue eyed."[130] Every object is tagged with its English name—but, as described in the stage directions, written in totally unreadable skewed "mashed up Roman/Hangul letters."[131] June's room signifies her confusion and estrangement regarding language, culture, and identity as a child brought from Korea to a new and overwhelming environment. The strangeness surrounding June is primarily captured by the oversized prints on the bed's quilt and the window curtains, which make her seem even smaller than she actually is and thus more vulnerable. Sivigny's stage directions for June's room specify: "what we would normally see as inviting and warm is foreign and threatening to her. . . . There is too much contrast. There are too many shadows."[132] The spatial bewilderment that enwraps both June's mind and her body is further accentuated when she takes from her suitcase objects that look small compared with the oversized items in her room, including a *hanbok* for children, little shoes, and a photocopied Korean tour brochure, a symbol of her past traces and future plans. By using the set design and stage props in this fashion, Sivigny depicts June's belonging as undefined and unfamiliar. June visibly does not fit in her room but rather seems to belong somewhere in between the oversized space of her present and the smaller world of her past contained in her suitcase.

In Sivigny's immersive theater production, audience members are ushered into domestic/public spheres where objects take on a symbolic life of their own and perform in conjunction with the actors to reveal the innermost lives of the adoptee characters. This visual language provides clues pointing to the three characters' respective nuanced and atmospheric delineations as "good," "bad," and "strange" adoptees. The varied settings within the house enable audiences to contextualize the three adoptees' different experiences of displacement and belonging, whether (un)settling in with their adoptive families, returning to Korea, or searching for their birth mothers and families.

Kinning Onstage and Offstage: A Theater of Care

While belonging may be something the main characters of all three plays discussed in this chapter search for, it is also something they realize they can create for themselves. Thus, the adoptee characters find themselves forming or re-forming kinship through constructions not limited to their adoptive or birth families. *Middle Brother, In My Heart,* and *Hello, My Name Is . . .*

---

130. Sivigny, *Hello, My Name Is . . .*, 7.
131. Sivigny, 7. *Hangul* is the Korean alphabet.
132. Sivigny, 7.

reimagine Korean adoptee kinship through the sharing of adoptees' search-and-reunion stories, and the ways in which their characters negotiate their adoptive and birth cultures, past and present, and reality and imagination. As previously mentioned in this chapter, Howell defines the concept of "kinning" as the method by which a person is accepted into a lasting kinship affinity with a set of people. Here, kinning is an act of performing kinship via theatrical representations and dramaturgical apparatus. It involves creating and exploring extended bonds and relationships through the lens of performance, using the tools and techniques of theater to bring these connections to life. This process allows participants and audiences to experience and understand kinship in fresh and profound ways, transcending "family" ties and highlighting the emotional and social dimensions of what family can mean. Through kinning, theater becomes a space where individuals can experiment with and redefine the meaning of kinship affinity, fostering a deeper sense of community and belonging. In this sense, my conceptualization of the term here extends beyond the narratives of the plays and their fictional characters to also encompass a theater's community-making process, which incorporates commitment from the theater company, performers/playwrights, and community members participating onstage and offstage.

The kinning practices that inform the works of Sharp, Cooper and Berks, and Sivigny allow their audiences to observe, engage with, and imagine adoptee kinship beyond birth and adoptive family boundaries, and beyond the stage and theater space itself. Whereas in all three plays, the senses of displacement and dissonance are prominently expressed by each of the Korean adoptee characters, when these voices come together, their impact is heightened, exemplifying the powers of connectivity and collectivity. Although these voices utilize different methods of kinning in their respective works—as in the medley of adoptee voice-overs at the ending of *Hello, My Name Is . . .* , or in the form of an Asian American production like Theater Mu's *Middle Brother*, or even in the convergence of content and form, as in *In My Heart*'s community-based piece bringing together different racial and ethnic groups—their shared strength engenders the theatrical communion of care. As the outcome of these kinnings, the productions examined in this chapter create what I call a "theater of care," indicating that in addition to bringing people together as artists and audiences, they allow caring to fulfill the determinative role of initiating a sense of belonging on both sides of the stage. It should be noted, however, that the theater of care does not simply celebrate adoptee audiences as well as general audiences as a singularly defined community with uniform reactions to theater productions. Rather, it recognizes and embraces the disparity and difference that might occur throughout the auditorium. Ultimately, while acknowledging diverse forms of responses, the three plays here align with the spirit of the theater of care in their commitment to strengthening an adoption community and adoptee kinship.

With *Middle Brother* and Minnesota's Twin City–based Theater Mu (hereafter Mu), the act of kinning between Asian America and Korean adoptees leaps off the stage and into the audience, functioning as a central force of the Midwest Asian American theater community. Due to its centralized adoption services network, Minnesota has been a geographical hub for Korean adoptees for several decades. In 2008 Kim Park Nelson notes that the number of Korean American adoptees in Minnesota was estimated at ten to fifteen thousand,[133] accounting for up to 50 percent of the state's Korean American population.[134] Park Nelson further expands on Minnesota's unique position:

> The practice of Korean adoption has become so normalized and commonplace that a viable and visible Korean adoptee community has developed along many different axes, including support for Korean adoptive families and children, adoptee-led networking and activism, journalism and publishing that privileges Korean adoption experiences, Korean adoptee artistic expression, participation by Korean adoptees in the Korean American community, and formal adoption research. I believe that this concentration of adoptees is the result of several historical, structural, and sociocultural factors that have worked in concert to make Minnesota an American homeland of sorts for Korean adoptees.[135]

The distinctive clustering of Korean adoptees in Minnesota has brought about a thriving artistic spirit and community, as evidenced by such theatrical productions as *Middle Brother* and *How to Be a Korean Woman* (chapter 2), which both premiered in Minneapolis. According to Sharp, Mu played an important role in creating *Middle Brother*: "we have a very special Midwestern Asian American aesthetic here that Mu is really responsible for, and I feel so thankful to them. . . . That's the community in terms of inspiration for how we worked on the play."[136]

Founded in 1992, Mu is the largest Asian American performing arts organization in the Midwest and is dedicated to narrating Asian American stories through artistic exploration and experimentation, engaging with equality and social justice. Noting how Korean adoptees have been omitted from the

---

133. Park Nelson, *Invisible Asians*, 101.
134. Park Nelson, 96.
135. Park Nelson, 101.
136. Sharp, interview.

history of Asian immigration, SunAh Laybourn states that an "appropriate corrective must also incorporate an inclusion of Korean adoptees in how we think about *contemporary* Asian American community and identity."[137] Within the context of Asian American theater-making, Mu is a notable exception to the omission of Korean adoptees from Asian American history and serves as a significant example of contemporary Asian America as a collective and cultural group. For more than thirty years, Mu has been producing theater pieces about Korean transnational adoption, from Rick Shiomi's *Mask Dance* (1993, 1995) and *Mask Dance 2* (1996) to Rick Shiomi and Sundraya Kase's *The Walleye Kid* (1998) and its musical adaptation (2005) and Katie Hae Leo's *Four Destinies* (2011).[138] *Mask Dance*, which is based on interviews with Korean adoptees, is of particular interest as it was one of the first plays about adoptee search-and-reunion stories produced by Mu. Moving away from the happy-reunion narrative, the play presents the return search trip to Korea as a significant factor in the willingness of adoptees to confront their past, even if the search results prove discouraging. Novy writes that *Mask Dance* reveals how adoptees can take very different attitudes to their double identities while still showing solidarity with one another.[139]

Also set in Minnesota, Korean adoptee playwright and performing artist Katie Hae Leo's full-length play *Four Destinies* is a metatheatrical piece in which Leo appears as herself, the playwright who brings to the stage the stories of four different adoptee characters growing up in the United States, all named Destiny. The four adoptees include a ten-year-old Korean American girl, a thirteen-year-old African American girl, a twenty-year-old Latin American woman, and an eight-year-old European American boy (who the audience later finds out is gay). Rather than focusing on one adoptee's search-and-reunion narrative, *Four Destinies* touches on the adoption experiences of four adoptee characters, encompassing domestic transracial adoption, international adoption, and gay adoptee sexuality. In Mu's lineage, *Middle Brother* serves as a continuation of the building of the bridge between Asian America and Korean adoptees in theater.

In my interview with him, Sharp specified that he was not only the playwright and lead actor but was also "involved in almost everything in terms of input" for the production.[140] Hence, he was particularly pleased that the

---

137. Laybourn, "Being a Transnational Korean Adoptee," 35. Italics in original.
138. "Production History," Theater Mu. The script of *Walleye Kid: The Musical* is available in the play anthology *Asian American Plays for a New Generation*, edited by Josephine Lee, Don Eitel, and R. A. Shiomi.
139. Novy, *Reading Adoption*, 175–76.
140. Sharp, interview.

all-Asian cast included three other adoptee actors in the show, so that "in this play about Korean adoption . . . four out of six were Korean adoptees."[141] With a majority of the cast being Korean transnational adoptees, the production reveals how thoughtful casting serves kinning to make a work more meaningful for an audience, as well as for the performers themselves. The playbill for Mu's 2014 production of *Middle Brother* features a note by Katie Hae Leo, aforementioned, who affirms the importance of Mu in the lives of adoptees due to its "commitment to producing plays for and by adoptees recogniz[ing] the power of seeing oneself represented through art for so many Minnesota adoptees and their families."[142] The playbill also offers a timeline of Korean adoption starting from the Korean War, written by pioneering Korean adoption studies scholar and Korean American adoptee Kim Park Nelson. The timeline includes significant historical, social, and legislative information about transnational and transracial adoption along with a glossary of Korean words used in the play. The entire work, from playscript to playbill to production, demonstrates how the artistic and scholarly Korean adoptee community came together to form a theater of care. *Middle Brother* thus fortifies Mu's long-term communal commitment to adoptees' voices by centering the complexity of transnational adoption experiences within the vector of Asian America in the Midwest.

In My Heart, also produced in Minneapolis, qualifies as what Miriam Haughton calls "a performance process where theatre is the vehicle for social change . . . dealing with distinct traumas, to create strength from this shared space of life storytelling and suffering [. . . that] illuminates and reinforces the power of community-building."[143] Through its community-building efforts, *In My Heart* becomes a collaborative work of kinning beyond networks of Korean transnational adoptees by specifically spotlighting an encounter in the play between a Korean American adoptee and a Native American adoptee. After Jennifer drinks the magical potion offered by the White Rabbit, the Caterpillar enters in the form of a woman chef in a white uniform and a hairnet. Jennifer talks to the Caterpillar about her childhood experience of isolation, being a person of color, and a Korean transnational adoptee different from her white family and friends in a small Minnesota town. The Caterpillar then shares her own adoption story—about her life as a Native American adoptee, her neglectful parents and their issues with substance abuse, and her feelings of being unwanted and abandoned by her foster families. Jennifer further tells her frustrations about her time in Korea, her struggles with the language barrier, and her envy toward Korean parents and children because they looked

---

141. Sharp, interview.
142. Leo, program for *Middle Brother*, 7.
143. Haughton, *Staging Trauma*, 21.

alike and had a clearly defined identity and kinship. This confessional moment allows two adoptees of color to bond over the challenges they face in and beyond the United States for being an adoptee of color. Writing specifically about transracial adoptees in the United States, Shannon Gibney articulates how these adoptees center losses as essential elements of their identities and forge a "'kinship of loss' [. . . as they] mourn toward wholeness."[144] As Gibney further states, "This process of deep looking and exploration, of recognition, of connection and community-building becomes central to the kinship of loss amongst transracial adoptees."[145] The heart-to-heart encounter between Jennifer and the Caterpillar presents their mutual sense of loss. The kinning is actualized in the sharing of their loss, as Jennifer and the Caterpillar establish new bonds via their budding kinship as transracial adoptees.

The kinning between Jennifer and the Caterpillar also suggests a historical juncture between Korean and Native American adoptions in Minnesota. During the 1970s, Native American adoptees were placed into foster homes at a rate five times higher than any other adoptee group.[146] In 1974 alone, nearly 35 percent of Minnesotan Native American children were taken away from their families and relinquished for adoption, placed into foster care, or institutionalized.[147] In 1978 Albert Trimble, the Executive Director of the National Congress of American Indians, stated that "25–35% of all Indian children had been separated from their families."[148] That same year, the Indian Child Welfare Act (ICWA) was passed to keep Native American children in their tribes with either their biological or extended family. In this setting, because the 1970s saw strong opposition to the adoption of Native American as well as Black children in white homes,[149] adoption agencies and adoptive parents looked elsewhere for children: Asia. According to Park Nelson:

> Since the anti-transracial-adoption positions of the NABSW [The National Association of Black Social Workers] and in the ICWA emphasized histories of racial discrimination against African Americans and American Indians, the perceived absence of racial discrimination against Asian Americans made the transracial adoption of Asians into White homes appear safe in comparison to domestic transracial adoption.[150]

---

144. Gibney, "Kinship between Transracial Adoptees," 158.
145. Gibney, 159.
146. Simon and Alstein, "Transracial Adoption."
147. Simon and Alstein. Also see Deloria and Lytle, *American Indians, American Justice*.
148. Indian Child Welfare Act of 1978.
149. Raleigh, *Selling Transracial Adoption*, 130.
150. Park Nelson, *Invisible Asians*, 95–96.

With adoption of Asians into white homes being considered "safe in comparison," the laws of supply and demand were applied to relinquished Korean and other Asian children instead of African American and Native American children in the United States. The 1970s and 1980s thus saw a dramatic surge in the number of Korean children relinquished for adoption into American homes.

Amid this historical backdrop, another scene with Jennifer and the Caterpillar presents an act of kinning that foregrounds an even stronger bond between these two adoptees of color, imagining a path toward healing through music and dance. As the Caterpillar shares a story with Jennifer about a powwow her tribe organized with adoptees and foster children, the Wablenica Song (Native Adoptee Healing Song) plays in the background.[151] Marla Powers writes that the Lakota term *wablenica*

> designated a child who had lost its mother and father, but there was always someone to assume responsibility for its care. Often these *wablenica* were showered with extraordinary kindness and attention. . . . Whether they were adopted formally, . . . or informally, they were treated the same as biological kin.[152]

According to Cooper, the decision to incorporate the Wablenica Song was made about one year before the production when she was invited by a Native American friend to observe a powwow for adoptees and then join an actual ceremony. Adoptees from the play's cast were all invited to join the following year's ceremony to experience the drumming and singing.[153] During the production, while the Wablenica Song plays, Jennifer describes to the Caterpillar the Korean percussion music genre of *samulnori*, comprising four different percussion instruments played in unison, highlighting the harmonious rhythm among the four players.[154] When Jennifer tells the Caterpillar how moved she was when she heard this for the first time in Korea, actual *samulnori* musicians begin playing drums on the platform. The Caterpillar then starts to dance to the drumming, and Jennifer joins in. The combination of the music and dance resembles a ritual performance through which Jennifer and the Caterpillar form a kinship sprouting from a sense of loss and from hope for belonging and healing across different ethnic and racial groups. In

---

151. Cooper and Berks, *In My Heart*, cover page.
152. Powers, *Oglala Women*, 57. Italics in original.
153. Cooper, interview.
154. K. I-Y. Lee, *Dynamic Korea and Rhythmic Form*; and Koehler, Byeon, and Lee, *Traditional Music*.

this kinning, through the intersection of the Wablenica Song and *samulnori* music, Cooper and Berks create a sensorial and spiritual moment that reflects the purpose of *In My Heart*—to have audiences interact with the feelings of others in their community and, as Cooper said, for "the adoptive community specifically to make space for the grief that everybody involved has."¹⁵⁵

In *Hello, My Name Is . . .* , kinning is particularly dramatized in the scene where the three adoptee characters share different and conflicting points of view regarding their adoption experiences but also find common ground in their failure to reunite with their birth families. When Dana, June, and Bryan separately return to Korea as adults, they meet by chance outside the adoption agency that placed them and decide to have lunch. The three sit down on the floor around a table in the middle of a room as audience members enter and seat themselves on chairs around the room's walls. An actress playing the role of a server gives Dana, June, and Bryan a menu and serves them a bottle of *soju* (Korean liquor) on a tray. She then offers each of the audience members around the room one of the already filled glasses on her tray, acknowledging their presence as if they were other dining customers. Unlike the scenes in the bedrooms, where the audience was present but not part of the setting, each audience member becomes a participant here. The audience thus shifts from a passive voyeuristic position to a role of engaged witness, although not directly participating *in* the scene. While eating and drinking, Dana, June, and Bryan, each talk about their experience at the adoption agency. June is bitter that both her birth parents are dead and that her now-deceased adoptive mother refused to let her come to Korea before. Dana is grateful that her adoptive parents chose her, yet she feels like a stranger in her own birth country and longs to belong. Bryan, who has been drinking heavily, is acrimonious because he could not find his birth parents and his adoptive parents did not process his naturalization papers, leading to his deportation and present life in limbo. When their debate about adoption becomes heated, Bryan burns the letter he had written for his birth mother, whom he still has not found, and angrily leaves the restaurant. The scene suggests that the Korean adoptee community does not simply conform to unified experiences and views about adoption-related topics, particularly regarding search and reunion. Moreover, deromanticizing the idea of a successful search and reunion for all three adoptees, their failed search becomes a catalyst through which they can emotionally bond. As McKee notes, an "instantaneous affinity" is created among Korean transnational adoptees whose intimately shared commonalities forge

---

155. Cooper, interview.

an immediate connection and "feeling of kinship."[156] In this sense, the restaurant scene does present an "instantaneous affinity" among the three, showing that affinity can still occur in conflict rather than in harmony and even in loss rather than in reunion.

The act of kinning, moreover, is not limited to the stage and auditorium but also extends into the online Korean transnational adoptee community.[157] For instance, at the conclusion of *Hello, My Name Is . . .* , the three adoptee characters simultaneously read out letters to their birth mothers, telling their stories of being and becoming adoptees in and out of the United States. To obtain material for this dramatic scene, Sivigny, who had already read Korean adoptee Facebook threads after her visit to her adoption agency in Korea, also sent out surveys to adoptees and received several answers.[158] The letters reveal the differences and disparities in the Korean adoptees' responses about their upbringing, the purpose of birth searches and reunions, and the questions they have for birth mothers regarding their choice of relinquishment (see table 1).

During the performance, the overlapping monologues of the three characters merge with the recorded voices of adoptees gathered through social media, each expressing emotions and ideas about what it means to be an adopted person. As McKee points out, the internet has provided new venues of expression for and by adoptees, many of whom have created online communities for the sharing of thoughts and feelings.[159] By using the text of the responses, Sivigny privileges the voices of adoptees and elevates their expressions of their lived experiences to art. This interweaving of fictional and real adoptee voices is suggested by the title of the play, *Hello, My Name Is . . .* , which takes on a striking significance in light of the fact that adoptees generally hold two (or more) different names, birth and adoptive. The ellipsis in the play's title thus designates two or more ways adoptees can identify

---

156. McKee, *Disrupting Kinship*, 119.

157. Kinning efforts online have existed in varied ways from virtual exhibitions of visual and video art to online activism. In 2020 "[dis]locations: Overseas Adopted Korean Artists Open Online Exhibition," with works by kate-hers RHEE and two other visual artists, kimura byol lemoine and Leah Nichols, was curated by theater artist and educator Amy Mihyang Ginther (whose solo performance *Homeful* is analyzed in chapter 2). See "dislocations," AHL Foundation. Also, the Network of Politicized Adoptees (NPA), an organization composed of transracial and transnational adoptees that provides a platform for adoption, immigration, community activist groups, has arranged discussion groups (online and offline). See Network of Politicized Adoptees.

158. Sivigny, interview.

159. McKee, *Disrupting Kinship*, 123–45.

TABLE 1. Three adoptee characters' simultaneously spoken monologues

BRYAN	DANA	JUNE
Dear Omma,	Dear Mother,	(*After a moment.*)
For a long time growing up I hated you for sending me away, because nothing could be worse than where I grew up. I was thankful when my foster mother kicked me out when I was seventeen. I wanted nothing more than to be out of that hellhole of a home but I didn't know where else to go . . .	My name is Dana. I'm writing you because the social worker said someday you might look for me. I haven't looked for you because I was afraid you didn't want to see me. But I'm not sure I want to see you either. I've been learning a lot about how different mothers can be. I know that you made a very difficult choice to give me up.	
So I tried punching my way out. I wanted to hurt people like they hurt me. I often wondered if you sent me away because I was a bad kid. That I deserved to be beaten and yelled at. Maybe that's what you thought I'd have in Korea too so anything could be better, right?	I am doing okay. I'm married now. I live in Chicago. I am thankful to you for the life you gave me. I hope you'll see this letter someday and think about me.	Dear Omma . . .
I'm trying hard to understand that. I'm here now. I'm looking for you. Are you looking for me?	[*silence*]	[*silence*]
[*silence*]	[*silence*]	I forgive you.

Source: Compiled and conceived from online spaces and surveys, in Debra Kim Sivigny's *Hello, My Name Is . . .* , 42–43.

themselves. This indeterminacy is an experience shared by both the real-life adoptees quoted in the play and the imagined adoptee characters. Through the sharing of intertextual accounts between the factual and the fictional, *Hello, My Name Is . . .* comes to serve not only as a representational art space but also as a communal platform where performers and participants conjoin through this act of kinning across virtual and actual spaces. At the end of the play, the multitude of adoptees' voices reading letters overtakes the space in "an ocean of sound."[160] This ending leaves a feeling of wistful open-endedness,

160. Sivigny, *Hello, My Name Is . . .* , 42.

very much reflecting the characters' ongoing searches for belonging and the production's striving toward a theater of care.

•

Whether transgressing time and space or shifting between the real and the imagined, the Korean transnational adoptee characters in *Middle Brother, In My Heart,* and *Hello, My Name Is* . . . are constantly in motion within worlds that are continuously in flux. As such, all three plays are thematically connected through the notion of fantasy in their search-and-reunion narratives that reveal the adoptee characters' liminal position. By mapping out their contested state of in-between-ness, the fantastical elements serve as conduits to deliver the idea of unsettled belonging. What becomes apparent in their search and reunion is that these adoptee characters' sense of belonging is contingent on the forces of adoptive and birth cultures that draw the characters as either "good," "bad," or "strange." However, the three plays reimagine belonging for adoptees as something that they can create by forming supportive and sustainable kinships. In doing so, these theaters of care serve not just as a performance site for telling different adoption stories but also as a communal hub where belonging becomes generative for all kins involved, both onstage and offstage.

CHAPTER 4

Decolonial Discomfort

Extraordinary Adoption Stories beyond the Korea–US Cartography

If the word "adoption" most often conjures comforting stories, the three works in this final chapter dispel that perennial notion by presenting something that delves into unsettling adoption experience and imagination. This chapter examines the works of Korean women adoptee playwrights and performers from Belgium, England, and Denmark, with a focus on how their work unpacks the experiences of sexual and racial violations, such as rape, incest, and "whitewashing," that Korean adoptees have encountered.[1] In Cathy Min Jung's solo performance *Les Bonnes Intentions* (2011),[2] the relationship between an adoptive mother and daughter is shown through the pair's shared confidences. However, the exchange of confidences results in the exact opposite of the closeness and well-being such interactions between family members are generally expected to create and sustain. In In-Sook Chappell's full-cast play *This Isn't Romance* (2009), the intimacy of a biological brother–sister relationship is expressed through their incestuous sexual attraction to each other

---

1. Examining the life stories of Korean American adoptees, Sandra Patton-Imani finds that rape, sexual abuse, incest, and race are interconnected in white patriarchal adoptive families. Patton-Imani, "'Someone's Roots.'" Kim Park Nelson writes of how white parents who view themselves and/or their adoptive nonwhite children as "raceless" are unknowingly "Whitewashing their children." Park Nelson, *Invisible Asians*, 82.

2. Many thanks to Alain G. Cloarec for his French-to-English translation of the play and my interview notes with Cathy Min Jung.

after years of separation. The main adoptee character's attempt to expiate her guilt leads to a tragic and violent ending. Yong Sun Gullach's performance art piece *Re-enacting the Transnational Adoptee* (2015) directly engages with the experiences of racialization and the power of whiteness usurping a body of color—specifically, the Asian adoptee's body.

While the search-and-reunion story structure in the plays examined in the previous three chapters is, for the most part, clearly defined, the works discussed in this final chapter depict adoptee searches in a broader sense. In *Les Bonnes Intentions,* a young Korean adoptee girl in Belgium copes with domestic violence by searching for memories of her birth mother and fantasizing about her mother's story of relinquishment; in *This Isn't Romance,* a transnational Korean adoptee raised in the UK returns to Korea to reunite with the violently troubled brother she left behind when he was a young boy; and in *Re-enacting the Transnational Adoptee,* the Korean Danish artist enacts her uncompromising position on transnational adoption, incorporating her personal experience of adoption forgery, which she discovered during her search for her birth records. What is extraordinary about these characters and personae is how they "reinvent" themselves in the process of reuniting or attempting to reunite with their birth family, whether real or imagined. Their extraordinariness lies in the extent to which their need for reunion—or recreation of a union—compels them to this reinvention of their own beings.

Another common thread in the three works is their staging of violence against Korean women adoptee characters and performers in their adoptive home or during their search and reunion.[3] Thus, they deal primarily with disturbing consequences of search and reunion, in contrast to the heartwarming search-and-reunion narratives that are more often presented. Exposing the viciousness imposed upon the Asian female adoptee body through gendered and sexualized racialization, the three works shatter the popular tropes of transnational adoption's humanitarian, multicultural, and ethnonationalist narratives. Laura Hyun Yi Kang proposes a conceptualization of Asian women as becoming "intelligible" through documentation of the racial and gendered violations committed upon them, reframing Asian women "as a critical prompt for mapping varying configurations of power, knowledge, and justice."[4] Borrowing from Kang's conceptualization, in this chapter I treat the depiction of such violations upon Asian adoptee women as an intelligible

---

3. While violence is integral to all three works, it is not explicitly enacted on stage but evokes violent imageries and actions in *Les Bonnes Intentions* and *This Isn't Romance.* Only Yong Sun Gullach's performance piece employs "violent" acts, but even her actions are planned and she remains in control at all times.

4. Kang, *Traffic in Asian Women,* 16.

site wherein adoptees' bodies produce knowledge and awareness about Asian women's experiences and expose the unequal and unjust power dynamics imposed upon them.

While portraying racial, gender, and sexual violence against Asian adoptee women, the three works allow their characters to appropriate violence and transform themselves from "victim" into "aggressor." The child adoptee raped in *Les Bonnes Intentions* executes her family; the adult adoptee in *This Isn't Romance* sets fire to herself to avoid an incestuous relationship with her biological brother; and Gullach acts violently toward herself and aggressively toward her spectators in a reflective enactment of the invasive power of the institutionalized adoption industry and white hegemony in *Re-enacting the Transnational Adoptee*. In this way, the works show that their Korean women adoptee characters and performers are not powerless but powerful, because it is they who decide, when, where, and how to end the vicious cycle of violation. The astonishing boldness of their actions transforms their vulnerability from victimhood to resistance.

The standard definition of "vulnerability" derives etymologically from the Latin *vulnus* and *vulnerare*, meaning "wound" and "to wound," respectively, thus rendering the meaning of the word as "being physically or emotionally wounded [and] open to attack or damage."[5] Recent studies of vulnerability from feminist perspectives, however, have brought a new direction to the word's implications, away from the idea of vulnerability as a damageable fragility, which disempowers those identified as vulnerable.[6] In the introduction to *Vulnerability in Resistance*, Judith Butler, Zeynep Gambetti, and Leticia Sabsay posit an alternative framework that moves beyond the idea of vulnerability as weakness. The authors caution against accepting the paternalistic notion of vulnerability as a passive and victimized state needing protection.[7] Butler further offers an alternative view of vulnerability linked to resistance, stating that "vulnerability, understood as a deliberate exposure to power, is part of the very meaning of political resistance as an embodied enactment."[8] In regard to the works discussed in this chapter, the notion of vulnerability I use reclaims agency from paternalism, refuses the label of victimization, and turns passivity into action. In this sense, vulnerability does not just expose the institutionalized mechanisms that shape adoptees as vulnerable subjects but also expresses their potential for resistance within vulnerability.

---

5. "Vulnerable" and "vulnerability" in *Merriam-Webster Dictionary*.
6. Hirsch, "Vulnerable Times."
7. Butler, Gambetti, and Sabsay, *Vulnerability in Resistance*, 1.
8. Butler, "Rethinking Vulnerability and Resistance," 22.

It is my further intention in this chapter to show how performed vulnerability has an affective capacity to account for the power relations influencing adoptees' experiences while also revealing the precariousness of constructed identity and belonging. This is not to say that adoptees *are* vulnerable beings but rather that performances of vulnerability in the adoptee representations generate a realm where spectators can re-evaluate what it means to affectively interact with one's own and others' precarious experiences. In the introduction to *The Power of Vulnerability*, Anu Koivunen, Katariina Kyrölä, and Ingrid Ryberg propose that "vulnerability directly invokes and mobilises affect in that it actualises in feelings of fear, shame, compassion, anger, and many others."[9] In the three works discussed in this chapter, the power of vulnerability is communicated to audiences through the mobilization of affect in theatrical and performative expressions by and about Korean transnational adoptees. Centering emoted vulnerability, I argue that the violence inflicted on and by the Korean women adoptee characters and performers shocks audience members into a state of discomfort, allowing them to more fully identify with the pain enacted in these stories and performances of Korean transnational adoption. Unlike painful injuries immediately sutured and then ignored, the pain depicted in these three pieces is thoroughly explored and exposed, leaving its sources, development, and traces wide open for examination. This evokes in audience members what Lisa Fitzpatrick describes as "a visceral or morphological response in the spectator through a momentary identification with the vulnerability of (all) bodies."[10] Audience members acknowledge the susceptibility to harm that vulnerability involves as a sense of exposure or risk, then vicariously empathize with the characters and performers as they enact being harmed or injured on stage. Thus, the result of these performances of vulnerability is a profound sense of empathy.

The staging of violence by women raises an important point about gender. While men are more often associated with violence in heteronormative discourse as well as in cultural and theatrical depictions, efforts have been made to "degender" violence through performance.[11] From the earliest days of Western drama, female characters who commit violent acts have been represented in the theater, with Euripides's *Medea* perhaps being the most renowned dramatic example. Women (in theater as in life), however, have most often found themselves the victims of violence rather than its agents. Degendering violence in theater is important, then. For one thing, as Nancy Taylor Porter states, it offers "far more dramatic and complex portrayals, [. . . and] opens

---

9. Koivunen, Kyrölä, and Ryberg, "Vulnerability as a Political Language," 7.
10. Fitzpatrick, "Performance of Violence," 66.
11. Taylor Porter, *Violent Women in Contemporary Theatres*, 2.

audience's minds to greater possibilities than they have previously imagined."[12] In a sense, to degender violence—as Lady Macbeth so aptly puts it, "unsex me here"[13]—is to give agency to women to perform actions usually reserved for men, even if only in the theater. This is certainly not meant to encourage women to be violent, but rather to place them on equal footing with men in terms of the array of emotions and actions they are capable of experiencing and performing as multifacetedly actualized beings.

Regarding audiences' encounters with violence in theater, Taylor Porter (referencing Lucy Nevitt) writes that audiences "*are* capable of having both intellectual and emotional responses to stage violence."[14] Playwright Carson Kreitzer also contends that "Theater is the best forum to deal with violence. . . . For what that violence *means*, for how it affects both the characters and the audience, theater operates on a higher level."[15] Porter, Nevitt, and Kreitzer conceptualize stage violence's capacity to lead audiences to reflect and, as Porter further suggests, to demonstrate that truthful theatrical portrayals of violent women can present audiences with important and thought-provoking challenges.[16] Contesting spectators' ideas of gendered and racialized violence thus provides them valuable insights into their own assumptions about women's behaviors that may violate societal norms. While staging violent theatrical works may be criticized for romanticizing or glorifying violence, the representation of violent women on stage in the three works is not about glamorizing violence but about perceiving how violence may be used to lead women's resistance against wrongdoing. As opposed to violence used to thrill a morally corrupt audience, the violence portrayed in these works represents a self-determined stance of resistance to immorality and injustice. *Les Bonnes Intentions, This Isn't Romance,* and *Re-enacting the Transnational Adoptee* depict violence in order to performatively highlight racial and sexual violations imposed on the bodies of women adoptees of color, thereby enabling acts of defiance. The violence enacted by the adoptee characters in the three works thus becomes an intentionally distressing expression of their fight against oppression, rather than a random residual effect of their past.

In my interview with Min Jung, she stated that she views international adoption as "an act of colonization."[17] Min Jung's perspective echoes the

---

12. Taylor Porter, 25.
13. Shakespeare, *Macbeth*, 1.5.39.
14. Taylor Porter, *Violent Women in Contemporary Theatres*, 21. Italics in original.
15. Kreitzer, "A Conversation with Carson Kreitzer," interview by Caridad Svich as cited in Taylor Porter, *Violent Women*, 21. Italics in original.
16. Taylor Porter, *Violent Women in Contemporary Theatres*, 19.
17. Min Jung, interview with the author, June 3, 2019, Brussels, Belgium.

postcolonial analysis of Tobias Hübinette, who considers transnational adoption as "a clear reflection of a global colonial reality and racial hierarchy" and one of the contemporary "ever-present colonial projects of the West."[18] Susie Woo sees the neocolonial othering of Korean adoptees and women as a means of conveying US and Korean nationalisms.[19] Informed by Min Jung, Hübinette, and Woo, this chapter scrutinizes violence not only as a violation of intimate relationships in which adoptees are entangled but also as a manifestation of colonial power over adoptees' bodies, which desires to mold them in accordance with imagined notions of adoptee-ness, Asianness, and exotic femaleness. Discussing her piece *Re-enacting the Transnational Adoptee*, Gullach asserts that "the structure of the performance is built in a way where I am also a figure on the scene, being any transnational adoptee basically, and being in a structure that any transnational adoptee is in, which is a structure of post-colonialism, a structure of power."[20] Theater and performance are, therefore, ways of foregrounding the traces and mechanisms of othering adoptees and offering possible strategies against them. The three pieces are not works of postcolonial theater and drama per se since the artists do not explicitly refer to colonial history and power relations. They nevertheless implicate and challenge the colonizing effects of international adoption by disclosing the imbalanced power dynamics experienced by adoptee women and girls of color and disrupting them with performances of violent acts.

Further probing the idea of adoption as a reflection of colonizing power, I contend that the theater and performance works examined in this chapter contest the "symbolic colonization" of hegemonic narratives of transnational adoption, which show Korean orphans and adoptees saved and raised by white Westerners to live happily in forever families, while also revealing another side of the adoption story that is bleak and unsettling. As Isabel Molina-Guzmán puts it, symbolic colonization is "the storytelling mechanism through which ethnic and racial differences are hegemonically tamed and incorporated through the media."[21] For instance, writing specifically about Latina women in the United States, Molina-Guzmán notes that news media manufacture negative racial and sexual images of Puerto Rican women, who are "stereotyped as untrustworthy and hypersexual criminals."[22] This type of news coverage flattens the diverse cultural, social, historical, and racial characteristics of whole populations, preventing news consumers from seeing them

---

18. Hübinette, "Comforting an Orphaned Nation," 28.
19. Woo, *Framed by War*.
20. Gullach, interview with the author, July 25, 2019, Seoul, Korea.
21. Molina-Guzmán, *Dangerous Curves*, 9.
22. Molina-Guzmán, 81.

differently and understanding them more deeply. In the context of Korean transnational adoption, media portrayals and prevalent narratives have reified adoptees' stories as scripts of lifesaving love, happiness, and gratefulness, thereby averting the public from contextualizing the other side of adoption narratives, particularly adverse ones in which vulnerability can be fully understood and felt. The three pieces analyzed here expose this phenomenon of symbolic colonization that reduces adoption to heartening stories of salvation and rescue, and thus enable their audiences to understand and reject its hegemonic difference-flattening effects.

Ann Laura Stoler notes two correlated sources of power in colonial domination, "one that works through the requisition of *bodies* . . . and a second that molds new 'structures of feeling'—new habits of heart and mind that enable those categories of difference and subject formation."[23] While the three works discussed here reveal methods of controlling Asian female adoptee bodies, they also invite audience members to challenge the ways in which their feelings about adopted subjects and adoption as a subject have been shaped as "feel-good." According to Gabriele Schwab, feelings are political underpinnings that must be decolonized: "In pursuit of a decolonization of the mind . . . we will also have to decolonize our emotions and affects, including our unconscious fears of the Other and perhaps our unconscious desires as well."[24] In the same vein, this chapter sheds light on audience response as a facet through which the "feel-good" master affect of Korean transnational adoption can be decolonized in theater. However, because the master affect is the master's tool, it cannot be used to "dismantle the master's house," which has been built on underrepresentation and misrepresentation.[25] Other tools, narratives, and feelings must be used to demolish the "feel-good" master affect.

Theorizing the visceral as disruptive, transformative, and generative of anticolonial imaginaries, Neetu Khanna advances a Fanonian analysis of decolonization's bodily and affective dimensions. By deliberating on bodies and bodily responses, and asking how decolonization can occur when the body automatically responds to racialized sensibilities, Khanna offers a way to read and rethink postcolonial problematics.[26] In a similar way, I would contend that the three works discussed here present a rare opportunity for audiences to experience decolonizing discomfort in a visceral encounter with adoption and adoptees that are a far cry from the numbing effects of happy-ever-after stories. As such, I view these theater and performance pieces as artistic efforts

---

23. Stoler, "Intimidations of Empire," 2. Italics in original.
24. Schwab, *Haunting Legacies*, 150.
25. Lorde, "Master's Tools," 110–13.
26. Khanna, *Visceral Logics of Decolonization*, 5, 32.

to unsettle the universalized "feel-good" Korean transnational adoption narrative and affect, drawing on the potential of vulnerability to resist the traces of colonial power still lingering in audiences' hearts and minds.

Korean Transnational Adoption and Adoptees in Western and Northern Europe

While much of the research on transnational adoption from Korea has focused on the United States, Korean adoption in European nations has its own trajectory. Since the three works chosen for this chapter are all from Western and Northern Europe, it is necessary to discuss the historical and cultural implications of transnational adoption routes in these contexts. Until after the Second World War, intercountry adoption in these regions occurred almost exclusively within the continent of Europe and largely involved white children. According to Sabina Ivenäs, intercountry adoption within the European continent occurred during the First and Second World Wars, when German and Finnish children were sent to Scandinavian foster homes while waiting for permanent adoption.[27] Transnational adoption of nonwhite children from overseas began in the 1950s and surged in Western and Northern Europe after the Korean War.[28] Since this chapter delves into three works from Denmark, Belgium, and the United Kingdom, a brief overview of these three nations' involvement with transnational adoption will be helpful to situate the pieces into adoption discourses of each country.

In Denmark, a decline in relinquished Danish-born children during the 1950s and 1960s led to a lack of adoptable children. This lack was publicized by the media, which suggested that "the need to adopt could be satisfied by increasing the number of sending countries."[29] During this period, the first transracial adoptions to Denmark occurred as Danish families adopted Black mixed-race children born from white German women and Black US military men stationed in West Germany, although it should be noted that these adoptions were illicit and eventually exposed by the media.[30] With a growing demand for adoptable children, Danish newspapers presented children in developing nations as suffering from homelessness and suggested a possible mass adoption of Korean children, arguing that Sweden and Norway had received "hundreds of adoptions from Korea" unhindered by the bureaucracy

27. Ivenäs, "White Like Me," 241.
28. Ivenäs.
29. Park Nelson and Myong, "Shared and Divergent Landscapes," 103.
30. Eriksen, "Great Desire for Children," 7–8.

Denmark imposed on prospective Danish families.[31] In the 1970s, Danish newspapers focused their reporting on the biracial Black Korean adoptees arriving from Korea and, according to Kim Park Nelson and Lene Myong, framed "Danish color blindness" in opposition to Korean racial politics that marginalized biracial babies and children.[32] Denmark's stance on transnational adoption centered around a colorblind ideology that erased present and past oppression on a racial and cultural level.[33] While Denmark ranked ninth among the world's receiving nations in 2013,[34] hosting about twenty thousand adoptees born overseas, it has also been prone to anti-immigrant and antiminority rhetoric. This is mostly due to the influence of the right-wing Danish People's Party, making the country "one of the Western world's most antimulticultural societies" while still promoting transnational adoption.[35] The last work discussed in this chapter, Yong Sun Gullach's *Re-enacting the Transnational Adoptee*, hails from Denmark, where Gullach grew up after her adoption from Korea. Gullach's message regarding the racialization of Korean transnational adoptees reflects the white Western domination that dictates her body and self.

In Belgium, 90 percent or more of all adoptions are transnational adoptions (equal to the percentages in neighboring nations France and Luxembourg).[36] Because Belgium's history includes colonization of the Congo (independent since 1960 and renamed the Democratic Republic of the Congo in 1964), the Afro-Belgian population is one of the nation's largest minority groups and includes a significant number of adoptees.[37] Overall, transnational adoption has been viewed in Belgium as a reproductive choice and represented in humanitarian terms. Since the 1970s, however, Belgian immigration policies have increasingly created restrictions, with immigration allowances typically being granted only for political and familial reasons.[38] Public sentiment pushed for governmental facilitation and support of transnational adoption, challenging its existing restrictive immigration policy, which was viewed as "unnecessarily keeping poor 'Third World' children in orphanages."[39] Although the overall number of adoptions decreased in Belgium from 2011 to

---

31. Park Nelson and Myong, "Shared and Divergent Landscapes," 105.
32. Park Nelson and Myong, 108.
33. Park Nelson and Myong, 99–125.
34. United Nations Department of Economic and Social Affairs/Population Division (UNDESA/PD), *Child Adoption: Trends and Policies.*
35. Wills, Hübinette, and Willing, "Introduction," 4.
36. UNDESA/PD, 74–75.
37. Wills et al., "Introduction," 5.
38. De Graeve "They Have Our Culture."
39. De Graeve, 76.

2019, the number of transnational adoptions was consistently higher than that of domestic adoptions.[40] The first play discussed in this chapter, *Les Bonnes Intentions* by Korean Belgian adoptee Cathy Min Jung, is about a Korean girl who is brought to Belgium at a young age and experiences abuse in her adoptive home.

In the 1960s, England and Wales witnessed a rise in domestic adoptions due to out-of-wedlock children being relinquished at birth, but the late 1960s and the '70s reversed this trend because of widespread availability of contraception and abortion and less discrimination against illegitimate children.[41] In the latter half of the twentieth century, England and Wales did not experience a high influx of children from abroad. This was partly because since the 1980s children in England and Wales who had been removed from abusive homes were placed for adoption, and the British government encouraged domestic over foreign adoptions, discouraging the latter through the imposition of high costs.[42] Furthermore, until the 1990s, there were no adoption agencies in England that facilitated international adoptions for British parents.[43] According to Jean-François Mignot, the idea of transplanting children from their birth countries also brought up England's history of forced emigration, casting doubt on the ethicality of international adoption.[44] Thus, the best interests of children (domestic and foreign), as well as the cost and lengthy procedures of transnational adoption, which presumably only wealthier British families could afford, deterred transnational adoption in England.[45] Korean British playwright In-Sook Chappell's *This Isn't Romance,* the second play discussed in this chapter, implies a connection to the class-based aspect of UK transnational adoption, as the main character, Miso, was adopted from Korea by a wealthy English couple. In the play, when Miso reunites in Korea with her biological brother, Han, he contemptuously labels her a rich foreign woman, as the divergence in their lives accentuates his poverty.

Western and Northern European nations' involvement with Korean transnational adoption reflects their ever-changing landscapes regarding racial and cultural politics, women's reproductive choices, international relations—including wars, colonialism, and immigration—and adult adoptees' growing

---

40. Fédération Wallonie-Bruxelles, "Nombre d'enfants adoptés par pays d'origine" [number of adopted children by country of origin]. Belgium experienced more overseas adoptions from Africa than from any other continent. Figures for adoptions from Korea are not listed on the chart. Adoptees from Thailand were the most relinquished to Belgium from Asia.
41. Mignot, "Child Adoption in Western Europe," 347.
42. Mignot, 353.
43. Masson, "The 1999 Reform of Intercountry Adoption," 227.
44. Mignot, 353; and Masson, 226.
45. Mignot, "Child Adoption in Western Europe," 353.

community-building and activism. As in the United States, Korean adoptee-centered associations and activism began to appear in Europe. Adoptee-led Korean adoption organizations in Europe include the Adopted Koreans' Association (AKF) and Swedish Korean Adoptee Network (SKAN) in Sweden, Arierang in The Netherlands, Belgian Adoptees from Korea (BAK) in Belgium, Koreanische Adoptierte Deutschland e.V. (KAD e.V.) in Germany, Associazione Culturale Koreani Italiani Adottivi (KOR.I.A) in Italy, Racines Coréennes (Korean Roots) in France, Dongari in Switzerland, and Korea Klubben in Denmark.[46] These community-based organizations offer cultural activities as well as support for Korean adoptees with post-adoption services, traveling to Korea, publications, and news about adoption. In regard to adoptee activist forces particularly in Denmark, Park Nelson and Myong note that "[Korean transnational] adoptees have managed to introduce a more critical dimension to adoption discourse in the public domain," resulting in the establishment of organizations and political networks.[47] Park Nelson and Myong view these adoptee-focused accounts in Denmark as "potent counternarratives to both adopter-centered discourses and child rescue tropes that predominated in previous transnational adoption reporting."[48] Continuing efforts spearheaded by Danish adoptees in 2013 led to the establishment of the activist organization Adoptionspolitisk Forum (Forum for Adoption Politics), with Yong Sun Gullach, whose performance art piece is analyzed in this chapter, as chairperson (at the time of this writing),[49] and the research-based association Tænketanken Adoption (Think Tank Adoption) established in 2012. In 2015 the Copenhagen municipality financed an adoptee community center called Adoptionshuset (Adoption House) founded by Adoptionspolitisk Forum.[50] More recent Korean adoptee activism includes advocacy by Danish adoptee Peter Møller, co-founder of the Danish Korean Rights Group (DKRG), which supports the rights of Korean adoptees in Denmark. In particular, Møller's work with the DKRG has brought attention to irregularities in past adoption practices.[51] In Sweden, a social media influencer named "Stulen identitet" (stolen identity) shares critical comments on adoption, racism, and corruption,

---

46. A list of these organizations (and other worldwide Korean associations) and their websites can be found on the International Korean Adoptee Association's (IKAA) website.
47. Park Nelson and Myong, "Shared and Divergent Landscapes," 115.
48. Park Nelson and Myong, 118. The authors also refer to Catherine Ceniza Choy's *Global Families*, ch. 5, "To Make Historical Their Own Stories."
49. Adoptionspolitisk Forum website.
50. Park Nelson and Myong, "Shared and Divergent Landscapes," 116.
51. H-J Lee, "Adoption Agency Denies Fabricating Documents of Danish Adoptees."

as well as organizing lectures, talks, and a conference related to adoption.[52] Korean adoptee activist voices in Europe are thus at the forefront of challenging transnational adoption issues advocating for the rights and recognition of adoptees across borders. In parallel, Korean adoptee artists in Europe have broken new ground in the artistic landscape, pushing the envelope with imaginative and innovative expressions of their adoption experiences.

While this chapter focuses on the three selected works, several other Korean adoptees in Europe have created notable theater and performance pieces based on their actual and imagined adoption stories. In Germany, at the HAU Hebbel am Ufer Theatre in Berlin, Korean German adoptee Miriam Yung Min Stein performed *Black Tie* (2008), which she co-created with Helgard Haug and Daniel Wetzel of the Berlin-based Rimini Protokoll theater group.[53] In Norway, *Journey to the East* (2014), performed by Korean Norwegian adoptee actress Mona Grenne, is a play inspired by Grenne's story of attempting to find her birth mother in Seoul. Written by Nelly Winterhalder and directed by Øystein Ulsberg Brager, it was produced at the Cafeteateret's Nordic Black Theater in Oslo. UK-based Korean American adoptee performing artist Veronica Thompson, a.k.a. Fancy Chance, created and performed her first full-length autobiographical cabaret show, *Flights of Fancy* (2017), at London's Soho Theatre, with direction by Nathan Evan. In Denmark, Jacob Nossell, a Korean adoptee artist who was diagnosed with cerebral palsy not long after his arrival as a child in Denmark,[54] wrote and performed a full-length autobiographical play, *Human afvikling* (*Human Outphasing*), which opened at Copenhagen's Royal Danish Theater in 2016. In his play, Nossell asks if he is "normal" and has the right to live, raising ethical questions regarding whether a fetus with a disability should continue to birth or be terminated.[55] Plays and performance pieces by Korean adoptees based in Europe thus represent a wide spectrum of Korean transnational adoption narratives that deserve more focused and detailed analyses. The three pieces discussed in this

---

52. Wyver, "More Beautiful Than Something We Could Create Ourselves," 93. Also see A Stulen identitet's Facebook page.

53. Ancheri, "Reality Bites."

54. While often omitted from conversations about Korean transnational adoption, disabled adoptees are nevertheless part of its historical trajectory. Since the start of the 1970s, the percentage of disabled children adopted progressively increased, accounting for one out of every four adoptions. Hübinette, "Comforting an Orphaned Nation," 72. Hübinette also cites official statistics showing that 33,880 disabled Korean children were transnationally relinquished from 1954 to 2001. Hübinette, 101.

55. Royal Danish Theatre, *Human afvikling* (*Human Outphasing*). A documentary film entitled *Natural Disorder* (2015), directed by Christian Sønderby Jepsen, follows Nossell in his daily life and preparation for the performance of his play. Also see *Natural Disorder*.

chapter were chosen for their unusual renderings of birth search and reunion, wherein the sexual and racial violations of Asian women adoptees reflect a colonial framing of international adoption. Together, Korean European adoptee activists and artists form a dynamic and multifaceted wave, driving forward the dialogue on transnational and transracial adoption and shaping a more inclusive and equitable future for adoptees.

Extraordinary Adopted Childhood in *Les Bonnes Intentions* (2011)

Whereas Marissa Lichwick's autobiographical solo performance *Yellow Dress* (chapter 2) touches on the sexual abuse the character Riss was subjected to in her Korean orphanage, *Les Bonnes Intentions*, a one-woman play written and performed by actress, writer, and director Cathy Min Jung, addresses the topic of child abuse through an account of sexual violence in a Belgian adoptive home.[56] Set in rural Belgium, the story of *Les Bonnes Intentions* is told in monologue by an adopted Korean girl. Presented through disjointed scenes, the play follows the young girl's story until her teenage years as she is verbally and physically abused by her adoptive mother, who treats her like an indentured servant, and sexually assaulted by her adoptive father. Written in the present tense, the plot focuses on four periods of the young girl's childhood in her abusive adoptive family. Performed by Min Jung, the young girl, now grown up, looks back to recount her story of child exploitation and sexual violence in an intimate family setting. By writing *Les Bonnes Intentions*, Min Jung wanted to tell a story "that was not your usual thank-you-for-adopting-me story [... and] bring out the reality of a child who ... experienced the day of her adoption like a *kidnapping*."[57] Loosely based on Min Jung's own life, *Les Bonnes Intentions* shares an abused adopted child's perspective on how adoption, while paved with "good intentions," can also be marred by cruelty

---

56. *Les Bonnes Intentions* was first produced in February 2012 at the Théâtre de l'Ancre in Charleroi, Belgium, during the "Kicks" Festival, before proceeding to a run at the Théâtre de Poche in Brussels in March 2012, directed by Rosario Marmol Perez. *Les Bonnes Intentions* was awarded the Meilleur auteur du Prix de la critique Théâtre (Best Playwright Award) by the association of Belgium Francophone Theater and Dance Critics and Best Set Design. The analysis of *Les Bonnes Intentions* is based on both the 2011 published script and the 2012 videotaped performance provided by the artist. Before *Les Bonnes Intentions*, in 2007, Cathy Min Jung wrote and directed the documentary film *Un Aller Simple?* (*A One Way Trip?*), examining adoption, cultural heritage, and identity during her trips to Korea to search for her birth family and meet her biological father.

57. Min Jung, interview. Emphasis added.

and misery. Caroline Knowles states that "[child] abuse has forced us to think about the boundaries between what childhood can and cannot be allowed to be. The social demand to identify and deal with child abuse has forced a distinction between endangered and normal childhood."[58] Min Jung's play reveals that when boundaries have already been trespassed several times over, the "distinction between endangered and normal childhood" no longer exists, and only pain remains.

In *Les Bonnes Intentions,* the characters have no names and are only referred to by their familial titles: father, brother, and mother. The dogs, who hold an important role, also do not have names. When the mother speaks to her adopted daughter, she addresses her as "you." This style of anonymity creates a disassociation with the family setting. The family members exist, but only as their labels of kinship, removed from any affectionate behavior and connection. From the beginning of the play, this impersonal way of identifying characters establishes the harsh tone of the piece, accentuated by the emotionally detached viewpoint of the young girl, especially when she refers to her adoptive mother:

> Mother always said that one needs to cook meat before giving it to the dogs
> Even the bits and pieces that you will throw out
> Otherwise they will get used to raw meat
> The taste of blood
> If you give raw meat every day to a dog
> It will wind up eating a man
> We have two, dogs
> I'm the one who feeds them
> They know that
> They know that I only want to do good to them
> Not like my mother.[59]

The script of *Les Bonnes Intentions* purposefully lacks punctuation in many sections and is almost entirely devoid of stage directions (in the entire work, there are only three stage directions). The play is also formatted in such a way that it stylistically resembles poetry. Min Jung intentionally composed the lines in this fashion and carefully worked with the typesetter during the production of the printed play so as to bring out a musicality to her text, which

---

58. Knowles, *Family Boundaries,* 82.

59. Min Jung, *Les Bonnes Intentions,* 9. When citing Min Jung's *Les Bonnes Intentions,* I have reproduced the format of the script, conforming to the original typeset of the published work to the best of my ability within the limitations of block quotation indentations.

she considers "formal but also very organic."⁶⁰ The resulting text creates the feeling of reading a poem instead of a play, and the halting prose expresses the sense of dissociation experienced by the character of the young girl. The printed words follow a poetic form with pauses, which demand that readers maintain an active imagination and immerse themselves in the main character's voice as she narrates her traumatic experiences and emotions.

In the production, however, Min Jung's acting adhered to a proselike diction, while the lighting and set design conveyed the poetic sense of detachment. As the lights go up, the stage reveals an indistinct structure composed of tall, dark-brown wooden panels resembling a large container crate. A spotlight then shines on Min Jung, who is situated far stage left. The two pools of light separate Min Jung from the structure, creating a sense of temporal distance. A single mournful note played by a string instrument is the only element connecting her to both spaces. Min Jung walks to the structure and feels its surface as if to make sure it is real. She places her hands on both sides of a latched panel and hesitates as if she were about to open Pandora's box. She then unfastens two latched horizontal side panels and a third that opens vertically to create a ramp, revealing an inside space big enough to move around in. This abstract and empty wooden configuration denotes her adoptive parents' farmhouse, where the main character grew up isolated and exploited.

In this space, Min Jung, as the girl, starts her story at the age of seven, alternating between speaking as herself and as her mother. She recounts her mother's abuses, even as she remains defiant: "She forces me to just stay motionless and look at her while she lets her slaps fall."⁶¹ The young girl is forced to do all the chores in the house and garden and to take care of the yard animals. Although promised playtime after work, her mother always takes it away from her. The girl is slapped for no reason and without ever knowing when it might happen. In the context of the mother–daughter relationship, the abused versus abuser distinction is initially quite clear; however, this distinction becomes increasingly more complex as both mother and daughter alternate between the roles of victim and aggressor. The mother outwardly expresses her bitter feelings, stating, "What did I do to God to deserve such a girl like her,"⁶² while the girl speaks her defiant thoughts to herself: "I am at war / Since the first day we met."⁶³ Though abusive, their relationship remains intimate, as the adoptive mother and adopted daughter forge a strong connection through this distorted liaison. Patrick Anderson and Jisha Menon argue

---

60. Min Jung, interview.
61. Min Jung, *Les Bonnes Intentions*, 26.
62. Min Jung, 27.
63. Min Jung, 23.

that in performance, "violence is a *binding, affective* experience [. . . and] that conventional distinctions between 'victim' and 'aggressor' are often ill-suited to fully explain the effects of violence."[64] Violence entrenches this mother-daughter bond, which grows over the years into a shared loathing so intimate that it creates an interdependent relationship wherein they need one another to nourish each other's detestation. "I feed her of her own hate and violence,"[65] says the girl early on, later stating, "Each gasp of air I breathe in / Comes from the one you exhale."[66] The mother tells her daughter, "Look at that disgusting face of yours!"[67] before switching to the third person as if taking someone else as a witness: "She annoys me so much I feel like strangling her."[68]

The mother–daughter relationship severely deteriorates over time, with the mother's abuses of power extending to inculcating in her daughter a sense of inferiority regarding her birth culture, recalling Frantz Fanon's analysis of the colonizing power's efforts "to bring the colonized person to admit the inferiority of his culture."[69] Criticizing her daughter's food preferences, her mother says, "Do you forget where you come from? / If you had stayed over there, you wouldn't be so finicky . . . you have no idea how lucky you are. / She was dying of hunger and now she's being a princess."[70] Attempts to ingrain gratitude are a recurring theme in adoption stories; similarly, gratitude has often been portrayed in colonial modernity as an obligatory emotion imposed on colonized subjects by colonial powers when introducing "new" thoughts, culture, and language to replace their "old" values, behaviors, and systems. Undertaking to guilt her adopted daughter into being grateful, the mother says, "When I think that I'm the one who wanted a girl, I should have accepted a boy."[71] This particular thought insinuates a sense of buyer's remorse, as if the mother feels cheated out of a better "product" and now regrets that an exchange or refund is no longer possible. The notion of adoptees as consumable products links colonialism to capitalism, an idea bolstered by Elizabeth Raleigh's finding that, through adoption, children are "priced according to their market value."[72] Ultimately, the mother uses her hierarchical position to cement her power by referencing her daughter's otherness and her assumed destitute origins, implying she could never fully belong to their family.

---

64. Anderson and Menon, *Violence Performed*, 5. Italics in original.
65. Min Jung, *Les Bonnes Intentions*, 25.
66. Min Jung, 32.
67. Min Jung, 26.
68. Min Jung, 27.
69. Fanon, *Wretched of the Earth*, 236.
70. Min Jung, *Les Bonnes Intentions*, 15.
71. Min Jung, 27.
72. Raleigh, *Selling Transracial Adoption*, 7.

As bleak as the girl's conditional existence may seem, she finds ways to experience the warmth of family through the sensory memories of her past, while remaining unsure whether her remembrances are real or not. Although she is unable to definitively trace her recollections to her birth land and mother, she feels some kind of yearning connection to the smells and tastes of her food memories from Korea.[73] Desperately attempting to emotionally reconnect with her birth land, she takes to cooking and secretly modifies her adoptive mother's recipes to "look for and hope to find a familiar taste."[74] The sense of taste is a particularly important element for the girl, as it proves to be the strongest sense that fleetingly connects her to her birth mother. As a contact sense (along with the sense of touch), taste is perceived at its physical contact point, the tongue.[75] This very intimate contact site triggers an association of food with memories. For the girl, the sensory elements of taste and smell kindle her imagination, which attempts to materialize signs of "maternal presence."[76] As much as she tries to reinvent herself as her past self through food memories, these do not crystalize into a concrete memory of her birth mother's love. As her food memories fail to create a connection to her birth mother, the little girl reimagines her life as an infant in Korea. In one scene, Min Jung says the words *saranghae* (meaning "I love you" in Korean). As these words echo, a projected video backdrop shows out-of-focus and fragmented filmed images of an Asian infant mixed with red heart-shaped streaks of paint on a blueish filmstrip background. The quality of these images is reminiscent of home movies from the past recorded on Super 8mm film, with the disjointed images emphasizing the girl's yearning for traces of herself, her birth mother, land, and culture. These tender and nostalgic images fade out, and Min Jung (as the girl) begins to talk intensely about her adoptive childhood struggles with bulimic disorder, stomach distention, and hospitalization, which culminated in her eating a red alcohol thermometer and bleeding from the mouth. The dreamy and longing projected images are then replaced by a harsh red color that gradually fills the screen, suggesting that the brutal reality of the girl's life makes it impossible for her to live in the search for her past.

Outside of her home, the girl happily finds refuge and even empowerment by reinventing herself through a vivid fictional life at school. There, she fully expresses her feelings, free of constraints, and builds a new persona that

---

73. Homans writes of how cultural values such as "the taste and smell of Korean food" temporarily connect adoptees to their birth mothers. Homans, *Imprint of Another Life*, 169. Homans here refers to Kimberly Kyung Hee Stock, "My Han," in Cox, *Voices from Another Place*, 96.
74. Min Jung, *Les Bonnes Intentions*, 11.
75. Korsmeyer, *Making Sense of Taste*, 20.
76. Homans, *Imprint of Another Life*, 169.

eschews the grateful adoptee archetype her adoptive mother would impose on her. Appropriating the otherness of her origin, she becomes the center of attention as she dresses in a made-up costume and teaches her classmates a nonsensical dance, the supposedly authentic culture of her invented birth country. The girl fabricates not only her own past but also that of her birth mother, creating a romantic and tragic love story as the reason for her abandonment:

> My country was at war, my mother fell in love with a soldier who died in combat. As she became a single mother her family repudiated her, especially since it was a noble family and my father was merely a soldier. Without family, without money, she had no other choice but to abandon me, it was for my own good, she was really very courageous, I don't blame her, I understand her. I don't have any news from her, but one day, when I will be big, I will look for her and I will take her out of her misery, out of her prostitution.[77]

During this scene, slides are projected in the style of shadow puppetry to show the invented story of her birth mother: a map of East Asia superimposed with animated pictures of a little girl, a World War II bomber, drawings of a pregnant woman and her soldier lover who is then shot, a French-language newspaper headline relating a war orphan story, and the silhouette of a stripper symbolizing prostitution. In the girl's story, her birth mother survives by courageously accepting her fate. Tellingly, the girl includes details she knows will satisfy the colonial imagination already embedded in her classmates' young minds.

The way the girl constructs the story of her birth country and mother to fulfill her peers' expectations of her exotic otherness recalls Edward Said's notion of the Orient as constructed through the eyes of European culture and ideology.[78] Specifically, her story refers to a Western world's Orientalist views of Asian birth mothers as poor, pathetic, hypersexualized, tragic, and sacrificial lovers. In this sense, the girl's made-up story bears a resemblance to the musical *Miss Saigon* and the story of its main character, Kim, an unwed Vietnamese birth mother who develops a relationship with a white soldier and must turn to sex work to survive before eventually being forced to relinquish her child and dying. *Miss Saigon* also offers a glimpse into the Orientalism that has pervaded the Western imagination since the times of the musical's antecedents, such as Pierre Loti's 1887 novel *Madame Chrysanthème*, the 1900

---

77. Min Jung, *Les Bonnes Intentions*, 16.
78. Said, *Orientalism*, 3. Also see Mohanty, "Under Western Eyes"; and Shimizu, *Hypersexuality of Race*.

David Belasco play *Madame Butterfly*, and the succeeding 1904 opera *Madama Butterfly* by Giacomo Puccini.[79] These works created and sustained a crude and distorted view of Asia and Asian women and children that prevails in the West today. As Karen Shimakawa observes, *Miss Saigon*'s story perpetuates Orientalism in its depiction of the "self-sacrifice of an Asian woman for the love of a white (Western) man . . . an archetypal template, against which Asian women's sexuality is always measured in terms of self-denial/self-destruction (and often internalized racism)."[80] In a similar vein, in *Les Bonnes Intentions*, the girl's imaginary birth mother's story of "self-denial/self-destruction" shows how Western Orientalist ideals have already permeated her life and mind as well as those of her young peers.

As well as fashioning a saga of her birth mother as a reflection of colonial fantasies of Asian women, the girl also delights in telling her own imagined life story of being born in a big, bustling city like New York, where crowds and anonymity are familiar and possibilities abound.[81] During this part of the performance, stock footage of Times Square and New York City's skyscrapers is projected. These images are accompanied by pulsating music, which is eventually overtaken by an incomprehensible murmuring that becomes progressively louder until the girl sadly says:

> I invent a whole bunch of stories,
> Fascinating stories
> To speak of an absence
> A loss of memory
> Stories that are fanciful
> To fill in a three year void
> A fabulous past on which I constructed myself.[82]

The projection and sound then fade out. The little girl continues to compensate for the reality of her dreadful home life by constantly imagining an invented past that provides her, though elusively, with heartfelt feelings of fulfillment. Betty Jean Lifton writes how adoptees "have an unconscious fantasy when they are searching that they are following a path that leads to *home*."[83] Although the girl initially searches for sensorial traces of her birth mother through imagined sense memories of food, sights, and sounds, when these

---

79. J. Kim, *Ends of Empire*, 79.
80. Shimakawa, *National Abjection*, 26.
81. Min Jung, *Les Bonnes Intentions*, 17.
82. Min Jung, 17.
83. Lifton, *Twice Born*, 233. Italics in original.

prove vague or inadequate, she turns to full-fledged fantasy. The girl's fantasizing serves as a gesture of birth search and (wished-for) reunion with what has possibly been lost from her life. Scouring her sense memories and dreaming up stories are ways for the girl to search for her birth mother and birth culture—and to reunite with them at least in her vivid imagination. The erasure of the girl's past in the process of her adoption makes her search all the more intangible yet also all the more necessarily imaginative and sensorially vivid. All the girl knows is that she once had another life somewhere else, where "Somebody made me know the taste of love."[84] Her need to find and to reunite with this "somebody" compels her to swear that her imagined stories are true and even to start believing in them: "I want this so much / I need this so much / Everything actually existed / Since I imagined it."[85]

The security of this imaginary life is ultimately destroyed when the girl enters puberty and her adoptive father's sexual interest in her becomes apparent:

> I try to hide when I'm bathing,
> But he is often able to surprise me,
> As if by chance,
> Almost as if he is stalking me,
> Like a reptile, motionless.
> As soon as I'm in the bathroom, he comes in, without knocking,
> I did not hear him coming up the stairs.
> As soon as I take off my clothes in my room,
> He comes in without any warning.
> It's always during those times that he has something to ask me.[86]

The danger of her situation is rendered even more precarious when she realizes her adoptive mother is aware of her predicament yet takes no action to protect her, instead becoming a silent accomplice to the insidious crime:

> What about you, mother,
> You also sensed this.
> You, you even sensed that his organ got harder when he would see me in a bathing suit.
> What are you playing at mother,
> You made me into your enemy . . .
> When he forces me to come sit on his knees, you don't say anything.

---

84. Min Jung, *Les Bonnes Intentions*, 11.
85. Min Jung, 18.
86. Min Jung, 29.

> When I protest, you scold me. . . .
> Can't you hear my cries for help? No?
> No
> You throw me into the mouth of the reptile.[87]

Sandra Patton-Imani writes that rape is an aspect of reality in the life stories of Korean American women adoptees, describing it as "a brutal agent of socialization, inscribing racial, sexual, class, and national identities on the bodies of its victims."[88] Examining a case study of a Korean adoptee girl sexually abused by her adoptive father, Patton-Imani notes that the adoptive mother blamed the girl for enticing the father with her racially exotic appearance. Patton-Imani finds the adoptive mother's account to be "particularly informed by colonial ideologies justifying white male desire for racialized and sexualized exotic 'others,'" and further notes that such Orientalist narratives have the social function of rationalizing rape as the fault of the victim, her exotic, sexually tempting nature making the rapist nonculpable.[89] In the play, rather than condemn her husband for his actions, the mother views herself as a victim of his adultery and her adopted daughter as an outsider to the family who has used her powers of seduction on her husband. Whereas incest is considered an act of sexual violence and a desecration and exploitation of the parent–child relationship, a historical fixation on consanguinity buttresses the idea that adoptive families are often viewed as being beyond the boundaries of incest.[90] McKee explains that this way of thinking "exposes the outdated nature of conceptualizations of incest that overlook how adoptive families are equal to biological families" and diminishes the significance and severity of the damage caused by incest in adoptive families by presuming that adoptive ties are weaker than biological ties.[91] In the play, the mother perpetuates this

---

87. Min Jung, 29–30.
88. Patton-Imani, "Someone's Roots," 115.
89. Patton-Imani, 120.
90. McKee, "From Adoptee to Trespasser," 156–57.
91. McKee, 157. To illustrate this idea, McKee examines gender, sexual, and racial politics in relation to the relationship between Soon-Yi Previn and Woody Allen and to the ways in which Previn was viewed by the media and Mia Farrow when nude photos Allen had taken of Previn were found. McKee argues that due to Orientalist stereotypes of the Asian woman as "deviant, foreign, hypersexual," Previn was cast as a sexual predator instead of the victim of sexual abuse in her adoptive setting. This created a competition between mother and daughter, who were seen as rivals, with Previn being considered a sexualized adult who was also framed by Farrow and her advocates as "intellectually disabled." Moreover, supporters of Allen came to his defense, denying any familial connection between him and Previn and, in effect, "delegitimizing what transpired between Allen and Previn as abuse." For McKee, this line of thinking results in a complicity in the delegitimization of other familial ties and the dismissal of accountability for child sexual violation from within. McKee, "From Adoptee to Trespasser," 163–66.

idea of the adoptee as nonfamily by judging the girl's harrowing experience to be a consequence of her seduction of her husband, rather than as an incestuous sex crime committed in the domestic setting with her daughter as the victim.

Compounding the girl's suffering, the father rapes her repeatedly over a period of three years. Unable to fight back, she resorts to the defense mechanism of mentally and emotionally disconnecting whenever it occurs, silently counting flowers on the tablecloth, tiles in the kitchen, steps to the door. Staging this scene, Min Jung sits on a wooden crate, her elbows placed on her knees and her hands crossed in front of her. Bending forward, she speaks in a very calm, matter-of-fact tone. When she counts, she lowers her head and looks at the floor, her long black hair hanging forward. Her position gives the impression of utter exhaustion and defeat. When she finally lifts her head, she brings one leg up against her body and holds it while resting her head against the wall, then smiles as though realizing the absurdity of the extreme cruelty she was subjected to. This anticlimactic recollection creates a striking contrast with the brutal sexual violence perpetrated by the adoptive father. By dedramatizing these events through the tranquil delivery of her lines, Min Jung demonstrates how the character of the girl has desensitized herself in order to confine her pain to that time frame, just as her entire childhood is contained in the wooden structure that represents the house.

In *Les Bonnes Intentions,* the adoptive family proves to be a site of broken trust and trauma. The ferocity of the adoptive parents' behavior and actions toward their adopted daughter is extraordinary. Eventually the girl, too, becomes extraordinary, when, at the end of the play, the emotional, physical, and sexual violence that she (now a fourteen-year-old) has experienced finally leads her to react. No longer accepting the role of victim, the girl resolves to inflict violent punishment on her tormentors. In the penultimate scene, she declares: "My body no longer exists. / . . . I no longer feel anything / . . . I am a rock / I am a stone."[92] At this point in the production, Min Jung kneels with her hands on her head in a position of surrender. She then slowly lowers her arms to her knees and, holding her head high and motionless, delivers her lines in an impassive manner directly to the audience: "One, brother fell without a noise / Two, father, without a cry / Three, I walked right up to her / One, two, three, four, I struck with all my might."[93] While the stage directions indicate that the girl mimes a saber hack, in the production, Min Jung kneels facing the audience with her hands on her knees, and the violence is visualized by the video projection of three vivid red splashes across Min Jung's face and

---

92. Min Jung, *Les Bonnes Intentions,* 32.
93. Min Jung, 32.

onto the rear wall. In contrast to the goriness of these images and the savagery of her related actions, Min Jung's face and posture at this point express feelings of inner peace and liberation rather than of viciousness or vengefulness.

After a gruesome hint that she has fed the corpses of her adoptive family to their dogs, Min Jung looks at the space of her childhood as if for the last time and leaves via a back door. A special-effects video projection then shows her hologramlike image re-entering the space from the same door. Min Jung's hologram stands inside the wooden structure, and the audience hears her counting, just as the little girl did during the times when her adoptive father raped her. The "actual" Min Jung then appears stage right and proceeds to shut the box's wooden panels one by one, while her hologram stands inside and looks around. When Min Jung bolts the last latch, locking her image in the box, the counting stops. Min Jung then faces the audience and says: "To count, / Numbers in the head rather than memories. / Above all I shouldn't remember."[94] These final lines suggest that she can forget traumatic memories by replacing them with the counting of numbers, so that instead of remaining a victim to her memories, she might now, borrowing the words of Cathy Caruth, "exit into the freedom of forgetting."[95] By deliberately locking her replicated self in the box and exiting the stage, Min Jung finally gives her "self" the freedom to forget. This final action completes her detachment from her extraordinarily abusive past and abused self, locked inside the box, allowing her to finally reinvent herself.

Extraordinary Birth Siblings in *This Isn't Romance* (2009)

As in *Les Bonnes Intentions,* destructive intimate sexual relationships are central to the plot of *This Isn't Romance*. The main character, Miso Blake, a Korean woman adoptee in her thirties from the United Kingdom, reunites in Korea after twenty-five years with her younger biological brother Han-Som Kim (referred to as Han in the play). Written by playwright and screenwriter In-Sook Chappell,[96] *This Isn't Romance* explores the sibling ties that bind the

---

94. Min Jung, 33.
95. Caruth uses these words to describe how memory is enacted in the 1959 French film *Hiroshima mon amour.* Caruth, *Unclaimed Experience,* 32.
96. In-Sook Chappell's plays have been performed in major theater venues in the United Kingdom, the United States, and Korea. Chappell's first full-length play, *This Isn't Romance* (2009), won the 2007 Verity Bargate Award, London's Soho Theatre playwriting award. *This Isn't Romance* was commissioned as a screenplay (under the title *Miso Blake*) by Film Four and was also made into a radio play broadcast by BBC Radio 3 in 2011. The analysis of *This Isn't Romance* is based on the 2009 published script and the videotaped 2017 National Theater Company of Korea's (NTCK) production in Seoul, Korea.

two main characters and puts them at odds with the brutal world outside their painful lives. While the plays *Middle Brother* and *In My Heart* (both in chapter 3) also explore adoptees' siblinghood, *This Isn't Romance* goes further in scrutinizing sibling relationships by showing the emotional and moral complexities of long-separated biological siblings whose incestuous attraction to each other masks their need to compensate for feelings of abandonment and guilt.

In the history of Western theater, the theme of parent–child incest has been explored by diverse dramatists from Sophocles in *Oedipus Rex* to Sam Shepard in *Buried Child* (1978). Sibling incest stories can also be found in plays such as Lillian Hellman's *Toys in the Attic* (1960) and Joe Orton's *The Ruffian on the Stair* (1964), which features a gay sibling incestuous relationship. A notable early example of sibling incest theatrical representation would be John Ford's play *'Tis Pity She's a Whore* (first published in 1633), in which a brother and sister have a sexual relationship that results in her pregnancy. By focusing the entire story on the growing powerful incestuous attraction between Miso and Han, *This Isn't Romance* incorporates a love–hate relationship stemming from their feelings entangled with Miso's transnational adoption. The work also depicts the siblings' conflicted relationship in a ruthless manner that shocks readers and audiences, prompting them to think how far dramatic art can explore transnational and transracial adoption. Despite navigating through violence and the violation of intimacy, the play's narrative ultimately leads to a renewed kinship. One striking aspect of the play is Miso's position as a returning European transnational adoptee whose gender and foreignness are both objects of scorn and sexual attraction not only for her brother but also for a wealthy white British male character whom Miso encounters by chance. Her in-between-ness is thus pressed into a love–hate, or, more precisely, desirable–disdained identity, reflected by the need of the male characters to impose their own sets of racialized sexism and misogyny onto her.

Set in Seoul, the play begins with the initial reunion between Miso and Han. Miso, described as "thirty-two, Anglo-Korean, [who] wears a white dress, white ballet shoes, carries an expensive handbag,"[97] meets her twenty-nine-year-old brother Han for the first time since he was four and she was seven. At that time, she had left her brother behind, as she had been adopted by a wealthy English family who would take her to the United Kingdom. Miso and Han meet at the orphanage where Han's file was kept and interact through a brusque interpreter, Miss Lee. While this first scene establishes the conflict between Miso and Han, it also presents a budding attraction between

---

97. Chappell, *This Isn't Romance*, 17.

them, first introduced in the script through the description of Han as "Korean, handsome with a wildness, a toughness, an intense sexuality,"[98] and through another clue when Miss Lee mistranslates one of the questions. Han asks an upset Miso why she is sad and crying, since she is sexy and rich. Miss Lee, however, translates this as, "Why are you sad? You're . . . goodlooking [sic], you're rich."[99] The ellipsis in the text indicates Miss Lee's hesitation and her decision not to include the word "sexy" to describe Han's impression of his grown-up sister. This moment stands out as an indication that Han views his sister not as a biological sibling but as a sexually available woman.

This scene also reveals the complicated nature of Miso and Han's siblinghood, in which feelings of guilt and mutual longing are enacted through the exchange of (un)met gazes. Experiencing such a strong sense of guilt in front of her resentful brother, who is irate at her past abandonment and long-overdue return, Miso is at a loss for words and can barely look at him as he angrily stares her down. The only time Miso can bring herself to look him in the eyes, the stage directions read, "Slowly MISO uncovers her eyes, she looks at him, it's as if they're looking in a mirror."[100] Unable to express herself through Miss Lee's interpretations and unable to look at her brother, Miso breaks down, and Han angrily decides to leave. The moments in this scene when Miso cannot meet Han's eyes are reminiscent of the first meeting in the Korean duo-drama *Chalkak* (chapter 1) between Malsim, the birth mother, and Bongu, her relinquished daughter, when, due to her sense of remorse, Malsim avoids looking directly at Bongu. Miso like Malsim finds herself incapable of facing her brother's accusing eyes. The sense of sight and, more specifically, the role of eyes serve an important function in *This Isn't Romance*, first by leading Miso to temptation (seeing her brother in a sexual manner), and second by leading her to redemption at the end of the play, when she almost completely blinds herself.

In the same first scene, Miso's inability to speak Korean accentuates her sense of loss. When she hears Han speaking Korean, Miso starts to cry, as the sound of his words reminds her of her lost ability to speak and understand her maternal language: "There are sounds that are only in Korean and they make me . . . I can't make those sounds anymore . . . [. . .] I've lost so much. I lost . . . and I can't even talk to . . ."[101] Miso's loss of the Korean language not only marks her acculturation to her adoptive land, which widens the gap between her and Han, but also signifies her loss of her birth mother. On his

---

98. Chappell, 18.
99. Chappell, 21. Ellipsis in original.
100. Chappell, 20.
101. Chappell, 20–21. Ellipses in original. Bracketed ellipsis added.

way out, Han hands her an origami bird he has made. Miso stares at the paper bird and utters, *Umma* ("mother" in Korean). Miso's utterance suggests that her return to Korea, although ostensibly to reunite with her brother and ask for forgiveness, is also a return to somehow find a connection to her deceased birth mother through her closest living kin, her biological brother. This scene also finds a common thread with the ending of *Middle Brother* (chapter 3), in which Billy's inability to speak Korean prevents him from knowing the truth about his past. In both instances, loss of language is a hurdle to the truth and prevents both returned adoptee characters, Miso and Billy, from gaining a sense of agency.

After their first reunion, Miso goes to see a drunk Han in his dingy apartment and realizes the poverty he lives in. As his anger at her for not having contacted him all these years intensifies, his attitude toward her takes on a disturbing and sexually aggressive quality. Expressing himself through broken English, he imagines the rape and murder of a woman, an allusion to Miso, who shockingly goads him on:

> MISO: In your mind, what are you doing to the bitch?
> HAN: Raping her.
> MISO: I feel it.
> HAN: I want to stab her over and over, close her eyes, twist her neck with my hands and . . .
> MISO: I feel you.
> HAN: Hurt you . . . **Sibalnyun** (fuck you) . . . lose me . . .
> MISO: In me?
> HAN: In something better.
> MISO: I can feel you pushing up inside me. Hard. You won't let me breathe.
> HAN: Where do you feel me?
> MISO: In my heart, in my belly.
> HAN: Where?
> MISO: Here in my cunt.
> HAN: **Sibalnyun** (slut).
> MISO: I am you. You're the marrow in my bones, you're in my genes, in my body. You're the love that's tied up in me. You're the language I can't speak, the feelings I don't understand.[102]

The blatant sexual attraction suffused with violent overtones, along with the dialogue that mixes metaphors of sex and death, raises the stakes of their

---

102. Chappell, 35–36. Chappell puts Korean words in bold in her play. Ellipses in original.

precarious relationship. Astoundingly, Miso leads Han on in this line of thought by adding sexual images of her own body ("belly," "cunt"), thus entering into a dangerous partnership with him. The scene's conflicting expressions and utterances create a constant and volatile tension, and it seems that at any moment an incestuous act could occur. Surprisingly, at the end of this scene, Han asks Miso to console him by hugging him from behind as he curls up in a fetal position and falls asleep. This highly emotional sequence brings Han and Miso from a point of sexually charged antagonism and hatred with the threat of physical violence to a state of sibling intimacy, compassion, and absolution. The fetal-shape tableau suggests a turn in Miso's position from that of a sister to that of a mother—a surrogate maternal figure for Han.

The morning after this turbulent night, Miso and Han's mutual bond deepens as they connect to their traumas and intense need for further solace together. The siblings share how their paths have diverged since Miso left Korea, revealing lives of desolation. Miso tells Han of her affluent yet unhappy and aimless life in the United Kingdom, while Han recounts how, when he was younger, he was sexually abused by an older American man who replaced him with a fourteen-year-old boy once Han turned twenty-one.[103] Han also tells Miso about his bleak former life as a gangster underling and how he took part in the rape of a woman whose death he also caused. By exercising his power as a gangster, Han compensated for his feelings of powerlessness, stemming from the usurpation of his sexuality when he was a teenager, and restored his sense of masculinity. Han's recollections underline his shifting embodiment of a toxic masculinity that conceals vulnerability. Toward the end of the scene, Han's fragility re-emerges when he abruptly tells Miso that he needs money from her to repay a debt to his gangster boss, thus revealing his emotional and financial dependence on her. As if reverting to his vulnerable four-year-old self, Han holds Miso tight and says, "I am not strong like you, I not survive if you left me again."[104]

Scarcely having enough money herself to get by, a desperate Miso decides to possibly take up a previous offer to be the mistress of a wealthy white man, Jack Cash. Jack, a fifty-year-old British hotelier who works and travels between Seoul and London, where his wife and child live, has no qualms about frequenting strip clubs and having sexual escapades while in Korea. Initially

---

103. Han's story of his sexual liaison with this older American man when he was in dire straits as a young, orphaned boy suggests Western exploitation of the Asian male body. Eng-Beng Lim, in his examination of Orientalism through the trope of the homoerotic white man and native boy, finds that colonialism's legacy haunts "the contemporary postcolonial queer Asian." Lim, *Brown Boys and Rice Queens*, 11.

104. Chappell, *This Isn't Romance*, 47.

meeting Jack at a club, Miso rejects his request to be his long-term mistress. At a follow-up meeting, however, she reinvents herself by bluntly asking Jack for money up front in exchange for sex and trying to arouse him with a sadomasochistic line of thought:

> JACK: Am I disgusting?
> MISO: Yes and I like it. I like to disgust myself and I like to be paid. . . .
> *Han walks back in, stands at the bar looking at MISO. JACK's back is towards him.*
> MISO: I could pretend but then you'd hate me for pretending, like you hate all the women who've lied to you. No we're going to go through the whole fucking repertoire. . . . I want you to hate me. I want you to humiliate me, degrade me and I'll like it. I want you to hurt me, tear me, make me bleed. All the hatred, all the anger you feel I want you to act it out on me. And the pain that you . . . can't even come close to what's already inside. I don't care what you do to me just keep me alive.[105]

While there is no indication in the script that Miso's last lines are delivered to Han, the 2017 National Theatre Company of Korea (NTCK) production, directed by Sae-rom Boo, was staged with Han appearing behind Jack and Miso as if saying her lines to Han.[106] This directorial approach turns Miso's lines into a confession in which she gives herself to Han and asks him to release his hatred for her. For Miso, the sexual transaction is not merely a monetary way for her to repay her debt of guilt to Han but, possibly, to truly connect with him. Furthermore, her sense of guilt over abandoning Han and need for forgiveness are so powerful that she is willing to reinvent herself and engage in this degrading sexual transaction. Her willingness to be taken advantage of mirrors how a younger Han sexually compromised himself with the American man in exchange for financial and emotional security. In comparison, Miso's reinvention is not intended to ensure her survival but rather

---

105. Chappell, 65–66. Last ellipsis in original.

106. The NTCK production of *This Isn't Romance* was produced under the "Korean Diaspora" season theme, sending the message that Korean transnational adoptees and adoption issues are part of the performances of Korean diaspora stories. Other plays included in the season were Mia Chung's *You for Me for You*, Ins Choi's *Kim's Convenience*, and Julia Cho's *Aubergine*. According to Yeonju Yu, the season disclosed the Western-oriented definition of performing the Korean diaspora by selecting only Korean diaspora playwrights from the United States, the United Kingdom, and Canada, dismissing works from non-Western countries. It is worth noting that criticism arose regarding the choice of works by established playwrights including Chappell rather than trying to make an effort to seek out new playwrights. Yu, "Korean Diaspora Festival."

to regain her brother's acceptance. However, repelled by the intensity of her words, Jack rejects her.

At first glance, *This Isn't Romance* seems to insinuate a dualistic perception of the power dynamics between the three main characters in terms of race, gender, and sexuality. Han fits the role of the once-orphaned poor young Asian man, Jack the older white European male financier, and Miso the Asian female adoptee, sexually coveted by both Jack and Han. Jack represents the quintessential Orientalist Western hedonist, a symbol of European colonialism in Asia, who sees himself as part of the upper class of entrepreneur expatriates, wholly distinct from those he describes as sex tourists, like "One of those middle aged failures that moves to Bangkok."[107] Yet, as much as Jack may deny it, he is a predator, financially and sexually, who takes advantage of his white European heterosexual male privilege to pursue aggressive money-making deals and instant sexual gratification in Asia. Indeed, Jack's behavior and attitude reflect the idea—which Said identifies as a "remarkably persistent motif in Western attitudes to the Orient"—that "the Orient seems still to suggest not only fecundity but sexual promise (and threat), untiring sensuality, unlimited desire, deep generative energies."[108] While Han and Jack are of different races and from different cultural backgrounds, both men seem to find common ground in their misogynistic and male-dominant outlook as they both try to take advantage of Miso.

Nevertheless, the play suggests an interpretation of Miso not as a victim but as a transnational Asian woman embodying an ambiguity. Unlike the two male characters, Miso personifies a combination of imaginaries of East and West. As such, she is seen by Jack and Han as both privileged like the West and exotic like the East, and is thus attractive to both men for her in-between-ness. In the club, discussing his taste in women with Miso, Jack points out that he prefers her to the Korean waitress because the latter is "too ethnic" and Miso is "in a different category."[109] Han also sees her as an object of desire, calling her sexy and, at one point, kissing her "savagely."[110] For Han, Miso paradoxically exemplifies the Western femininity he both despises and regards with envy. He tells her, "You look like me, but like stranger. Arrogant bitch with hard currency."[111] Han also puts Miso in the category of "other" when he asks, "why you look like **wheregugin** (foreigner)." And he calls her an "opportunist," the same word he uses to describe the older American man who replaced him

---

107. Chappell, *This Isn't Romance*, 60.
108. Said, *Orientalism*, 188.
109. Chappell, *This Isn't Romance*, 60.
110. Chappell, 38.
111. Chappell, 35.

with a younger boy.[112] Yet Miso remains ambivalent about her Asianness and her Westernness. This ambivalence creates within her a conflicting push-and-pull as she negotiates a positionality, which is, in the words of Homi Bhabha, "caught in the tension of demand and desire."[113] Interestingly, the Greek etymology of hatred is *mīsos*, while in Korean *miso* means smile, allowing Miso's name to indicate the ambivalence of her character.[114]

After their intense confrontation with Jack, Miso and Han return to Han's room and drink heavily while talking about their dismal lives and desperate need for each other. As Miso speaks about their childhood and their birth parents' tragic deaths at sea, they draw closer to one another, confessing that they cannot live without each other. As they lie on the bed, Han undresses and kisses Miso, telling her he loves her. Moving his head down her stomach, he says, "You smell like the sea. **Eung . . . Non nahante badaya** (You are my sea). . . . You are . . . my world."[115] Han's physical transgression catalyzes a shift in Miso's unstable position from that of a sisterly and maternal figure to that of a sexual counterpart. Fearing their passion, Miso moves away from Han to drink from a whiskey bottle, then pours it over her head. She then looks at Han and lights a match before the stage blacks out. The following and final scene is set one month later in a hospital near the seashore, where Han visits Miso, whose face and hands are bandaged. Miso has almost permanently blinded herself in warding off temptation. Her act of self-inflicted violence has not only prevented the consummation of their incestuous attraction but also allowed the siblings to finally achieve closure. Han declares that he found hope and love again when Miso came back and that now, for the first time, he feels he has family and a home: "We saved each other. All clean now, start again."[116] As a consequence of their reunion, Miso and Han seem to have ultimately found redemption, albeit at the price of Miso's sacrificial self-harm.

The play ends with the sound of the sea and an airplane flying overhead as the audience is put in Miso's place, hearing only what she can hear since she cannot see. The sounds of the sea, a site of permanency with its ever-crashing waves, recall Han and Miso's birthplace on the island of Jeju (an island south of the Korean Peninsula) and their childhood with their birth parents. In the previous scene, Miso had told Han about their childhood on the island where their mother was a pearl diver and their father a boatman. As well as evoking a time before they became orphans, the sea also represents

---

112. Chappell, 42.
113. Bhabha, "Foreword," xxviii.
114. Thanks to the external reader's input regarding Greek mythology.
115. Chappell, *This Isn't Romance*, 75. First and last ellipsis in original.
116. Chappell, 80.

the present, the time of their reunion and intimate communion, and seems to promise an indeterminate future in which they might be able to start over again as reunited siblings. Han affirms Miso's return to her beginnings—to her infancy—with the last words in the play: "Heal . . . get better. When you stronger I take you to the sea."[117] As an open-ended symbol, the sea carries a strong maternal symbolism.[118] In this sense, Miso's return to the sea represents a symbolic return to and reunion with her birth mother, further becoming one for her brother. Conversely, the airplane sound denotes the temporal trajectory that encompasses both Miso's departure from Korea when she was adopted as a child and her return as an adult to reunite with her brother. While Miso's sight is impaired, her auditory sense remains, and the combined sounds of the sea and the airplane resonate as a recapitulation of her life's path from Korean child and orphan, to transnational adoptee, to returnee. Despite its bleakness and violence, *This Isn't Romance* finishes with Han's rage appeased and Miso's guilt assuaged. Miso's deliberate self-injury prevents a potentially morally destructive outcome, allowing for atonement. Moreover, Miso's act of penitence and sacrifice allow her to re-create herself anew—as a person physically disfigured but free of self-hatred and guilt. Thus, her search and reunion bring about painful regeneration in both the relationship between Miso and Han, and Miso's relationship with herself.

Extraordinary Adopted Being in *Re-enacting the Transnational Adoptee* (2015)

While *Les Bonnes Intentions* and *This Isn't Romance* convey the idea of birth search and reunion as a pathway to survival and redemption, respectively, Yong Sun Gullach's performance art piece, *Re-enacting the Transnational Adoptee,* portrays the birth search as a means of seeking the truth, however painful.[119] The works of Gullach, a Korean Danish adoptee artist and activist, explore the complications of emotion, memory, and history in the othering of people of color, employing various performative methods from body art to the visual and conceptual arts. For instance, in "The Starchild Project," a collection of multidisciplinary works, Gullach delves into the (re)presentations of bodies of color in relation to race and gender in a white hegemonic Western

---

117. Chappell, 80. Ellipsis in original.
118. Carl Jung considered water one of the many symbols for mother. Jung, *Psychology of the Unconscious,* 244.
119. The analysis of *Re-enacting the Transnational Adoptee* is based on the videotaped performance made available through the artist's official website.

society. This project includes a series of pieces ranging from an exhibition of performative objects (*Hwarang*) and a collection of photographic works-in-progress (*Alien*) to a body art performance involving the process of scarification (*The Starchild*). *The Starchild* particularly criticizes the Western-centered ideology of what it means to be a mother. This ideology has degraded Asian motherhood and Asian women's reproductivity in favor of transnational and transracial adoption as the preferred, and even best, option for children in need.[120] To reveal this silenced women of color's devalued fertility and their bodily pain in adoption narratives, in *The Starchild*, Gullach enacts direct physical pain by piercing the skin around her belly button in such a way as to make the shape of a star with eight needles. Each of the eight needles has strings attached to eight transparent spheres holding items such as spices, tea, silk, and opium seeds that, according to Gullach, symbolize a reference to the colonization of Asia. Another one of the spheres contains little plastic baby figurines representing Asian children who were sold and shipped out, just like other commodities.[121] For Gullach, *The Starchild* addresses transnational adoption by utilizing the symbol of the "starchild," which, for her, signifies the bodily pain of the female womb. This performance artwork thus serves not only to convey that Gullach's female body of color feels "real" pain, but also to disturb spectators watching her actual body in pain. Using such subversive tactics of enacting pain, spectators are compelled to reflect upon the unjust and unethical practices associated with transnational adoption.

Gullach continues her strategy of discomforting audiences with her piece *Re-enacting the Transnational Adoptee*. As part of "The Starchild Project," *Re-enacting the Transnational Adoptee* is a thirty-minute performance art work that has been performed in several venues, including the 2015 Hysteria Festival in Berlin, Germany, the Miami Performance International Festival also in 2015, and the 2018 Living Archives Research Project in Malmö, Sweden. At the start of the performance, Gullach appears in a dark room, clothed in a traditional Korean *hanbok* and wearing a gas mask, which she keeps on throughout the performance. As she enters, Gullach makes eye contact with several audience members and speaks through her mask in an untranslatable language. Sounds projected in the performance space include buzzing, radio-type static, recorded Korean advertisements, fragments of Korean, English, and Danish sentences, and the babbling of babies in Danish. Communication between her and the audience members is consequently hindered by the constant sounds and by Gullach, who intentionally whispers incomprehensible

---

120. H. Kim, *Birth Mothers*, 191.
121. Gullach, interview.

sentences through her mask. This obligates listeners to try decoding the language of racially othered subjects—here, in particular, a Korean transnational adoptee. After her entrance, Gullach stands in the middle of a lighted white space surrounded on the floor by white pieces of paper neatly arranged in evenly spaced piles forming a semicircle around her. A small amount of white talcum powder, a flogging whip, and paper airplanes lined up in a row are also on the floor. Gullach removes her *hanbok* until she is topless in white underwear. She then rolls around on the floor, stops to crouch in the middle of the performance space, puts white powder on the whip, and harshly lashes her back several times. Fine white powder particles disperse all around her in the air under the bright lighting. In the white-dust-filled space, Gullach then takes papers from the piles and frantically tapes them to her body, from her feet to her torso and arms. The papers include fake Korean and Danish paper money, research materials on the history and practices of Korean transnational adoption, general and Gullach's personal adoption documents, and pieces of paper with Korean, English, and Danish words, including "Banana" and "Chinaman." Once she finishes wrapping herself, she grabs the paper airplanes and angrily throws them at the audience. Finally, she puts her *hanbok* back on, covering her wrapped body, and interacts with audience members through eye contact, hugs, and whispers as she exits.

Influenced by Erika Fischer-Lichte's phenomenological investigations in theater and performance, Gullach differentiates between the phenomenological body as an embodiment and the semiotic body as a body that represents something more.[122] Fischer-Lichte writes that in mid-eighteenth-century German theater, a new type of acting surfaced in which "the actor 'embodied' a dramatic character," denoting that the actor had to "become proficient at expressing physically the meanings that the poet had expressed textually, [thus transforming] his sensual body into a semiotic one which would serve as a material carrier for textual meaning."[123] In my interview with her, Gullach mentioned that she felt compelled to understand why many people of color, including transnational adoptees, were only viewed as phenomenological rather than semiotic figures and decided to investigate this matter. Gullach stated that she very deliberately tried to show that her entire piece is built in such a way that the (re)presentational structure of the performance suggests a semiotic body as well as a phenomenological body of an adoptee.[124] In other words, Gullach foregrounds her body as the embodiment of a transnational adoptee of color but also a body that incorporates the semiotics—the

---

122. Gullach, interview.
123. Fischer-Lichte, *Transformative Power of Performance*, 77–78.
124. Gullach, interview.

meanings—about *being* a transnational adoptee of color. In so doing, Gullach's performance demonstrates the slippage of ontological being in the course of adoption. In her own words, "It's like an exchange between the two [the phenomenological body and the semiotic body] all the time."[125] This slippage sparks a conflict between her own phenomenological body and a semiotic body that is wrapped in an "adoptee-ness" conceived through cultural imaginaries of transnational adoptees of color. Oscillating between the phenomenological and the semiotic body, a definitive signification is thus deferred. Peggy Phelan writes that "Performance boldly and precariously declares that Being is performed (and made temporarily visible) in that suspended in-between."[126] Like Phelan's positioning of performance between the performing body's tangible corporeality and the "psychic experience" of being embodied,[127] Gullach's performance occurs between her real body, her phenomenological body, and her semiotic and psychic embodiment in an in-between suspension of what it means to be an adopted person.

Significantly, *Re-enacting the Transnational Adoptee* holds a personal meaning linked to Gullach's own birth search. In preparation for the performance, Gullach visited the adoption agency in Seoul where she had been relinquished as a child, wishing to obtain physical documents about her adoption case as part of her archival research.[128] However, because the archives belonged to the organization, her search for her birth records consistently encountered obstacles. Gullach had to visit the agency five times, being given a different type of documentation each time, and accepting whatever she was given, sometimes only a single page or a photo.[129] For Gullach, the difficulty in accessing her own adoption papers reveals the adoption industry's ongoing practice that results in failing to serve adoptees' interests and needs and marginalizing their right to know when they return for their search.[130] Here, the adoption agency does not simply function as an adoption intermediary but as an authoritative archive where adoptee records reside under its control. In Gullach's case, the use of such controlling strategies becomes clear when, through scrutinizing her retrieved adoption documents, she found out

---

125. Gullach, interview.
126. Phelan, *Unmarked*, 167.
127. Phelan.
128. Gullach, interview.
129. Gullach, interview.
130. The right to adoption information disclosure was passed through the Special Adoption Law in 2012, but, according to legal expert Te-ri Kang, "the scope remains limited to such a degree that it's hard to claim that this provision respects adoptees' right to know." Kang, "What Does Korean Law Say about Adoptees' Right to Information Disclosure."

that her adoption records had been falsified.[131] Gullach realized that, among other inconsistencies, some of her baby photos did not resemble each other, her name tag showed evidence of her social security number having been retouched by pen, and her birth document listed her as male.[132] Thus, by including this archival search of her personal adoption documents in her performance piece, she exposes the institutionalized abusive power that the Korean transnational adoption industry perpetuated as it created unreliable—if not labyrinthic—ways for adoptees to trace their birth records.[133] Gullach, in a sense, is performing her hard-won reunion with her past self, represented in her adoption documents though fabricated and partial, integrating into her performance the frustration and anger she experienced in obtaining them.

While the incorporation of personal aspects brings a realness to her performance, Gullach's transfigurations also constitute an extraordinary way for her to reinvent herself as an embodiment of transnational adoptees' experiences. Alternating between silences and an unintelligible language that negates clear verbal communication, Gullach's body becomes a "talking" entity that re-enacts her personally embodied and historically embedded experiences of being and becoming a transnational adoptee of color in a white hegemonic Western setting. In my interview with her, Gullach noted that transnational adoptees are rarely invited to participate in discussions about race, despite having the "very unique position of experiencing racism in close family because a lot of them are children of color adopted into white families."[134] To illustrate her point, whiteness is identified in her performance as a violative force overwriting her body, reflecting the perpetual silencing of adoptees of color. In order to foreground this silencing power of whiteness actualized onto nonwhite adoptee bodies, Gullach utilizes visual materials that serve as conceptual signifiers of whiteness: white talcum powder and white papers. To enact the whiteness imposed on her body, Gullach specifically utilizes the mundane act of bathing, but using white powder instead of water. Taking

---

131. Gullach, interview.
132. Gullach, interview.
133. For other art works expressing the difficulty in accessing adoption records, see the following: in the United States, Jean A. S. Strauss's documentary film, *ADOPTED: for the life of me* (2010), follows the heartbreaking stories of middle-age American adoptees trying to obtain their birth records while confronting constant rejection due to constitutional rights and privacy laws in several states. Borshay Liem's documentary film, *In the Matter of Cha Jung Hee* (2010), shows Liem as she returns to Korea to search for the truth about why her identity had been switched during her adoption process. The Korean Swedish adoptee artist Lisa Wool-Rim Sjöblom's graphic novel, *Palimpsest: Documents from a Korean Adoption* (2019), deals with the predicaments that Korean transnational adoptees experience in the course of searching for birth records.
134. Gullach, interview.

FIGURE 4. *Re-enacting the Transnational Adoptee,* Yong Sun Gullach, 2015. Live performance at EVA International 2016. Photo: Miriam O'Connor. Courtesy the artist and EVA International.

hold of the long-lashed whip covered with talcum powder, she whips her half-naked body (see figure 4). This action invokes the Scandinavian practice of using birch twigs in the sauna to cleanse the skin and improve circulation, but in the context of her performance, Gullach subverts this practice by whipping herself "dirty" with white powder.

Examining everyday practices and performances of the Asian body, Ju Yon Kim conceptualizes what the Asian body means as it becomes a venue of mundane racialization. Kim discusses ways in which identity is constructed and the Asian body, in particular, becomes a racial marker through which its ambiguity is foregrounded. Kim states that "while the repetitions of the quotidian unfold, signify, and have social effects in a subliminal hum, rituals are more insistently patterned and symbolic."[135] Gullach embodies the idea of "whitewashing" through the quotidian act of bathing, but the repetition of her actions points to a ritualistic performance. Moreover, the harshness of the repeated strokes evokes a sense of punishment, the whipping itself reminiscent of the flagellation of Christ and the medieval religious flagellant sects attempting to appease the wrath of God so as to be spared from the plague. In a way, Gullach punishes herself for not being white enough and consequently

---

135. J. Y. Kim, *Racial Mundane,* 78.

endeavors to beat whiteness into herself. Fanon observes that the Black man's racialized psychic formation and affective response are tied to white colonial power, as the emulation of whiteness only leads to the alienation from Blackness.[136] Gullach's ritualistic action here symbolizes her alienation from her Asianness through a painful emulation of her attempted transformation into whiteness. Yet the more she tries to reinvent herself to being white, the more impossible that goal becomes, leaving her Asian body somewhere between whiteness as an enforcing power and whiteness as an emulating desire.

After her half-naked body becomes coated and draped in white powder and white papers, her extended body morphs from an Asian body into a rematerialized whitened body containing the residual traces of the physical and emotional labor she has endured. Gullach's vehement acts of wrapping her body with white paper and lashing her body with the white-powered whip represent the overwhelming, invasive whiteness taking over the body of a nonwhite adoptee. Hübinette contends that "a white subject position is exactly what diasporic non-whites need to be able to survive in a world of white supremacy and white privileges."[137] Likewise, Gullach's harsh bodily actions reflect her struggle to "survive" by whitening herself, but in a self-inflicted way indicating the (in)visible violence of her assimilation into white hegemonic society. Moreover, with every lash of her whip, Gullach not only whitens her back more but also releases white particles into the air, filling the entire space, signifying the prevalence of whiteness. The thickness of the white powder in the air visually suggests to onlookers that the air is more difficult to breathe, an effect that Gullach intended as

> a comment of being in the white space in general as a body of color, but also being in a certain space as an adoptee, constantly trying to find your own life, so to speak. The breathing is life. And not breathing is surrendering to your life, basically. So, I wanted the audience to have that physical feeling of how it is to be in a space where you can hardly breathe.[138]

In this sense, the suffocating, white-dust-filled space and Gullach's whitened body visualize the (in)visible power of whiteness that affects transnational adoptees: "It covers everything, [and is] a way of showing how both your body is being covered by this whiteness, and also how you as a person will need to

---

136. Fanon, *Black Skin, White Masks*.
137. Hübinette, "Disembedded and Free-Floating Bodies," 144.
138. Gullach, interview.

fight to get out of this whiteness, to get out of the understanding of yourself as being part of the whiteness."[139]

While Gullach reveals the invasive encroachment of whiteness on non-white adoptees' bodies, she also suggests the idea of resistance for her "claimed" self. Toward the end of the performance, she puts her *hanbok* back on, evoking her potential reconstruction, although it is never fully achieved. Gullach's act of re-donning the traditional Korean clothing over her whitened body signifies that she has stripped off her "Koreanness" and put it back on. In his postcolonial analysis of Asian Swedish adoptees reified as "mimic Swedes," Richey Wyver argues that the authorized version of otherness that international adoption inscribes onto the transracial Swedish adoptees renders them "almost the same, but not quite—or almost the same, but not white."[140] This process is captured in one of Wyver's case studies, *Gul utanpå* (*Yellow on the Outside*), a 2013 autobiographical novel by Korean adoptee Patrik Lundberg that shows the adoptee's progression "into a 'mimic Swede,' along with the frictions of being trapped between a not-quite-white Swedishness and a not-quite otherness."[141] Gullach's mimic white body demonstrates her ensnarement between a not-quite whiteness, a not-quite otherness, and a not-quite Koreanness through her painstaking acts of whitewashing, affixing, and un- and re-dressing. In doing so, she pointedly shows how transnational adoptees are irreversibly marked by a "friction" between not-quite-white and not-quite other. Her performance thus takes the form of a rebuilding, but with all the pain that the lived experiences and processes of transnational adoption have caused her and other adoptees.

Gullach has performed *Re-enacting the Transnational Adoptee* mostly in museums and galleries in Euro-American contexts, where the white gaze is predominantly visible in the works of white artists and in white audiences, administrative personnel, and institutional powers. George Yancy writes that "the white gaze is an embodied phenomenon, a mode of social engagement, a form of practice that presupposes a thick, historical sedimentation or encrustation of white supremacy. [. . . Nevertheless,] the white gaze is contingent and thereby open to be disrupted, undone."[142] Gullach's performance exposes how the reinvention of an adoptee is created in relation to whiteness and how

---

139. Gullach, interview.

140. Wyver, "Civilizing Missions and Mimicry," 133. Wyver builds his thought on Homi Bhabha's writing about colonial mimicry, "almost the same, but not quite," as the other (the colonized) becomes almost the same as the colonizer but will never quite assimilate into the colonizer's dominant networks. Bhabha, *Location of Culture*, 86.

141. Wyver, "Civilizing Missions and Mimicry," 135.

142. Yancy, "White Embodied Gazing," 244–45.

exercising the power of performance disrupts the white gaze. One of the ways Gullach achieves this disruption is through her direct, up-close interactions with audience members immediately upon entry into the performance space as she makes eye contact with several of them. Another way she undoes the gaze is by breaking the "ordinary" norms of decency by revealing her half-naked body and using shock to draw attention and control the audience's focus. Through this performative strategy to subvert their gaze, Gullach highlights the body as her best resource for empowerment:

> The piece only exists while my body exists in that moment. So therefore, I have a certain kind of power in that moment. I have a power of how to set up the space. I have a power of how I want the audience to be placed. I have a power of whom in the audience I reenact with. I have the power of offering my body but also withdrawing my body if I want to.[143]

Drawing on this sense of power in performance, Gullach also engages with her body to enact rage through aggressive acts directed not only toward herself but also toward her spectators by throwing paper airplanes at them. The planes are specifically folded with a point at the head so they can fly faster. Some planes are made from the paperwork of different falsified adoption cases, and the anger with which Gullach throws the paper planes is meant to directly "hurt" audience members.[144] Anger in Gullach's performance is an affective strategy, which differs from the one-dimensional representation of an angry adoptee. In my interview with her, Gullach emphasized the significance of feeling anger by mentioning the Korean Danish adoptee poet Maja Lee Langvad, whose 2014 poem "Hun er vred: Et vidnesbyrd om transnational adoption" ("She is angry: A testimony of transnational adoption") expresses her anger about the injustices of transnational adoption.[145] Through Gullach's "violent" actions based on her self-reflective and revelatory anger, the Asian female body is no longer viewed as an object of repression but as an agent of resistance. But more than fighting back, her actions are meant as a form of punishment. Inflicting harm (albeit as much as a paper projectile can inflict) from such painful content is a way for Gullach to dare the audience to challenge either their passive or active involvement in the injustices associated with transnational adoption, or their ignorance of them. Gullach thus turns spectators into tacit conspirators in the making of adoptees as racialized others and in the unjust transnational and transracial adoption practices in and

---

143. Gullach, interview.
144. Gullach, interview.
145. Langvad, *"Hun er vred."*

out of Korea while simultaneously extending her hand to potential future allies in changing this adoption landscape for justice.

Interestingly, the conclusion of Gullach's performance conveys a different feeling. Before finally leaving the space, she makes random eye contact with audience members and interacts with them through looks, hugs, and whispered but intelligible words. She also sometimes comes so close to them that she touches her forehead to theirs in a wishful expression of intimacy, care, and solidarity. In contrast to her confrontational entrance with its broken words and made-up language, these direct engagements during her exit evoke a "sticky feeling" between her and the audience members. Sara Ahmed uses the words "sticky" and "stickiness" to argue that "affect is what sticks, or what sustains or preserves the connection between ideas, values, and objects."[146] I use "stickiness" here in a similar sense to emphasize the emotional, intellectual, and physical bonds Gullach creates between herself and her audience members. Her intimacy with spectators arouses a sense of stickiness, inviting a feeling of empathy rather than judgment, as though they have all shared a special, albeit uncomfortable, moment.

While not intrinsically an interactive piece (as spectators do not take part in her performance), by playing with tactile sensations, Gullach makes audience involvement a necessary component of *Re-enacting the Transnational Adoptee*. Because touch is a "body-oriented" sense,[147] using it here is a way for Gullach to connect more personally to her audience and herself. Through physical interaction with audience members, Gullach establishes a close connection that shifts their perception of her performance from cognitive to corporeal. Furthermore, because the sense of touch is shared, this two-way exchange also affects her, as Gullach's touch conveys her hope to engender a temporary communion between her and her audience. In this context, as Eve Kosofsky Sedgwick suggests, "the sense of touch makes nonsense out of any dualistic understanding of agency and passivity."[148] Through her improvisational act of touching, Gullach allows herself to yield her agency (her total control over the performance's actions and consequences) while also negating the passivity of being solely on the performer's side of the performance—that is, an object receiving the audience's gaze. As such, Gullach transgresses these dualistic boundaries and, in the process, makes the audience part of an interfacing whole. Calling on spectators to be active thinkers at the very least and active participants at the highest level, particularly in confronting whitewashing and injustice toward adoptees of color, Gullach encourages them to

---

146. Ahmed, *Promise of Happiness*, 230n1.
147. O'Shaughnessy, *Consciousness and the World*, 630.
148. Sedgwick, *Touching Feeling*, 14.

develop more critical understandings of the racialized experiences of transnational adoptees. By concluding her performance piece with physical touches, Gullach transcends words, emphasizing a truthful and hopeful interdependence between her and her audience members.

Transmitting a variety of emotions ranging from bewilderment and anger to communal togetherness, Gullach's performance serves to unsettle a white-centric perspective on transnational adoption. Rather than verbally recounting her story, Gullach instead puts her body in focus to disclose the (self-) inflicted violence imposed on transnational and transracial adoptees of color. In this way, she allows her body to become a contested scene of re-enactments of the sending of a child from Korea for adoption into a white-dominant society and the reclaiming of one's own self in the course of searching. In sum, Gullach's *Re-enacting the Transnational Adoptee* is nothing less than a performed manifestation of the living memory of Korean transnational adoption.

Feeling Decolonial Discomfort

Writing on queerness in Cuban theater and performance, Bretton White contends that "new affective modes are produced when performing bodies highlight—often in uncomfortably intimate, grotesque, or raw ways—the unavoidability of spectators' bodies, as well as their capacity for queerness."[149] Focusing on the uncomfortable feelings that stem from the proximity of staged sexuality, White argues that these intimate junctions possess the ability to generate affective forces enabling new insights into queerness and artistic creativity.[150] Applying White's argument to this chapter, I would maintain that feelings of discomfort can facilitate the creation of renewed insights into Korean transnational adoption, particularly regarding what it means to be a transnational and transracial female adoptee whose experiences are sexualized and racialized through encounters with adoptive and birth families and cultures.

In *Les Bonnes Intentions*, *This Isn't Romance*, and *Re-enacting the Transnational Adoptee*, violence and violation function as a dramatic and performative vehicle for the dismantling of the trope of the "feel-good" adoption story, a vestige of emotive colonialization derived from transnational adoption scripts of salvation, rescue, and charity. As Kim-Su Rasmussen argues, "The cultural discourse of adoption establishes imaginary tropes and structures of feeling, which serve to justify the practice of transnational adoption from Korea."[151]

---

149. White, *Staging Discomfort*, 2.
150. White, 3.
151. Rasmussen, "Sublime Object of Adoption," 16.

These cultural tropes and structures of feeling have been selectively (re)constructed from dualistic tribulations such as poverty, prostitution, domestic violence, and military rule in sending nations as well as colorblind, progressive, and benevolent family-making practice in receiving nations. These constructions have been relentlessly reified and widely circulated to validate transnational narratives of saviorlike white adoptive parents, happy multicultural families, and blissful birth family reunions (see the introduction for historical details). In the historical and ongoing consumption of these tropes, patriarchal norms and unequal racial discourses remain unchallenged, repeatedly perpetuating the same problematic perceptions of adoption. In light of this, performing transnational adoption works highlight the need to challenge prevailing Korean transnational adoption imaginaries and narratives, mere reiterations of the "feel-good" script that engender a compulsory sanitizing of uncomfortable emotions. One of the ways the adoption industry achieves this cleansing is by using the images of children as a "tranquilizing convention," the function of which is to "depoliticize highly political contexts," thus generating a public comfort.[152] By centering on discomfort, my intent in this chapter is not to justify the sensationalizing of adoption stories on stage but to gauge the varied structures of emotion that have influenced how we, as audience members and readers, contextualize adoption beyond "feeling good." Thus, I argue that experiencing discomfort through theatrical adoption stories can alter our understanding of adoption that has previously been tranquilized by "feel-good" narratives and affects.

The three selected works examined in this chapter instill an unsettling discomfort in audiences by creating harsh experiences in a performance space that exposes spectators to "dangerous" situations. In my interview with Chappell, she commented that, in theater, "not everything needs to be safe, middle of the road."[153] Chappell's comment is reminiscent of the words of Augusto Boal, who, when questioned about the safety of his work, in which intense explorations of personal relationships often led to raw emotional expressions, answered, "This work is theatre and not therapy. Theatre is not safe."[154] Theater, indeed, is not always a "safe" space, wherein certain actions, characters, and narratives are only created for an audience's comfortable reception. All

---

152. E. J. Kim, citing Liisa Malkki. E. J. Kim, *Adopted Territory*, 75. Malkki writes that images of children "as moral subjects are used in international ceremonial discourses as *ritual fetishes of peace*, [... with] appeals and images of children as teachers and ambassadors of peace [... acting] precisely as a *tranquillizing convention*." Malkki, *Need to Help*, 92. Italics in original.

153. Chappell, interview with the author, June 2, 2019, Hackney, London, UK.

154. Boal as cited by Robert Landy and David T. Montgomery. Landy and Montgomery, *Theatre for Change*, xxiii–xxiv.

three of the pieces examined here demonstrate the principle Antonin Artaud felt was missing in the theater of his time, which had "broken away from solemnity, from direct, harmful effectiveness—in a word, from Danger."[155] Artaud linked danger to fear and saw danger produced on the stage as the sudden unforeseen "passing from a mental image to a true image."[156] In this sense, an augmented danger and fear permeate every page, scene, and performative action of these three works, whose audiences shudder to imagine what might happen next to the main characters and performers.

A further commonality between the three works is the shock they produce as they depart from the expected "feel-good" aspect often associated with adoption narratives. This shock engenders jolts of fear and dismay in audiences, who, after anticipating the usual happy and grateful adoption story, are suddenly confronted with an extraordinary harshness that makes them wince and perhaps hope for a rapid end to the performance. In both *Les Bonnes Intentions* and *This Isn't Romance*, shock stems from experiencing what one is not ready to view or accept, the sometimes-bleak realities of transnational and transracial adoption. Moreover, in these "unsafe" and "danger-embracing" theatrical acts and imaginings, discomfort does not derive just from experiencing emotionally distressing adoption stories of rape, incest, and racialization but also from imagining or actually witnessing violent acts evoked on stage. This is especially evident in *Re-enacting the Transnational Adoptee*, in which Gullach "injures" her own body. Her performance, in particular, also sows the seeds of what Artaud wished for theater: to "cause a shock to the anatomy, leaving an indelible impression on it."[157] In a similar spirit, RoseLee Goldberg sees performance as a way of "shocking audiences into reassessing their own notions of art and its relation to culture."[158] In this context, Gullach's performance art piece compels her audience members to re-examine archaic views on adoption, as well as the ways they expect adoption to be represented and communicated with them through art.

Regarding audience responses, in our interview, Min Jung mentioned that different audiences had different reactions to *Les Bonnes Intentions*. The Korean Belgian adoptee community members she met thanked her because they recognized themselves in the play and felt understood. Some of the adoptive parents and older people, however, felt attacked.[159] Similar senti-

---

155. Artaud, *The Theatre and Its Double*, trans. Victor Corti, 29.
156. Artaud gives the example of danger on stage as being when a man suddenly curses and then "sees the image of his curse realistically materialized before him." Artaud, 30.
157. Artaud, 55.
158. Goldberg, *Performance Art*, 8.
159. Min Jung, interview.

ments were expressed regarding audience reactions to *This Isn't Romance*. Chappell said in our interview that the play had offended some white people, as well as more conservative Koreans.[160] The Soho production of *This Isn't Romance* reached another level of disturbance with its discomforting story about Korean transnational adoption, particularly among a group of Korean diasporic audiences in the United Kingdom who may have perceived the play as a criticism of Korea's involvement in the adoption industry. According to Chappell, she became, in her own words, "a persona non grata of the Korean Embassy because I was seen as a foreigner criticizing Korea."[161] Audience response to performing transnational adoption thus cannot be generalized into a simple either/or dichotomy. Discomfort, however, remains consistently present for some.

For Gullach, the reception of *Re-enacting the Transnational Adoptee* was largely positive for audiences of color and adoptees who had a closer understanding and better grasp of the ideas Gullach was trying to convey.[162] While some white audiences said they could feel the emotional aspects of the piece, Gullach observed that they "didn't understand the political structure" through which she was presenting it.[163] Gullach viewed this reaction from white audiences as a "technique" that is used "to silence . . . artists of color."[164] Gullach explained that because of her position as an adoption activist and artist commenting on adoption, silencing techniques are often employed to diminish her knowledge and critical voice. For example, she said that commenting on her work as only "too angry, or too sad, or too involved, or too investigated" can be understood as an attempt to lessen the validity of her critique and to render her voice "invisible."[165] Gullach's reflection connects to Wyver who, writing about Sweden's intercountry adoption, asserts that when critically thinking adoptees criticize adoption by using the principles of Swedishness (defined as "antiracism, anticolonialism, feminism, and progressive left-leaning liberalism"), they are considered a threat to white Swedish identity, the sense of national belonging, and the belief of adoption as a rescue mission.[166] As Wyver further astutely puts it:

---

160. Chappell, interview.
161. Chappell, interview.
162. Gullach, interview.
163. Gullach, interview.
164. Gullach, interview.
165. Gullach, interview.
166. Wyver, "Civilizing Missions and Mimicry," 143.

When the observed becomes the observer, when the researched becomes the researcher, the mimic adoptee poses arguably the greatest threat of all: a threat to split, challenge, and even rupture, from the inside, the very foundation of white progressive Swedishness, making a mockery of the civilizing mission of adoption itself as adoptees reveal its colonial origins and underpinnings.[167]

As the "performed" becoming the "performers," Gullach, Chappell, and Min Jung expressly make a performative examination of the "colonial origins and underpinnings" rooted in transnational adoption. Remarks regarding the three works made by specific audiences (who may only be familiar with "feel-good" Korean transnational adoption stories and adoption in general) reveal that adoptees' expressions of critical thinking through artistic evocations are often perceived as threats to the hegemonic order dictating how adoption can be conceived and conveyed artistically. In this sense, these artists' performances break what Lene Myong conceptualizes as "racial silence"[168] and what Mette Kim-Larsen describes as "colorblind avoidance."[169] Indeed, Gullach's overall objective for her performance piece was to disrupt the power of adoptive parent–centric discourses by making adoptees' presence a force to be seen and heard:

> Within the adoption discussion in general, the adopters are the major powers and the major drivers, and the voices of the transnational adoptees are very much fighting to be visible. [. . .] It is] by being seen that we do exist. So, for me, it's a basic question of existence.[170]

Re-enacting the Transnational Adoptee thus claims the very existence of Korean transnational adoptees both for Gullach and for other adoptees of color. The work boldly foregrounds how adoptees exist within racialized hierarchies that reinforce inequity, injustice, and invisibility as well as how they can resist these systems of power, utilizing performance as a tool.

Should feelings of being attacked, insulted, or criticized, in other words, feeling uncomfortable, not occur in the theater, particularly when recounting stories about adoption? Quite the contrary. Ahmed asserts that "the 'non-fitting' or discomfort opens up possibilities, an opening up which can be difficult and exciting. . . . To feel uncomfortable is precisely to be affected by that

---

167. Wyver, 143.
168. Myong's term quoted by Kim-Larsen, "Danish Milk," 359.
169. Kim-Larsen, 359.
170. Gullach, interview.

which persists in the shaping of bodies and lives."[171] Actively engaging with discomfort should therefore take place and, in the context of the three works, be regarded as an anticolonial resistance through which audience members can defy simplistic outlooks. The significance of these three pieces lies in their unsettling of the Korean transnational adoption story, which itself has been colonized as a "feel-good" imagination. This disquietude is brought up by unpleasant emotions or, as Sianne Ngai puts it, "ugly feelings" that are made up of "multiple levels of negativity."[172] For Ngai, these ugly feelings are "useful for *conjoining* predicaments from multiple registers—showing how sociohistorical and ideological dilemmas, in particular, produce formal or representational ones."[173] In all three works, the ugly feeling—discomfort—leads audiences to temporarily conjoin the shocking vulnerability embodied by the women characters and performers. The ugly feeling audiences might experience as they come to realize how these three pieces unravel the "feel-good" imagination of adoption, therefore, paves the way for the decolonization of this master affect.

Analysis of the audiences' affective reactions and emotional engagements with these works prompts us to ponder how performing Korean transnational adoption stories potentially creates a decolonial discomfort as audiences witness the violated Asian female adoptee body. As Helen Gilbert and Joanne Tompkins have articulated, "The body's ability to move, cover up, reveal itself, and even 'fracture' on stage provides it with many possible sites for decolonisation."[174] In this sense, the "fractured" Asian female adoptee body onstage becomes a site for the reconstruction of the ways in which a body is colonized and thus enable the production of a new subjectivity beyond the colonial power imposed upon the body. While audiences may have varying thresholds for discomfort, audience members of these three works feel discomfort when they witness the Asian female adoptee body in pain. Through the examination of performances of bodily suffering from medieval to postmodern times in which spectators experience pain, Marla Carlson argues that pain in varied performances is cross-historical and communicable in the (trans)formation of spectator response. Carlson proposes that the uniqueness of pain

> creates an urgent need to communicate things to which no one is eager to listen. . . . Because pain so powerfully solicits the spectator's engagement, aestheticized physical suffering plays a vital role in creating communities

---

171. Ahmed, *Cultural Politics of Emotion*, 154–55.
172. Ngai, *Ugly Feelings*, 12.
173. Ngai, 12. Italics in original.
174. Gilbert and Tompkins, *Post-Colonial Drama*, 204.

of sentiment and consolidating social memory, which in turn shapes the cultural and political realities that cause spectators to respond in different ways at different times.[175]

Drawing on Carlson's idea, in this chapter I conceptualize discomfort as a modality to communicate adoptees' experiences through the painful enactments of violence, thereby creating a unique social memory of Korean transnational adoption. In these three works, decolonial discomfort thus operates as a performative strategy to envision healing and regeneration, and to engender, as Ahmed puts it, "a call for action, and a demand for collective politics."[176] In my interview with her, Min Jung stated that she wanted *Les Bonnes Intentions* to "provoke a reaction in audiences so they would open their eyes and start thinking about the issue [of transnational and transracial adoption], ask questions to each other, and more than anything else start discussing this among themselves."[177] According to Min Jung's account, this provocative invitation to the public was more than successful, as, after *Les Bonnes Intentions*' run, the Belgium Council on Adoption used the play as part of their pedagogical research for future adoptive parents:

> It was the first time here in Belgium that they asked questions that had never been asked from a different angle, and not just about Asian adoption but all international adoptions. Because the focus had always been on future adoptive parents: how they felt, how they lived, if they felt ready, but didn't center much on the child. Since then, they no longer say, "We're looking for a child for parents," now they're saying, "We're looking for parents for a child."[178]

Just as Min Jung's work decenters the focus on adoptive parents in the adoption discourse in Belgium, experiencing the three works in this chapter corroborates Helen Tiffin's assertion that "decolonization is process, not arrival."[179] Decolonization does not occur as a destination but rather as an ongoing route with an antiracist and antisexist direction that challenges colonial, postcolonial, and neocolonial effects upon cultures, languages, methods, forms, and emotions, including theater and performance, across the globe. What I wish to highlight from the three selected works is how theater and performance can generate a transformation in the way audiences feel and learn about adoption. Schwab notes that "such learning about and from other cultures, including

---

175. Carlson, *Performing Bodies in Pain*, 2.
176. Ahmed, *Cultural Politics of Emotion*, 39.
177. Min Jung, interview.
178. Min Jung, interview.
179. Tiffin, "Post-Colonial Literatures and Counter-Discourse," 17.

tolerating and modulating the conflicting affects that arise in the process, is a necessary condition . . . for mental decolonization."[180] Schwab continues by stating that "telling stories across cultural divides might be a first step toward global transcultural literacy because, in bearing witness to historical violence and damage, storytelling negotiates affective difference and aims toward a rearrangement of affect and desire in the future."[181] Instilling discomfort within audiences can be one step toward realizing the potential of decolonizing adoption stories beyond the predetermined and pretamed "feel-good" narratives. Thus, through their daring content and innovative forms, these three pieces and others like them serve as signposts pointing in liberating directions for future representations of adoption and adoptees.

•

Les Bonnes Intentions, This Isn't Romance, and *Re-enacting the Transnational Adoptee* unfetter the imagination of Korean transnational adoption by portraying the uneasy and painful aspects of adoption and adoptee experiences, in contrast to the more commonplace, "feel-good" adoption narratives. Moreover, these three works display an astonishing boldness in their representations of Korean transnational and transracial adoptees' birth search and reunion, contesting assumptions of their inherent vulnerability. In the end, the adoptee characters and performers display courage and strength that challenge the victimization of their sexual and racial experiences of violation. In affirming the three women's agency, these pieces unsettle the denotations and restrictions set by adoption master scripts and become sites of resistance to such inscriptions. Embodying the artists' extraordinary spirit and power of imagination, the works evoke discomfort in their audiences in order to emancipate them and allow them to consider transnational adoption in a decolonized light.[182] However, staging depictions of violence and violation is dependent on audiences' willingness to engage with the painful experience of adoptee characters and performers. If audiences are willing to explore this discomfort, these extraordinary stories and performances can certainly inspire change or, at the very least, create an affective awareness enabling audiences to think about adoption differently. In this way, dramatic and performative works such as these will continue to offer the invaluable opportunity to participate in the decolonization of transnational and transracial adoption narratives.

---

180. Schwab, *Haunting Legacies,* 116.
181. Schwab, 116–17.
182. Rancière, *Emancipated Spectator,* trans. Gregory Elliott.

POSTSCRIPT

Onstage and Offstage

*Imagining Transnational Adoption within
and beyond Birth Search and Reunion*

One autumn weekend in October 2020, I drove to Paju, a one-hour drive north of Seoul (adjacent to the North Korean border), to visit Omma Poom Park, a site developed by the Paju city government specifically as a memorial for birth mothers and returning overseas adoptees to visit and feel reunited with their birth land. This memorial park resides outside the city on the former location of US Army Camp Howze, which was built during the last year of the Korean War, in 1953, and "returned" to the city in 2005. The city decided to use parts of this US military base area as a local outdoor sports place as well as a memorial park. The space has been available to the public since 2018 when a dedication ceremony was officially held for the opening of Omma Poom Park. My journey to reach this memorial park, however, proved to be so puzzling that it led me to question the ways in which the space remembers Korean adoptees and birth mothers.

Once I arrived at the location, taken from the official address on a Korean search engine, I found myself in front of a locked gate encroached upon by bushes, apparently an abandoned entrance. Unable to enter, I luckily encountered a person employed nearby who informed me that the gate was a rear entrance and had been closed for a long time. As the person did not know how to find the actual entrance to the park, I called a local government office that oversees tourism in Paju, and an official informed me of the correct address. Upon arriving at the actual entrance, I found the uninviting large, high metal gate with dark gray steel posts to also be closed. I then noticed a security camera monitoring access to the park. According to a cast-iron information plaque, while the park is only open during certain times on weekdays, on weekends the main gate is operated exclusively upon request. All this information was written in Korean only. I called the same government official again, and the gate opened via remote-control to reveal a view of decrepit army buildings and unkempt vegetation. Driving through a vast, hilly open space, I saw dilapidated remnants of the former US Army base, overgrown with trees and weeds. An eerie silence filled the vast space, and there was no one to be seen. From the top of a hill, I looked out, and sections of the city of Paju sprawled before me in the silent distance, accentuating the eerie quietness of the park. On the other side of the hill, I came to a sign for Omma Poom Park (the literal translation of the Korean name of the park is "the hill of mother's arms"). Once inside the park, I realized that I was on the inside of the closed back entrance where I had mistakenly gone about an hour earlier. Hidden all the way back inside the former army base, in its seclusion the memorial park had the air of a forgotten secret.

At the entrance, a number of tall flagpoles with the flags of the nations that took part in the Korean War greet visitors. Further inside, in an area about the size of a small soccer field, stand sparsely arranged sculptures and the memorial's two main installations. Visiting adoptees can walk, sit, and pause at several places around the site; thus, this immersive space invites them to contextualize their own search and reunion in a meditative way. Adoptees have the leeway to choose their own pace as well as the amount and depth of the memories and feelings they would like to engage with in this open circle of reunion. The space allows adoptees to connect physically with their birth land and spiritually with their birth mothers within the open setting of nature, and to envision birth search and reunion not as a fixed linear event but as an embodied experience to process by themselves. Thus, by offering visitors, especially adoptees, a site-specific outdoor venue in which to experience alternative reunions, Omma Poom Park attempts to liberate adoptees from the essentialized narrative tethered to desperate searches and happily-ever-after reunions. This memorial site makes one ponder other ways of imagining birth search and reunion and remember Korean transnational adoption as an everyday part of Korea's historical and contemporary experiences of local, national, and international politics entangled with US militarism and tourism. Elizabeth Son contends that memorial spaces become a performance in which statues, monuments, or installations take on a life of their own through the public's actions of care.[1] As such, I view Omma Poom Park not as a space

---

1. Son, *Embodied Reckonings*, 147–75.

FIGURE 5. *Shadow Child* (2018) by Wonsook Kim. Photo by author.

for a site-specific performance (that is, a theater or performative event performed at a specific non-auditorium-based site) but as a performative site unto itself. Accordingly, I posit that the site serves as a "performance of care" wherein a live and interactive connection between the space of the site, its visual installations, and its visitors transmits a message of reconciliation, healing, and liberation.[2]

While offering returned adoptees an alternative search-and-reunion experience, Omma Poom Park also, and particularly, reterritorializes what it means to be a birth mother, as expressed by the two main installations (see figures 5 and 6). *Shadow Child* (2018) by Wonsook Kim is a bronze statue in the shape of a standing woman looking down at her arms folded in such a way as to suggest that she is holding a baby, yet her arms are empty. At ground level, however, the statue's bronze shadow shows her holding a baby in her arms. *Mother's Arms* (2018) by Kwanghyun Wang is a more abstract work, a massive sculpture composed of white aligned circles. Situated in the middle of the park, this large circular installation is surrounded by small stones that seem to be in orbit around it. Visitors can walk around or sit on the stones to contemplate the work.

---

2. Son.

FIGURE 6. *Mother's Arms* (2018) by Kwanghyun Wang. Photo by author.

A sign provides the meaning of the two sculptures:

[The former] shows a lone Korean mother who is hugging herself with empty arms; she represents the hope that Korean adoptees and their birth mothers will embrace and understand each other. [The latter] image of the circles being rolled into a mother's arms in white linen and the gradual gathering of circles represent the meaning in "returning to your mother's arms."³

Although these installations do invite onlookers to think about the loss and love involved in Korean transnational adoption, birth mothers and adoptees exist only as symbols in this park. Nowhere could I find any visual or textual "voices" of birth mothers and adoptees that might communicate what separation and reunion mean to them.

Walking in the park, I found only one exception to this. On a wall approximately thirty feet in length, made as a grid of wrapped and crossed iron bars filled with stones, visitors are encouraged to hang padlocks with messages written on them. This "Memory Wall" functions as a participatory installation

---

3. Author's translation of official plaque at Omma Poom Park.

FIGURE 7. Memory wall padlock.
Photo by author.

of visitors' memories, thoughts, feelings, and wishes, locked to the wall in their padlocks. The solid rock, iron, and steel that compose the wall, bar grid, and padlocks seem to signify a promise to permanently preserve the memories. The act of locking a personal message to this public wall affirms visitors' expressions of determination and commitment to never forget. Furthermore, the fastened padlock itself becomes a performative object that embodies feelings of loss, grief, joy, and hope, and is meant to engender memories of reunion and to encourage the restoration of ties among birth mothers, birth land, and adoptees. While this wall holds an evocative purpose, at the time of my visit, only one padlock hung on the iron bars, sadly. A person by the name of 홍성차 (Sonja), presumably a Korean transnational adoptee, had written on it in English: "Home is where my heart is . . ." (see figure 7). This lonely padlock whose handwritten message had already half faded, left only a vaguely discernable trace of Sonja's thought. This was the sole voice—whether from an adoptee or a birth mother—that I could find at the memorial, other than administratively curated metaphors conjuring the romanticized scenario of reunion with birth mothers and birth land.

Hosu Kim observes that even though Omma Poom Park was established as a site of reconciliation, it is also considered a place of economic potential and progress.[4] Kim notes the comments made by a city official before the park's construction: "We will develop various cultural education programs to cater to adoptees who must have a sense of loss towards the homeland, so that the Omma Poom could become one of the most notable tourist sites worldwide."[5] From this point of view, this memorial park, originally intended to provide space for the remembering of reunion and honoring of loss, should become a tourist spot geared to generate profit from the visits of Korean transnational adoptees and their remembrances. On my way out of the park, I reread the city of Paju's original purpose for the site, inscribed on the plaque at the entrance: "To replicate the nostalgic nature of Korean adoptees returning to their motherland, we are planning to create a park named Omma Poom to accentuate humanism."[6] Thus, this site repurposed as a spatial *aide-mémoire* of reunion and loss simultaneously reflects Korean society's capitalistic and nationalistic desire and even demand to reshape its ongoing history of complicity with transnational adoption as well as US militarism. Remembering the words of the city official, I could not help but wonder for whose benefit had this nostalgic replica actually been built, and my overall experience of visiting Omma Poom Park left me with a strong sense of ambivalence. While the memorial ostensibly does commemorate birth mothers and adoptees, its essentialized imagery, geographical remoteness, difficult access, lack of publicity, and Korean-only language signs actively *dis*remember them.

Finally, Omma Poom Park's setting especially recalls the historical initiation and subsequent institutionalization of transnational adoption from Korea to foreign countries—particularly to the United States, whose lingering postwar military presence accommodated intimate interracial encounters between US soldiers and Korean women. As Kim-Su Rasmussen observes, "Korea has a long history of providing women or children as human payment to a superior foreign power in exchange for military protection and economic benefits."[7] After the Korean War, the South Korean government colluded with the US Army to provide institutionalized sexual access to Korean women for GIs in the immediate vicinity of most of the US military bases in Korea. A vivid reminder of this part of Korea's postwar and neocolonial history appeared to me as I left the park. Driving out of the main entrance, I noticed that the former base was surrounded by a *gijichon,* a camptown local residential neighborhood that included a red-light district where Korean women used to mainly serve US soldiers in sexual or romantic relationships. Stopping, I walked around the deserted neighborhood and spotted piles of

---

4. H. Kim, "Reparation Acts," 325.
5. Quoted in H. Kim, "Reparation Acts," 325.
6. Author's translation of official plaque at Omma Poom Park.
7. Rasmussen, "Sublime Object of Adoption," 4.

garbage bags outside the doors of bars, an indication that these were open for business at least at nighttime. English words like "fuck" and "sex" retouched on some of the houses' walls looked like they might have been put up a long time ago to designate brothels for non-Korean-speaking US soldiers. For me, the area vividly brought to mind the setting of *Ilgopzipmae* and the former *gijichon* sex worker character Sunyeong, who relinquished her biracial Korean American son for transnational adoption. I was also reminded that the initial plan for Omma Poom Park was to also be a commemorative site for *gijichon* women whose "stigmatized occupation and the challenging environment for raising biracial children meant that their children were often placed for transnational adoption."[8] However, neither inside nor outside the park could I find the voice of a single *gijichon* woman whose motherhood intersected with transnational adoption. Even more distressing to recall were the memorial's sculptures, which embraced birth mothers as a signifier of maternal nostalgia but excluded any trace of *gijichon* birth mothers, whose existence had seemingly evaporated as if unworthy of remembrance. In fact, this politically and financially motivated public space lacked the "humanism" that its bureaucratic agenda had declared it was meant to accentuate. The site's ambiguous ways of historicizing Korean transnational adoption prompted me to ask further questions: in what forms of remembrance can we truly engage with Korean transnational adoptees, birth mothers, and *gijichon* birth mothers? As both an onlooker and participant in this performative space, how can we actively resist the systemic erasure and selective remembrance that contribute to the depoliticization of Korean transnational adoption?

Nevertheless, as I still ponder these questions, I remind myself that theater and performance artists have taken up the torch and carry on the work of commemorating and reviving the voices of figures like Sunyeong, whose recorded message to her biracial son breaks the shame and silence in *Ilgopzipmae*. The theatrical experience of birth search and reunion continues to enable audiences to engage with the stories of Korean transnational adoptees and their loved (or lost) ones. In this way, theater offers a meaningful time and space for the postmemory generations of Korean transnational adoption to explore and envision healing and justice as part of its ongoing legacy.

•

Unsettling Acts: Performing Transnational Adoption examined the representations of Korean adoptees' birth searches and reunions that unsettle dominant narratives of transnational adoption throughout the second half of the

---

8. H. Kim, "Reparation Acts," 324.

twentieth century and even still today. The word *unsettling* implies that a certain norm was set but is now being disturbed, shaken, or made unstable, offering an opportunity for change. In this book, unsettling marks the ways in which both adoptee and non-adoptee artists not only disclose the predicaments and possibilities associated with the adoptees' search-and-reunion process but also disrupt an essentialized and pathologized view of what it means to be a Korean transnational adoptee, even if the theatrical and performative imagination surprises and upsets audiences. To be specific, the theater and performance of birth search and reunion necessarily complicate the notion of adoptees' belonging, which is too complex to be simply framed by the narrative of a "rescued" Korean orphan becoming a perfectly assimilable child in an adoptive territory, or by an ethnocentric invitation for blood-related Korean overseas adoptees as Korea's long-lost but newly found "ambassadors and bridges connecting Korea to the West."[9]

In chapter 1, I analyzed *Chalkak* (2020), *Airport Baby* (2018, 2020), and *Ilgopzipmae* (2013), by the non-adoptee Korean artists Sumin Ha, Soo-yang Jun and Hee-sun Chang, and Yang Gu Yi, respectively. I argued that the staging of encounters between Korean birth mothers and their relinquished children, whose differently experienced birth search and reunion revives their mothers' assumed condition of "social death," defies the stigmatization and silence imposed on them in Korea. Conceptualizing birth mother necropoetics, I further complicated the discussion of these three works' endings by critiquing the notion that ethnonationalist healing and reconciliation can only be found after the birth mother characters' deaths. Chapter 2, about the autobiographical solo performances, *Yellow Dress* (2015), *How to Be a Korean Woman* (2012), and *Homeful* (2018), each by Korean American women adoptee artists, Marissa Lichwick, Sun Mee Chomet, and Amy Mihyang Ginther, centered on the artists' border-crossing bodily testimonies of birth search and reunion, which intervene in the gendered, racialized, and ethnicized scripts of Korean transnational adoption in both adoptive and birth countries. In chapter 3, I investigated the highly imaginative time-and-space transgressing works *Middle Brother* (2014) by Eric Sharp, *In My Heart* (2016) by Leah Cooper and Alan Berks, and *Hello, My Name Is . . .* (2017) by Debra Kim Sivigny, all three of which show how adoptees' sense of belonging is shaped while delineating adoptees as "good," "bad," or "strange" in their course of birth searches and reunions. Moreover, theorizing the idea of kinning, I discussed how these plays widen the constituency of the Korean adoption community by creating an adoptee kinship and connecting it with Asian American theater, Native

---

9. E. J. Kim, "Our Adoptee, Our Alien," 507.

American groups, and other fellow adoptees. Chapter 4 examined the solo performance *Les Bonnes Intentions* (2011) by Korean Belgian adoptee Cathy Min Jung, the full-length play *This Isn't Romance* (2009) by Korean British adoptee In-Sook Chappell, and the performance art piece *Re-enacting the Transnational Adoptee* (2015) by Korean Danish adoptee Yong Sun Gullach. In this chapter, my analyses conveyed the adoptee characters' and performers' experiences of racial violation and sexual violence, which shatter the "feel-good" master narrative and affect of Korean transnational adoption, thereby evoking a decolonial discomfort.

This plethora of unsettling acts tell stories of adoptees' birth search and reunion that rewrite Korean transnational adoption via performed knowledge and embodied experiences and feelings. Collected from a range of countries including Korea, the United States, the United Kingdom, Belgium, and Denmark, the works examined in this book give voice to diverse Korean adoptees through their stories, characters, designs, and performing bodies. Via analyses of these artists' works, I have focused on their counteractions against the postwar humanitarian, colorblind multicultural, and ethnonationalist perspectives of Korean transnational adoption that reduce adoptees to gratefully saved and happily assimilated objects of adoption fantasies.[10] Hence, I have wanted to show how connections between all of these works from different parts of the world can be found in their varied imaginaries and narratives that take on the performance of Korean transnational adoption. Challenging hegemonic scripts of adoption, many more theatrical and performative pieces will come to life, unsettling audience perceptions of what it means to be a transnationally adopted person in the twenty-first century.

Unsettling Acts spotlighted theater and performance as a past, present, and future locus wherein the field of critical adoption studies can cultivate its horizons through the performing arts. Furthering the examination of the search-and-reunion narrative, I proposed herein a framework—unsettling acts—applicable to the study of theatrical representations as well as other performing arts and popular entertainment genres (dance, music, film, and TV drama) that explore the ongoing ramifications of transnational adoption's history and the richness of transnational adoptees' stories. For instance, the continuing *Hallyu* Korean cultural wave increasingly presents a multitude of Korean adoption stories and adoptee characters, particularly in a slew of Korean TV drama shows. These have gained worldwide popularity through internet-based entertainment platforms such as Netflix, featuring Korean domestic and transnational adoptees as major and minor characters (although

---

10. McKee, *Adoption Fantasies*.

not necessarily within the dramatic arch of birth search and reunion). As one notable example, the first episode of the mega-hit Korean TV drama *Guardian: The Lonely and Great God* (2016) presents a handsome and compassionate goblin in human form who saves a transnationally adopted Korean child from an abusive white adoptive father in Canada. In another highly rated series entitled *Vincenzo* (2021), the male protagonist, the gorgeous legal counsel of an Italian Mafia family, is a Korean Italian adoptee who returns to Korea and takes up the cause of poor working people fighting against a corrupt conglomerate. These two popular media portrayals—of a Korean mystical male figure saving a Korean transnational adoptee and a Korean transnational adoptee coming back to Korea to aid disenfranchised Korean people—reflect Korean society's neo-ethnonationalist desire to portray Korean transnational adoption. The depiction of adoptees returning as pseudo-superhero saviors of the nation's vulnerable therefore deserves further analyses.

Another potential path for the analysis of performances of transnational adoption lies in the rise of women's rights and feminist movements in sending countries. For a long time in the Korean context, Korean feminists and women's rights activists have tackled the male-dominated and misogynistic practices that have presided over the familial system in Korea and ruled out women's autonomy from it.[11] Recently, in the era of the international #MeToo movement and Korean feminism reboot, feminist activists have become more vocal and taken to challenging numerous social practices and systems that perpetuate sexism, sexual violence against women, and femicide, among many others.[12] Korean transnational adoption does not simply exist as a practice of sending unwanted babies away but is historically entangled with women's rights, in particular unwed and single mothers' unprotected reproductive and motherhood rights. For example, out-of-wedlock pregnant Korean women have often been coerced into considering adoption as their only viable option. Such strong-arm tactics are a sign that the judicial system should scrutinize adoption practices more closely and legislative action should be taken to bring about change, particularly with regard to the legal protection, systemic support, and cultural acceptance of unwed and single mothers' parenting. In this regard, some Korean adoptees who have returned to Korea and witnessed

---

11. *Hojuje* (the male household-head system), which originated from the Japanese colonial period in Korea, governed Korean familial structures and customs and was particularly biased against women. Under the *hojuje*, women's divorce rights (among others) were curtailed: in a divorce, the wife would lose all parental rights to her children. Thanks to women's rights activists, the system was invalidated but only in 2005. S. Lim, "Defying Claims of Incompetence," 43n1, 47.

12. Seo and Choi, "Why Korean Feminism?," 380, 386–87.

gender inequality and adoption injustice have banded with Korean activists who fight for gender equality, queer justice, and the rights of unwed and single mothers to preserve their families in Korea.[13] As the public becomes more aware of these causes and forces, more insightful and innovative portrayals of adoptees and (birth) mothers in theater, TV dramas, and films will bring to life the imagination of a transnational feminist future.

For more than seventy years, Korea reigned over transnational adoption in terms of the sheer number of adoptees sent overseas. Although transnational adoption from Korea has seen a steady decline since its peak in the 1980s,[14] the Korean transnational adoption industry's effects nevertheless linger on, haunting those who have been directly impacted by it. Catherine Ceniza Choy states that even though transnational adoption might end, "the Cold War history and legacy of this phenomenon cannot be undone."[15] The history of Korean transnational adoption is still clouded by economic, military, and political profit-seeking in the guise of humanitarian ideals. Because of these continuing realities, unsettling acts become even more relevant and needed to contest the persistence of dominant discourses like the rhetoric of rescuing poor children. In 2017, following a Korean transnational adoption symposium,[16] a group of transnational Korean adoption scholars and activists in and out of the United States gathered and called for action by the Korean government to immediately end the sending of babies and children to other nations.[17] The following year, the academic journal *Adoption & Culture* published a special issue entitled "The Ends of Korean Adoption" in which leading critical adoption studies researchers examined the (im)possibility of bringing an end to transnational adoption from Korea.[18] These scholars and activists still persevere with their demands for the further problematization of continuing practices of Korean transnational adoption. Via their theater and performance works, all the artists discussed in this book indeed call for change and transformation in the perception of adoption and adoptee representation.

---

13. Notable adoptee activists include Jane Jeong Trenka and Kim Stoker. Chan, "Raised in America." Another noteworthy adoptee activist is Pauline Park, a Korean American transgender person based in the United States, who has been vocal about queer rights in Korea, particularly participating in the 16th Queer Korea Festival and the Seoul Pride Parade in 2015. Park, "Coming Full Circle."

14. Selman, "Global Decline of Intercountry Adoption."

15. Ceniza Choy, "On Histories and Futures," 296.

16. This conference, entitled "The Ends of Adoption: A Symposium on Transnational Korean Adoption," took place at the University of California, Irvine, on May 13, 2017. McKee, "Introduction," 267.

17. "Declaration Calling for an Immediate End to the Industrial International Adoption System from South Korea."

18. See "Ends of Korean Adoption."

Aligning myself with these endeavors, in this book about the theater and performance of Korean transnational adoption, I not only revisit representations of transnational adoption from Korea but also envision artistic actions that can serve as rehearsals for redress and reconciliation. With *Unsettling Acts,* I hope to strengthen the possibilities that theater and performance can generate via the staging of a full humanity through the embodied experiences of adoptees, adoptive and birth families, and adoption communities along with their allies.

The discussion of theater and performance of Korean transnational adoption in this book strives to offer a critical and creative way of contextualizing adoption in connection to human separation. In the United States, family separation has been part of the nation's history since the days of the slave trade, when the Black children of enslaved people were sold off, and even after the abolition of slavery, when Black children were separated from their families during apprenticeships.[19] Indigenous children were also separated from their families and tribal lands and taken to special schools and orphanages in order to purportedly make them good "whitened" citizens.[20] Moreover, at the time of this writing, the US government still separates families in the form of immigration regulation at the Mexican-US border, where a crisis created under the Trump Administration allowed children to be torn away from their parents and put into detention.[21] This book thus interrogates the potential of theater and performance to inspire new ways of pondering the practices of making and breaking families and their impacts on people of color, especially. As such, hopefully this book engenders discussions that will open a path to realizing the urgent need to view adoption's dimensions of human separation and (un)belonging as affronts to humankind and to imagine families without bars and borders.

In order for this to transpire, change must not only occur in the courts but also in the hearts and minds of people who need to recognize that transnational adoption is a complex personal and political experience with a long history of racial, gender, and class inequality and injustice. The exploitations of the adoption business, and the tensions and traumata that mark this transnational experience for adoptees from other countries, still await investigation. Furthermore, the problematics of the adoption trade between sending and receiving nations including the United States must make us more carefully consider systemic issues such as corruption, armed conflicts, famine, and disease that are ravaging countries and making orphans of millions of

---

19. Briggs, *Taking Children,* 28.
20. Adams, *Education for Extinction.*
21. US House Committee on Oversight and Reform.

children. In many cases, critical views on transnational adoption also force us to consider offenses by adoption services employees.[22] In present times, historical and ongoing abuses are still both being unearthed and perpetrated in several nations in the Global North. In Canada the discovery of the remains of more than two hundred Indigenous children revealed that they had been taken from their families and sent to white-run boarding schools where they had died from unknown causes.[23] In Ukraine, during the current war with Russia, Ukrainian children in territory occupied by Russian forces have been kidnapped in plain sight from orphanages and Ukrainian parents and sent to Russia to be raised in Russian foster families.[24] Such heinous past and present events create a crucial urgency to re-evaluate adoption and condemn crimes committed against children under its guise. In light of these dire actualities, I view this book about theater and performance as holding the means to re-examine adoption through its live communitarian experience and call for intervention from audiences.

Performing transnational adoption is, therefore, a strategic praxis offering an imaginative gesture of belonging and healing as well as justice for adoptees and the people who have been enmeshed in adoption's history and practices. *Unsettling Acts: Performing Transnational Adoption* extends this gesture by asserting the significance of the theater and performance of Korean adoptees' birth search and reunion in providing a paradigm for future adoptee and non-adoptee artists and audiences across the globe to pursue artistic and activist works and actions reimagining adoption.

---

22. Mitchell, "Ethiopia Puts Its Young"; US Department of Justice, "Four Employees of Adoption Services"; and Riben, "Adoption Criminality and Corruption."
23. Honderich, "Why Canada Is Mourning."
24. Bubola, "Using Adoptions."

BIBLIOGRAPHY

"33: Convention of 29 May 1993 on Protection of Children and Co-operation in Respect of Intercountry Adoption." Accessed April 22, 2024. https://www.hcch.net/en/instruments/conventions/full-text/?cid=69.

A Stulen Identitet—problematisering av adoption. Facebook. Accessed May 5, 2024. https://www.facebook.com/StulenIdentitet42/.

"About." Also-Known-As, Inc. Accessed April 28, 2024. https://www.alsoknownas.org/about.

"About." Organisation for Economic Co-operation and Development (OECD). Accessed April 23, 2024. https://www.oecd.org/about/.

Abulafia, Yaron. *The Art of Light on Stage: Lighting in Contemporary Theatre*. London: Routledge, 2016.

Adams, David Wallace. *Education for Extinction: American Indians and the Boarding School Experience, 1875–1928*. Lawrence: University Press of Kansas, 2020.

Adoptionspolitisk Forum. Accessed May 5, 2024. https://www.adoptionspolitiskforum.org/a-critical-voice-of-transnational-adoption-in-denmark-by-yong-sun-gullach-chairwoman/.

Ahmed, Sara. *The Cultural Politics of Emotion*. New York: Routledge, 2004.

———. *The Promise of Happiness*. Durham, NC: Duke University Press, 2010.

Althusser, Louis, Fredric Jameson, and Ben Brewster. "Ideology and Ideological State Apparatuses: Notes Towards an Investigation." In *Lenin and Philosophy and Other Essays*, translated from the French by Ben Brewster, 85–126. New York: New York University Press, 2001.

Ancheri, Saumya. "Reality Bites: In Conversation with Helgard Haug and Miriam Yung Min Stein." *Material*. Accessed May 5, 2024. https://www.rimini-protokoll.de/website/en/text/reality-bites.

Anderson, Joel, and Wiebke Leister. "The Theatre of Photography: An Interdisciplinary Duologue." *Sens public*, 2019. https://doi.org/10.7202/1067430ar.

Anderson, Patrick, and Jisha Menon. *Violence Performed*. New York: Palgrave Macmillan, 2009.

Ang, Ien. *On Not Speaking Chinese: Living Between Asia and the West*. London: Routledge, 2001.

Artaud, Antonin. *The Theatre and Its Double*. Translated by Victor Corti. London: Alma Classics, 2013.

Augé, Marc. *Non-Places: Introduction to an Anthropology of Supermodernity*. London: Verso, 1995.

Bae, Shannon. "Radical Imagination and the Solidarity Movement between Transnational Korean Adoptees and Unwed Mothers in South Korea." *Adoption & Culture* 6, no. 2 (2018): 300–315. https://doi.org/10.1353/ado.2018.0017.

Baik, Crystal Mun-hye. *Reencounters: On the Korean War & Diasporic Memory Critique*. Philadelphia: Temple University Press, 2019.

Banes, Sally. *Dancing Women: Female Bodies on Stage*. London: Routledge, 1998.

Barthes, Roland. *Camera Lucida: Reflections on Photography*. New York: Hill and Wang, 1981.

Baugh, Christopher. *Theatre, Performance and Technology: The Development and Transformation of Scenography*. London and New York: Palgrave Macmillan, 2014.

Bhabha, Homi K. "Foreword." In *Black Skin, White Masks*, by Frantz Fanon, xxi–xxxvii. London: Pluto Press, 1986.

———. *The Location of Culture*. New York: Routledge, 1994.

Biggin, Rose. "Environment and Site-Specificity: Space, Place and Immersion." In *Immersive Theatre and Audience Experience: Space, Game and Story in the Work of Punchdrunk*, by Rose Biggin, 177–205. Cham, Switzerland: Palgrave Macmillan, 2017.

Bloom, Laura Begley. "5 Ways Travel Can Help Create Your Dream Career." *Forbes*, September 6, 2018. https://www.forbes.com/sites/laurabegleybloom/2018/09/06/5-ways-travel-can-help-create-your-dream-career/#4c916b241b3c.

Boo, Kyung-Sook. "Intersections of Historical Remembering and Caregiving in Korean American Fiction." Paper presented at the Annual Conference of the Association for Asian American Studies, 2017.

Borland, Katherine. "'That's Not What I Said': Interpretive Conflict in Oral Narrative Research." In *Women's Words: The Feminist Practice of Oral History*, edited by Sherna Berger Gluck and Daphne Patai, 63–75. New York: Routledge, 1991.

Borowiec, Steven. "South Korean Single Mothers Turn to Theater to Strike Back Against Stereotypes." *Los Angeles Times*, December 28, 2015. https://www.latimes.com/world/asia/la-fg-south-korea-mothers-20151228-story.html.

Bradway, Tyler, and Elizabeth Freeman. "Introduction: Kincoherence/Kin-aesthetics/Kinematics." In *Queer Kinship: Race, Sex, Belonging, Form*, edited by Tyler Bradway and Elizabeth Freeman, 1–22. Durham, NC: Duke University Press, 2022.

Brecht, Bertolt. *Brecht on Theatre: The Development of an Aesthetic*. Edited and translated by John Willett. New York: Hill and Wang, 1964.

Briggs, Laura. *Somebody's Children: The Politics of Transracial and Transnational Adoption*. Durham, NC: Duke University Press, 2012.

———. *Taking Children: A History of American Terror*. Oakland: University of California Press, 2020.

Brockelman, Thomas P. *The Frame and the Mirror: On Collage and the Postmodern*. Evanston, IL: Northwestern University Press, 2001.

Bryant, Lei Ouyang. "Performing Race and Place in Asian America: Korean American Adoptees, Musical Theatre, and the Land of 10,000 Lakes." *Asian Music* 40, no. 1 (2009): 4–30. https://doi.org/10.1353/amu.0.0015.

Bubola, Emma. "Using Adoptions, Russia Turns Ukrainian Children into Spoils of War." *New York Times,* October 22, 2022. https://www.nytimes.com/2022/10/22/world/europe/ukraine-children-russia-adoptions.html.

Butler, Judith. "Foucault and the Paradox of Bodily Inscriptions." *Journal of Philosophy* 86, no. 11 (1989): 601–7. https://doi.org/10.5840/jphil198986117.

———. *Gender Trouble: Feminism and the Subversion of Identity.* New York: Routledge, 1990.

———. "Rethinking Vulnerability and Resistance." In *Vulnerability in Resistance,* edited by Judith Butler, Zeynep Gambetti, and Leticia Sabsay, 12–27. Durham, NC: Duke University Press, 2016.

Butler, Judith, Zeynep Gambetti, and Leticia Sabsay. "Introduction." In *Vulnerability in Resistance,* edited by Judith Butler, Zeynep Gambetti, and Leticia Sabsay, 1–11. Durham, NC: Duke University Press, 2016.

Cacho, Lisa Marie. *Social Death: Racialized Rightlessness and the Criminalization of the Unprotected.* New York: New York University Press, 2012.

Carlson, Marla R. *Performing Bodies in Pain.* New York: Palgrave Macmillan, 2010.

Carp, E. Wayne. *Jean Paton and the Struggle to Reform American Adoption.* Ann Arbor: University of Michigan Press, 2014.

Caruth, Cathy. *Unclaimed Experience: Trauma, Narrative and History.* Baltimore: Johns Hopkins University Press, 1996.

Catalano, Theresa, and Linda R. Waugh. *Critical Discourse Analysis, Critical Discourse Studies and Beyond.* Cham, Switzerland: Springer, 2020.

Cavicchi, Andrea Kim. "Power, Resistance, and Subjectivity: An Exploration of Overseas Korean Adoptees in Korea." PhD diss., University of California, Los Angeles, 2016.

Chan, Wilfred. "Raised in America, Activists Lead Fight to End S. Korean Adoptions." *CNN,* September 16, 2013. https://www.cnn.com/2013/09/16/world/international-adoption-korea-adoptee-advocates/index.html.

Chappell, In-Sook. *This Isn't Romance.* London: Oberon Books, 2009.

Chen, Fu-Jen. "Maternal Voices in Personal Narratives of Adoption." *Women's Studies* 45, no. 2 (2016): 162–87. https://doi.org/10.1080/00497878.2015.1122504.

Ceniza Choy, Catherine. "On Histories and Futures of International Adoption." *Adoption & Culture* 6, no. 2 (2018): 292–99. https://doi.org/10.1353/ado.2018.0020.

———. "To Make Historical Their Own Stories." In *Global Families: A History of Asian International Adoption in America,* by Catherine Ceniza Choy, 131–60. New York: New York University Press, 2013.

Cho, Grace M. *Haunting the Korean Diaspora: Shame, Secrecy, and the Forgotten War.* Minneapolis: University of Minnesota Press, 2008.

Cho, Oakla. "Modernization Experiences of Urban and Rural Low-Income Korean Women." In *Women's Experiences and Feminist Practices in South Korea,* edited by Pil-wha Chang and Eun-Shil Kim, 205–28. Seoul: Ewha Womans University Press, 2005.

Choe, Sang-Hun. "An Adoptee Returns to South Korea, and Changes Follow." *New York Times,* June 28, 2013. https://www.nytimes.com/2013/06/29/world/asia/an-adoptee-returns-to-south-korea-and-changes-follow.html.

———. "Deportation a 'Death Sentence' to Adoptees after a Lifetime in the U.S." *New York Times,* July 2, 2017. https://www.nytimes.com/2017/07/02/world/asia/south-korea-adoptions-phillip-clay-adam-crapser.html.

Choi, Seungyeon. "Attempts Revealing Potential and Possibility: Awardees of the 2015 New Musical Production Support *Well-Dying, Airport Baby,* and *Go with God*" [*Jamjaeryeok-gwa ganeungseongi yeotboin sidodeul*]. *The Korean Theatre Review,* Spring 2016, 347–64. In Korean.

Chomet, Sun Mee. *How to Be a Korean Woman.* Unpublished manuscript, 2012. PDF file.

Chun, Jeongyun. "From Adopted Child to French 'Fleur' . . ." [*Ibyangaeseo peurangseuui peullo-ereuga doegikkaji*]. *Hankyoreh,* May 18, 2012. https://www.hani.co.kr/arti/international/europe/533502.html. In Korean.

Coleman, Jeffrey K. *The Necropolitical Theater: Race and Immigration on the Contemporary Spanish Stage.* Evanston, IL: Northwestern University Press, 2020.

Coletu, Ebony. "Introduction Biographic Mediation: On the Uses of Personal Disclosure in Bureaucracy and Politics." *Biography* 42, no. 3 (2019): 465–85. https://doi.org/10.1353/bio.2019.0055.

Cooper, Leah, and Alan Berks. "In My Heart: The Adoption Play Project." Unpublished manuscript, 2016. PDF file.

Creagh, Diane. "Science, Social Work, and Bureaucracy: Cautious Developments in Adoption and Foster Care, 1930–1969." In *Children and Youth in Adoption, Orphanages, and Foster Care,* edited by Loris Askeland, 31–44. Westport, CT: Greenwood Publishing Group, 2006.

Cvetkovich, Ann. *An Archive of Feelings: Trauma, Sexuality, and Lesbian Public Cultures.* Durham, NC: Duke University Press, 2003.

Davison, Carol Margaret. "The 'Last Home': Death in the Works of Charlotte Brontë." In *Time, Space, and Place in Charlotte Brontë,* edited by Diane Long Hoeveler and Deborah Denenholz Morse, 197–216. Abingdon: Routledge, 2017.

De Graeve, Katrien. "'They Have Our Culture': Negotiating Migration in Belgian-Ethiopian Transnational Adoption." *Ethnos* 80, no. 1 (2015): 71–90. https://doi.org/10.1080/00141844.2013.813565.

"Declaration Calling for an Immediate End to the Industrial International Adoption System from South Korea." Accessed May 6, 2024. https://koreanadoptiondeclaration.wordpress.com/.

Deloria, Vine, and Clifford M. Lytle. *American Indians, American Justice.* Austin: University of Texas Press, 1983.

Docan-Morgan, Sara. *In Reunion: Transnational Korean Adoptees and the Communication of Family.* Philadelphia: Temple University Press, 2024.

———. "Korean Adoptees' Birth Family Reunions: Questions of Family Identity and Cultural Identity." In *The Intercountry Adoption Debate: Dialogues across Disciplines,* edited by Robert L. Ballard, Naomi H. Goodno, Robert F. Cochran, and Jay A. Milbrandt, 591–617. Newcastle upon Tyne: Cambridge Scholars Publishing, 2015.

Dolan, Jill. *Utopia in Performance: Finding Hope at the Theater.* Ann Arbor: University of Michigan Press, 2005.

Doolan, Yuri W. *The First Amerasians: Mixed Race Koreans from Camptowns to America.* New York: Oxford University Press, 2024.

Dorow, Sarah, ed. *I Wish for You a Beautiful Life: Letters from the Korean Birth Mothers of Ae Ran Won to Their Children.* St. Paul, MN: Yeong & Yeong Book Company, 1999.

"Dreams Come True." Oprah.com, March 27, 2007. https://www.oprah.com/oprahshow/dreams-come-true_7.

Elfving-Hwang, Joanna. *Representations of Femininity in Contemporary South Korean Women's Literature.* Kent, UK: Global Oriental, 2010.

"The Ends of Korean Adoption." Special issue, *Adoption & Culture* 6, no. 2 (2018).

Eng, David L. *The Feeling of Kinship: Queer Liberalism and the Racialization of Intimacy*. Durham, NC: Duke University Press, 2010.

Enloe, Cynthia. *Bananas, Beaches and Bases: Making Feminist Sense of International Politics*, 2nd ed. Berkeley: University of California Press, 2014.

Eriksen, Kasper Emil Rosbjørn. "A Great Desire for Children: The Beginning of Transnational Adoption in Denmark and Norway during the 1960's." *Genealogy* 4, no. 4 (2020): 4–19. https://doi.org/10.3390/genealogy4040104.

Espeland, Pamela. "Poignant 'Adoption Play Project' Is a Labor of Love." *MinnPost*, December 15, 2016. https://www.minnpost.com/artscape/2016/12/poignant-adoption-play-project-labor-love.

Fagan, Kristina. "Adoption as National Fantasy in Barbara Kingsolver's *Pigs in Heaven* and Margaret Laurence's *The Diviners*." In *Imagining Adoption: Essays on Literature and Culture*, edited by Marianne Novy, 251–66. Ann Arbor: University of Michigan Press, 2001.

Fanon, Frantz. *Black Skin, White Masks*. New York: Grove Press, 2008.

———. *The Wretched of the Earth*. Translated by Constance Farrington. New York: Grove Press, 1963.

Farber, Yaël. *Theatre as Witness: Three Testimonial Plays from South Africa: In Collaboration with and Based on the Lives of the Original Performers*. London: Oberon Books, 2008.

Fédération Wallonie-Bruxelles. "Nombre d'enfants adoptés par pays d'origine." Chiffres Clés. Accessed May 5, 2024. https://statistiques.cfwb.be/aide-a-la-jeunesse/adoption/nombre-denfants-adoptes-par-pays-dorigine/. In French.

Fedosik, Marina. "Representations of Transnational Adoption in Contemporary American Literature and Film." PhD diss., University of Delaware, 2009.

Fischer-Lichte, Erika. *The Transformative Power of Performance: A New Aesthetics*. London: Routledge, 2008.

Fitzpatrick, Lisa. "The Performance of Violence and the Ethics of Spectatorship." *Performance Research* 16, no. 1 (2011): 59–67. https://doi.org/10.1080/13528165.2011.561676.

"#FliptheScript 2014 (the Origins)." *Lost Daughters* blog. Accessed May 11, 2024. http://www.thelostdaughters.com/p/flipthescript.html.

Fluck, Winfried. "The Role of the Reader and the Changing Functions of Literature: Reception Aesthetics, Literary Anthropology, Funktiongeschichte." *European Journal of English Studies* 6, no. 3 (2002): 253–71. https://doi.org/10.1076/ejes.6.3.253.14835.

Foucault, Michel. *The History of Sexuality Vol. 1: An Introduction*. Translated by Robert Hurley. New York: Vintage Books, 1990.

Francus, Marilyn. *Monstrous Motherhood: Eighteenth-Century Culture and the Ideology of Domesticity*. Baltimore: Johns Hopkins University Press, 2013.

Fuhr, Michael. *Globalization and Popular Music in South Korea: Sounding Out K-Pop*. New York: Routledge, 2016.

García, Alberto N., ed. *Emotions in Contemporary TV Series*. London: Palgrave Macmillan, 2016.

Garza, Chris. "Mu Performing Arts' Lost and Found *Middle Brother*." Howlround Theatre Commons, October 23, 2014. https://howlround.com/mu-performing-arts-lost-and-found-middle-brother.

Gibney, Shannon. "Kinship between Transracial Adoptees: A Case for the Kinship of Loss." In *Ethnicity and Kinship in North American and European Literatures*, edited by Silvia Schultermandl and Klaus Rieser, 153–61. New York: Routledge, 2021.

"Gifts of Hope." Holt International. Accessed April 23, 2024. https://giftsofhope.holtinternational.org/.

Gilbert, Helen, and Joanne Tompkins. *Post-Colonial Drama: Theory, Practice, Politics*. London: Routledge, 1996.

Gill, Jungyun. *Unequal Motherhoods and the Adoption of Asian Children: Birth, Foster, and Adoptive Mothers*. Lanham, MD: Lexington Books, 2017.

Gilmore, Leigh. *Autobiographics: A Feminist Theory of Women's Self-Representation*. Ithaca, NY: Cornell University Press, 1994.

Ginther, Amy Mihyang. *between*. Unpublished manuscript, 2011. PDF file.

———. "Dramaturgy of Deprivation (없다): An Invitation to Re-Imagine Ways We Depict Asian American and Adopted Narratives of Trauma." *Journal of American Drama and Theatre* 34, no. 2 (2022). https://jadtjournal.org/2022/05/20/dramaturgy-of-deprivation/.

———. *Homeful*. Unpublished manuscript, 2018. PDF file.

Goddard, Lynette. *Staging Black Feminisms: Identity, Politics, Performance*. Basingstoke: Palgrave Macmillan, 2007.

Goffman, Erving. *Stigma: Notes on the Management of Spoiled Identity*. New York: Simon and Schuster, 1963.

Goldberg, RoseLee. *Performance Art: From Futurism to the Present*. New York: H. N. Abrams, 1988.

González, Rosita, Amanda Transue-Woolston, and Diane René Christian, eds. *Flip the Script: Adult Adoptee Anthology*. CreateSpace Independent Publishing Platform, 2015.

Gordon, Avery F. *Ghostly Matters: Haunting and the Sociological Imagination*. Minneapolis: University of Minnesota Press, 2008.

Graves, Kori A. *A War Born Family: African American Adoption in the Wake of the Korean War*. New York: New York University Press, 2020.

Haas, Benjamin. "Tears Flow as Separated South and North Korean Families Reunite." *Guardian*, August 20, 2018. https://www.theguardian.com/world/2018/aug/20/separated-south-and-north-korean-families-take-part-in-rare-reunions.

Han, Sangsoon, ed. *Dreaming a World: Korean Birth Mothers Tell Their Stories*. St. Paul, MN: Yeong & Yeong Book Company, 2010.

Harrison, Martin. *The Language of Theatre*. New York: Routledge, 1998.

Harvey, David. *The Condition of Postmodernity: An Enquiry into the Origins of Cultural Change*. Oxford: Blackwell, 1990.

Haughton, Miriam. *Staging Trauma: Bodies in Shadow*. London: Palgrave Macmillan, 2018.

Herman, Ellen. *Kinship by Design: A History of Adoption in the Modern United States*. Chicago: University of Chicago Press, 2008.

Herrera, Patricia. "A Sonic Treatise of Futurity: *Universes*' Party People." In *Race and Performance after Repetition*, edited by Soyica Diggs Colbert, Douglas A. Jones Jr., and Shane Vogel, 71–100. Durham, NC: Duke University Press, 2020.

Herskovitz, Jon. "Olympic Star in Tearful Reunion with Korean Dad." *Reuters.com*, February 28, 2007. https://www.reuters.com/article/us-korea-dawson/olympic-star-in-tearful-reunion-with-korean-dad-idUSSEO27323720070228.

Hincks, Joseph. "'The Moment We Met, Tears Rolled Down.' War-Torn Korean Families Describe What It Was Like to Be Reunited." *Time*, August 23, 2018. https://time.com/5374167/south-north-korea-family-reunions.

Hirsch, Marianne. *The Generation of Postmemory: Writing and Visual Culture after the Holocaust.* New York: Columbia University Press, 2012.

———. "Vulnerable Times." In *Vulnerability in Resistance,* edited by Judith Butler, Zeynep Gambetti, and Leticia Sabsay, 76–96. Durham, NC: Duke University Press, 2016.

Hochschild, Arlie Russell. *The Managed Heart: Commercialization of Human Feeling.* Berkeley: University of California Press, 1983.

Hogarth, Hyun-key Kim. *Korean Shamanism and Cultural Nationalism.* Seoul: Jimoondang Publishing Company, 1999.

Höhn, Maria, and Seungsook Moon, eds. *Over There: Living with the U.S. Military Empire from World War Two to the Present.* Durham, NC: Duke University Press, 2010.

Homans, Margaret. "Adoption and Return: Transnational Genealogies, Maternal Legacies." In *Rites of Return: Diaspora Poetics and the Politics of Memory,* edited by Marianne Hirsch and Nancy K. Miller, 185–99. New York: Columbia University Press, 2011.

———. "Adoption Narratives, Trauma, and Origins." *Narrative* 14, no. 1 (2006): 4–26. https://doi.org/10.1353/nar.2005.0026.

———. *The Imprint of Another Life: Adoption Narratives and Human Possibility.* Ann Arbor: University of Michigan Press, 2013.

———. "Reunions with Siblings in Search Memoirs across Cultures." In *Adoption and Multiculturalism: Europe, the Americas, and the Pacific,* edited by Jenny Heijun Wills, Tobias Hübinette, and Indigo Willing, 69–96. Ann Arbor: University of Michigan Press, 2020.

Homans, Margaret, Peggy Phelan, Janet Mason Ellerby, Eric Walker, Karen Balcom, Kit Myers, Kim Park Nelson, Laura Briggs, Cynthia Callahan, Rosemarie Peña, Elisabeth Wesseling, Bruno Perreau, Lucy Curzon, Kimberly Leighton, and Barbara Yngvesson. "Critical Adoption Studies: Conversation in Progress." *Adoption & Culture* 6, no. 1 (2018): 1–49. https://doi.org/10.1353/ado.2018.0015.

Honderich, Holly. "Why Canada Is Mourning the Deaths of 215 Children." *BBC News,* June 3, 2021. https://www.bbc.com/news/world-us-canada-57325653.

Hong, Cathy Park. *Minor Feelings: An Asian American Reckoning.* New York: Random House, 2021.

Hong, Christine. *A Violent Peace: Race, U.S. Militarism, and Cultures of Democratization in Cold War Asia and the Pacific.* Stanford, CA: Stanford University Press, 2020.

Hornby, Louise. *Still Modernism: Photography, Literature, Film.* New York: Oxford University Press, 2017.

Howell, Signe. *The Kinning of Foreigners: Transnational Adoption in a Global Perspective.* New York: Berghahn Books, 2006.

———. "Return Journeys and the Search for Roots: Contradictory Values Concerning Identity." In *International Adoption: Global Inequalities and the Circulation of Children,* edited by Diana Marre and Laura Briggs, 256–70. New York: New York University Press, 2009.

Hübinette, Tobias. "Adopted Koreans and the Development of Identity in the 'Third Space.'" *Adoption & Fostering* 28, no. 1 (April 2004): 16–24. https://doi.org/10.1177/030857590402800104.

———. "Comforting an Orphaned Nation: Representations of International Adoption and Adopted Koreans in Korean Popular Culture." PhD diss., Stockholm University, 2005.

———. "Disembedded and Free-Floating Bodies Out of Place and Out of Control." *Adoption & Culture* 1, no. 1 (2007): 129–62. https://doi.org/10.1353/ado.2007.0007.

———. "Korean Adoption History." In *Guide to Korea for Overseas Adopted Koreans,* edited by Eleana Kim, 12–19. Seoul: Overseas Koreans Foundation, 2004.

———. "North Korea and Adoption." *Korean Quarterly* 4, no. 5 (2002).

Hübinette, Tobias, and Carina Tigervall. "Contested Adoption Narratives in a Swedish Setting." Paper presented at the International Conference on Adoption Research, University of East Anglia, Norwich, 2006.

Huyssen, Andreas. "The Metamorphosis of the Museal: From Exhibitionary to Experiential Complex and Beyond." In *Women Mobilizing Memory,* edited by Ayşe Gül Altinay, María José Contreras, Marianne Hirsch, Jean Howard, Banu Karaca, and Alisa Solomon, 47–64. New York: Columbia University Press, 2019.

I Miss That Person ("그사보 정희정"). Global Overseas Adoptees' Link. December 29, 2008. YouTube video, 10:00. https://www.youtube.com/watch?v=bzUnq3UbUtU&list=PLS-C8nrz5ONx84kt-DNGUHtSi__9E6d04.

Indian Child Welfare Act of 1978: Hearing on S. 1214 Before the Subcommittee on Indian Affairs & Public Lands of the H. Comm. on Interior & Insular Affairs, 95th Cong. 296. 1978.

International Korean Adoptee Association (IKAA). Accessed May 5, 2024. https://ikaa.org/our-network/.

"Introduction of Happitory." Happitory. Accessed June 9, 2024. http://www.happitory.org/happitory_intro.

"It Took the #FliptheScript Village. . ." *Lost Daughters* blog. November 30, 2014. http://www.thelostdaughters.com/2014/11/it-took-flipthescript-village.html.

Ivenäs, Sabina. "White Like Me: Whiteness in Scandinavian Transnational Adoption Literature." *Scandinavian Studies* 89, no. 2, Nordic Whiteness (Summer 2017): 240–65.

Jackson, Julie. "Kolleen Park Presents New Musical 'Airport Baby.'" *Korea Herald,* February 25, 2016. http://www.koreaherald.com/view.php?ud=20160225001148.

Jeffrey, Paul. "A Place for the Forgotten." *Global Lens,* originally published in *Response Magazine,* October 2018. Accessed April 28, 2024. http://www.kairosphotos.com/blog/a-place-for-the-forgotten/.

Jin, Dal Yong. *New Korean Wave: Transnational Cultural Power in the Age of Social Media.* Urbana: University of Illinois Press, 2016.

Johnson, Kay Ann. *China's Hidden Children: Abandonment, Adoption, and the Human Costs of the One-Child Policy.* Chicago: University of Chicago Press, 2016.

Jones, Maggie. "Adam Crapser's Bizarre Deportation Odyssey." *New York Times,* April 1, 2015. https://www.nytimes.com/2015/04/01/magazine/adam-crapsers-bizarre-deportation-odyssey.html.

———. "Why a Generation of Adoptees Is Returning to South Korea." *New York Times,* January 14, 2015. https://www.nytimes.com/2015/01/18/magazine/why-a-generation-of-adoptees-is-returning-to-south-korea.html.

Ju, Hyun-Shik. "Autobiographical Documentary Theatre *A Suk-ja Story* and Heterotopia." *Journal of Drama* 58 (2019): 73–100. In Korean.

Jung, Carl Gustav. *Psychology of the Unconscious: A Study of the Transformations and Symbolisms of the Libido.* New York: Moffat, Yard and Company, 1916.

Kang, Laura Hyun Yi. *Traffic in Asian Women.* Durham, NC: Duke University Press, 2020.

Kang, Te-ri. "What Does Korean Law Say about Adoptees' Right to Information Disclosure." *Korea Times,* October 16, 2021. https://www.koreatimes.co.kr/www/opinion/2021/10/715_317117.html.

Kaplan, E. Ann. *Motherhood and Representation: The Mother in Popular Culture and Melodrama.* London: Routledge, 1992.

Kendall, Lauren. *The Life and Hard Times of a Korean Shaman: Of Tales and Telling Tales.* Honolulu: University of Hawai'i Press, 1988.

Khanna, Neetu. *The Visceral Logics of Decolonization.* Durham, NC: Duke University Press, 2020.

Kim, Chongho. *Korean Shamanism: The Cultural Paradox.* New York: Routledge, 2018.

Kim, Da-sol. "[History through Films] 'Ode to My Father,' Story of Korean Fathers in the Post-War Era." *Korea Herald,* March 18, 2024. https://www.koreaherald.com/view.php?ud=20240318050598.

———. "Korea Ranks Bottom in OECD for Welfare Spending." *Korea Herald,* October 31, 2016. http://www.koreaherald.com/view.php?ud=20161031000659.

Kim, Dong Hoon. *Eclipsed Cinema: The Film Culture of Colonial Korea.* Edinburgh: Edinburgh University Press, 2017.

Kim, Eleana J. *Adopted Territory: Transnational Korean Adoptees and the Politics of Belonging.* Durham, NC: Duke University Press, 2010.

———. "Our Adoptee, Our Alien: Transnational Adoptees as Specters of Foreignness and Family in South Korea." *Anthropological Quarterly* 80, no. 2 (2007): 497–531. https://doi.org/10.1353/anq.2007.0027.

Kim, Eunjung. *Curative Violence: Rehabilitating Disability, Gender, and Sexuality in Modern Korea.* Durham, NC: Duke University Press, 2017.

Kim, Geumyeong. "Is That Material Like This?" [*Geu sojaereul ireoke?*]. *CNB Journal,* March 7, 2016. http://weekly.cnbnews.com/news/article.html?no=117940. In Korean.

Kim, Huikyeong. *Strange Normal Family* [*Esanghan jeongsang gajok*]. Seoul: Dongasia, 2018. In Korean.

Kim, Hosu. *Birth Mothers and Transnational Adoption Practice in South Korea: Virtual Mothering.* New York: Palgrave Macmillan, 2016.

———. "Reparation Acts: Korean Birth Mothers Travel the Road from Reunion to Redress." *Adoption & Culture* 6, no. 2 (2018): 316–35. https://doi.org/10.1353/ado.2018.0016.

Kim, Hyo-jin. "14,189 Korean-Born Adoptees in US Undocumented." *Korea Times,* October 10, 2017. https://www.koreatimes.co.kr/www/nation/2020/05/177_237441.html.

Kim, Jodi. *Ends of Empire: Asian American Critique and the Cold War.* Minneapolis: University of Minnesota Press, 2010.

———. "An 'Orphan' with Two Mothers: Transnational and Transracial Adoption, the Cold War, and Contemporary Asian American Cultural Politics." *American Quarterly* 61, no. 4 (2009): 855–80. https://doi.org/10.1353/aq.0.0110.

Kim, Ju Yon. *The Racial Mundane: Asian American Performance and the Embodied Everyday.* New York: New York University Press, 2015.

Kim, Kyung Hyun. "Korean War through Cinema." In *Rediscovering Korean Cinema,* edited by Sangjoon Lee, 502–14. Ann Arbor: University of Michigan Press, 2019.

Kim, Mikyoung. "Gender, Work and Resistance: South Korean Textile Industry in the 1970s." *Journal of Contemporary Asia* 41, no. 3 (2011): 411–30. https://doi.org/10.1080/00472336.2011.582711.

Kim, Nan. *Memory, Reconciliation, and Reunions in South Korea: Crossing the Divide.* Lanham, MD: Lexington Books, 2017.

Kim, Oh Myo, Reed Reichwald, and Richard Lee. "Cultural Socialization in Families with Adopted Korean Adolescents: A Mixed-Method, Multi-Informant Study." *Journal of Adolescent Research* 28, no. 1 (2013): 69–95. https://doi.org/10.1177/0743558411432636.

Kim, Sook K. "Abandoned Babies: The Backlash of South Korea's Special Adoption Act." *Washington International Law Journal* 24, no. 3 (2015): 709–25.

Kim, Sukkyung. "A Study on Critical Understanding of Family Ideologies in Geun Hyung Park's Plays." *Journal of Korean Theatre Studies Association* 48, no. 1 (2012): 85–125. https://doi.org/10.18396/ktsa.2012.1.48.003. In Korean.

Kim, Tong-sim, Sa-jin Kwak, Il-han Kim, Yong-hui Han, Kyong-tae Pak, and Tu-yon Kim. "A Research Report on the Status of Mixed-Blood People in Camp Towns" [*Kijichon honhyorin inkwonsiltaejosa*]. Seoul: State Human Rights Commission, 2003. In Korean.

Kim-Larsen, Mette A. E. "Danish Milk." *Adoption & Culture* 6, no. 2 (2018): 353–63. https://doi.org/10.1353/ado.2018.0019.

Kina, Laura, and Wei Ming Dariotis, eds. *War Baby / Love Child: Mixed Race Asian American Art*. Seattle: University of Washington Press, 2013.

Knowles, Caroline. *Family Boundaries: The Invention of Normality and Dangerousness*. Peterborough, Canada: Broadview, 1996.

Koehler, Robert, Ji-yeon Byeon, and Jin-hyuk Lee. *Traditional Music: Sounds in Harmony with Nature*. Seoul: Seoul Selection, 2011.

Koivunen, Anu, Katariina Kyrölä, and Ingrid Ryberg. "Vulnerability as a Political Language." In *The Power of Vulnerability: Mobilising Affect in Feminist, Queer and Anti-Racist Media Cultures,* edited by Anu Koivunen, Katariina Kyrölä, and Ingrid Ryberg, 1–26. Manchester: Manchester University Press, 2018.

Komporaly, Jozefina. *Staging Motherhood: British Women Playwrights, 1956 to the Present*. Basingstoke: Palgrave Macmillan, 2007.

Koo, Huieon. "From Korean Adoptee to French Minister: Fleur Pellerin's Story of Rags to Riches" [*Hangukgye ibyanga chulsin peurangseu janggwan peulloereu pelleuraeng insaeng yeokjeon*]. *Woman Dong-A,* May 16, 2013. https://woman.donga.com/3/all/12/145715/1. In Korean.

Korean Unwed Mothers' Families Association (KUMFA). Accessed April 28, 2024. https://kumfa.or.kr/.

Korsmeyer, Carolyn. *Making Sense of Taste: Food and Philosophy*. Ithaca, NY: Cornell University Press, 2002.

Kreitzer, Carson. "A Conversation with Carson Kreitzer." Interview by Caridad Svich. *Dramatist: Journal of the Dramatist Guild* 3, no. 4 (2001): 35–37.

Lamm, Kimberly. *Addressing the Other Woman: Textual Correspondences in Feminist Art and Writing*. Manchester: Manchester University Press, 2018.

Landy, Robert, and David T. Montgomery. *Theatre for Change Education, Social Action and Therapy*. New York: Palgrave Macmillan, 2012.

Langvad, Maja Lee. "*Hun er vred:* Et vidnesbyrd om transnational adoption." *Versopolis*. https://www.versopolis-poetry.com/poet/173/maja-lee-langvad. Accessed May 5, 2024. In Danish and English.

Larson, James F. *The Telecommunications Revolution in Korea*. New York: Oxford University Press, 1995.

Laybourn, SunAh M. "Adopting the Model Minority Myth: Korean Adoption as a Racial Project." *Social Problems* 68, no. 1 (2021): 118–35. https://doi.org/10.1093/socpro/spz060.

———. "Being a Transnational Korean Adoptee, Becoming Asian American." *Contexts* 17, no. 4 (November 2018): 30–35. https://doi.org/10.1177/1536504218812866.

———. *Out of Place: The Lives of Korean Adoptee Immigrants*. New York: New York University Press, 2024.

Lee, Esther Kim. *A History of Asian American Theatre.* Cambridge: Cambridge University Press, 2006.

Lee, Hyo-jin. "Adoption Agency Denies Fabricating Documents of Danish Adoptees." *Korea Times,* October 10, 2022. https://www.koreatimes.co.kr/www/nation/2024/03/113_337613.html.

Lee, James Kyung-Jin. "An Adopter and the Ends of Adoption." *Adoption & Culture* 6, no. 2 (2018): 282–91. https://doi.org/10.1353/ado.2018.0023.

Lee, Jennifer, and Min Zhou. *Asian American Youth: Culture, Identity, and Ethnicity.* New York: Routledge, 2004.

Lee, Jieun. "Performing Transnational Adoption: Korean American Women Adoptees' Autobiographical Solo Performances." *Theatre Annual* 70 (2017): 60–80.

———. "Transnational Journey into Belonging: Korean American Adoptee's Birth Search and Reunion in Eric Sharp's *Middle Brother.*" In *Transnational Mobility and Identity in and out of Korea,* edited by Yonson Ahn, 23–35. Lanham, MD: Lexington Books, 2020.

Lee, Jin-kyung. *Service Economies: Militarism, Sex Work, and Migrant Labor in South Korea.* Minneapolis: University of Minnesota Press, 2010.

Lee, Joo Young. "Black Korea: Race, Nation, Hip Hop, and Cultural Hybridity." *Korean Cultural Studies* 96 (2022): 527–48. In Korean.

———. "Black-Korean Romance: Racially Triangulated Interracial Relationships and Immigrant Narratives in *The Sun Is Also a Star.*" *Journal of American Studies* 53, no. 2 (2021): 117–37. https://doi.org/10.22505/jas.2021.53.2.05.

Lee, Josephine, Don Eitel, and R. A. Shiomi, eds. *Asian American Plays for a New Generation.* Philadelphia: Temple University Press, 2011.

Lee, Katherine In-Young. *Dynamic Korea and Rhythmic Form.* Middletown, CT: Wesleyan University Press, 2018.

Lee, Na Young. "The Construction of Military Prostitution in South Korea during the U.S. Military Rule, 1945–1948." *Feminist Studies* 33, no. 3 (2007): 453–81.

Lee, Richard M. "The Transracial Adoption Paradox: History, Research, and Counseling Implications of Cultural Socialization." *Counseling Psychologist* 31, no. 6 (2003): 711–44. https://doi.org/10.1177/0011000003258087.

Lee, Richard M., Andrea Bora Yun, Hyung Chol Yoo, and Kim Park Nelson. "Comparing the Ethnic Identity and Well-Being of Adopted Korean Americans with Immigrant/U.S.-Born Korean Americans and Korean International Students." *Adoption Quarterly* 13, no. 1 (2010): 2–17. https://doi.org/10.1080/10926751003704408.

Lee, Sharon Heijin. "Beauty between Empires: Global Feminism, Plastic Surgery, and the Trouble with Self-Esteem." *Frontiers: A Journal of Women Studies* 37, no. 1 (2016): 1–31. https://doi.org/10.1353/fro.2016.a618381.

———. "The (Geo)Politics of Beauty: Race, Transnationalism, and Neoliberalism in South Korean Beauty Culture." PhD diss., University of Michigan, 2012.

Lee, Woo-young. "Two Korean Documentary Heritage Holdings Inscribed in UNESCO's Memory of the World." *Korea Herald,* October 9, 2015. http://www.koreaherald.com/view.php?ud=20151010000011.

Lehmann, Hans-Thies. *Postdramatic Theatre.* Translated by Karen Jürs-Munby. London: Routledge, 2006.

Leighton, Kimberly. "Adoption and Critical Models of Identity: 'Searching' for Adoptees' Rights to Know beyond an Ideology of Authenticity." In Homans et al., "Critical Adoption Studies." *Adoption & Culture* 6, no. 1 (2018): 1–49. https://doi.org/10.1353/ado.2018.0015.

———. "Being Adopted and Being a Philosopher: Exploring Identity and the 'Desire to Know' Differently." In *Adoption Matter: Philosophical and Feminist Essays,* edited by Sally Haslanger and Charlotte Witt, 146–70. Ithaca, NY: Cornell University Press, 2005.

lemoine, kimura byol, kate-hers RHEE, and Leah Nichols. "[dis]locations: Traversing Solidarities within Korean Adopted Activisms." AHL Foundation, 2020. Accessed June 9, 2024. https://www.ahlfoundation.org/dislocations.

Leo, Katie Hae. Program for *Middle Brother.* The Southern Theater, Minneapolis, 2014.

Lichwick, Marissa. *Yellow Dress.* Unpublished manuscript, 2015. PDF file.

Lie, John. *K-Pop: Popular Music, Cultural Amnesia, and Economic Innovation in South Korea.* Oakland: University of California Press, 2015.

Liem, Deann Borshay. *First Person Plural.* 2000. USA: Mu Films. Accessed August 30, 2024. https://www.mufilms.org/films/firstpersonplural/.

———. *In the Matter of Cha Jung Hee.* 2010. USA: Mu Films. Accessed May 5, 2024. https://www.mufilms.org/films/matter-of-cha-jung-hee/.

Lifton, Betty Jean. "Good Adoptee—Bad Adoptee." In *Lost & Found: The Adoption Experience,* by Betty Jean Lifton, 54–61. Ann Arbor: University of Michigan Press, 2009.

———. *Journey of the Adopted Self: A Quest for Wholeness.* New York: Basic Books, 1994.

———. *Twice Born: Memoirs of an Adopted Daughter.* New York: St. Martin's Griffin, 1975.

Lim, Eng-Beng. *Brown Boys and Rice Queens: Spellbinding Performance in the Asias.* New York: New York University Press, 2014.

Lim, Sungyun. "Defying Claims of Incompetence: Women's Lawsuits over Separate Property Rights in Colonial Korea." In *Rights Claiming in South Korea,* edited by Celeste L. Arrington and Patricia Goedde, 43–62. Cambridge: Cambridge University Press, 2021.

Lo, Adrienne, and Jenna Kim. "Manufacturing Citizenship: Metapragmatic Language Competencies in Media Images of Mixed Race Men in South Korea." *Discourse & Society* 22, no. 4 (2011): 440–57. https://doi.org/10.1177/0957926510395834.

Lorde, Audre. "The Master's Tools Will Never Dismantle the Master's House." In *Sister Outsider: Essays and Speeches,* by Audre Lorde, 110–13. Freedom, CA: Crossing Press, 1984.

Machon, Josephine. *Immersive Theatres: Intimacy and Immediacy in Contemporary Performance.* New York: Palgrave Macmillan, 2013.

Malkki, Liisa H. *The Need to Help: The Domestic Arts of International Humanitarianism.* Durham, NC: Duke University Press, 2015.

Masson, Judith. "The 1999 Reform of Intercountry Adoption in the United Kingdom: New Solutions and Old Problems." *Family Law Quarterly* 34, no. 2 (2000): 221–37. https://www.jstor.org/stable/25740288.

Mbembe, Achille. *Necropolitics.* Translated by Steve Corcoran. Durham, NC: Duke University Press, 2019.

McIntosh, Peggy. "White Privilege and Male Privilege: A Personal Account of Coming to See Correspondences through Work in Women's Studies." Working Paper 189. Wellesley, MA: Wellesley Centers for Women, 1988.

McIvor, Charlotte. "Community Theatre as Active Citizenship." In *Migration and Performance in Contemporary Ireland: Towards a New Interculturalism,* by Charlotte McIvor, 181–212. London: Palgrave Macmillan, 2016.

McKee, Kimberly D. *Adoption Fantasies: The Commodification of Asian Adoptees from Girlhood to Womanhood.* Columbus: The Ohio State University Press, 2023.

———. *Disrupting Kinship: Transnational Politics of Korean Adoption in the United States*. Champaign: University of Illinois Press, 2019.

———. "From Adoptee to Trespasser: The Female Asian Adoptee as Oriental Fantasy." In *Adoption and Multiculturalism: Europe, the Americas, and the Pacific*, edited by Jenny Heijin Wills, Tobias Hübinette, and Indigo Willing, 150–73. Ann Arbor: University of Michigan Press, 2020.

———. "Gendered Adoptee Identities: Performing Trans-Pacific Masculinity in the 21st Century." In *Gendering the Trans-Pacific World*, vol. 1, edited by Catherine Ceniza Choy and Judy Tzu-Chun Wu, 221–45. Leiden: Brill, 2017. https://doi.org/10.1163/9789004336100_012.

———. "Introduction: The Residues of Korean Adoption." *Adoption & Culture* 6, no. 2 (2018): 267–71. https://doi.org/10.1353/ado.2018.0027.

———. "Locating Adoptees in Asian America: Jane Jeong Trenka and Deann Borshay Liem." In *Our Voices, Our Histories: Asian American and Pacific Islander Women*, edited by Shirley Hune and Gail M. Nomura, 357–72. New York: New York University Press, 2020.

———. "Monetary Flows and the Movements of Children: The Transnational Adoption Industrial Complex." *Journal of Korean Studies* 21, no. 1 (2016): 137–78. https://doi.org/10.1353/jks.2016.0007.

———. "Public Intimacy and Kinship in the Korean Adoption Community." *Women, Gender, and Families of Color* 8, no. 1 (2020): 40–64. https://doi.org/10.5406/womgenfamcol.8.1.0040.

———. "Rewriting History: Adoptee Documentaries as a Site of Truth-Telling." In *The Routledge Companion to Asian American Media*, edited by Lori Kido Lopez and Vincent N. Pham, 119–30. Abingdon: Routledge, 2017.

McNeill, David. *Hand and Mind: What Gestures Reveal about Thought*. Chicago: University of Chicago Press, 1992.

Mignot, Jean-François. "Child Adoption in Western Europe, 1900–2015." In *Cliometrics of the Family*, edited by Claude Diebolt, Auke Rijpma, Sarah Carmichael, Selin Dilli, and Charlotte Störmer, 333–66. Cham, Switzerland: Springer, 2019.

Ministry of Health and Welfare. "Expert Discussion on the Hague Convention on Intercountry Adoption Held." https://www.mohw.go.kr/board.es?mid=a20401000000&bid=0032&tag=&act=view&list_no=260611.

Min Jung, Cathy. *Les Bonnes Intentions*. Brussels: Hayez&Lansman, 2011. In French.

"Mission." Korean Adoptees of Chicago. Accessed April 28, 2024. https://www.ikaa.org/portfolio/chicago/.

"Mission." The Welders, a Playwrights' Collective. Accessed March 10, 2024. https://www.thewelders.org/mission/.

"Mission." Wonderlust Productions. Accessed March 11, 2024. https://wlproductions.org/mission-vision/.

Mitchell, Anthony. "Ethiopia Puts Its Young Up for Adoption." *Washington Post*, January 2, 2005. https://www.washingtonpost.com/archive/politics/2005/01/02/ethiopia-puts-its-young-up-for-adoption/5c51dcc4-bef7-4020-a95b-cbf96cac9917/.

Mohanty, Chandra. "Under Western Eyes: Feminist Scholarship and Colonial Discourses." *Feminist Review* 30, no. 1 (November 1988): 61–88. https://doi.org/10.1057/fr.1988.42.

Molina-Guzmán, Isabel. *Dangerous Curves: Latina Bodies in the Media*. New York: New York University Press, 2010.

Moon, Katharine H. S. *Sex among Allies: Military Prostitution in U.S.-Korea Relations*. New York: Columbia University Press 1997.

Myers, Kit W. "'Real Families': The Violence of Love in New Media Adoption Discourse." *Critical Discourse Studies* 11, no. 2 (2014): 175–93. https://doi.org/10.1080/17405904.2013.852983.

Myong, Lene. "Adopteret: Fortaellinger om transnational og racialiseret tilblivelse." PhD thesis, Aarhus Universitet, 2009. In Danish.

Na, Eunha. "Empathic Imagination: Performing Interracial Intimacy in Contemporary Women's Drama." PhD diss., University of Minnesota, 2016.

———. "Re-made in Korea: Adult Adoptees' Homecoming and Gendered Performance in Recent American Plays." *American Studies* 43, no. 1 (2020): 25–56. In Korean.

Naficy, Hamid. *An Accented Cinema: Exilic and Diasporic Filmmaking*. Princeton, NJ: Princeton University Press, 2001.

Nakamura, Jessica. *Transgenerational Remembrance: Performance and the Asia-Pacific War in Contemporary Japan*. Evanston, IL: Northwestern University Press, 2020.

Natural Disorder: Christian Sønderby Jepsen and His Protagonist Challenge Our Ideas of Normality. Danish Film Institute, 2015. https://www.dfi.dk/en/viden-om-film/filmdatabasen/film/naturens-uorden.

Nelson, Hilde Lindemann. *Damaged Identities, Narrative Repair*. Ithaca, NY: Cornell University Press, 2001.

Network of Politicized Adoptees. Accessed May 2, 2024. https://www.npa-mn.org/.

Ngai, Sianne. *Ugly Feelings*. Cambridge, MA: Harvard University Press, 2007.

Novy, Marianne. *Reading Adoption: Family and Difference in Fiction and Drama*. Ann Arbor: University of Michigan Press, 2005.

Oh, Arissa H. *To Save the Children of Korea: The Cold War Origins of International Adoption*. Stanford, CA: Stanford University Press, 2015.

Ong, Aiwha. *Flexible Citizenship: The Cultural Logics of Transnationality*. Durham, NC: Duke University Press, 1999.

Oparah, Julia Chinyere, Sun Yung Shin, and Jane Jeong Trenka. "Preface." In *Outsiders Within: Writing on Transracial Adoption*, edited by Jane Jeong Trenka, Julia Chinyere Opara, and Sun Yung Shin, xii–xv. Minneapolis: University of Minnesota Press, 2021.

O'Shaughnessy, Brian. *Consciousness and the World*. New York: Oxford University Press, 2000.

Paik, Doosan. "Interview with Artists: Playwright and Director of *Ilgopzipmae*, Yang Gu Yi" [*Yesulgawaui mannam Yi Yang Gu jakga yeonchul*]. December 13, 2012. Arko Art Archives. Hyehwa, Seoul. Video. In Korean.

Papke, David Ray. "Transracial Adoption in the United States: The Reflection and Reinforcement of Racial Hierarchy." *Journal of Law and Family Studies* 15, no. 1 (2013): 57–80.

Park, Chanhyo. *Korean Family and Misogyny* [*Hangugui gajokgwa yeoseonghyeomo*], 1950–2020. Seoul: Chaekgwahamkke, 2020. In Korean.

Park, Hyeongju. "*Chalkak*, the Final Work for the Wandering Trilogy" [*Chalkak tteodom 3bujak sirijeu wangyeoljak*]. *ART Insight*, August 7, 2020. https://www.artinsight.co.kr/news/view.php?no=49266. In Korean.

Park, Jungman. "Yeonwoo Mudae and the Korean Theatre Movement in the 1980s." *Asian Theatre Journal* 30, no. 1 (2013): 67–89. https://doi.org/10.1353/atj.2013.0014.

Park Nelson, Kim. "The Disability of Adoption: Adoptees in Disabling Societies." *Adoption Quarterly* 21, no. 4 (2018): 288–306. https://doi.org/10.1080/10926755.2018.1526841.

———. *Invisible Asians: Korean American Adoptees, Asian American Experiences, and Racial Exceptionalism*. New Brunswick, NJ: Rutgers University Press, 2016.

———. "'Loss Is More Than Sadness': Reading Dissent in Transracial Adoption Melodrama in *The Language of Blood* and *First Person Plural*." *Adoption & Culture* 1, no. 1 (2007): 101–28. https://doi.org/10.1353/ado.2007.0006.

———. "Shopping for Children in the International Marketplace." In *Outsiders Within: Writing on Transracial Adoption*, edited by Jane Jeong Trenka, Julia Chinyere Oparah, and Sun Yung Shin, 89–104. Cambridge, MA: South End Press, 2006.

Park Nelson, Kim, and Lene Myong. "Shared and Divergent Landscapes of Transnational Adoption Politics and Critique: Newspaper Reporting and Transnational Adoptee Interventions in Denmark and Minnesota." In *Adoption and Multiculturalism: Europe, the Americas, and the Pacific*, edited by Jenny Heijun Wills, Tobias Hübinette, and Indigo Willing, 99–125. Ann Arbor: University of Michigan Press, 2020.

Park, Pauline. "Coming Full Circle: The Journey of a Transgendered Korean Adoptee." *Pauline Park* blog, November 5, 2015. https://paulinepark.com/2015/11/05/coming-full-circle-the-journey-of-a-transgendered-korean-adoptee-11-7-15/.

Park, Shelley M. *Mothering Queerly, Queering Motherhood: Resisting Monomaternalism in Adoptive, Lesbian, Blended, and Polygamous Families*. Albany: State University of New York Press, 2013.

Park, So Young. "Transnational Adoption, *Hallyu*, and the Politics of Korean Popular Culture." *Biography* 33, no. 1 (2010): 151–66. https://doi.org/10.1353/bio.0.0154.

Pate, SooJin. *From Orphan to Adoptee: U.S. Empire and Genealogies of Korean Adoption*. Minneapolis: University of Minnesota Press, 2014.

Paton, Jean. *Orphan Voyage*. New York: Vantage Press, 1968.

Patterson, Orlando. *Slavery and Social Death: A Comparative Study*. Cambridge, MA: Harvard University Press, 1982.

Patton-Imani, Sandra. "'Someone's Roots': Gender, Rape, and Racialization in Korean American Adoption Narratives." In *Race in Transnational and Transracial Adoption*, edited by Vilna Bashi Treitler, 112–29. London: Palgrave Macmillan, 2014.

Pazicky, Diana Loercher. *Cultural Orphans in America*. Jackson: University Press of Mississippi, 1998.

Pertman, Adam. *Adoption Nation: How the Adoption Revolution Is Transforming America*. New York: Basic Books, 2000.

Phelan, Peggy. "Letter to the Special Issue Editor." *Adoption & Culture* 6, no. 1 (2018): 5–9. https://doi.org/10.1353/ado.2018.0015.

———. *Unmarked: The Politics of Performance*. London: Routledge, 1993.

Powers, Marla N. *Oglala Women: Myth, Ritual, and Reality*. Chicago: University of Chicago Press, 2010.

Prague Quadrennial of Performance Design and Space Program. Prague: Arts and Theatre Institute, 2019.

Pratt, Mary Louise. "Arts of the Contact Zone." *Profession*, 1991, 33–40.

———. *Imperial Eyes: Travel Writing and Transculturation*. London: Routledge, 2008.

Prébin, Elise. *Meeting Once More: The Korean Side of Transnational Adoption*. New York: New York University Press, 2013.

"President Kim Dae Jung's Speech, October 23, 1998 at the Blue House." *Chosen Child* 1, no. 5 (1999): 15–16.

Production flyer for *Chalkak* at the CJ azit Daehakno. 2020. In Korean.

"Production History." Theater Mu. Accessed May 2, 2024. https://www.theatermu.org/production-history.

Radway, Janice. "Foreword." In *Ghostly Matters: Haunting and the Sociological Imagination*, by Avery F. Gordon, vii–xiii. Minneapolis: University of Minnesota Press, 2008.

Raleigh, Elizabeth. *Selling Transracial Adoption: Families, Markets, and the Color Line*. Philadelphia: Temple University Press, 2018.

Rancière, Jacques. *The Emancipated Spectator*. Translated by Gregory Elliott. New York: Verso, 2009.

Rasmussen, Kim-Su. "The Sublime Object of Adoption." *Orbis Litterarum* 73, no. 1 (2018): 1–28. https://doi.org/10.1111/oli.12153.

Re-enacting the Transnational Adoptee (trailer). Performed by Yong Sun Gullach. Video documentation by Tanja Wol. Accessed May 5, 2024. https://www.thestarchildproject.com/2017/03/16/re-enacting-the-transnational-adoptee/.

"The Republic of Korea Signs the 1993 Hague Intercountry Adoption Convention." Hague Conference on Private International Law (HCCH), May 28, 2013. https://www.hcch.net/de/news-archive/details/?varevent=309.

Ressler, Everett M., Neil Boothby, and Daniel J. Steinbock. *Unaccompanied Children: Care and Protection in Wars, Natural Disasters and Refugee Movements*. Oxford: Oxford University Press, 1988.

Riben, Mirah. "Adoption Criminality and Corruption." *Huffington Post*, January 13, 2015. https://www.huffpost.com/entry/adoption-crimes-and-corru_b_6467540.

Robinson, Tammy Ko. "Amy Mihyang's Play 'between' and Korean Activism for Single Mothers" [Eimi mihyangui yeongeuk 'between'gwa hangugui mihonmo undong]. *Pressian*, June 5, 2011. https://www.pressian.com/news/article.html?no=18572. In Korean.

Rodrigues, Sara. "Undressing Homogeneity: Prescribing Femininity and the Transformation of Self-Esteem in *How to Look Good Naked*." *Journal of Popular Film and Television* 40, no. 1 (2012): 42–52. https://doi.org/10.1080/01956051.2011.595743.

Rollins, Lisa Marie. Program note for *Homeful*, Theatre Row, New York City, 2018.

Rosen, Robert. "Director's Notes." Program for *Middle Brother*, The Southern Theater, Minneapolis, 2014.

Royal Danish Theatre. *Human Outphasing* (*Human afvikling*), 2016–17 season. Accessed May 5, 2024. https://kglteater.dk/en/whats-on/season-20162017/drama/human-outphasing.

Ruddick, Sara. *Maternal Thinking: Toward a Politics of Peace*. New York: Ballantine, 1989.

Said, Edward W. *Orientalism*. New York: Pantheon Books, 1978.

Salverson, Julie. "Transgressive Storytelling or an Aesthetic of Injury: Performance, Pedagogy and Ethics." *Theatre Research in Canada* 20, no. 1 (1999): 35–51. https://doi.org/10.3138/tric.20.1.35.

Schechner, Richard. *Performance Theory*. New York: Routledge, 1988.

Schneider, Rebecca. *The Explicit Body in Performance*. New York: Routledge, 1997.

Schultz, Stacy E. "Asian American Women Artists: Performative Strategies Redefined." *Journal of Asian American Studies* 15, no. 1 (2012): 105–27. https://doi.org/10.1353/jaas.2012.0000.

Schwab, Gabriele. *Haunting Legacies: Violent Histories and Transgenerational Trauma*. New York: Columbia University Press, 2020.

Sedgwick, Eve Kosofsky. *Touching Feeling: Affect, Pedagogy, Performativity*. Durham, NC: Duke University Press, 2003.

Selman, Peter. "The Global Decline of Intercountry Adoption: What Lies Ahead?" *Social Policy and Society* 11, no. 3 (2012): 381–97. https://doi.org/10.1017/S1474746412000085.

Seo, Jungmin, and Seoyoung Choi. "Why Korean Feminism?" *Journal of Asian Sociology* 49, no. 4 (2020): 371–98.

Shakespeare, William. *Macbeth.* In *The New Cambridge Shakespeare,* edited by A. R. Braunmuller, 115–254. Cambridge: Cambridge University Press, 1997.

Sharp, Eric. *Middle Brother.* Unpublished manuscript, 2014. PDF file.

Shim, Jung-Soon. "Recasting the National Motherhood: Transactions of Western Feminisms in Korean Theatre." *Theatre Research International* 29, no. 2 (2004): 143–54. https://doi.org/10.1017/s030788330400029x.

Shimakawa, Karen. *National Abjection: The Asian American Body Onstage.* Durham, NC: Duke University Press, 2002.

Shimizu, Celine Parreñas. *The Hypersexuality of Race: Performing Asian/American Women on Screen and Scene.* Durham, NC: Duke University Press, 2007.

Shin, Eun Hye, and Hyun Hee Kim. "Report on Former Kijichon Sex Workers in Gyeonggi Do." Conference Proceedings. Seoul: Haessal Sahoebokjihoe, 2008.

Simon, Rita J., and Howard Alstein. "Transracial Adoption: An Overview." In *Adoption, Race, and Identity: From Infancy to Young Adulthood,* 2nd ed., 1–39. Abingdon: Routledge, 2017.

Sivigny, Debra Kim. *Hello, My Name Is . . .* Unpublished manuscript, 2017. PDF file.

Sjöblom, Lisa Wool-Rim. *Palimpsest: Documents from a Korean Adoption.* Montreal: Drawn & Quarterly Publications, 2019.

Skreen, Chet. "Adopted Koreans Fully 'Americanized.'" *Seattle Times,* August 10, 1975.

Snyder-Young, Dani. *Theatre of Good Intentions: Challenges and Hopes for Theatre and Social Change.* London: Palgrave Macmillan, 2013.

Son, Elizabeth W. *Embodied Reckonings: "Comfort Women," Performance, and Transpacific Redress.* Ann Arbor: University of Michigan Press, 2018.

Song, Young In, and Ailee Moon. *Korean American Women from Tradition to Modern Feminism.* Westport, CT: Praeger Publishers, 1998.

Sontag, Susan. *On Photography.* New York: Farrar, Straus and Giroux, 1973.

Sorensen, Eli Park. "Korean Adoption Literature and the Politics of Representation." *Partial Answers: Journal of Literature and the History of Ideas* 12, no. 1 (2014): 155–79. https://doi.org/10.1353/pan.2014.0001.

Stock, Kimberly Kyung Hee. "My Han." In *Voices from Another Place: A Collection of Works from a Generation Born in Korea and Adopted to Other Countries,* edited by Susan Soon-Keum Cox, 96–104. Saint Paul, MN: Yeong & Yeong Book Company, 1999.

Stoker, Kim. "Beyond Identity: Activism in Korean Adoptee Art." *Duksung Women's University Journal* 34 (2005): 223–48.

Stoler, Ann Laura. "Intimidations of Empire: Predicaments of the Tactile and Unseen." In *Haunted by Empire: Geographies of Intimacy in North American History,* edited by Ann Laura Stoler, 1–22. Durham, NC: Duke University Press, 2006.

Strauss, Jean A. S. *ADOPTED: for the life of me.* 2010. Vimeo video, 56:54. Accessed May 5, 2024. https://vimeo.com/202415517.

Stuart Fisher, Amanda. *Performing the Testimonial: Rethinking Verbatim Dramaturgies.* Manchester: Manchester University Press, 2020.

Suh, Emily, and Katelyn Hemmeke. "What CDA/CDS Scholars Are Doing to Make a Difference in the World." In *Critical Discourse Analysis, Critical Discourse Studies and Beyond*, edited by Theresa Catalano and Linda R. Waugh, 325–88. Cham, Switzerland: Springer, 2020.

Swedish Korean Adoptees Network. Accessed May 5, 2024. https://swedishkoreanadopteesnetwork.wordpress.com/.

Tænketanken Adoption. Accessed May 5, 2024. http://www.taenketankenadoption.dk/english/.

Taylor, Diana. *The Archive and the Repertoire: Performing Cultural Memory in the Americas*. Durham, NC: Duke University Press, 2003.

Taylor Porter, Nancy. *Violent Women in Contemporary Theatres: Staging Resistance*. New York: Palgrave Macmillan, 2017.

Tchen, John Kuo Wei, and Dylan Yeats. *Yellow Peril!: An Archive of Anti-Asian Fear*. London: Verso Books, 2014.

Theater Hae blog. Accessed June 8, 2024. https://blog.naver.com/theaterhae. In Korean.

Tiffin, Helen. "Post-Colonial Literatures and Counter-Discourse." *Kunapipi* 9, no. 3 (1987): 17–34.

Trenka, Jane Jeong. *The Language of Blood: A Memoir*. St. Paul, MN.: Borealis Books, 2003.

Trezise, Bryoni. *Performing Feeling in Cultures of Memory*. New York: Palgrave Macmillan, 2014.

Tutu, Desmond. "Foreword." In Yaël Farber, *Theatre as Witness: Three Testimonial Plays from South Africa: In Collaboration with and Based on the Lives of the Original Performers*, 7. London: Oberon Books, 2008.

Ugwu, Catherine. *Let's Get It On: The Politics of Black Performance*. Seattle: Bay Press, 1995.

United Nations Department of Economic and Social Affairs. *Child Adoptions: Trends and Policies*, ST/ESA/SER.A/292., New York, (2009). https://www.un.org/en/development/desa/population/publications/pdf/policy/child-adoption.pdf.

United Nations Educational, Scientific, and Cultural Organization (UNESCO). The Archives of the KBS Special Live Broadcast "Finding Dispersed Families." Accessed May 12, 2024. https://www.unescoicdh.org/eng/sub.php?menukey=289&mod=view&no=10861&listCnt=10&code1=00000003&code2=00000032.

United Nations Convention on the Rights of the Child. *Human Rights Instruments*. Accessed May 31, 2024. https://www.ohchr.org/en/instruments-mechanisms/instruments/convention-rights-child.

US Department of Justice. "Four Employees of Adoption Services Provider Charged with Conspiracy to Defraud the United States in Connection with Ethiopia Operations." February 11, 2014. https://www.justice.gov/opa/pr/four-employees-adoption-services-provider-charged-conspiracy-defraud-united-states-connection.

US Department of State Bureau of Consular Affairs. *FY 2019 Annual Report on Intercountry Adoption*. https://travel.state.gov/content/travel/en/Intercountry-Adoption/adopt_ref/AnnualReports.html.

US House Committee on Oversight and Reform. *Child Separations by the Trump Administration*. Staff Report. July 2019. https://www.govinfo.gov/content/pkg/GOVPUB-OTHER-PURL-gpo126261/pdf/GOVPUB-OTHER-PURL-gpo126261.pdf.

Walton, Jessica. *Korean Adoptees and Transnational Adoption: Embodiment and Emotion*. Abingdon: Routledge, 2019.

Wang, Leslie K. *Outsourced Children: Orphanage Care and Adoption in Globalizing China*. Stanford, CA: Stanford University Press, 2016.

Warner, Michael. *Publics and Counterpublics*. Brooklyn: Zone Books, 2002.

———. "Publics and Counterpublics." *Public Culture* 14, no. 1 (2002): 49–90. https://doi.org/10.1215/08992363-14-1-49.

Wegar, Katarina. *Adoption, Identity, and Kinship: The Debate over Sealed Birth Records.* New Haven, CT: Yale University Press, 1997.

Weil, Richard H. "International Adoptions: The Quiet Migration." *International Migration Review* 18, no. 2 (1984): 276–93. https://doi.org/10.1177/019791838401800205.

Welton, Martin. *Feeling Theatre.* New York: Palgrave Macmillan, 2012.

White, Bretton. *Staging Discomfort: Performance and Queerness in Contemporary Cuba.* Gainesville: University of Florida Press, 2020.

"Who We Are." International Korean Adoptee Association Network. Accessed April 28, 2024. https://ikaa.org/who-we-are/.

Wills, Jenny Heijun. *Older Sister. Not Necessarily Related.* Toronto: McClelland & Stewart, 2019.

———. "Paradoxical Essentialism: Reading Race and Origins in Jane Jeong Trenka's Asian Adoption Memoirs." *Canadian Review of American Studies* 46, no. 2 (2016): 202–22. https://doi.org/10.3138/cras.2015.004.

Wills, Jenny Heijun, Tobias Hübinette, and Indigo Willing. "Introduction." In *Adoption and Multiculturalism: Europe, the Americas, and the Pacific,* edited by Jenny Heijun Wills, Tobias Hübinette, and Indigo Willing, 1–18. Ann Arbor: University of Michigan Press, 2020.

Wirth-Nesher, Hana. "The Literary Orphan as National Hero: Huck and Pip." *Dickens Studies Annual* 15 (1986): 259–73.

Wolf, Naomi. *The Beauty Myth: How Images of Beauty Are Used against Women.* New York: Doubleday, 1991.

Woo, Miseong. "Performing the Diasporic Sensibility of Displacement: International Korean Adoption in Sun Mee Chomet's How to Be a Korean Woman." *English Language and Literature* 61, no. 2 (2015): 289–308. https://doi.org/10.15794/jell.2015.61.2.007.

Woo, Susie. *Framed by War: Korean Children and Women at the Crossroads of US Empire.* New York: New York University Press, 2019.

Wyver, Richey. "Civilizing Missions and Mimicry in Sweden's Colonial Present: Exploring the Construction of the Transnational/-racial Adoptee as a Mimic Swede." In *Adoption and Multiculturalism: Europe, the Americas, and the Pacific,* edited by Jenny Heijun Wills, Tobias Hübinette, and Indigo Willing, 126–49. Ann Arbor: University of Michigan Press, 2020.

———. "'More Beautiful Than Something We Could Create Ourselves': Exploring Swedish International Transracial Adoption Desire." PhD diss., University of Auckland, 2021.

Yancy, George. "White Embodied Gazing, the Black Body as Disgust, and the Aesthetics of Un-Suturing." In *Body Aesthetics,* edited by Sherri Irvin, 243–60. Oxford: Oxford University Press, 2016.

Yi, Yang Gu. "Ilgopzipmae." In *The 34th Seoul Theater Festival Collection of Plays,* 159–234. Seoul: Yeongeukgwa Ingan, 2013. In Korean.

———. "Playwright's Note." Production program for *Ilgopzipmae* at the Seoul Theatre Festival. 2013. In Korean.

———. "The Use of the Date of Kijichon Women's Life History Research in the Play 'Ilgopzipmae.'" *Korea Journal of Oral History* 4, no. 2 (2013): 7–35. In Korean.

Yngvesson, Barbara. "Going 'Home': Adoption, Loss of Bearings, and the Mythology of Roots." *Social Text* 74 (2003): 7–27.

———. "Transnational Adoption and European Immigration Politics: Producing the National Body in Sweden." *Indiana Journal of Global Legal Studies* 19, no. 1 (2012): 327–45. https://doi.org/10.2979/indjglolegstu.19.1.327.

Yngvesson, Barbara, and Susan Bibler Coutin. "Backed by Papers: Undoing Persons, Histories, and Return." *American Ethnologist* 33, no. 2 (2006): 177–90. https://doi.org/10.1525/ae.2006.33.2.177.

Yngvesson, Barbara, and Maureen A. Mahoney. "'As One Should, Ought, and Wants to Be': Belonging and Authenticity in Identity Narratives." *Theory, Culture & Society* 17, no. 6 (2000): 77–110. https://doi.org/10.1177/02632760022051509.

Yonhap News. "One-Act Play Festival at Saem-teo and Blue Bird Theater" [*Saemteo parangsaegeukjangdeungseo danmakgeuk chukje*]. August 4, 1991. https://n.news.naver.com/mnews/article/001/0003562585?sid=103. In Korean.

Yoo, JinWol. *Korean Diaspora beyond Margin from Margin: Arts by Korean Overseas Adoptees and Overseas Koreans* [*Korian diaseupora, gyeonggyeeseo gyeonggyereul neomda: haeoe ibyangingwa jaeoehaninui yesul*]. Seoul: Prunsasang, 2015. In Korean.

Yook, Sung Hee, and Hosu Kim. "Decolonizing Adoption Narratives for Transnational Reproductive Justice." *CLCWeb: Comparative Literature and Culture* 20, no. 6 (2018). https://doi.org/10.7771/1481-4374.3323.

Youn, JK. *Ode to My Father*. 2014. South Korea: CJ Entertainment.

Yu, Yeonju. "Korean Diaspora Festival: Planning against Authors' Intentions, Staging against Authors' Intentions" [*Hanminjok diaseuporajeon: changjak uidoe banhaneun gihoek, changjak uidoe banhaneun mudaehwa*]. *Gongyeongwa Yron* 67 (2017): 255–67. In Korean.

Yun, Jieheerah. "A Foreign Country in Seoul: Itaewon's Multicultural Streets." In *Globalizing Seoul: The City's Cultural and Urban Change*, by Jieheerah Yun, 123–41. Abingdon: Routledge, 2017.

INDEX

abjection, 25, 83
accountability, 27–29
ADOPTED (film), 193n133
adoptees, Korean transnational: about, 2; activism, 110–11, 156n157, 168–70, 216–18, 217n13; activists, 169–70; ambiguity in performance, 187–88, 194–95; artists, 7, 30–33, 156n157, 170–71; birth search and reunion, 2–9, 8n27, 19–24; celebrity, 17–18; citizenship for, 15n65, 124–25, 131, 147n129; critically thinking, 33, 202–3; deportation, 15, 146–47, 147n129; experience of racism, 135–36, 193; experience of sexual abuse, 159n1, 179–80, 179n91; "good" versus "bad," 115–16; in Europe, 166–71, 168n40; killjoy, 115, 136–40; kinship, 116–17, 148–50; organizations, 169; park honoring, 207–13; with disability, 170, 170n54, 179n91. *See also titles of individual works*
adoption, Korean transnational: about, 2; and colonization, 163–66, 203–6; commodification of children, 13, 138, 138n100, 190; to European countries, 166–71; historical overview (US), 9–19; media representing, 44–50, 215–16; proxy, 11, 11n39; records, 18–19, 39n3, 132, 132n76, 133–35, 139–40, 160, 192–93, 193n133. *See also titles of individual works*
adoption, transracial, 13–15, 25–26, 102–3, 151, 153–54, 166–67, 218–19
Adoption & Culture, 217
affects. *See* emotions
Ahmed, Sara, 21n93, 130, 136, 198, 203–5
Airport Baby (Jun and Chang), 34, 39–44, 57–66, 58n65, 61 fig. 1, 74–80
airports, as settings, 58–59, 101–2
Albee, Edward, 4, 132n76
Alice in Wonderland (Carroll), 120, 131–32
Allen, Woody, 179n91
Also-Known-As (AKA), 109, 109n108
American Dream, The (Albee), 4, 132n76
Anderson, Patrick, 173–74
anger, 26, 103, 135, 139–41, 162, 197
archives, 8n27, 33, 45–46, 55–56, 72–73, 75, 91–93, 192–93
Ardnt-Johns, Jennifer, 84n12
"Arirang" (Korean folksong), 105–6, 105n95
Artaud, Antonin, 201, 201n156
artivism, 110–11

Asiamnesia (Chomet), 93
Asian American theater and performance, 4, 25, 27–28, 83, 150–52
Asian Americans, 14, 21, 25, 153
Asia-Pacific War, 27–28
audience involvement, 69, 143–48, 198–99
audience response, 31n136, 62, 108–9, 111–12, 201–2
Augé, Marc, 58
autobiographical performance, 31, 68–69, 81–113

Baik, Crystal Mun-hye, 28–29
Baker, Randy, 141
Banes, Sally, 52
Barthes, Roland, 55
Battle Hymn (film), 10
beauty myth, 96–99
Because I Am an Unwed Mother (play), 79
Belgium, 167–68, 168n40; Belgian Adoptees from Korea (BAK), 169; Belgium Council on Adoption, 205
belonging and unbelonging, 36–37, 48, 57–58, 65, 99, 102–4, 106, 114–58
Berks, Alan, 130. See also *In My Heart*
"best interests of children," 19, 26, 132–34, 168
between (Ginther), 100–102, 100n76
Bhabha, Homi, 89, 188, 196n140
Biggin, Rose, 142–43
birth search. *See* search and reunion; *and titles of individual works*
Black Tie (Stein), 170
blood-relatedness, 12, 16, 16n70, 22, 43n18, 48, 94–95, 214
Boal, Augusto, 200
body: birth mother of, 39, 43, 77; body politics, 115, 125; border-crossing testimony, 107–13; collage, 91–93, 92n49; decolonization, 204; in discipline, 126–29; in injury, 201; inscription of, 24–25; performance art, 189–99; racialization, 89, 160–63, 185n103; in slow motion, 94–96; in solo performance, 83; violence, 160–63
Boo, Kyung-Sook, 18n78
Boo, Sae-rom, 186
Brager, Øystein Ulsberg, 170

Brecht, Bertolt, 133
Briggs, Laura, 43
Brockelman, Thomas P., 92n49
brotherhood, 62, 121–30
Buried Child (Shepard), 182
Butler, Judith, 24, 161

Cacho, Lisa Marie, 40
cameras, 54–57, 60
Carlson, Marla, 204–5
Carroll, Lewis, 120, 130–32
Caruth, Cathy, 181, 181n95
Cavicchi, Andrea Kim, 21
Chalkak (Ha), 34, 39–44, 50–57, 50n38, 74–80, 183
Chang, Hee-sun, 57. See also *Airport Baby*
Chappell, In-Sook, 181, 181n96, 200–202. See also *This Isn't Romance*
Chen, Fu-Jen, 104
childhood, in performance, 87–89, 125–27, 146–48, 152–53, 171–81
China, adoptions from, 2n2, 19, 19n87
Cho, Grace, 67
Chomet, Sun Mee, 32, 82n6, 93, 93n51, 98 fig. 2, 107–13. See also *How to Be a Korean Woman*
Choy, Catherine Ceniza, 217
Christian Americanism, 9–10, 9n31, 10n32, 88, 143–44
Chu, Tammy, 84n12, 85n17
Chun Doo-hwan, 13
citizenship, 15n65, 124–25, 131, 147n129
Cold War, 2, 10, 11, 66–67, 89, 217
Coleman, Jeffrey, 76
Coletu, Ebony, 86
collage, in performance, 91–93, 92n49, 146
colonialism and colonization: adoption and, 37–38, 163–66, 167–68, 179, 190, 203–6; colonial imagination, 174–78; colonial modernity, 174; emulation of colonial power, 195; "feel-good" master affect, 165–66, 199–201, 203–4; mimicry, 196n140; symbolic, 164–65. See also decolonialism and decolonization

colorblindness, 3, 14–15, 27, 85, 103, 120, 167, 203
"comfort women," 27–28
community-based theater, 130–41, 152–55
contact zones, 35, 42, 65n75
Cooper, Leah, 130–31, 155. See also *In My Heart*
counterpublics, 7–8
Coutin, Susan, 122
critical adoption studies, 4–5, 4n11, 15n63, 215, 217–18
Crossing Chasms (Ardnt-Johns), 84n12
Cvetkovich, Ann, 55

dance and dancing, 52–53, 58n65, 127–28, 144, 154–55, 176
danger, in performance, 200–201, 201n156
Davison, Carol Margaret, 76
Dawson, Toby, 18
death, 39–41, 41n10, 44, 53, 55–57, 55n52, 60–64, 74–78, 144, 184–85. See also social death
decolonialism and decolonization, 165–66, 204–6
demythification, 82–83
Denmark, 2n2, 166–67, 169–70
deportation, 15, 146–47, 147n129
deus ex machina, 48, 48n35
discomfort, 199–206
[dis]locations exhibition, 156n157
Docan-Morgan, Sara, 21, 33
Dolan, Jill, 117
dressing and undressing, 97–99, 125–26, 190–91, 196
duo-drama, 50–51, 50n40

Elfving-Hwang, Joanna, 63
emotions: anger, 26, 103, 135, 139–41, 162, 197; Aristotelian affects in birth search and reunion spectacle, 46; audience, 62, 108–9, 110, 201–2, 204; on body, 107–8; colonized, 174; discomfort, 26, 199–206; emotional labor, 25–26, 25n118, 195; "feel-good" master affect, 165–66, 199–201, 203–4; killjoy, 115, 136–40; media representing, 20–21, 45–46; minor feelings, 26; in object, 211; pain, 16–17, 26, 28, 106–7, 162, 190, 204–5; response to adoptees, 16–17; script, 25–26; sticky feelings, 198; technology enabling, 63–64, 104–5; ugly feelings, 204
Eng, David, 65
England and Wales, 168
Enloe, Cynthia, 76
essentialism, 23
ethnicity, in performance, 90, 102–4
ethnonationalism, 2, 16–18, 16n70, 49, 105, 216
Euripides, 162
Evan, Nathan, 170

Fagan, Kristina, 118
family separation, 44–46, 218
Fanon, Frantz, 165–66, 174, 195
fantasy, 117–21, 122n37, 136–37, 177–78
Farrow, Mia, 179n91
fathers, 48–49, 79; adoptive, 138, 178–81, 216; birth, 18, 91, 128–29, 171n56, 176. See also parents
Fedosik, Marina, 73
"feel-good" master affect, 165–66, 199–201, 203–4
feelings. See emotions
femininity, 93–94, 96–99, 187–88
feminism, 33, 52–53, 78–79, 93–94, 136, 161, 202, 216–17
Finding Dispersed Families (TV program), 41–42, 44–46, 45nn27–28
First Person Plural (Liem), 81n2, 84–85, 96
Fischer-Lichte, Erika, 191–92
Fitzpatrick, Lisa, 162
Flights of Fancy (Thompson), 170
"flip the script," 9, 9n29
Fluck, Winfried, 73
food (liquor), 51, 105, 126–27, 155, 174, 175, 175n73
Ford, John, 182
forever family, 137–38
Four Destinies (Leo), 151
Francus, Marilyn, 145
Fuhr, Michael, 65n75

Futerman, Samantha, 85

gaze, 183, 196–99
gender: birth mothers, 42–43; justice, 216–17; motherhood, 41; norms, 65–66; performance representing, 93–99; script, 24; violence, 160–61, 162–63. *See also* femininity; masculinity; queer and queerness
Geographies in Kinship (Liem), 85
Gibney, Shannon, 153
gijichon: about, 67; birth mothers, 212–13; former *gijichon* women's theater work, 68–69; *gijichon* women, 67–68; government policy, 67n86; relation to adoption, 68; space, 69–70; theater representation of, 66–74. *See also Ilgopzipmae*
Gilbert, Helen, 204
Gill, Jungyun, 39, 39n3, 144
Gilmore, Leigh, 86
Ginther, Amy Mihyang, 31, 32, 100–101, 100n74, 100n76, 107, 109, 156n157. *See also Homeful*
Goddard, Lynette, 83
Goldberg, RoseLee, 201
González, Rosita, 9n29
Graves, Kori, 66
Grenne, Mona, 170
Guardian: The Lonely and Great God (TV drama), 216
Gul utanpå (Lundberg), 196
Gullach, Yong Sun, 164, 169, 189–90, 194 fig. 4, 202–3. *See also Re-enacting the Transnational Adoptee*

Ha, Sumin, 50–51. *See also Chalkak*
hallyu, 20–21, 20n89, 215–16
hanbok, 122, 122n38, 125, 146, 148, 190–91, 196
Happitory, 69, 69n95
Haughton, Miriam, 152
Hellman, Lillian, 182
Hello, Mommy (Yoo), 8n27, 40n5
Hello, My Name Is . . . (Sivigny), 15n65, 36, 114–17, 120, 141–48, 141n109, 155–58
Hirsch, Marianne, 29
Hochschild, Arlie Russell, 25n118
hojuk, 124
hojuje, 216n11

hologram, 181
Holt Adoption Program, 10, 10n32, 110
Homans, Margaret, 6n21, 39, 53–54, 81, 81n2, 84–85, 93, 116, 175n73
Homeful (Ginther), 31–32, 35, 81–84, 100–107, 100n74, 107–13
Hong, Cathy Park, 26
Hong, Christine, 70
Hornby, Louise, 57
How to Be a Korean Woman (Chomet), 32, 35, 41, 81–84, 93–99, 93n51, 98 fig. 2, 107–13, 150
Howell, Signe, 116, 149
Hübinette, Tobias, 12–13, 16n67, 17, 18, 20n88, 39n1, 58, 164, 170n54, 195
Human afvikling (Nossell), 170, 170n55
"Hun er vred" (Langvad), 197
Huyssen, Andreas, 41n10

I Miss That Person (TV program): about, 46–48; DNA test in performance, 94–95; theatrical critique, 59–60
ibyanga (*ibyangin*), 59
Ilgopzipmae (Yi), 34, 40–44, 66–74, 66nn80–81, 74–80, 213
I'm Sorry, I Love You (TV drama), 20
immersive theater, 142–43
immigration, 13, 76, 103, 124, 150–51, 167, 218
In My Heart (Cooper and Berks), 36, 114–17, 120, 130–41, 130n68, 152–55, 182
In the Matter of Cha Jung Hee (Liem), 85, 85n17, 193n133
incest, 89, 159–60, 179–80, 179n91, 182, 188
Indian Child Welfare Act (ICWA), 153
International Korean Adoptee Association (IKAA), 21, 108, 109n106, 110, 169n46
interview, in scene, 70–73
Itaewon, Korea, 59–60, 64–65, 65n75
Ivenäs, Sabina, 166

Jadhwani, Lavina, 87n28
Japan, 27–28, 216n11
Jepsen, Christian Sønderby, 170n55
Jeju Island, Korea, 188–89
Joseon Dynasty, in fantasy, 120, 122, 122nn37–38, 128–29

INDEX • 245

Journey to the East (Winterhalder), 170
Jun, Soo-yang, 57. See also *Airport Baby*
justice, 9, 27–29, 111, 129–30, 150, 160–61, 197–98, 216–17

Kaisen, Jane Jin, 7, 28
Kang, Laura Hyun Yi, 160–61
Kang, Te-ri, 192n130
Kaplan, E. Ann, 63
Khanna, Neetu, 165
killjoy, 115, 136–40
Kim Dae-jung, 16, 17n74
Kim, Eleana, 7, 7n25, 11, 28, 32, 110, 114, 116, 124–25, 128
Kim, Hosu: on birth mothers, 34, 40, 42n13, 43, 68, 106; on birth search and reunion narrative, 22, 43–44, 46–47, 76–77; on Omma Poom Park, 211–13; on president's speech, 17; on virtual mothering, 72, 104–5
Kim, Ju Yon, 194
Kim, Nan, 46
Kim, Oh Myo, 15
Kim, Sukkyung, 8n26
Kim, Wonsook, 209, 209 fig. 5
Kim Young-sam, 16
Kim-Larsen, Mette, 203
kinning, 37, 116–17, 148–58, 156n157
kinship, 6, 7n25, 78n111, 116–17; kinning, 148–58; in Korea, 12, 43; queer, 65–66; in spectatorship, 109–10; virtual, 72–73
Knowles, Caroline, 172
Koh, Yeon-ok, 66n81
Komporaly, Jozefina, 41
Korea, North, 16, 44, 67, 207
Korea, South: adoption from, 2, 9–12, 166; diaspora, 17–18, 45n28, 186n106; femininity, 32, 93–94, 97–99, 187–88; *gijichon*, 66–68; globalization (*segyehwa*), 16–17, 77; *hallyu*, 20–21, 20n89, 215–16; industrialization, 12–13; Koreanization, 125, 128–29; lookism, 98; "Miracle on the Han River," 15; Omma Poom Park, 207–13; screen cultures, 44–50, 49n37; shamans, 144
Korean Adoptees of Chicago (KAtCH), 1, 109, 109n107

Korean American Adoptee Adoptive Family Network Conference, 87n28
Korean Broadcasting System (KBS), 45–46, 45n27
Korean Special Adoption Law, 15n65, 18–19, 78n111, 192n130
Korean Unwed Mothers Families Association (KUMFA), 78n111, 100n76
Koreanness, 16–17, 48, 54, 64–65, 90, 124–25, 129, 196
Kreitzer, Carson, 163

language, in performance, 47, 51, 90, 125–29, 148, 183–84, 191, 198, 208
Language of Blood, The (Trenka), 53, 84–85
Langvad, Maja Lee, 7, 197–98
Laybourn, SunAh, 150–51
Lee, Esther Kim, 83
Lee, James Kyung-Jin, 107
Lee, Marie Myung-Ok, 73
Lee, Na Young, 68
Lee, Richard, 15
Lee, Sharon Heijin, 98, 98n69
Lehmann, Hans-Thies, 95
Leighton, Kimberly, 22
lemoine, kimura byol, 7, 110–11, 156n157
Leo, Katie Hae, 93n51, 151, 152
Les Bonnes Intentions (Min Jung), 37, 159–66, 160n3, 168, 171–81, 171n56, 199–206
Lichwick, Marissa, 1, 87–88, 87n28. See also *Yellow Dress*
Liem, Deann Borshay, 7, 81n2, 84–85, 84n12, 85n17, 96, 193n133
Lifton, Betty Jean, 22, 115, 121, 177
Lim, Eng-Beng, 185n103
lookism, 97–99
Lost Daughters (blog), 9n29
Lundberg, Patrick, 196

Macbeth (Shakespeare), 163
Machon, Josephine, 142
Mahoney, Maureen, 85, 116
Malkki, Liisa, 200n152
Marmol Perez, Rosario, 171n56
masculinity, 94n54, 185

Mask Dance (Shiomi), 119, 151
Master Is Here (Koh), 66n81
McIntosh, Peggy, 25n113
McIvor, Charlotte, 131
McKee, Kimberly: on adoptee affinity, 155–56; on adoptee artists, 7; on adoptee killjoy, 36, 115, 136–39; on adoptee organizations, 109; on adoptees as happy objects, 21n93, 26; on adoption as business, 13, 138n100; on adoption fantasy, 120, 215; on arrival day, 59; on autobiographical works, 85, 86; on incest, 179, 179n91; on online space, 156; on search and reunion, 21, 94n54
McNeill, David, 62–63
Medea (Euripides), 162
memoirs, 53, 84–85, 116
memory, in performance, 27–29, 44–48, 54–57, 91–93, 95–96; anticlimactic recollection, 180–81; via food, 175; Memory Wall, 210–11, 211 fig. 7; sonic, 105–6; visual, 106–7. *See also* Omma Poom Park
Menon, Jisha, 173–74
Middle Brother (Sharp), 31, 31n136, 36, 114–17, 120, 121–30, 126 fig. 3, 148–52, 182, 184
Mignot, Jean-François, 168
mimic Swedes, 196, 203
mimicry, 89, 196n140
Min Jung, Cathy, 163–64, 171–72, 171n56, 201, 205. *See also Les Bonnes Intentions*
Minnesota, 25, 84, 93n51, 130–31, 130n68, 131n72, 150–53
Miss Saigon (musical), 176–77
Mistry, Zaraawar, 93n51
Miyamoto, Ryan, 85
mobility, in performance, 122–23
model minority, 14
Molina-Guzmán, Isabel, 164
Møller, Peter, 169
Moon Jae-in, 44
Moon, Katherine, 67, 67n86
Moon, Samhwa, 66
mothers: adoptive, 88–89, 94, 104–5, 134–35, 143–44, 155, 171–81; birth, 18–19, 34–35, 39–44, 39n1, 39n3, 40n6, 42n13, 43n18, 50–74, 90–91, 106–7, 144–45; deaths of birth, 41n10, 74–78; dichotomous representations of, 63, 143–44; via food, 51, 105, 105n94, 175, 175n73; gestures, 62–63; *gijichon* birth, 68–69, 213; Korean, 63, 78n111, 98, 98n69, 216–17; onstage, 41, 78–79, 176; in performance art, 190; surrogate, 64, 185; unequal and spectral, 144–45; virtual mothering, 72, 104–5. *See also* parents
Mother's Arms (Wang), 209–10, 210 fig. 6. *See also* Omma Poom Park
Mu. *See* Theater Mu
multiculturalism: as adoption fantasy, 120; in American perception, 13, 14–15; for family-making ideology, 43, 137, 200; performance rejecting, 27, 35, 82–83
musicals, 40n5, 57, 58n65, 131n74, 151, 176–77. *See also Airport Baby; Miss Saigon; Walleye Kid, The*
Myers, Kit, 14, 138
Myong, Lene, 166–67, 169, 203

N/A (Leo), 93n51
Na, Eunha, 109–10, 123
Naficy, Hamid, 58
Nakamura, Jessica, 27
names and naming, 125–27, 156–58, 172, 188
National Association of Black Social Workers (NABSW), 13, 153
National Theatre Company of Korea (NTCK), 181n96, 186, 186n106
Native Americans (Indigenous peoples of North America), 13, 43, 117, 117n13, 118, 133, 152–55, 218, 219
Natural Disorder (film), 170n55
necropoetics, 44, 74–80
Network of Politicized Adoptees (NPA), 156n157
Nevitt, Lucy, 163
New York Times, 16n67, 106–7
New York Times Magazine, 147n129
Ngai, Sianne, 204
Nichols, Leah, 156n157
non-adoptees, 7–8, 31n136, 31–33, 77, 87, 110, 117
Nossell, Jacob, 170, 170n55
Novy, Marianne, 4, 5–6, 118–19, 132n76, 151

Ode to My Father (film), 48–49, 49nn36–37

Oedipus Rex (Sophocles), 4, 6, 6nn20–21, 182
Oh, Arissa, 9n31, 10n32, 14, 64, 82
Omma Poom Park, 38, 207–13
Ong, Aiwha, 123
open and closed adoption, 132–34, 132n76, 139–40, 193n133
Oprah Winfrey Show, The (TV program), 18
Organization for Economic Co-operation and Development (OECD), 16, 19n86
Orientalism, 89, 176–77, 179, 179n91, 185n103, 187
orphanages, 10, 13, 70, 87–88, 90–91, 111, 125–26, 129, 133, 167, 182, 218, 219
orphans, 2, 10–11, 28, 48, 117–19, 117n18, 124–27, 136, 164, 176, 185n103, 188–89, 219
Orton, Joe, 182
otherness, 89, 104, 174, 176, 196
Outside the Door (Yi), 69

pain: of adoption, 16–17, 106–7; in performance, 28, 162, 190, 204–5
Paju, Korea, 207–8
Palimpsest (Sjöblom), 193n133
Papke, David Ray, 10n32
parents: adoptive, 10n32, 13–15, 43, 112, 121–22, 135–41, 153–54, 180–81; adoptive parent-centric discourse, 6, 15n63, 23n104, 33; birth, 5, 6n21, 18–19, 21–23, 26, 39n1, 39n3, 116, 118–19, 134–35, 188; response from, 112, 201–2, 205. See also mothers; fathers
Park Chung-hee, 11–12
Park, Geun Hyung, 8n26
Park, Kolleen, 57–58. See also *Airport Baby*
Park, Pauline, 217n13
Park, Shelley, 85, 104
Park, So Young, 20–21
Park Nelson, Kim: on adoptees' autobiographical works, 85; on adoptees in Minnesota, 150; on adoption, 14, 87, 153, 159n1; on adoption in Denmark, 166–67, 169; on birth search and reunion, 21, 23, 81; on critical adoption studies, 15n63; research methods of, 30; on returning Korean adoptees, 16n70, 17, 21n96, 82, 90; for Theater Mu, 152
Pate, SooJin, 4, 7, 36, 79–80, 88–89, 115, 125, 127

Paton, Jean, 6n20, 133
patriarchy, 12–13, 49, 75–79, 93–94, 96–99, 144–45, 159n1
Patton-Imani, Sandra, 159n1, 179
Pazicky, Diana Loercher, 118
Pellerin, Fleur, 18
performance: about, 3–9, 170, 215–17, 217–19; abjection, 25; accountability in, 27–29; birth mothers featured in, 39–44; birth search and reunion, 23–24, 81–84, 117–21; border-crossing testimony, 107–12; of care, 148–58, 208–9; community-making, 148–58; decolonial practice in, 163–66, 199–206; emotional and bodily scripts, 24–26; of "good" and "bad" adoptees, 115; memorial as, 208–13; necropoetics, 74–79; violence in, 162–63; vulnerability in, 161–62. See also titles of individual works
performance art, 7, 189–99, 201
Phelan, Peggy, 4, 192
phenomenology, 191–92
photography, 20n88, 54–57, 55n52
Placé, Jean-Vincent, 18
poetry, 172–73, 197
postmemory, 29, 213
postwar humanitarianism, 9–11
Powers, Marla, 154
Prague Quadrennial of Performance Design and Space (PQ), 142, 142n112
Pratt, Mary Louise, 42
Prébin, Elise, 22–23
Previn, Soon-Yi, 179n91
prostitution, 11, 67–68, 67n86, 176, 200, 212–13. See also *gijichon*
proxy adoption, 11, 11n39
puppetry, 40n5, 176

queerness: connection to Orientalism, 185n103; and discomfort, 199; and kinship, 65–66, 66n79; queer characters, 58n65, 64–66, 151; Queer Korea Festival, 217n13
"quiet migration," 6, 6n22

race: adoptee artists' reflections of, 142, 193, 203; of adoptees, 15, 135–36, 159n1, 179; in adoption narratives, 4n11, 13–15, 118–19,

153–54; Asian, 88–89, 102–4, 160–61, 179, 187; colonialism and colonization, 163–66, 167; mixed (biracial and multiracial), 9, 66–68, 66n81, 69, 70, 166–67, 213; and motherhood, 39–41, 189–90; in performance, 24–25, 76, 82n6, 87–89, 93, 102–4, 194–96

Radway, Janice, 145

Raleigh, Elizabeth, 25n118, 174

rape, 52, 159n1, 179–81, 184–85

Rasmussen, Kim-Su, 199, 212

Redwood Curtain (Wilson), 119

Re-enacting the Transnational Adoptee (Gullach), 37, 159–66, 160n3, 167, 189–99, 194 fig. 4, 199–206

Reichwald, Reed, 15

repetition, 22, 103–4, 129–30, 194–95

resurrection, metaphorical, 40–41, 41n10

reunion. *See* search and reunion

RHEE, kate-hers, 7, 28, 110–11, 156n157

Rollins, Lisa Marie, 100n74, 107–8, 107n102

Rosen, Robert, 122

Ruddick, Sara, 43n18

Ruffian on the Stair, The (Orton), 182

Russia-Ukraine War, 219

Said, Edward, 176, 187

Salverson, Julie, 52

samulnori (music), 17n74, 154–55

scenic design, 142, 145–48, 173

Schechner, Richard, 5

Schneider, Rebecca, 120–21

Schultz, Stacy, 83

Schwab, Gabriele, 165, 205–6

scripts, bodily and emotional, 24–26

sculptures, 209–11

search and reunion, 2–9, 8n27, 19–24; in autobiographical works, 84–87; as contact zone, 42; "extraordinary" stories, 159–66; in fantasy, 117–21; in Korean screen cultures, 44–50; in Korean theater, 50–74; Omma Poom Park, 207–13. *See also* titles of individual works

Searching for Go-Hyang (Chu), 84n12

Seattle Times, 14

Sedgwick, Eve Kosofsky, 198

semiotics, 191–92

Seoul Olympic Games (1988), 15–16

Seoul Players, 100n76

Sex Show, The (Chomet), 93

sexuality, 89, 93, 151, 177, 183, 185–87, 199

Shadow Child (Kim), 209, 209 fig. 5. *See also* Omma Poom Park

Shakespeare, William, 4, 163

shamans, 144

Sharp, Eric, 31, 121, 126 fig. 3, 150–52. *See also* Middle Brother

Shepard, Sam, 182

Shim, Jung-Soon, 78

Shimakawa, Karen, 4, 25, 177

Shiomi, Rick, 119, 151

shock, in performance, 197, 201

siblinghood, 48–49, 84, 116, 181–89

sisterhood, 48–49, 53, 69, 131–41, 183, 185, 188

Sivigny, Debra Kim, 141–42, 141n109, 156–57. *See also Hello, My Name Is . . .*

Sjöblom, Lisa Wool-Rim, 7, 193n133

Smith, Anna Deavere, 84

social death, 40–41, 41n10, 44

Solheim, Nina, 18

solo performance, 1, 31, 35–36, 37, 81–84, 107–13

Somebody's Daughter (Lee), 73

Son, Elizabeth, 27–28, 208–9

songs, 45, 57–66, 58n65, 105–6, 105n95, 154–55

Sontag, Susan, 55–56, 55n52

Sophocles, 4, 182

Sorensen, Eli Park, 23n104, 85, 101, 137

sound, in performance, 56–57, 58, 102–3, 157, 177, 188–89

Starchild, The (Gullach), 189–90

Stein, Miriam Yung Min, 170

stereotypes, 14, 21, 28, 78, 89, 164, 179n91

Stoker, Kim, 110–11, 217n13

Stoler, Ann Laura, 165

Strauss, Jean A. S., 193n133

Stuart Fisher, Amanda, 83–84, 108, 110

Stulen identitet (influencer), 169–70

Suk-ja Story, A, 68–69

Sunlit Sisters' Center, 68–69, 68n92, 69n95

Tænketanken Adoption, 169
Take Off (film), 18, 18n78
Taylor, Diana, 95, 111, 119
Taylor Porter, Nancy, 162–63
technology: in kinship, 72–73; in mothering, 104–5
television, 2, 19–20, 20nn89–90, 44–48, 45n24, 45nn27–28, 59–60, 61 fig. 1, 94, 94n57, 215–16
temporality, 95, 122, 173, 189
Theater Hae, 69, 69n95
Theater Mu, 25, 121, 126 fig. 3, 150–52
This Isn't Romance (Chappell), 37, 159–66, 160n3, 168, 181–89, 181n96, 186n106, 199–206
Thompson, Veronica (Fancy Chance), 170
Tiffin, Helen, 205
time-space compression, 114–15
'Tis Pity She's a Whore (Ford), 182
Tompkins, Joanne, 204
touch, in performance, 198–99
Toys in the Attic (Hellman), 182
transhistoricity, 122, 128–30
Transnational Adoption Industrial Complex (TAIC), 13
Transue-Woolston, Amanda, 9n29
Trenka, Jane Jeong, 7, 53, 84–85, 217n13
Trimble, Albert, 153
Trump Administration, 218
Tutu, Desmond, 112
Twinsters (Futerman and Miyamoto), 85

Ugwu, Catherine, 83
United Nations Educational, Scientific and Cultural Organization (UNESCO), 45
US Army Camp Howze, 207
US militarism, 11, 28, 66–68, 70, 207–13

victims and victimhood, 161, 173–74, 179–81, 187
Vincenzo (TV drama), 216
violence: adoption and, 68, 138; toward children, 171–72; colonial power as, 163–64, 199–200; gender, 162–63; sexual, 88, 159n1, 178–81, 179n91; staging of, 160–61,

160n3, 163, 173–74, 180–81, 188, 195; symbolic, 28, 76, 138–39
voice-over, 10, 89, 146–47, 156–58
vulnerability, 78, 161–62, 165–66, 185, 204

Wablenica Song (Native Adoptee Healing Song), 154–55
Walleye Kid, The (Shiomi), 151
Walton, Jessica, 25–26, 104
Wang, Kwanghyun, 209–10, 210 fig. 6
water, as symbol, 188–89, 189n118
Weil, Richard, 6, 6n22
Welders, The, 141, 141n109
Welton, Martin, 26
"Where are you from?," 32–33, 102–4, 111
White, Bretton, 199
whiteness, 14–15, 24–25, 82n6, 103, 198–99, 218; in performance, 87–89, 193–98; white gaze, 196–97; white privilege, 25, 25n113
whitewashing, 159–60, 159n1, 194–95
Wills, Jenny Heijun, 23
Wilson, Lanford, 119
Winterhalder, Nelly, 170
Winter's Tale, The (Shakespeare), 4
Wirth-Nesher, Hana, 117–18
Wonderlust Productions, 130, 130n68
Woo, Susie, 10, 10n36, 70, 164
Woolf, Virginia, 57
wounds, 6n21, 106–7, 161
Wyver, Richey, 33, 196, 196n140, 202–3

Yancy, George, 196
yellow desire and yellow peril, 89
Yellow Dress (Lichwick), 1, 35, 81–84, 87–93, 87n28, 107–13
Yeonwoo Stage, 66, 66n80
Yi, Yang Gu, 66–69, 70–71. See also *Ilgopzipmae*
Yngvesson, Barbara, 14, 23, 85, 116, 122
Yoo, JinWol, 8n27, 88
Yook, Sung Hee, 106
Yu, Yeonju, 186n106
Yun, Jieheerah, 65

FORMATIONS: ADOPTION, KINSHIP, AND CULTURE
EMILY HIPCHEN AND JOHN MCLEOD, SERIES EDITORS

This interdisciplinary series encourages critical engagement with all aspects of nonnormative kinship—such as adoption, foster care, IVF, surrogacy, and gamete transfers—especially as they intersect with race, identity, heritage, nationality, sexuality, and gender. Books in the series explore how these constructions affect not only those personally involved but also public understandings of identity, personhood, migration, kinship, and the politics of family.

Unsettling Acts: Performing Transnational Adoption
    JIEUN LEE

Haphazard Families: Romanticism, Nation, and the Prehistory of Modern Adoption
    ERIC C. WALKER

Adoption Fantasies: The Fetishization of Asian Adoptees from Girlhood to Womanhood
    KIMBERLY D. MCKEE

Adoption across Race and Nation: US Histories and Legacies
    EDITED BY SILKE HACKENESCH

The Politics of Reproduction: Adoption, Abortion, and Surrogacy in the Age of Neoliberalism
    EDITED BY MODHUMITA ROY AND MARY THOMPSON

www.ingramcontent.com/pod-product-compliance
Lightning Source LLC
Chambersburg PA
CBHW020645230426
43665CB00008B/317